BROKEN ANGELS™

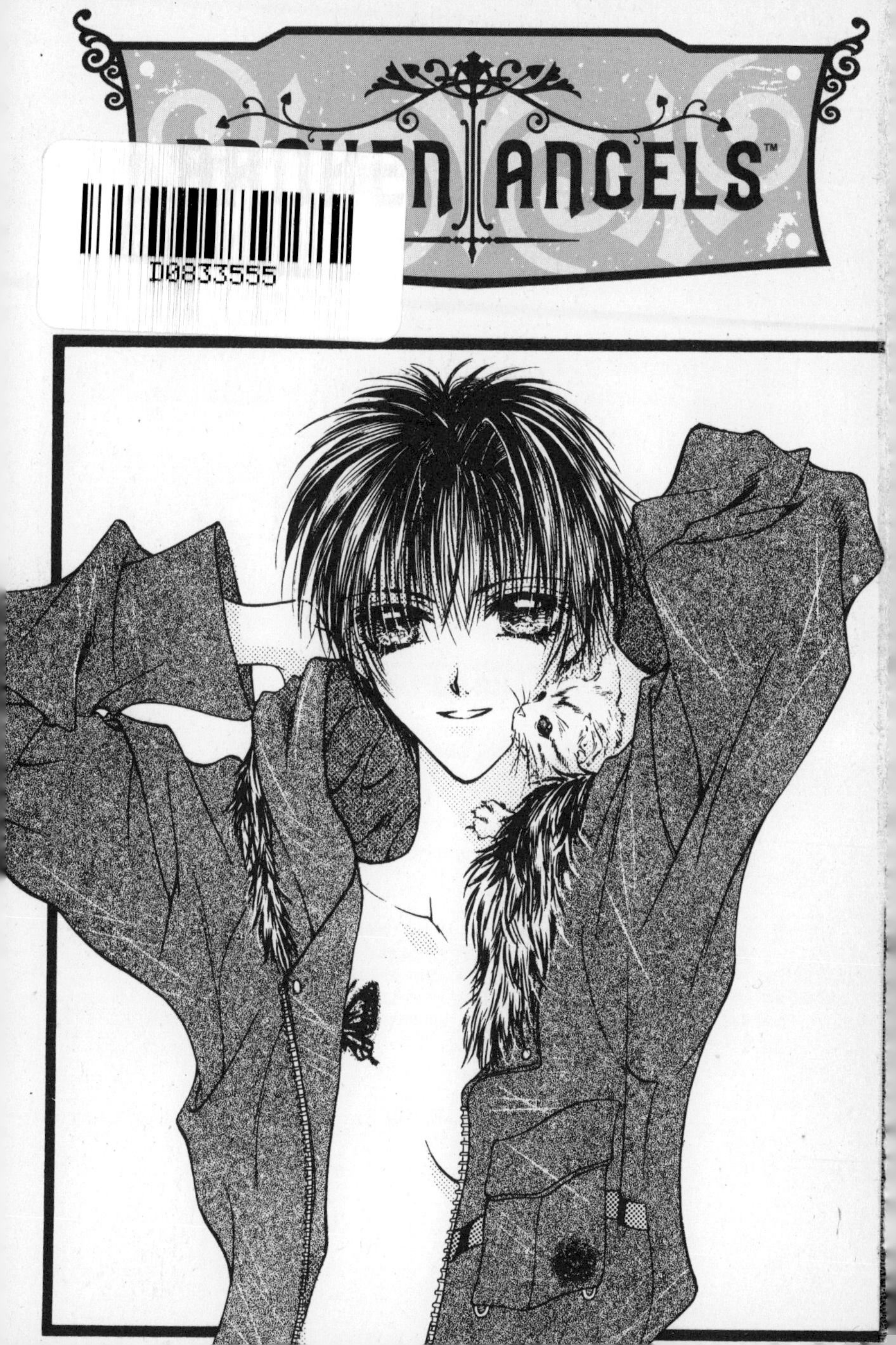

Broken Angels Vol. 1
Created by Setsuri Tsuzuki

Translation - Nayoung Aimee Kwon
English Adaptation - Jessica Cathryn Feinberg
Copy Editor - Hope Donovan
Retouch and Lettering - Erika Terriquez
Production Artist - Alyson Stetz
Cover Layout - Gary Shum

Editor - Tim Beedle
Digital Imaging Manager - Chris Buford
Production Managers - Jennifer Miller and Mutsumi Miyazaki
Managing Editor - Lindsey Johnston
VP of Production - Ron Klamert
Publisher and E.I.C. - Mike Kiley
President and C.O.O. - John Parker
C.E.O. - Stuart Levy

A **TOKYOPOP** Manga

TOKYOPOP Inc.
5900 Wilshire Blvd. Suite 2000
Los Angeles, CA 90036

E-mail: info@TOKYOPOP.com
Come visit us online at www.TOKYOPOP.com

ISBN: 1-59816-159-8

First TOKYOPOP printing: February 2006
10 9 8 7 6 5 4 3 2 1
Printed in the USA

BROKEN ANGELS™

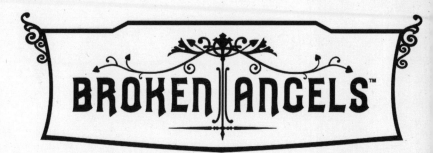

Volume 1

Created by
Setsuri Tsuzuki

TOKYOPOP®

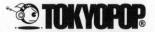

HAMBURG // LONDON // LOS ANGELES // TOKYO

Contents

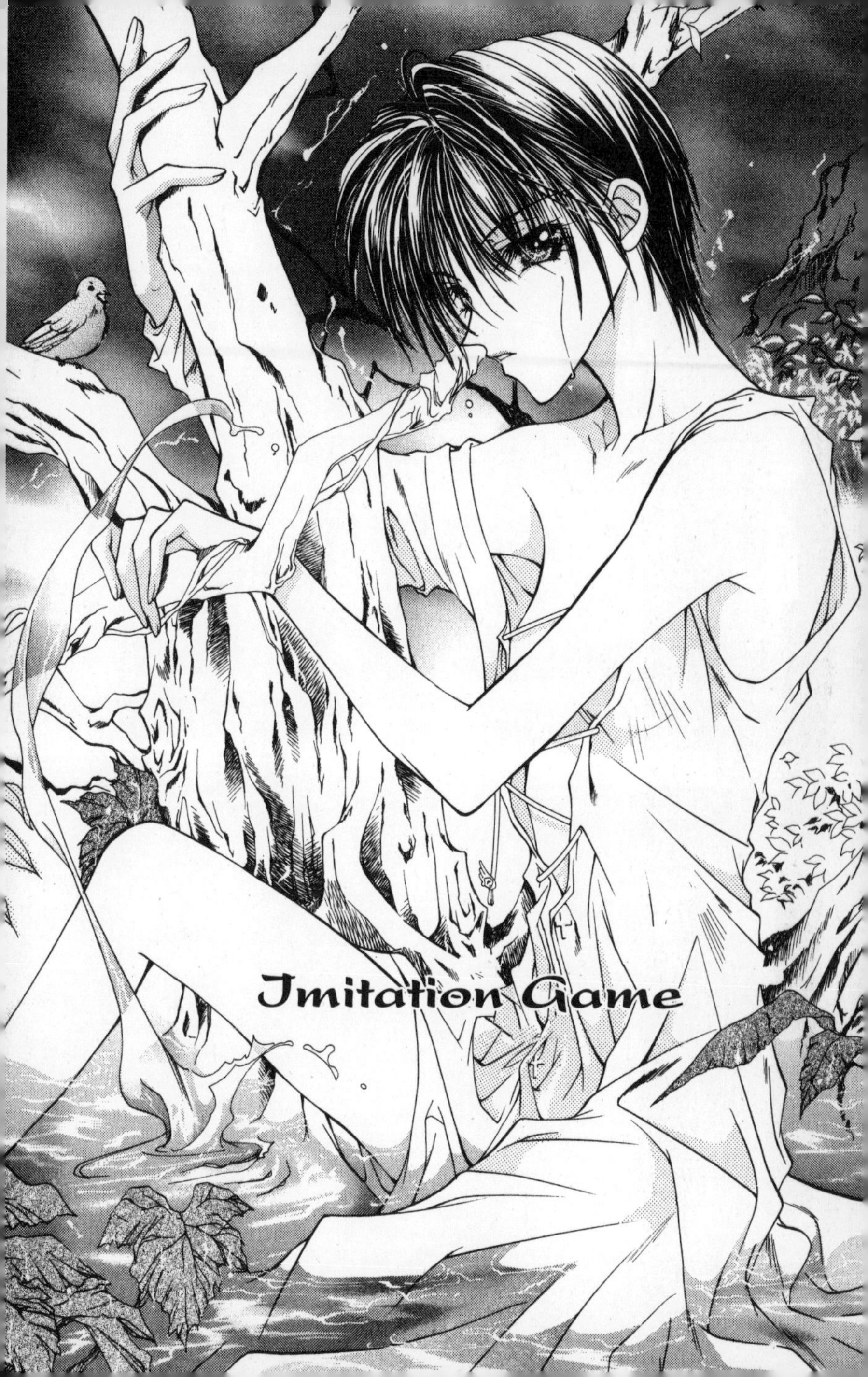
Imitation Game

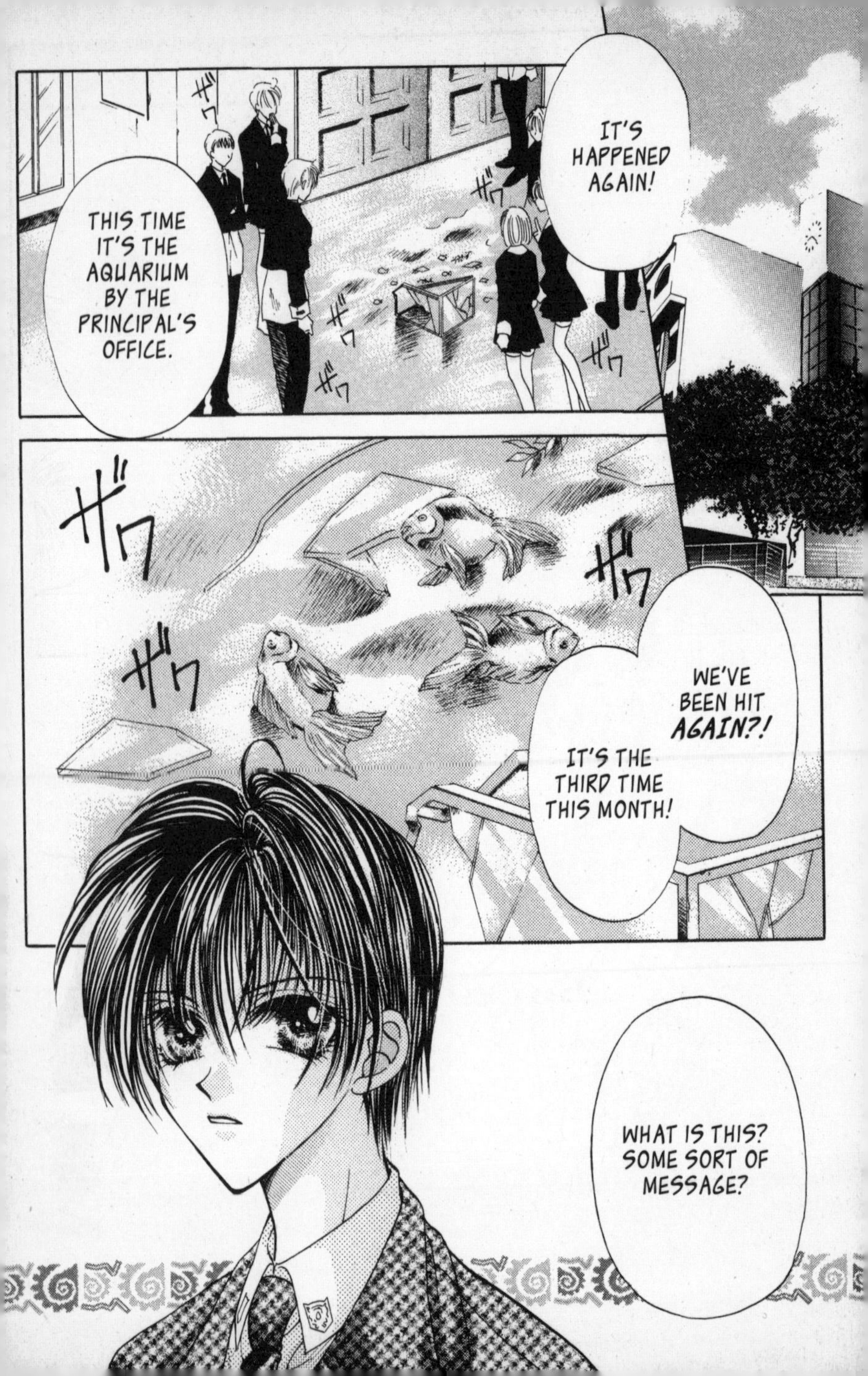
IT'S HAPPENED AGAIN!
THIS TIME IT'S THE AQUARIUM BY THE PRINCIPAL'S OFFICE.
ザワ
ザワ
WE'VE BEEN HIT AGAIN?!
IT'S THE THIRD TIME THIS MONTH!
WHAT IS THIS? SOME SORT OF MESSAGE?

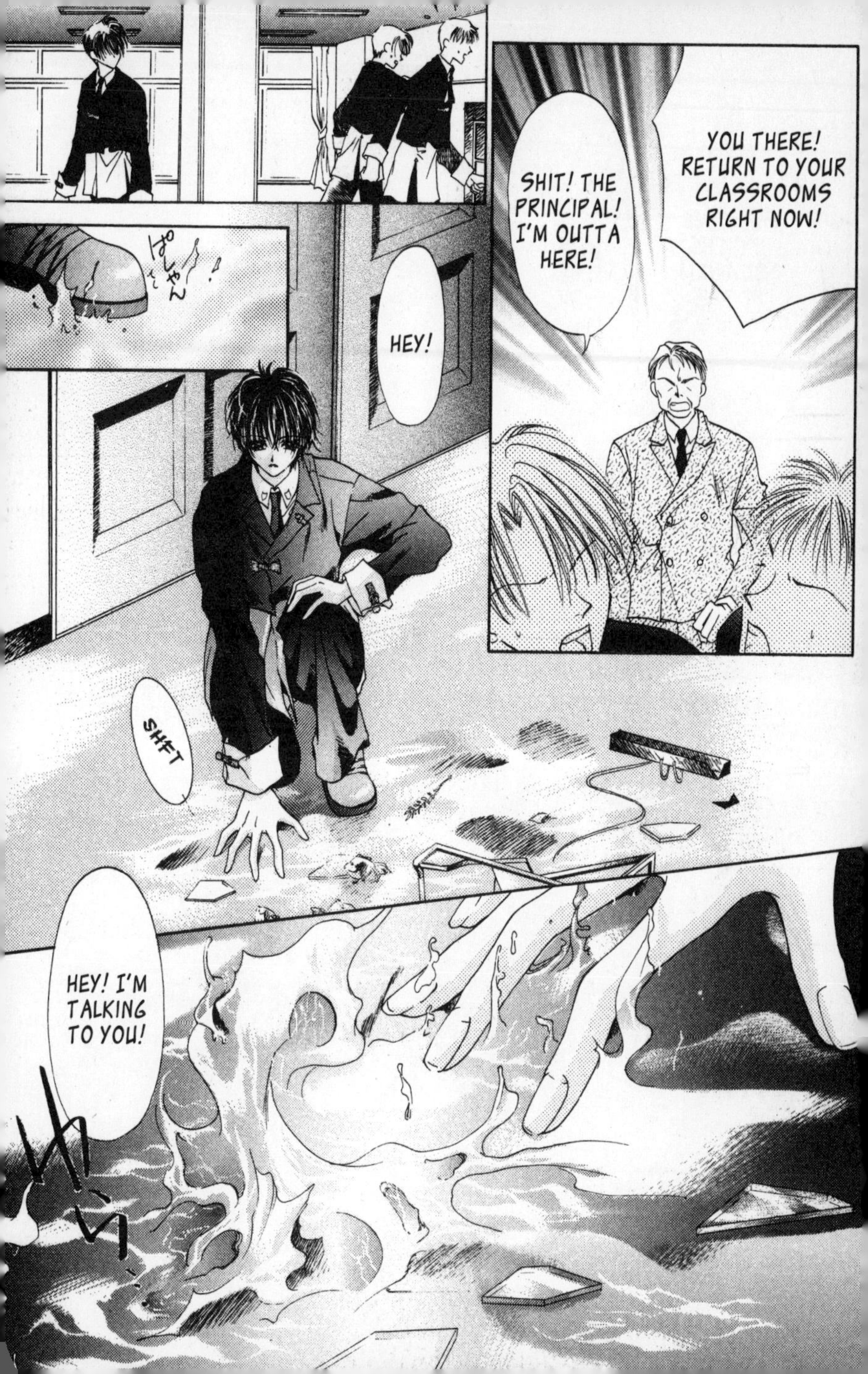
YOU THERE! RETURN TO YOUR CLASSROOMS RIGHT NOW!
SHIT! THE PRINCIPAL! I'M OUTTA HERE!
ぱしゃん
HEY!
SHFT
HEY! I'M TALKING TO YOU!

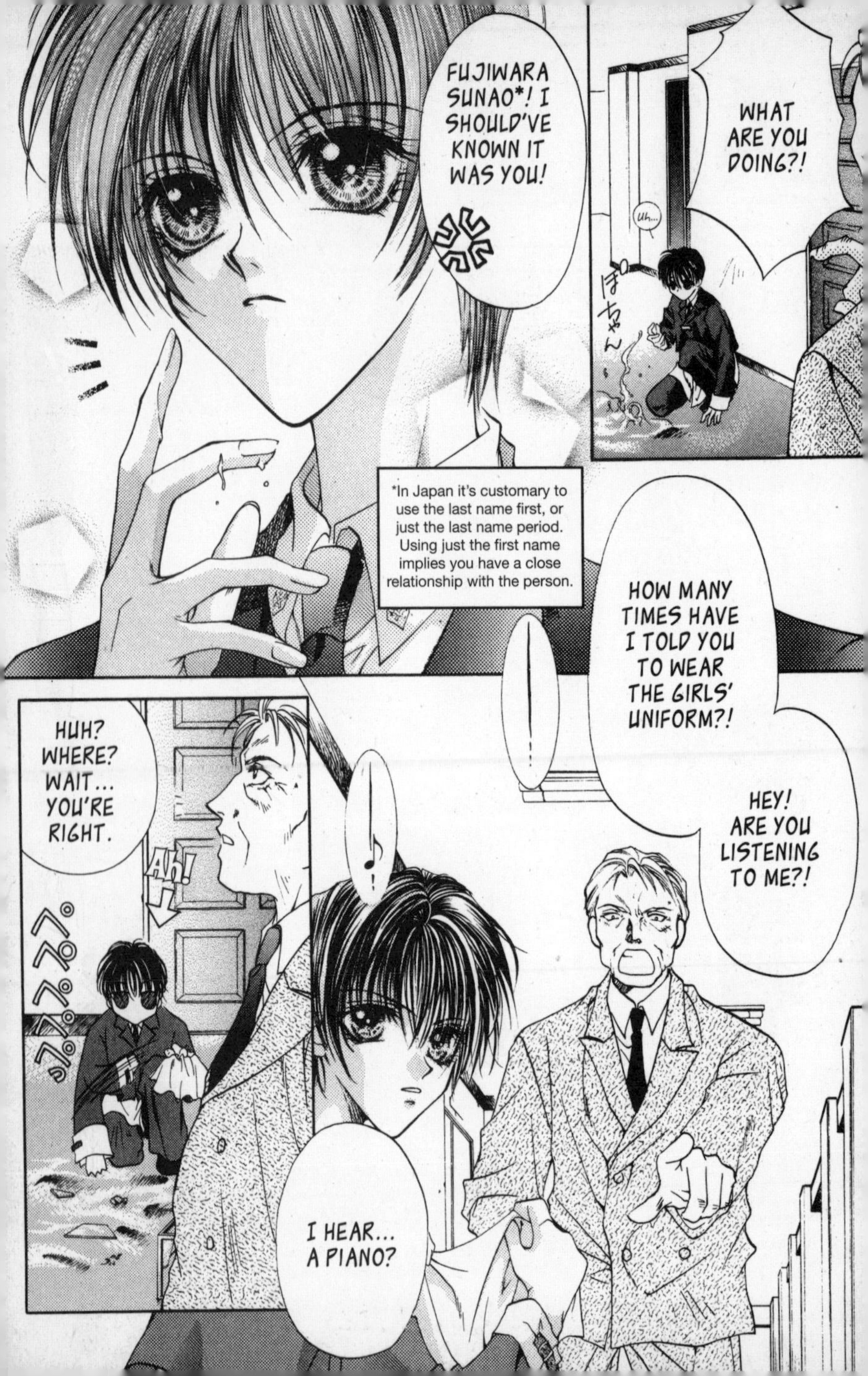
WHAT ARE YOU DOING?!
Uh...
ぽちゃん
FUJIWARA SUNAO*! I SHOULD'VE KNOWN IT WAS YOU!
*In Japan it's customary to use the last name first, or just the last name period. Using just the first name implies you have a close relationship with the person.
HOW MANY TIMES HAVE I TOLD YOU TO WEAR THE GIRLS' UNIFORM?!
!
HEY! ARE YOU LISTENING TO ME?!
I HEAR... A PIANO?
HUH? WHERE? WAIT... YOU'RE RIGHT.
Ah!

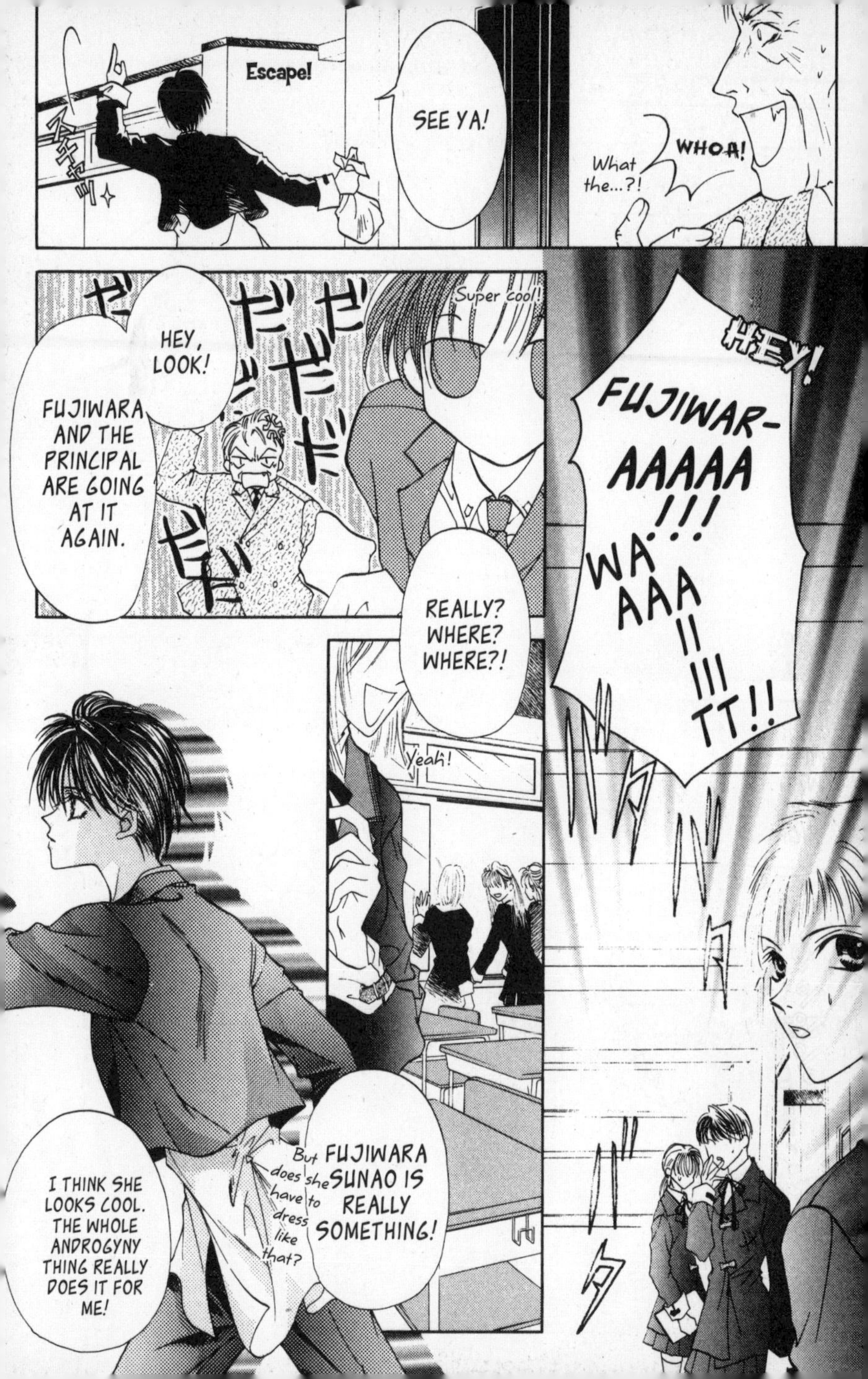
WHOA!
What the...?!
Escape!
SEE YA!
HEY!
FUJIWARAAAAAA!!!
WAAAAIIIIITT!!
Super cool!
HEY, LOOK!
FUJIWARA AND THE PRINCIPAL ARE GOING AT IT AGAIN.
REALLY? WHERE? WHERE?!
Yeah!
FUJIWARA SUNAO IS REALLY SOMETHING!
But does she have to dress like that?
I THINK SHE LOOKS COOL. THE WHOLE ANDROGYNY THING REALLY DOES IT FOR ME!

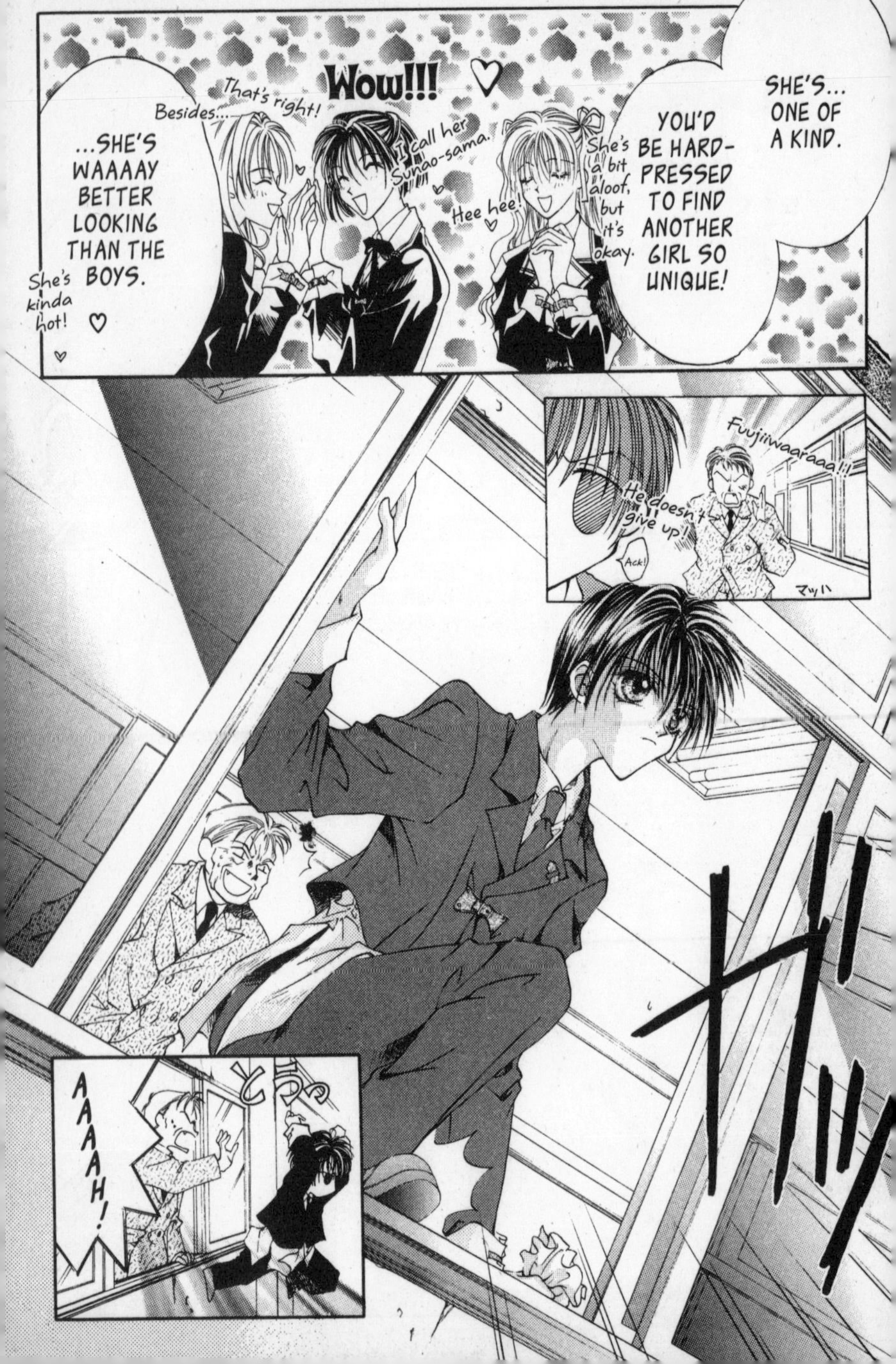
SHE'S... ONE OF A KIND.
YOU'D BE HARD-PRESSED TO FIND ANOTHER GIRL SO UNIQUE!
She's a bit aloof, but it's okay.
Hee hee!
I call her Sunao-sama.
Wow!!!
That's right!
Besides...
...SHE'S WAAAAY BETTER LOOKING THAN THE BOYS.
She's kinda hot!
Fuujiiwaaraaa!!
He doesn't give up!
Ack!
マッハ
ザッ
とうっ
AAAAH!

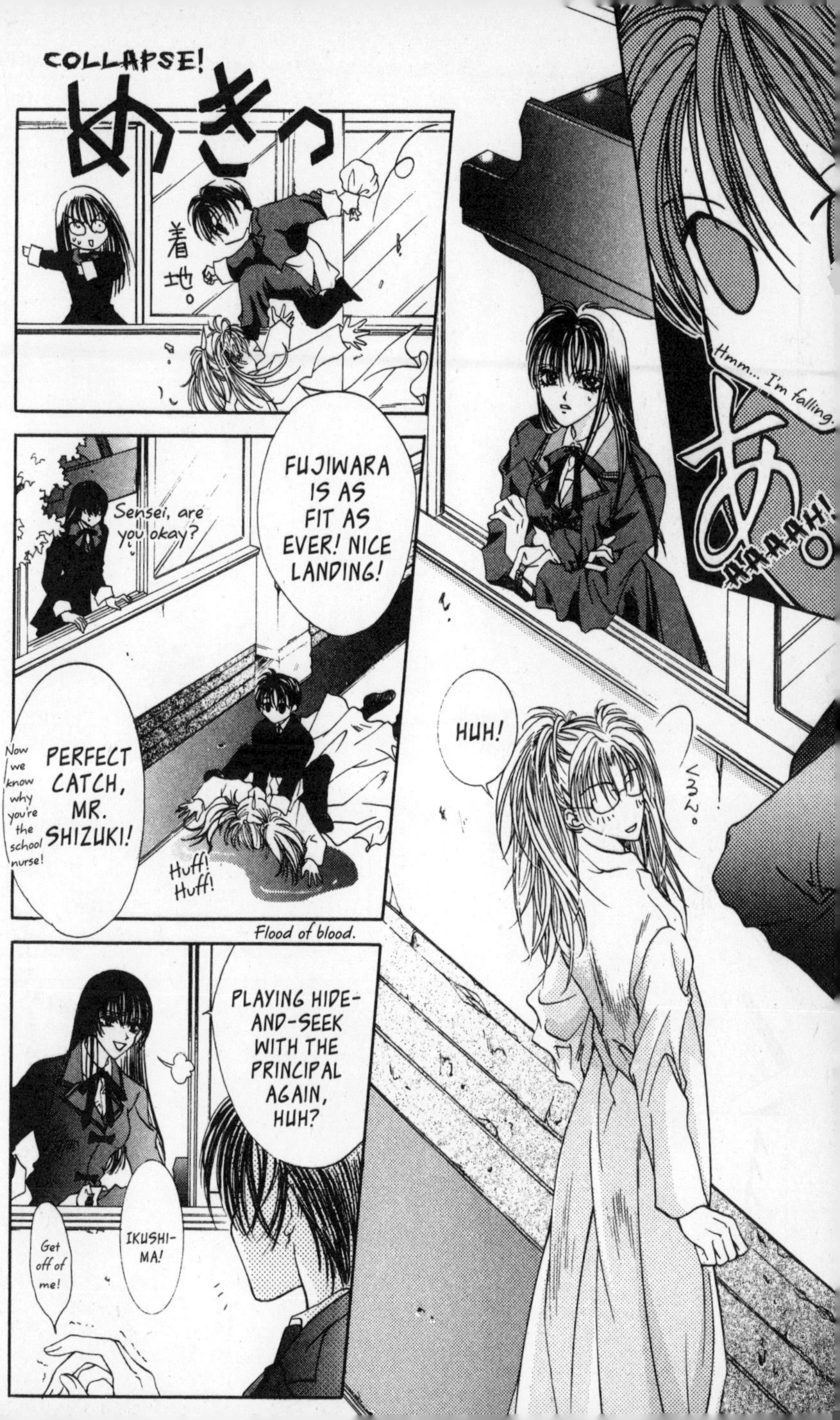

Hmm... I'm falling.
あ。
AAAAH!
HUH!
くるん。
COLLAPSE!
めきっ
着地。
Sensei, are you okay?
FUJIWARA IS AS FIT AS EVER! NICE LANDING!
PERFECT CATCH, MR. SHIZUKI!
Now we know why you're the school nurse!
Huff! Huff!
Flood of blood.
PLAYING HIDE-AND-SEEK WITH THE PRINCIPAL AGAIN, HUH?
IKUSHIMA!
Get off of me!

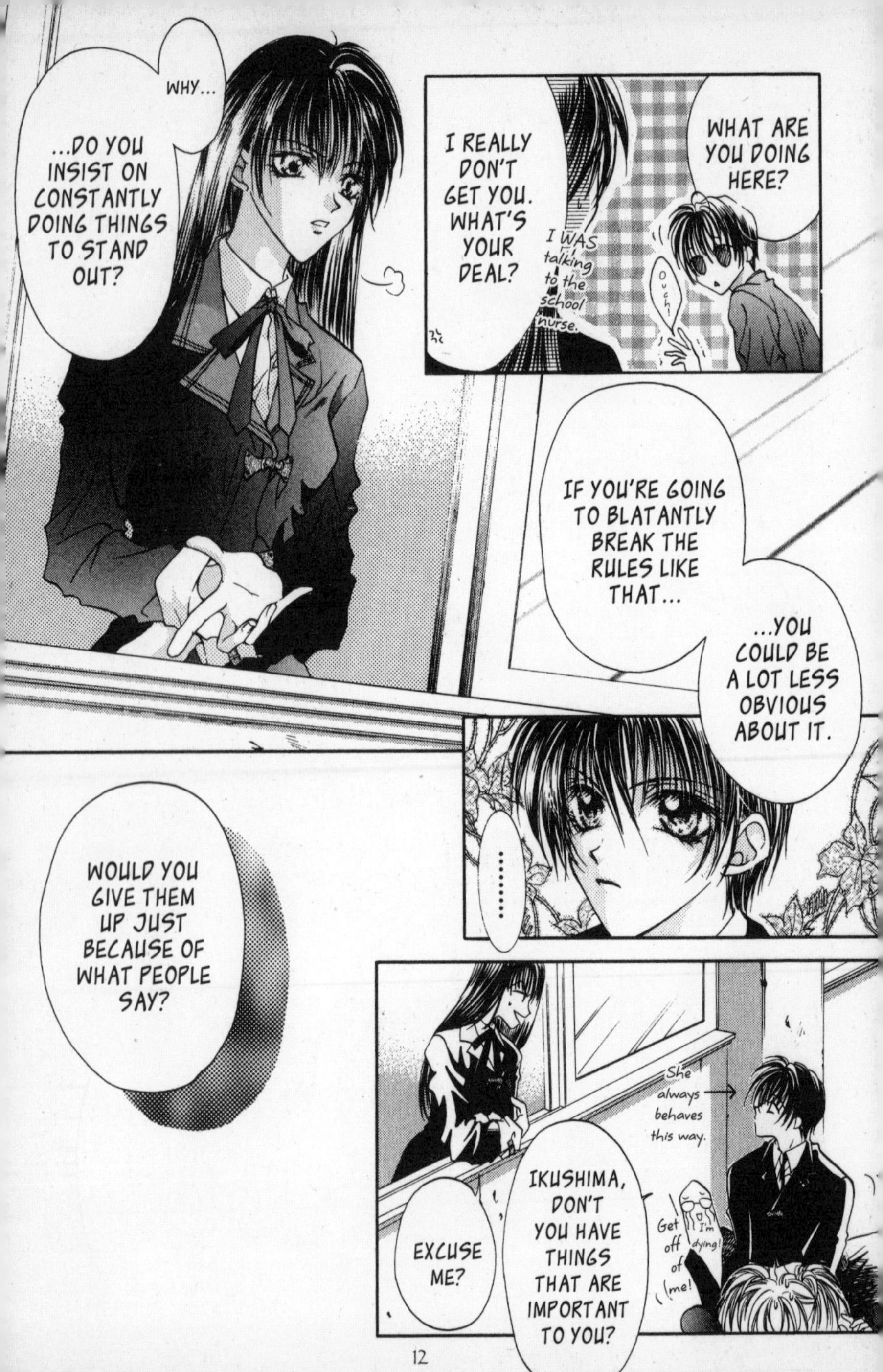
WHAT ARE YOU DOING HERE?
Ouch!
I WAS talking to the school nurse.
I REALLY DON'T GET YOU. WHAT'S YOUR DEAL?
IF YOU'RE GOING TO BLATANTLY BREAK THE RULES LIKE THAT...
...YOU COULD BE A LOT LESS OBVIOUS ABOUT IT.
WHY...
...DO YOU INSIST ON CONSTANTLY DOING THINGS TO STAND OUT?
......
She always behaves this way.
IKUSHIMA, DON'T YOU HAVE THINGS THAT ARE IMPORTANT TO YOU?
I'm dying!
Get off of me!
EXCUSE ME?
WOULD YOU GIVE THEM UP JUST BECAUSE OF WHAT PEOPLE SAY?

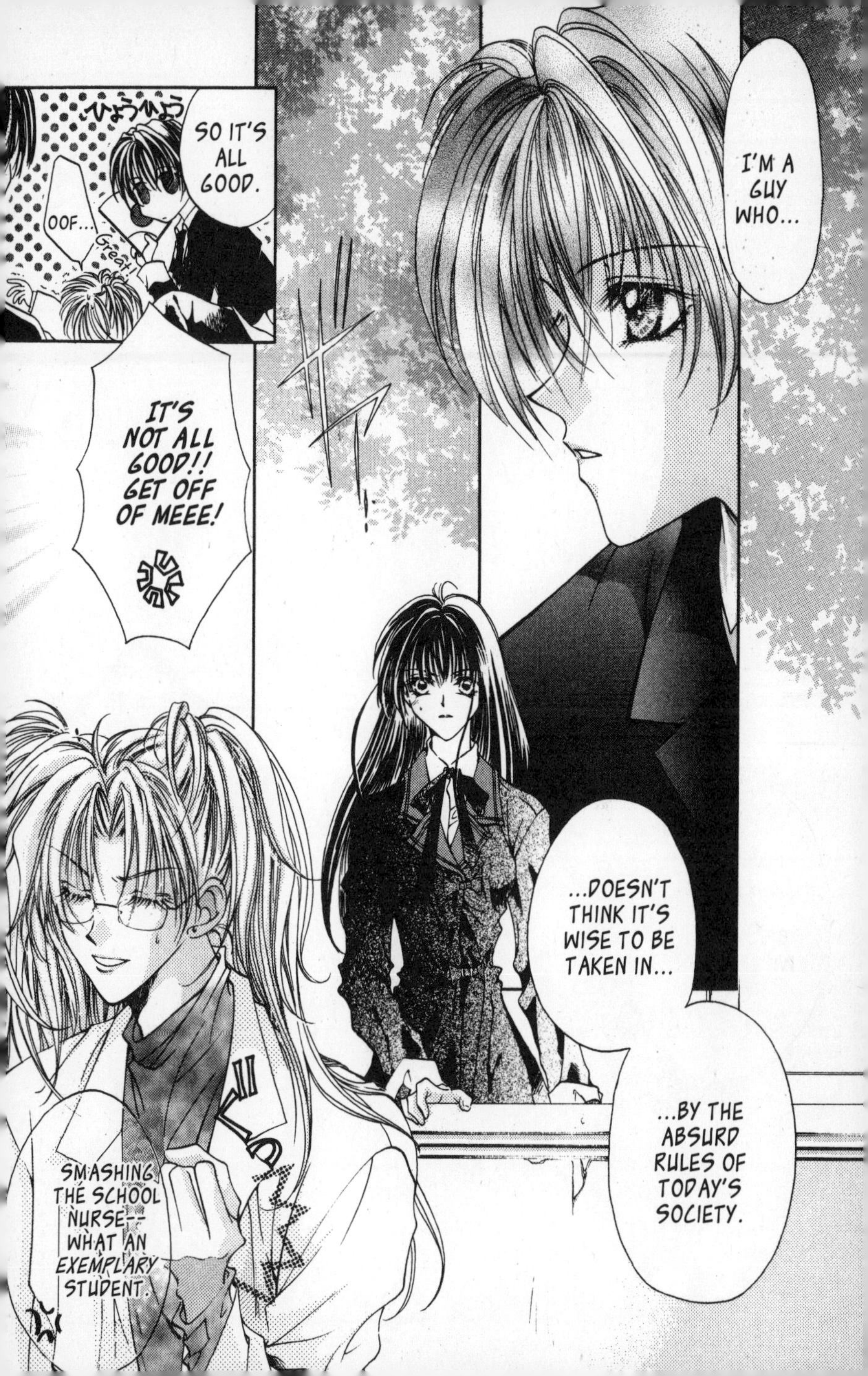
I'M A GUY WHO...
ひょうひょう
SO IT'S ALL GOOD.
OOF...
Great!
IT'S NOT ALL GOOD!! GET OFF OF MEEE!
...DOESN'T THINK IT'S WISE TO BE TAKEN IN...
...BY THE ABSURD RULES OF TODAY'S SOCIETY.
SMASHING THE SCHOOL NURSE-- WHAT AN EXEMPLARY STUDENT.

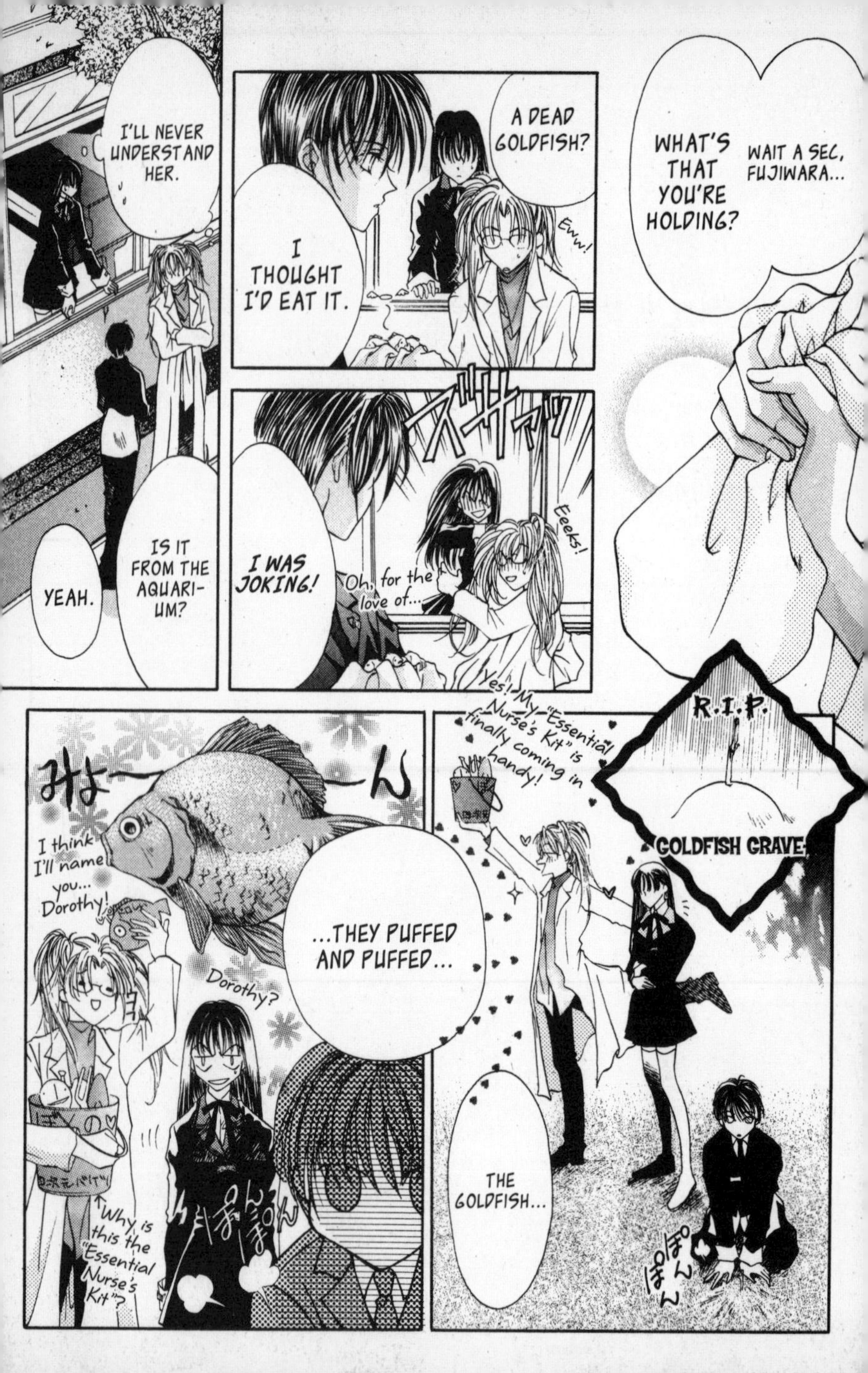
WAIT A SEC, FUJIWARA...
WHAT'S THAT YOU'RE HOLDING?
A DEAD GOLDFISH?
Eww!
I THOUGHT I'D EAT IT.
ズザァッ
Eeeks!
I WAS JOKING!
Oh, for the love of...
I'LL NEVER UNDERSTAND HER.
IS IT FROM THE AQUARIUM?
YEAH.
R.I.P.
GOLDFISH GRAVE
Yes! My "Essential Nurse's Kit" is finally coming in handy!
THE GOLDFISH...
ぽんぽん
...THEY PUFFED AND PUFFED...
みょ〜〜ん
I think I'll name you... Dorothy!
Dorothy?
ぽんぽん
Why is this the "Essential Nurse's Kit"?

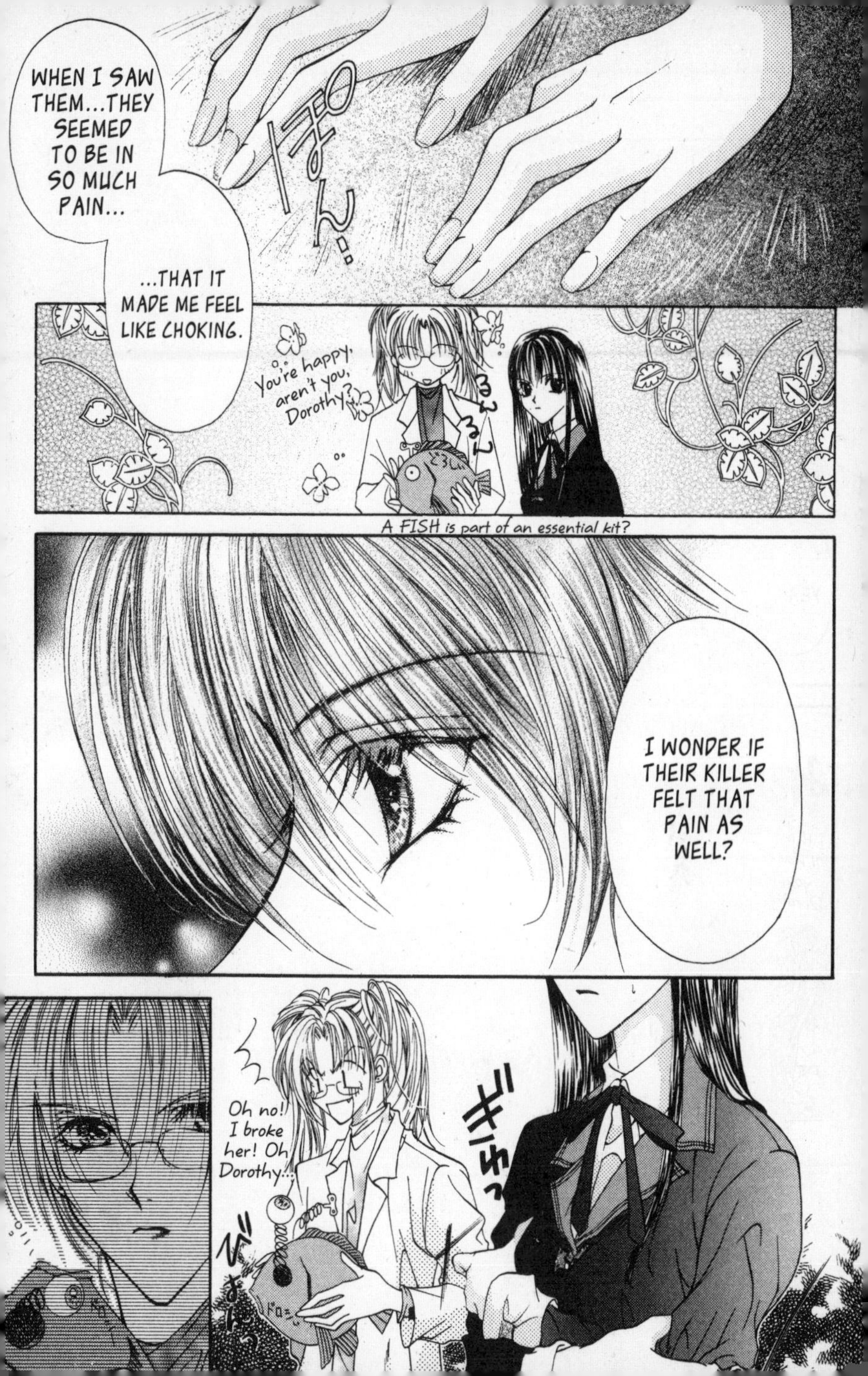
WHEN I SAW THEM...THEY SEEMED TO BE IN SO MUCH PAIN...
...THAT IT MADE ME FEEL LIKE CHOKING.
ぽん
You're happy, aren't you, Dorothy?
るんるん
A FISH is part of an essential kit?
I WONDER IF THEIR KILLER FELT THAT PAIN AS WELL?
ぎゅっ
Oh no! I broke her! Oh Dorothy...

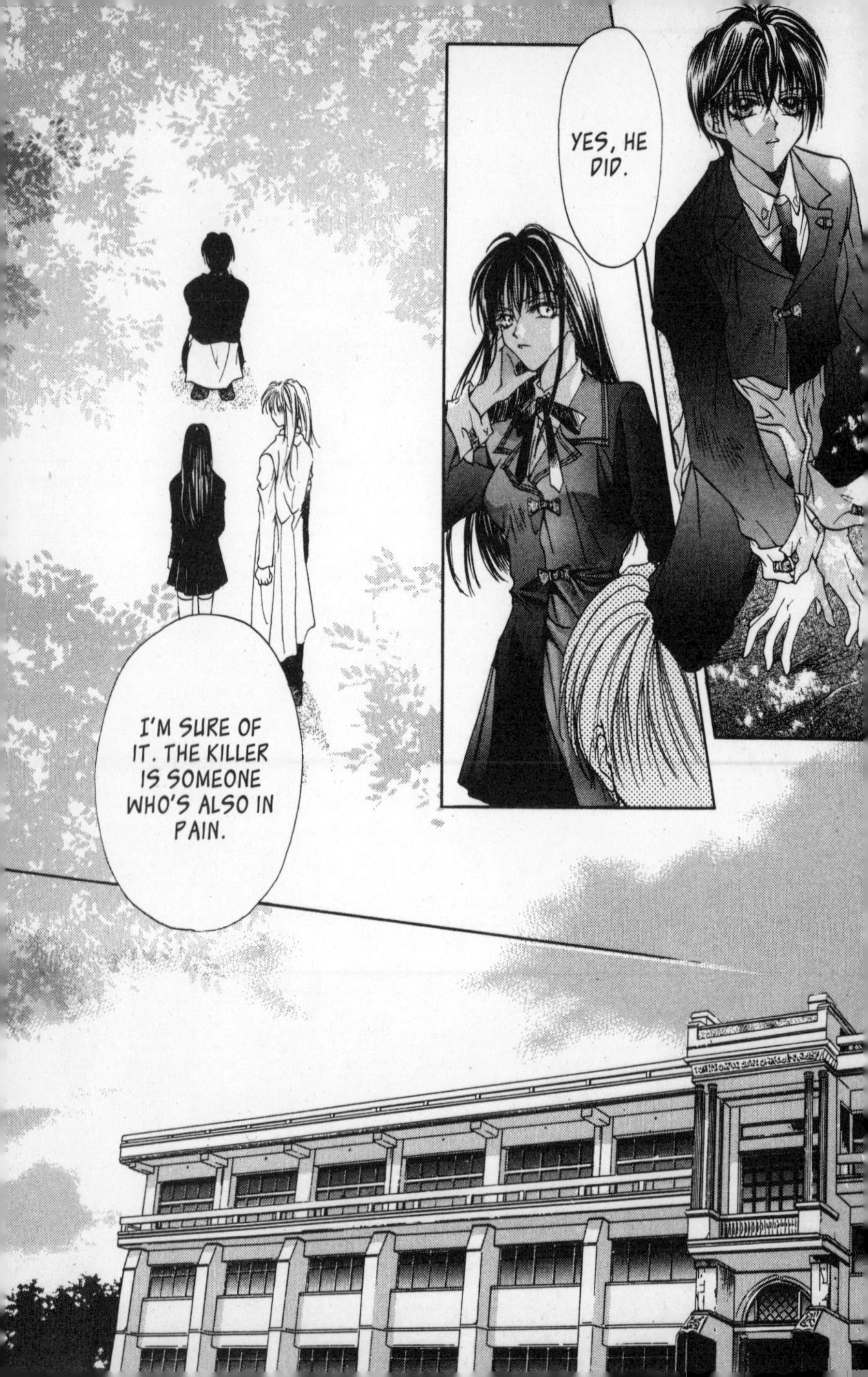
YES, HE DID.
I'M SURE OF IT. THE KILLER IS SOMEONE WHO'S ALSO IN PAIN.

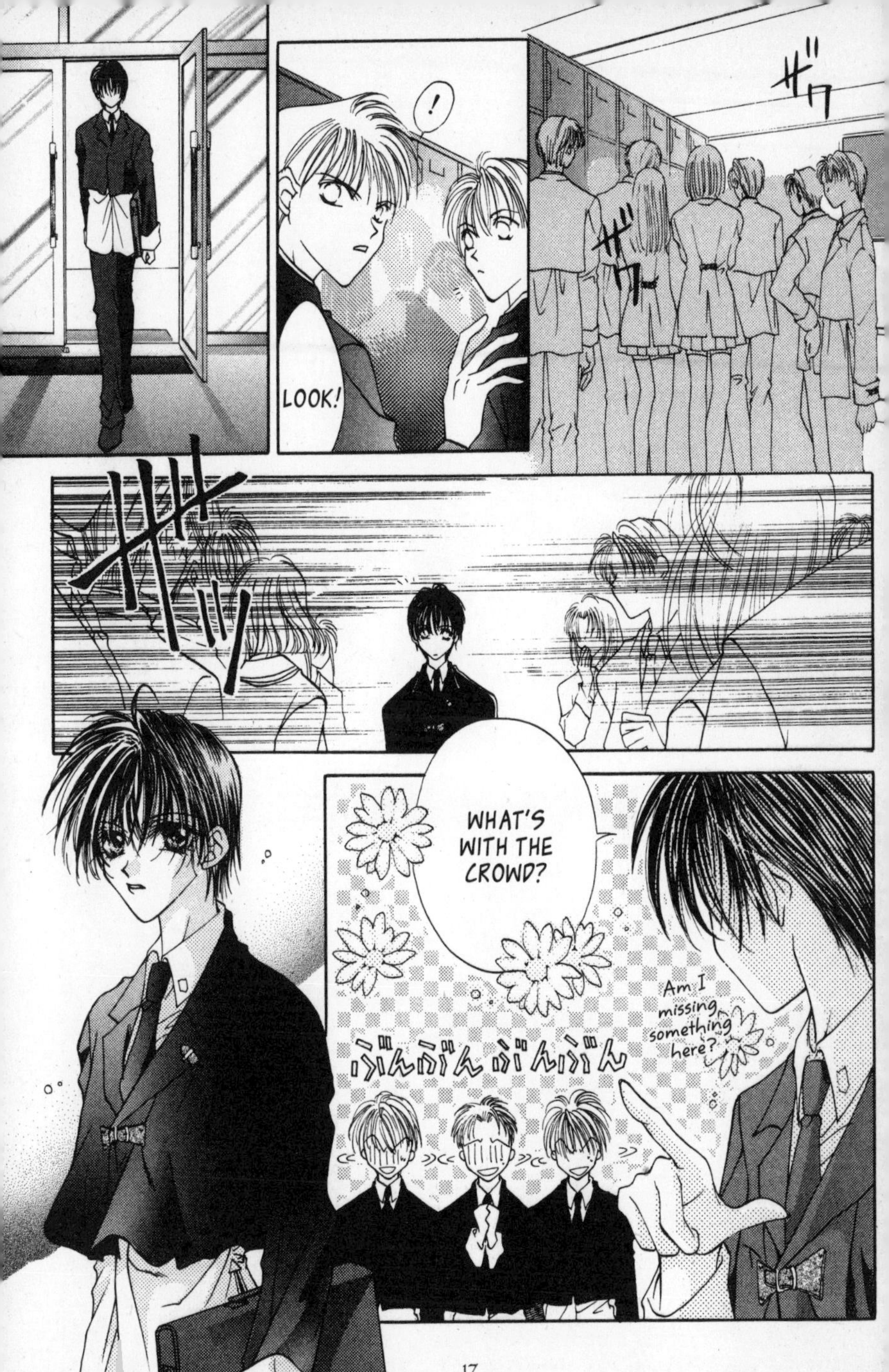
ザワ
ザワ
!
LOOK!
ザザッ
WHAT'S WITH THE CROWD?
ぶんぶん ぶんぶん
Am I missing something here?

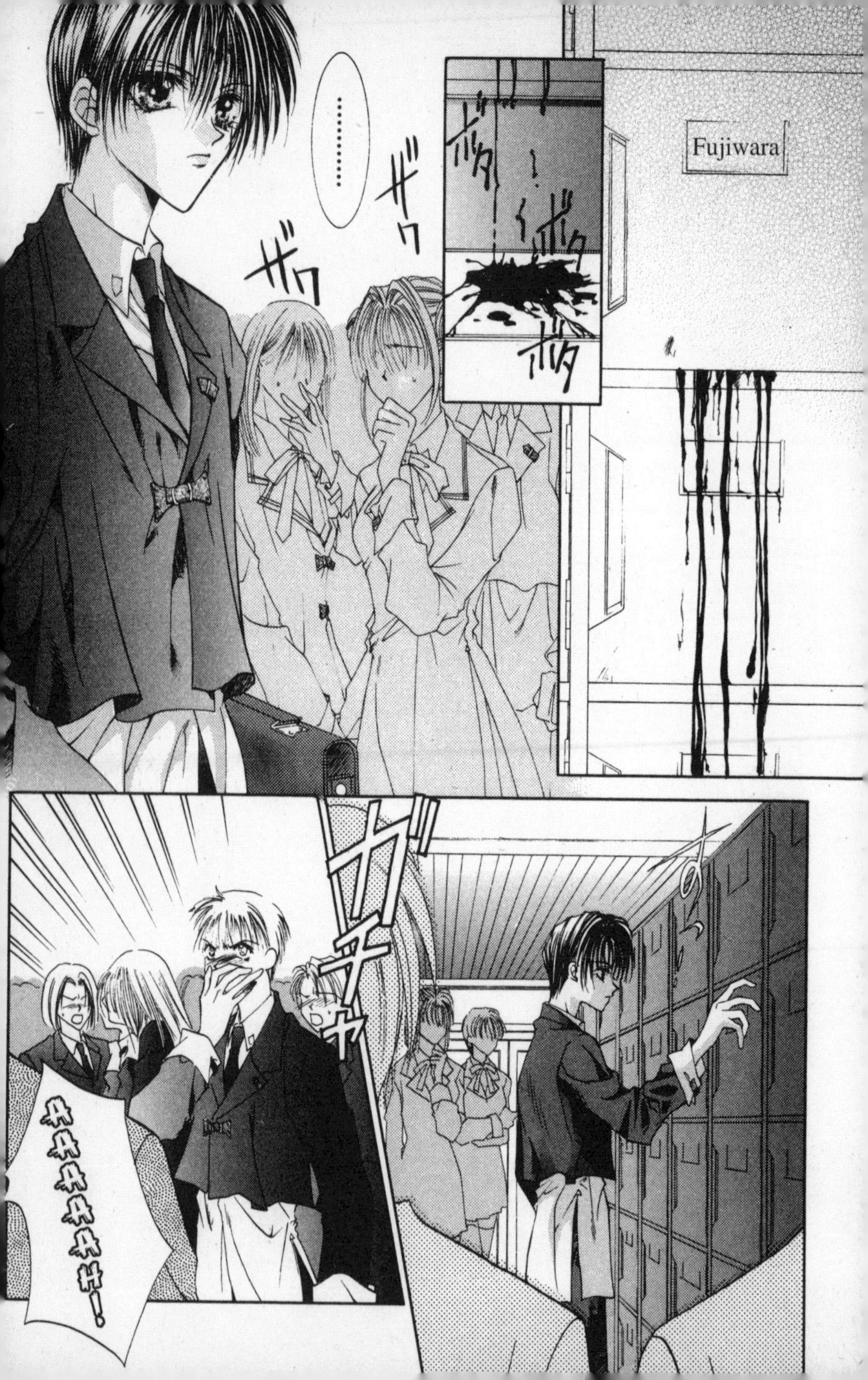
Fujiwara
ボタ
ボタ
ボタ
ザワ
ザワ
……
ガチャ
AAAAAH!

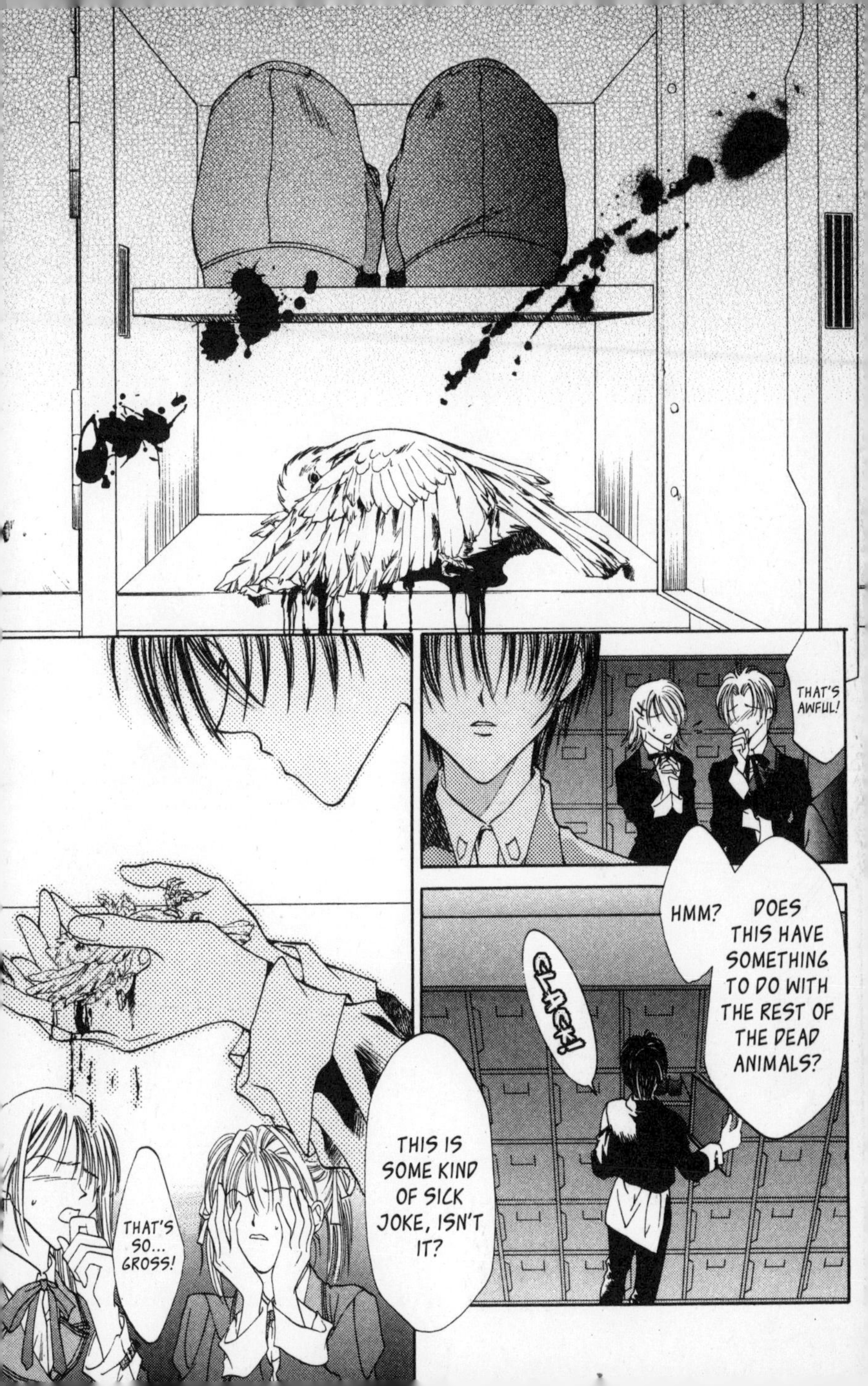
THAT'S AWFUL!
HMM? DOES THIS HAVE SOMETHING TO DO WITH THE REST OF THE DEAD ANIMALS?
CLACK!
THIS IS SOME KIND OF SICK JOKE, ISN'T IT?
THAT'S SO... GROSS!

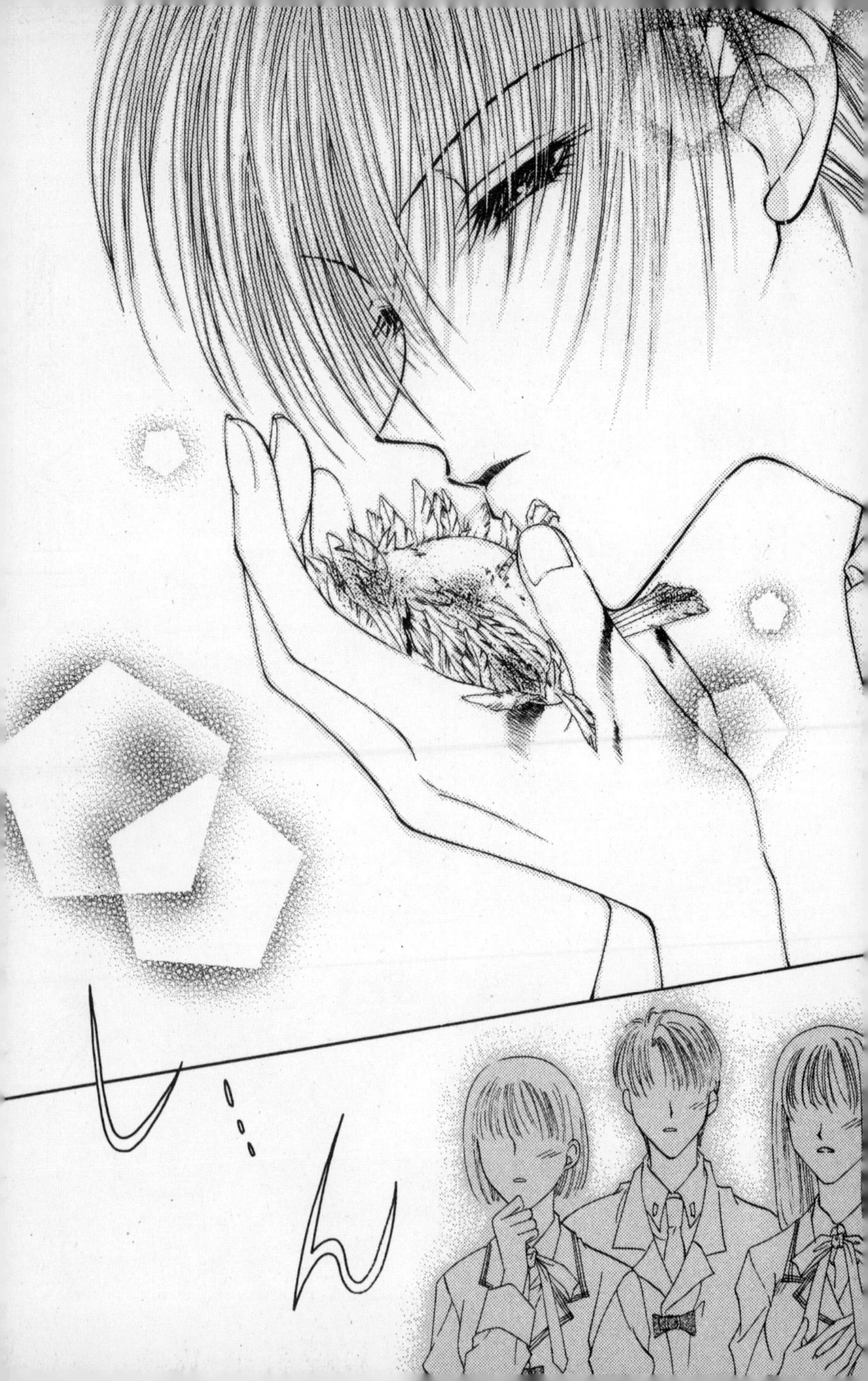
し…ん

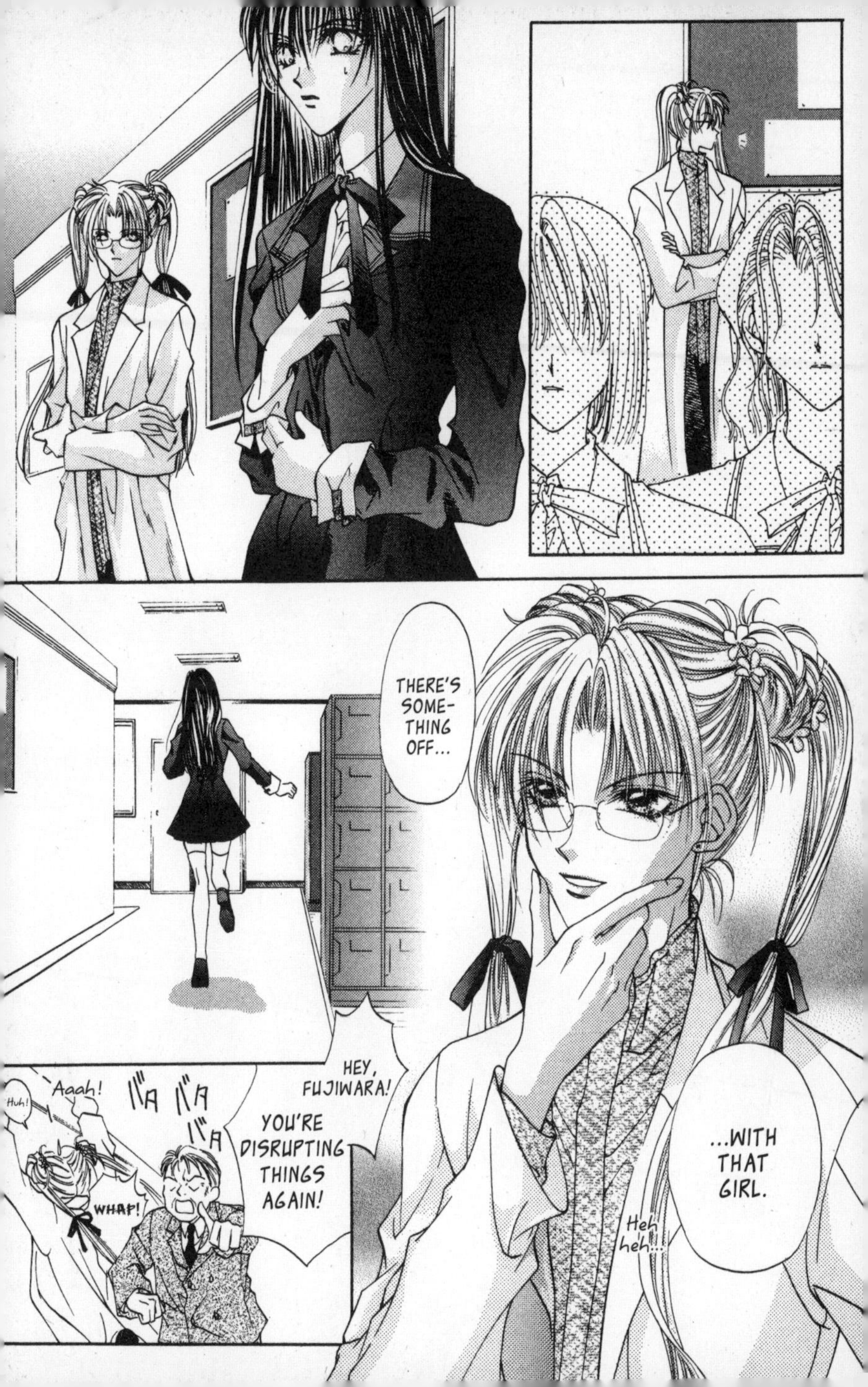
THERE'S SOMETHING OFF...
...WITH THAT GIRL.
Heh heh...
HEY, FUJIWARA!
YOU'RE DISRUPTING THINGS AGAIN!
バタ バタ バタ
Aaah!
Huh!
WHAP!

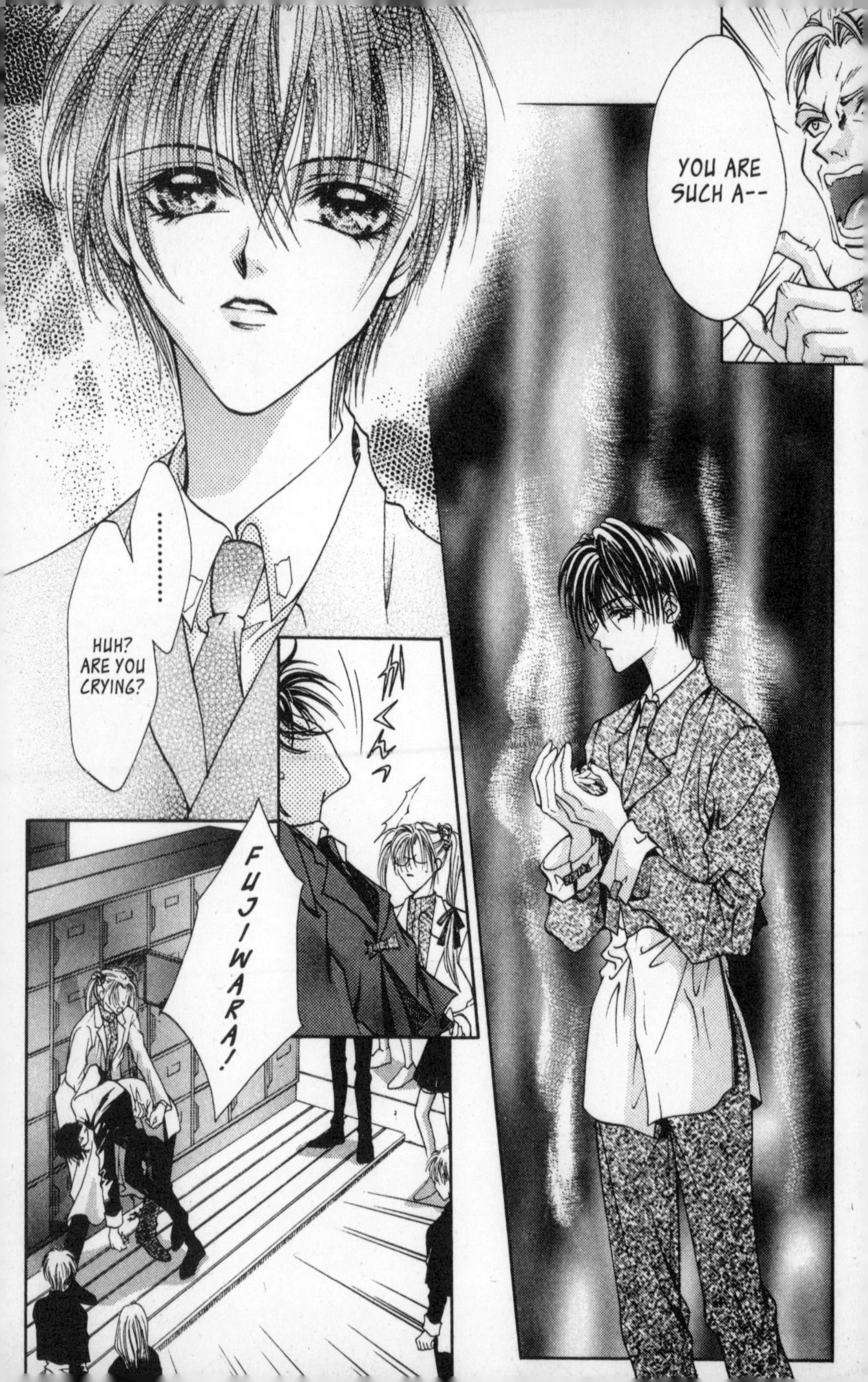
YOU ARE SUCH A--
......
HUH? ARE YOU CRYING?
FUJIWARA!

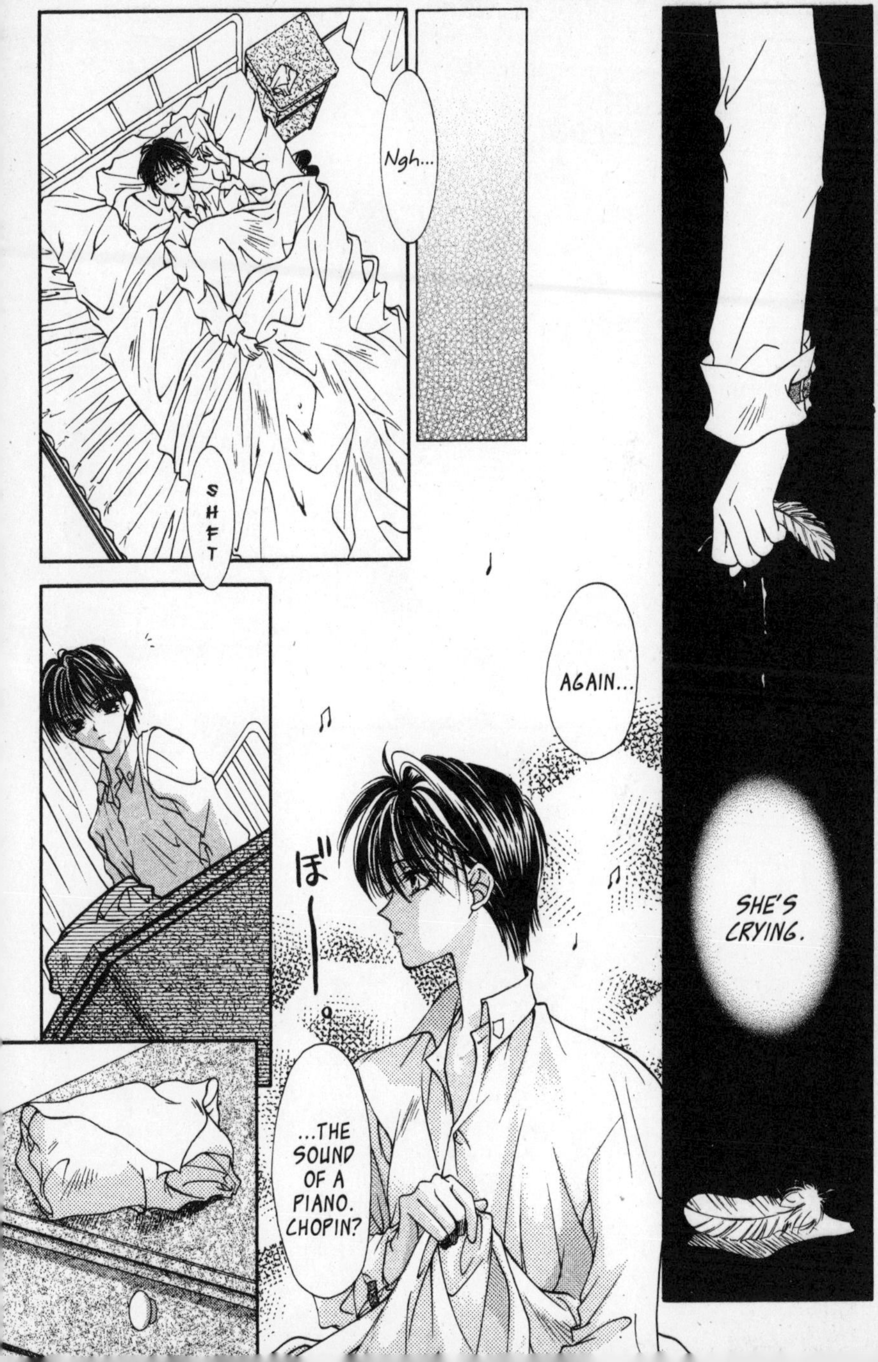
SHE'S CRYING.
Ngh...
SHFT
AGAIN...
ぼー。
...THE SOUND OF A PIANO. CHOPIN?

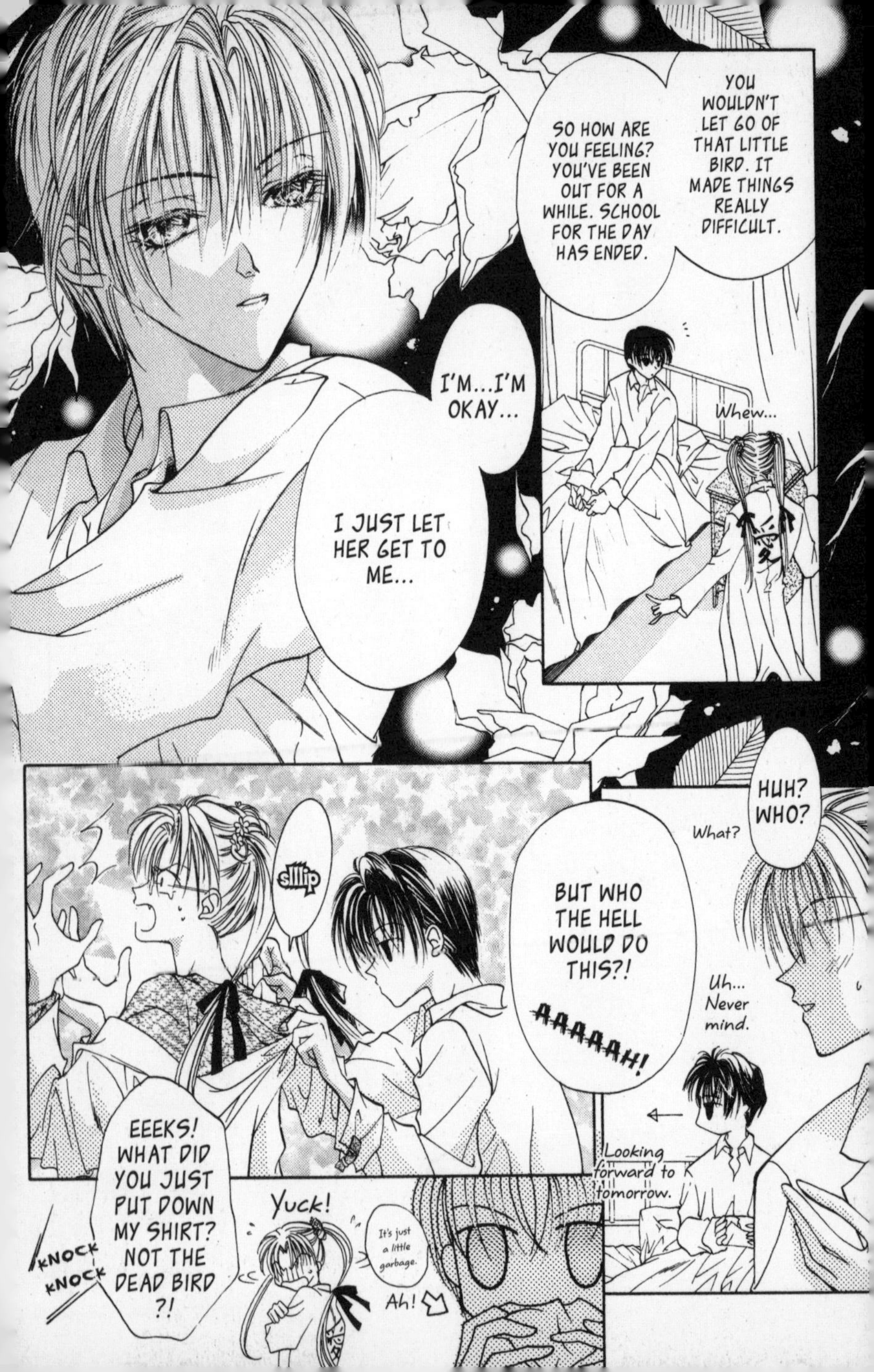
YOU WOULDN'T LET GO OF THAT LITTLE BIRD. IT MADE THINGS REALLY DIFFICULT.
SO HOW ARE YOU FEELING? YOU'VE BEEN OUT FOR A WHILE. SCHOOL FOR THE DAY HAS ENDED.
Whew...
I'M...I'M OKAY...
I JUST LET HER GET TO ME...
HUH? WHO?
What?
Uh... Never mind.
Looking forward to tomorrow.
BUT WHO THE HELL WOULD DO THIS?!
AAAAAAH!
slllip
EEEKS! WHAT DID YOU JUST PUT DOWN MY SHIRT? NOT THE DEAD BIRD?!
Yuck!
It's just a little garbage.
Ah!
KNOCK KNOCK

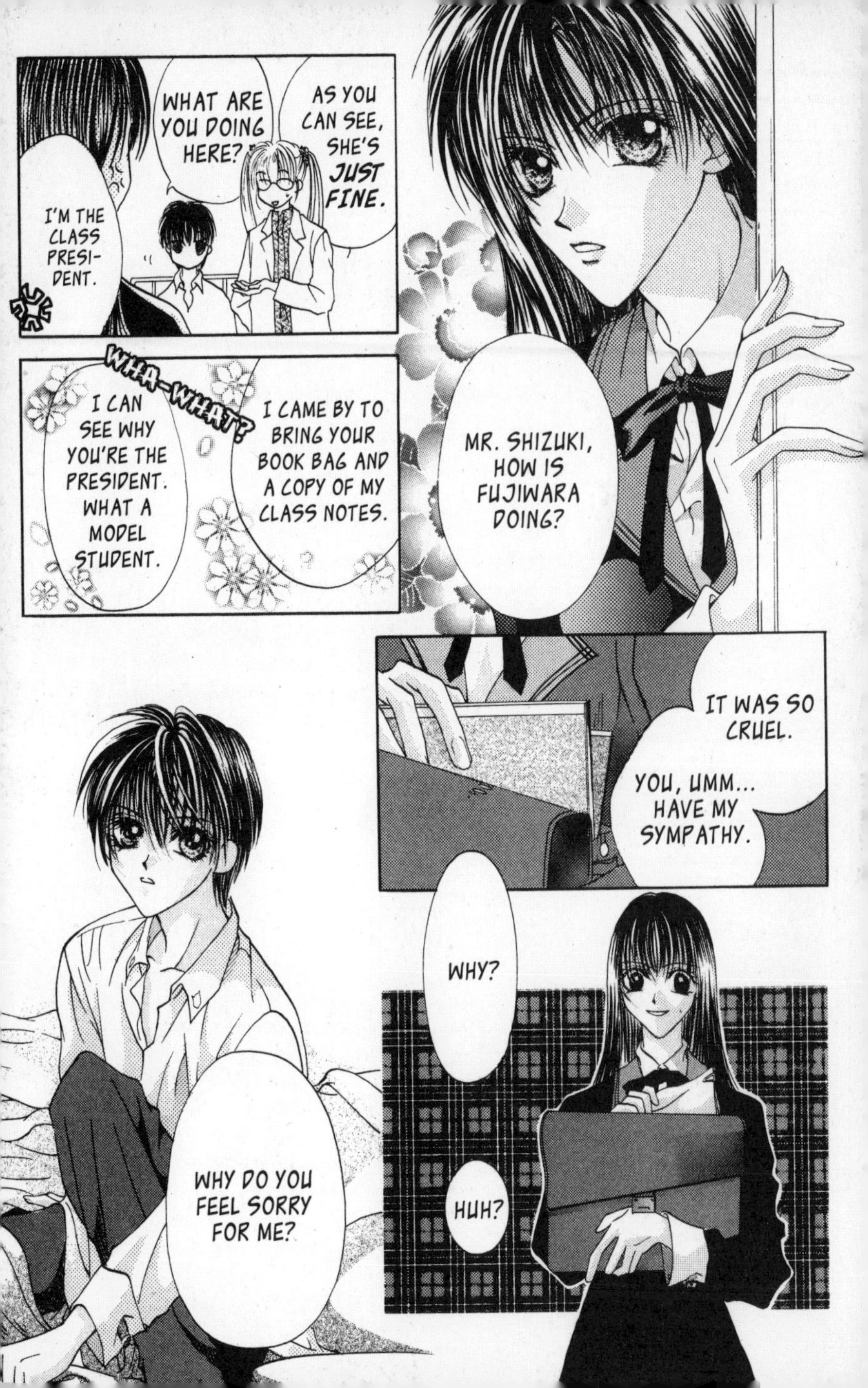
MR. SHIZUKI, HOW IS FUJIWARA DOING?
AS YOU CAN SEE, SHE'S JUST FINE.
WHAT ARE YOU DOING HERE?
I'M THE CLASS PRESIDENT.
I CAME BY TO BRING YOUR BOOK BAG AND A COPY OF MY CLASS NOTES.
WHA-WHAT?
I CAN SEE WHY YOU'RE THE PRESIDENT. WHAT A MODEL STUDENT.
IT WAS SO CRUEL.
YOU, UMM... HAVE MY SYMPATHY.
WHY?
HUH?
WHY DO YOU FEEL SORRY FOR ME?

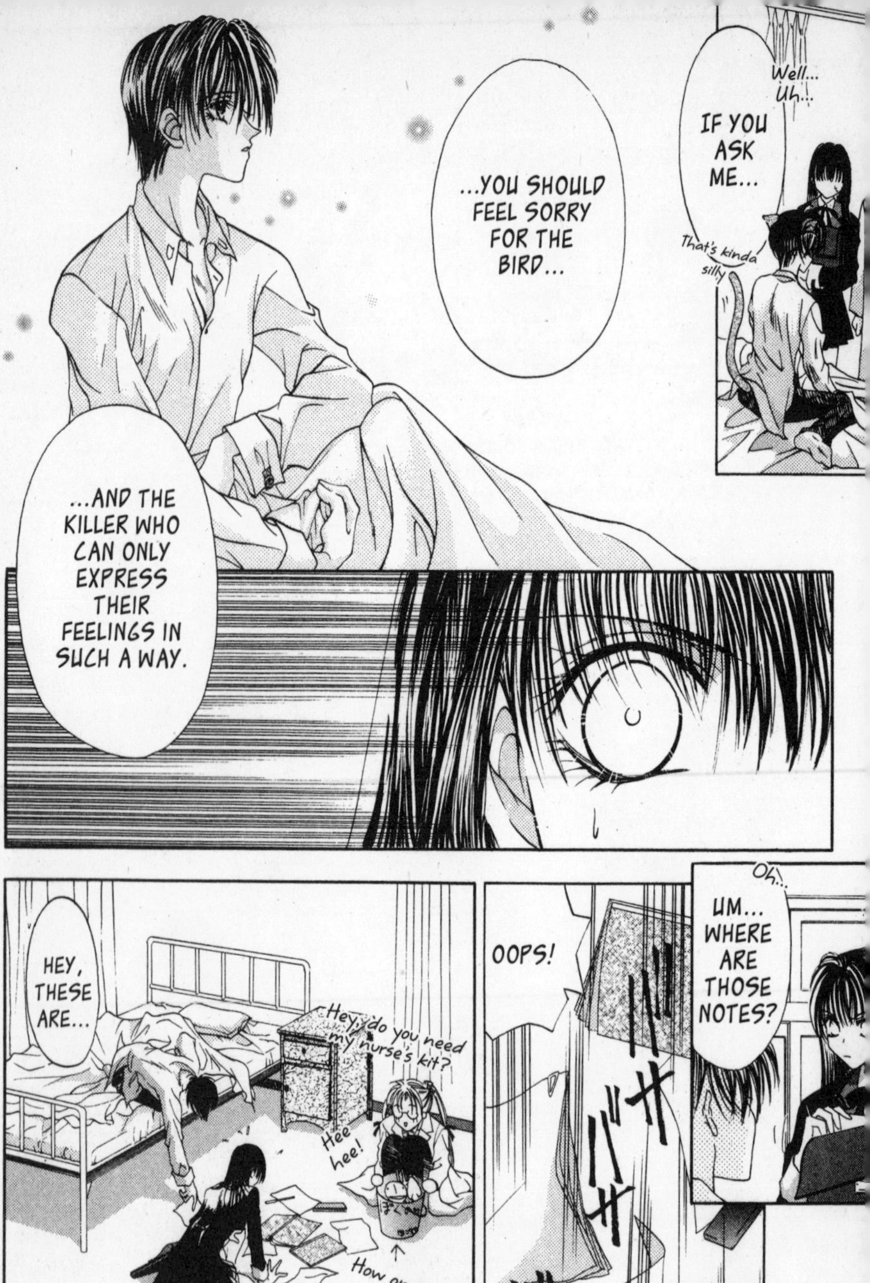

Well... Uh...
IF YOU ASK ME...
That's kinda silly
...YOU SHOULD FEEL SORRY FOR THE BIRD...
...AND THE KILLER WHO CAN ONLY EXPRESS THEIR FEELINGS IN SUCH A WAY.
Oh...
UM... WHERE ARE THOSE NOTES?
OOPS!
HEY, THESE ARE...
Hey, do you need my nurse's kit?
Hee hee!
How on earth would THAT help?

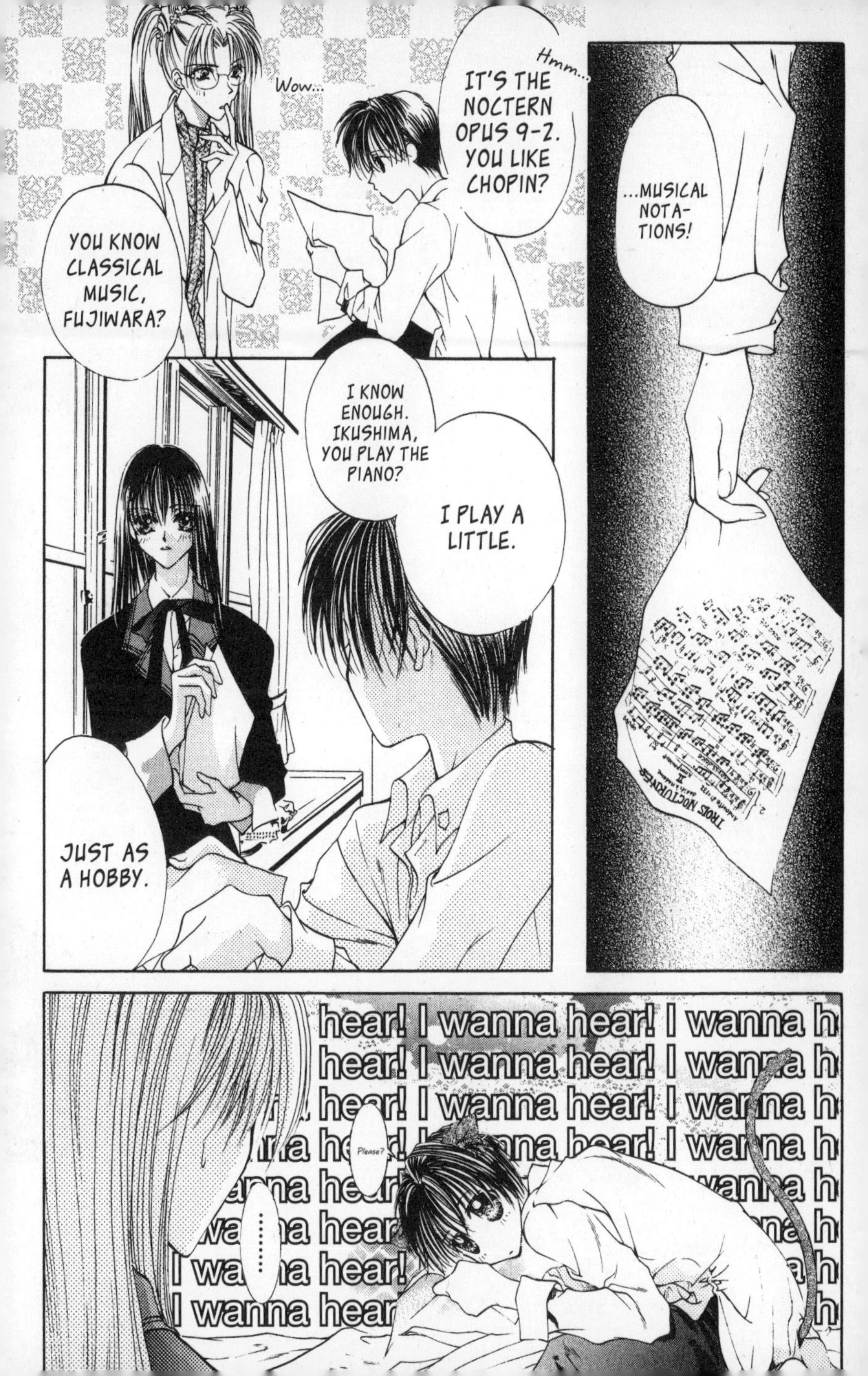
...MUSICAL NOTATIONS!
TROIS NOCTURNES
Hmm...
IT'S THE NOCTERN OPUS 9-2. YOU LIKE CHOPIN?
Wow...
YOU KNOW CLASSICAL MUSIC, FUJIWARA?
I KNOW ENOUGH. IKUSHIMA, YOU PLAY THE PIANO?
I PLAY A LITTLE.
JUST AS A HOBBY.
hear! I wanna hear! I wanna h
hear! I wanna hear! I wanna h
hear! I wanna hear! I wanna h
I wanna hear!
I wanna hear
Please?
......

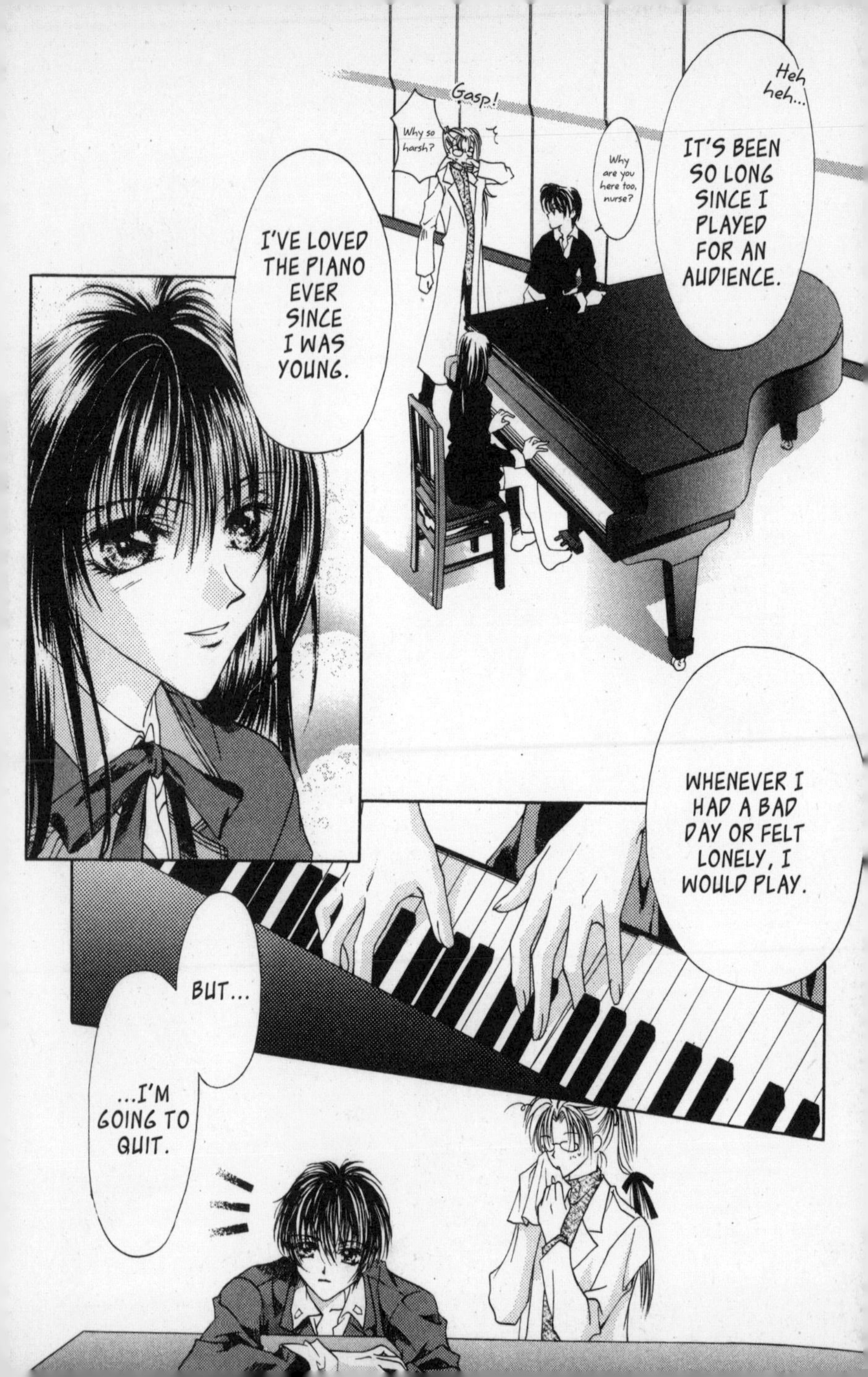
Heh heh...
IT'S BEEN SO LONG SINCE I PLAYED FOR AN AUDIENCE.
Why are you here too, nurse?
Gasp!
Why so harsh?
I'VE LOVED THE PIANO EVER SINCE I WAS YOUNG.
WHENEVER I HAD A BAD DAY OR FELT LONELY, I WOULD PLAY.
BUT...
...I'M GOING TO QUIT.

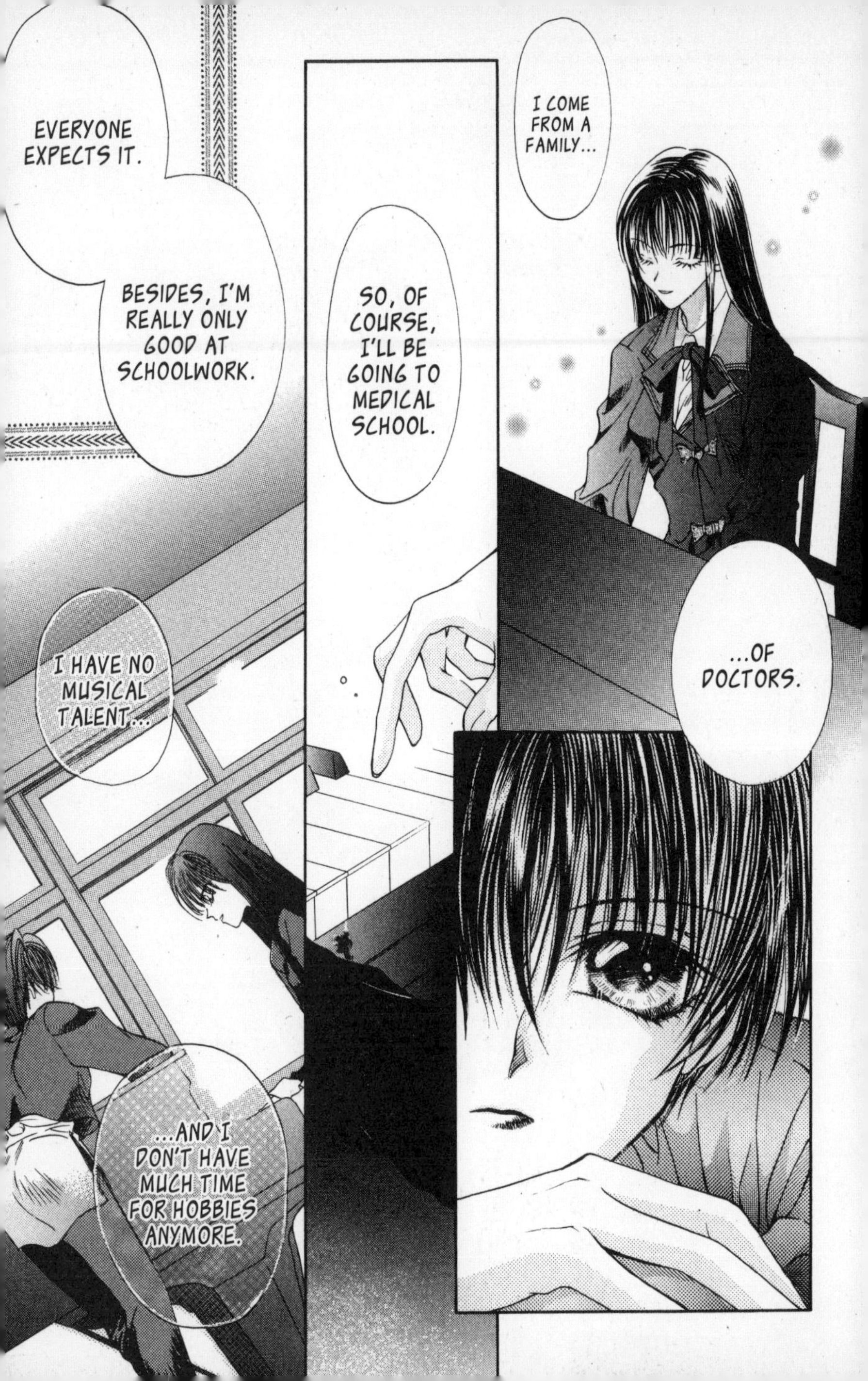
I COME FROM A FAMILY...
...OF DOCTORS.
SO, OF COURSE, I'LL BE GOING TO MEDICAL SCHOOL.
EVERYONE EXPECTS IT.
BESIDES, I'M REALLY ONLY GOOD AT SCHOOLWORK.
I HAVE NO MUSICAL TALENT...
...AND I DON'T HAVE MUCH TIME FOR HOBBIES ANYMORE.

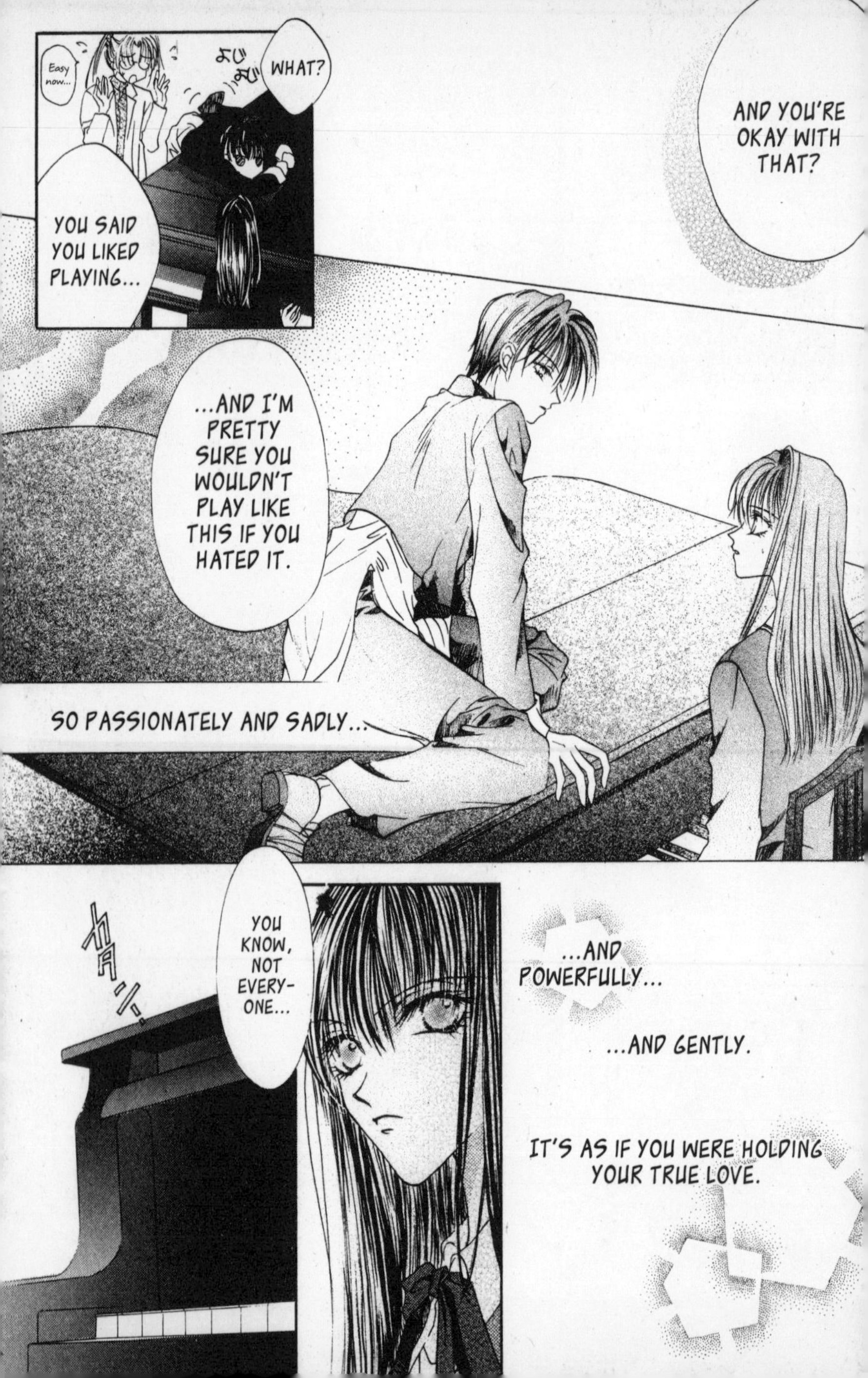
AND YOU'RE OKAY WITH THAT?
WHAT?
Easy now...
YOU SAID YOU LIKED PLAYING...
...AND I'M PRETTY SURE YOU WOULDN'T PLAY LIKE THIS IF YOU HATED IT.
SO PASSIONATELY AND SADLY...
...AND POWERFULLY...
...AND GENTLY.
IT'S AS IF YOU WERE HOLDING YOUR TRUE LOVE.
YOU KNOW, NOT EVERY-ONE...

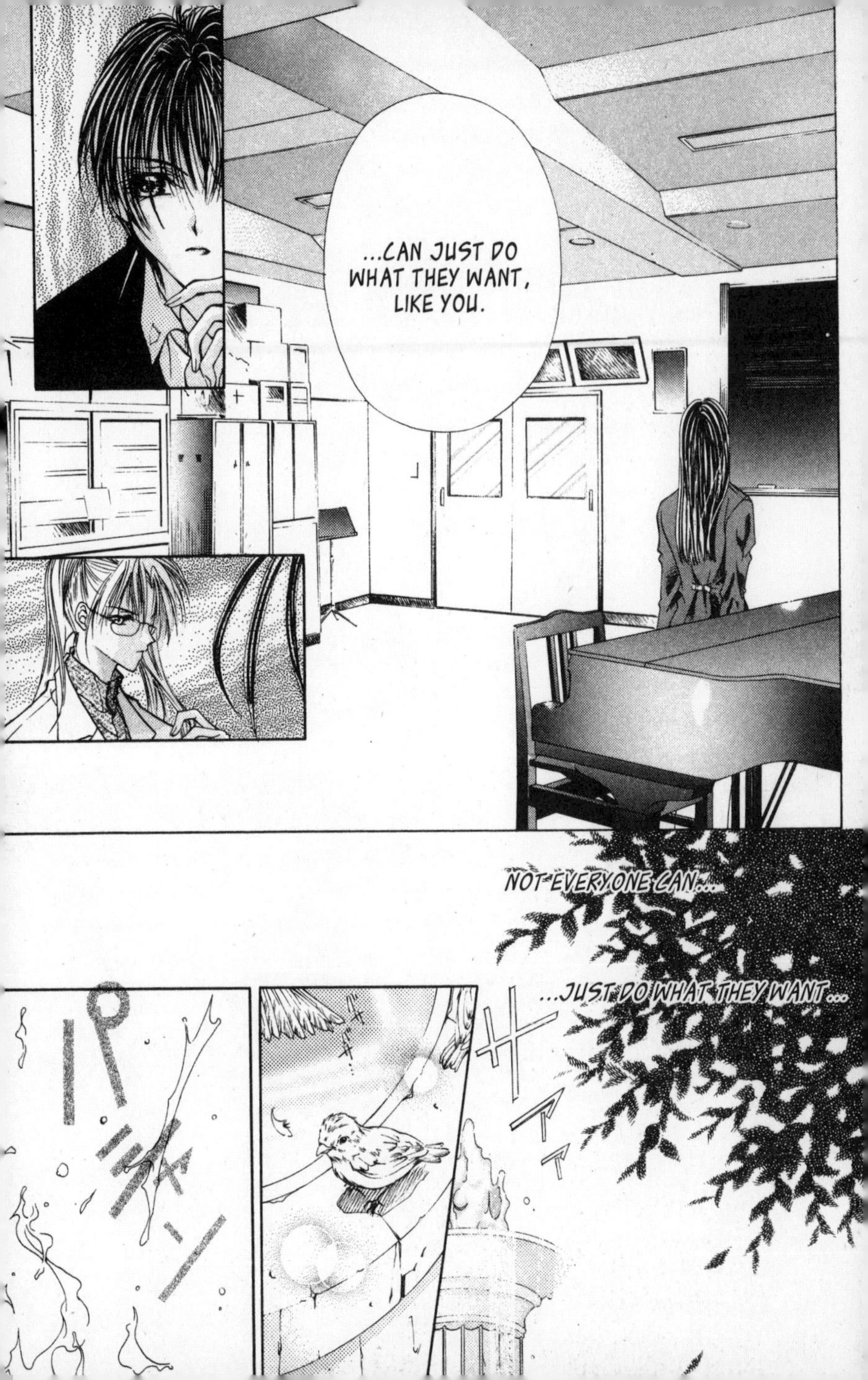
...CAN JUST DO WHAT THEY WANT, LIKE YOU.
NOT EVERYONE CAN...
...JUST DO WHAT THEY WANT...

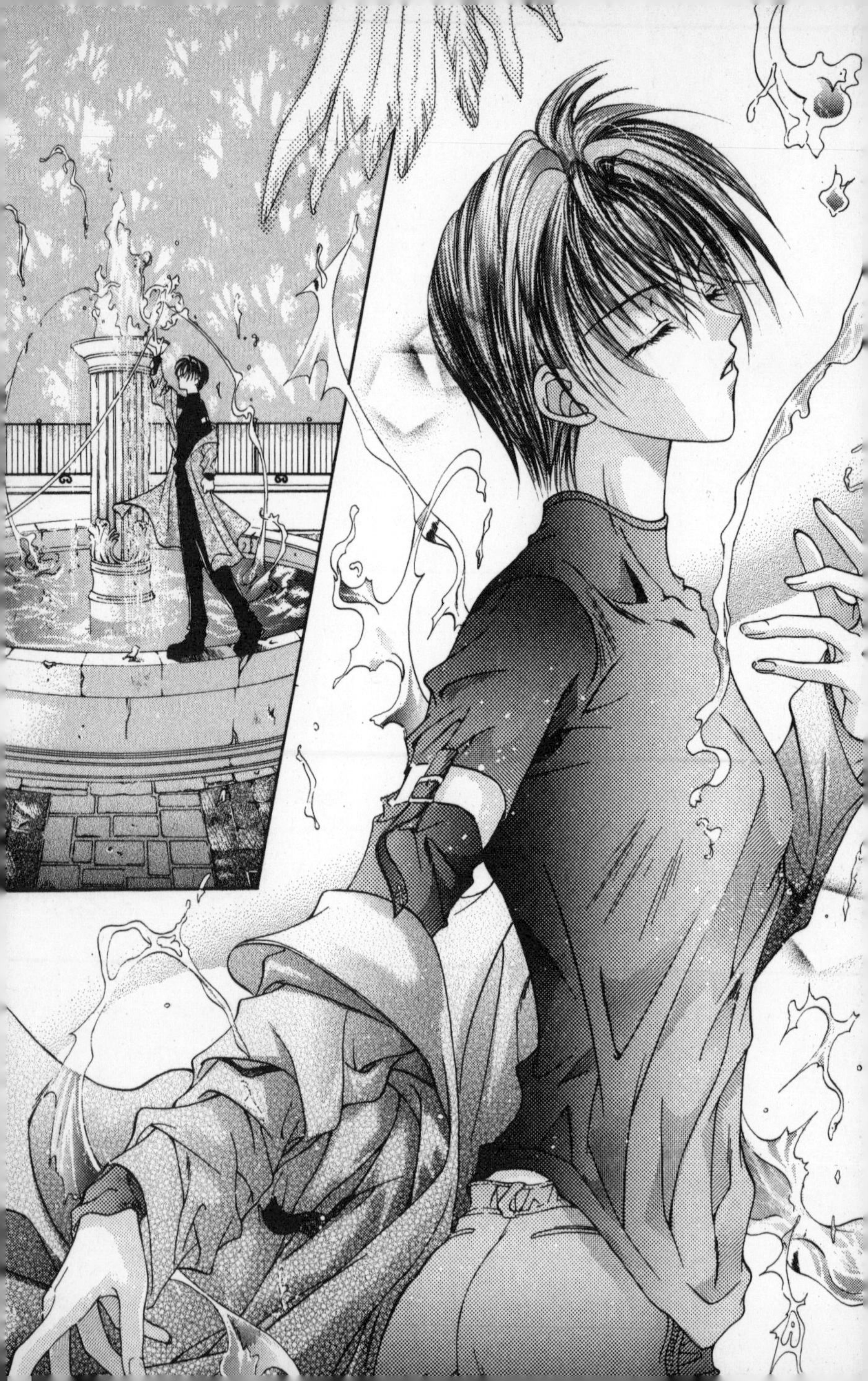

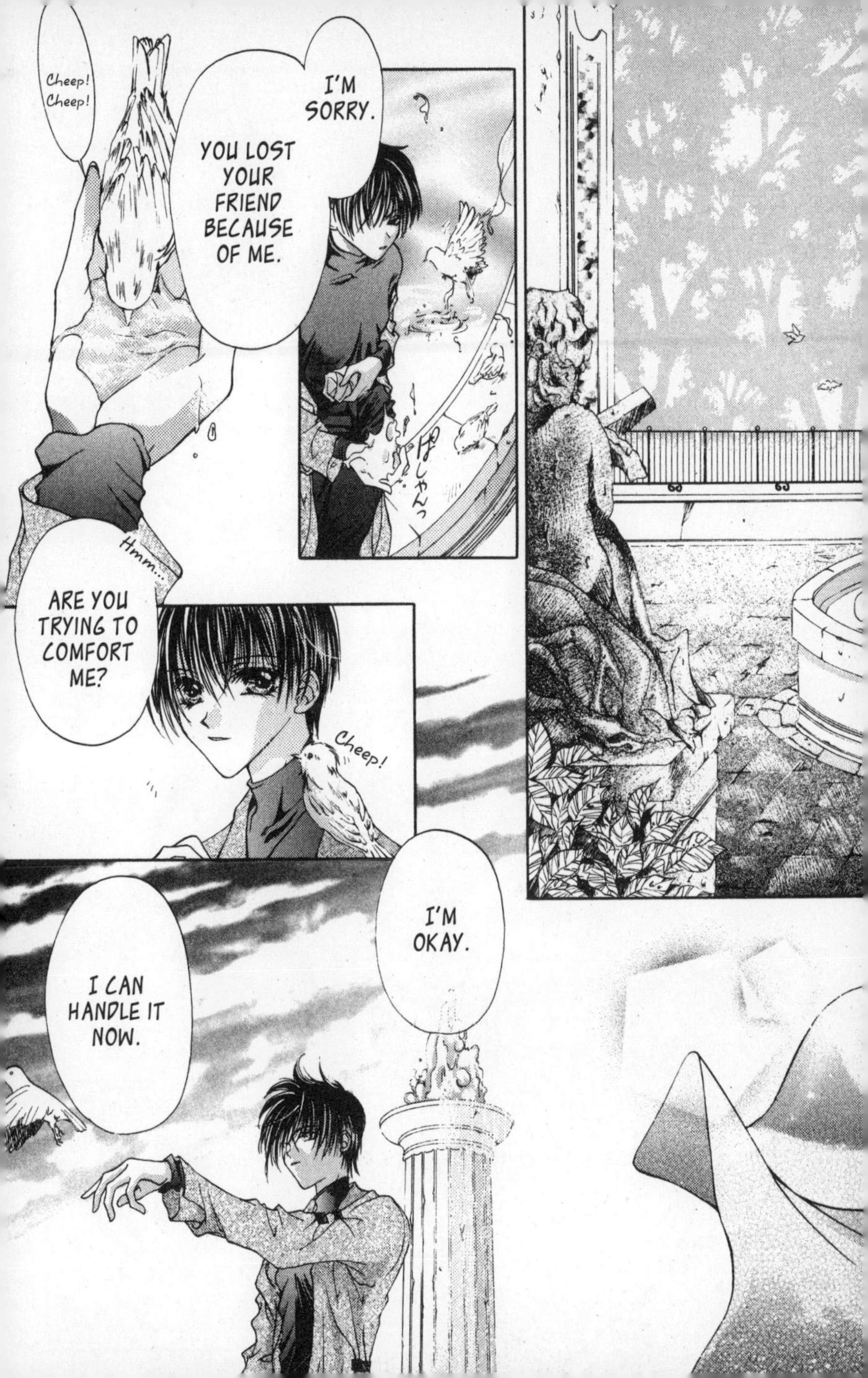
ぱしゃんっ
I'M SORRY.
YOU LOST YOUR FRIEND BECAUSE OF ME.
Cheep! Cheep!
Hmm...
ARE YOU TRYING TO COMFORT ME?
Cheep!
I'M OKAY.
I CAN HANDLE IT NOW.

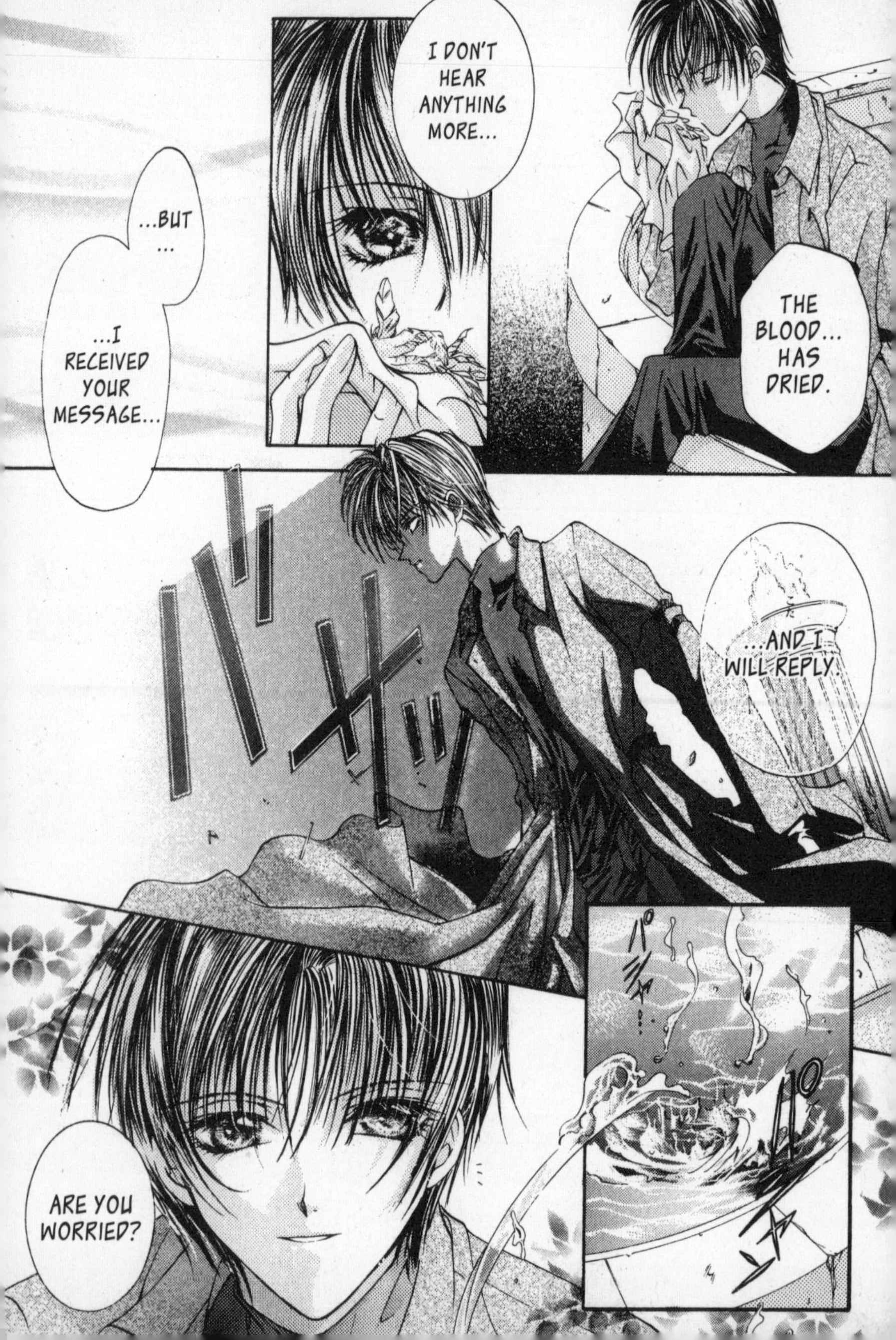
THE BLOOD... HAS DRIED.
I DON'T HEAR ANYTHING MORE...
...BUT ...
...I RECEIVED YOUR MESSAGE...
...AND I WILL REPLY.
ARE YOU WORRIED?

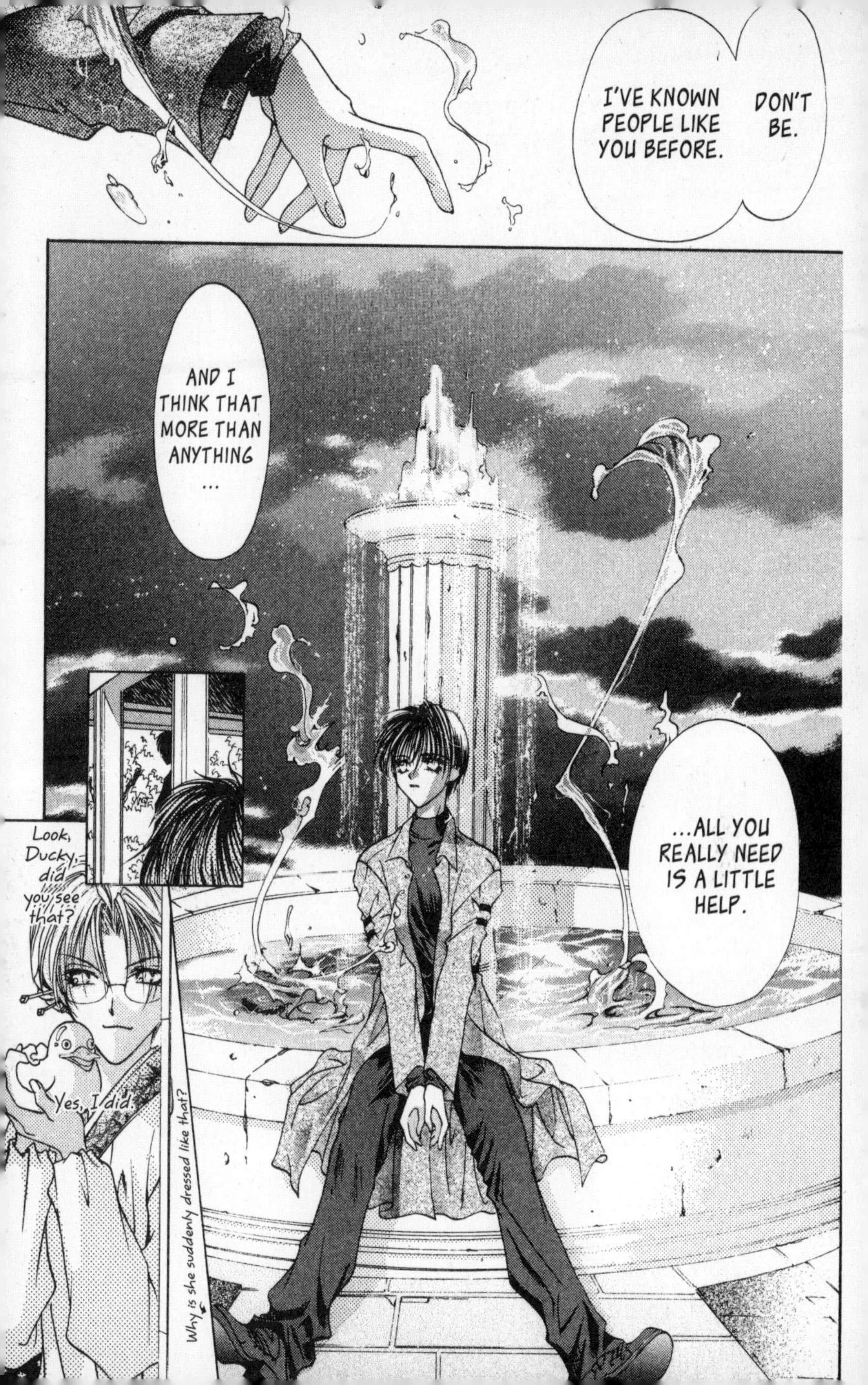
DON'T BE.
I'VE KNOWN PEOPLE LIKE YOU BEFORE.
AND I THINK THAT MORE THAN ANYTHING ...
...ALL YOU REALLY NEED IS A LITTLE HELP.
Look, Ducky, did you see that?
Yes, I did.
Why is she suddenly dressed like that?

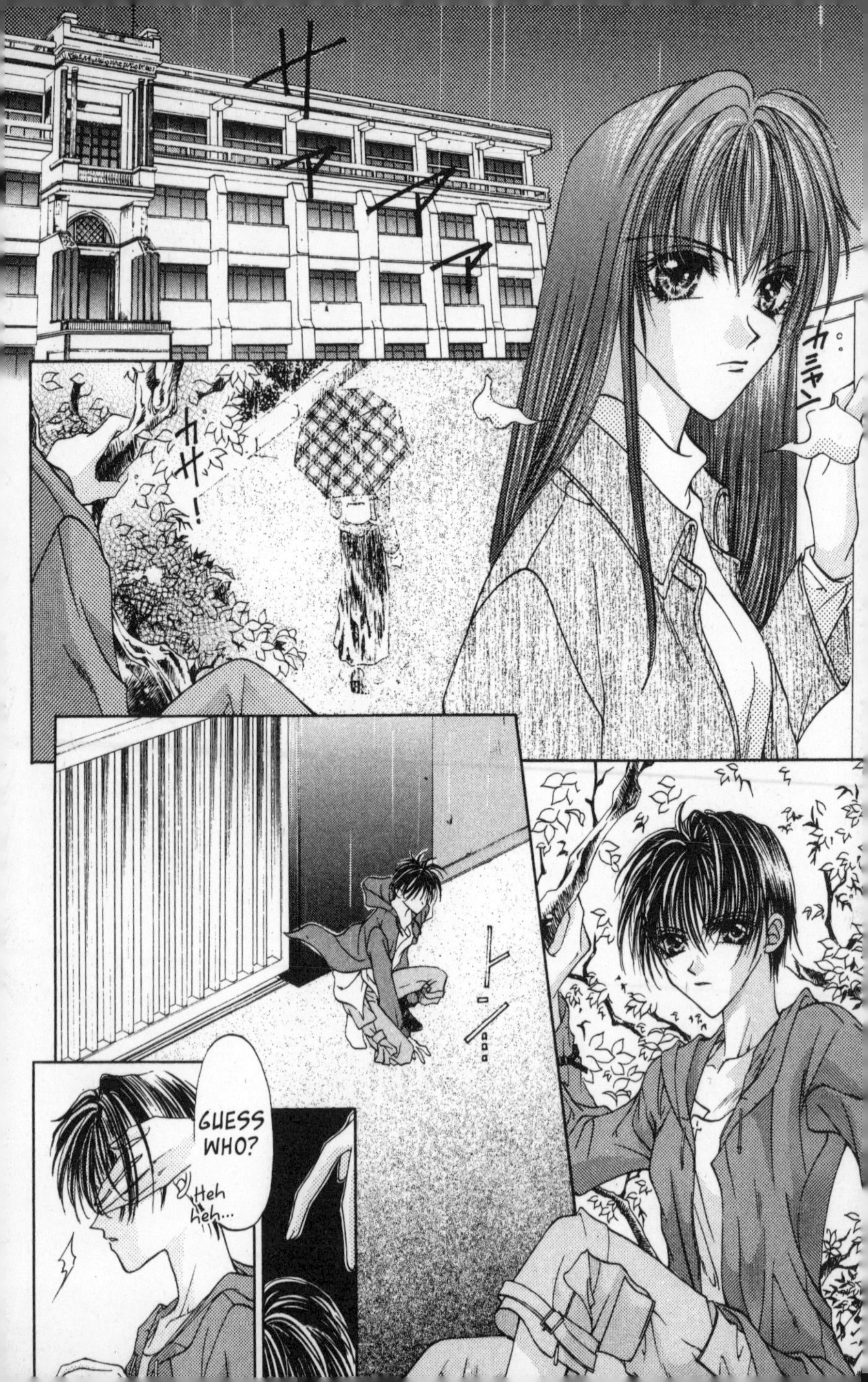
カシャン..
サァァァ
ガサッ!
ト…
GUESS WHO?
Heh heh...

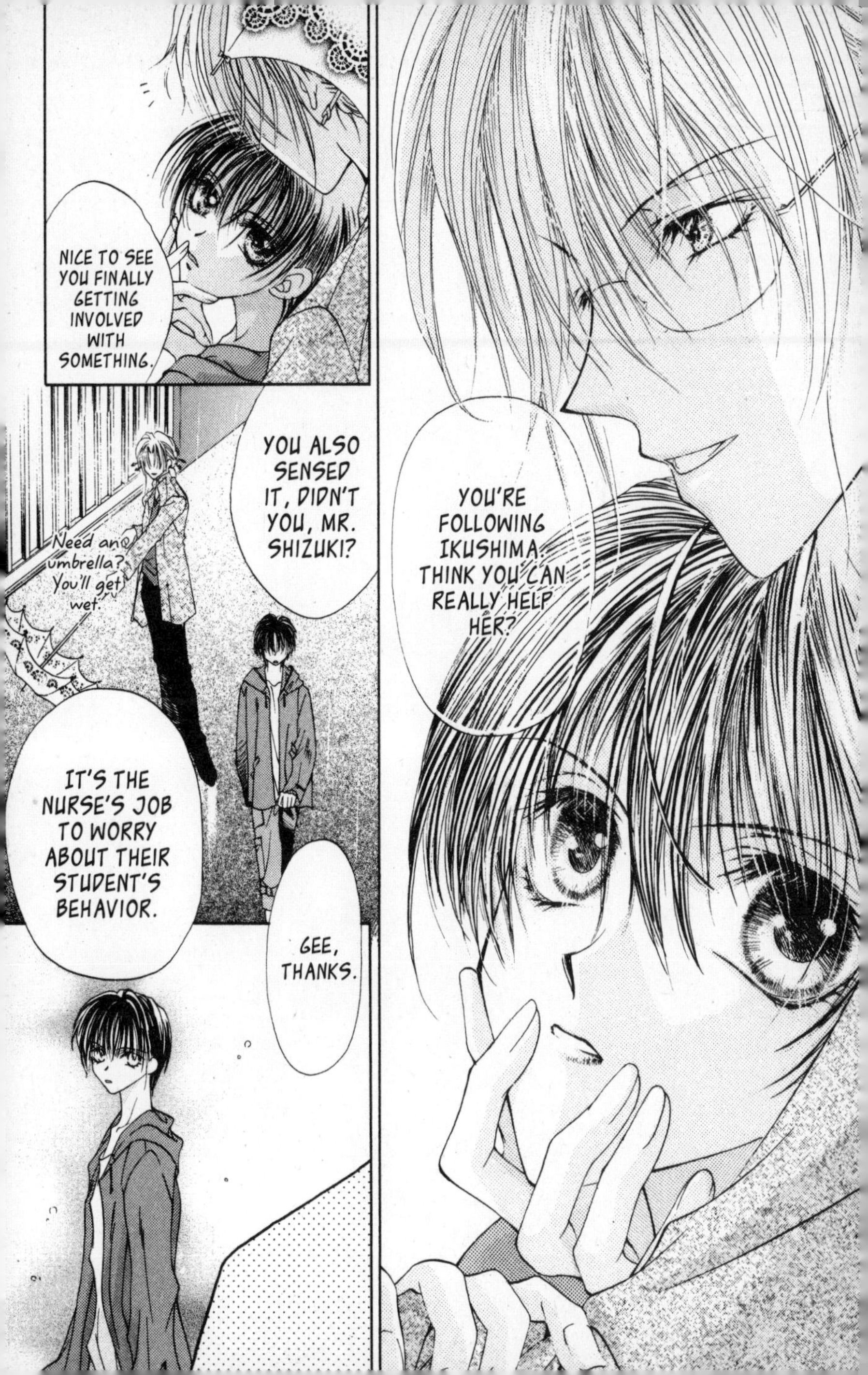
YOU'RE FOLLOWING IKUSHIMA. THINK YOU CAN REALLY HELP HER?
NICE TO SEE YOU FINALLY GETTING INVOLVED WITH SOMETHING.
YOU ALSO SENSED IT, DIDN'T YOU, MR. SHIZUKI?
Need an umbrella? You'll get wet.
IT'S THE NURSE'S JOB TO WORRY ABOUT THEIR STUDENT'S BEHAVIOR.
GEE, THANKS.

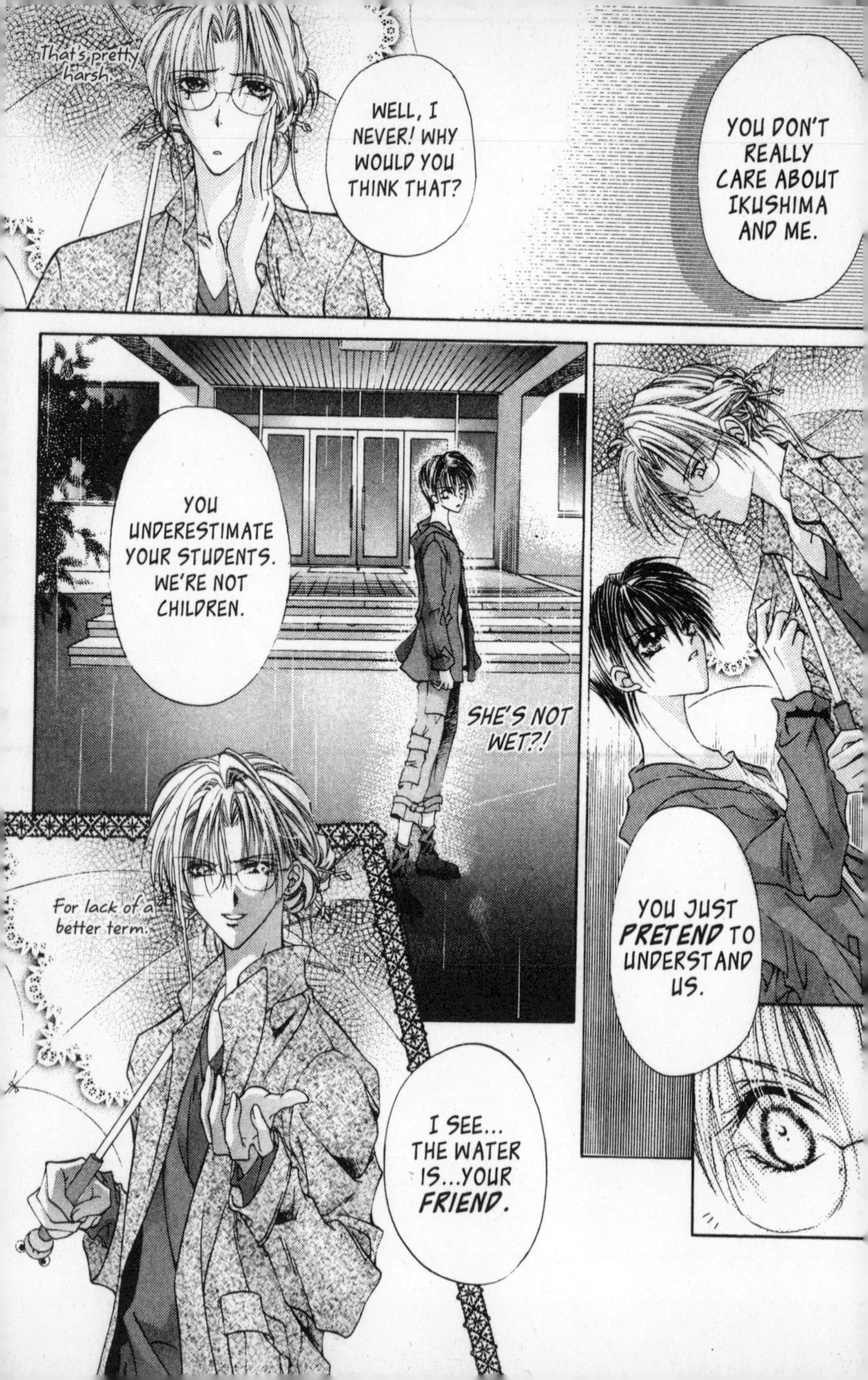

YOU DON'T REALLY CARE ABOUT IKUSHIMA AND ME.
WELL, I NEVER! WHY WOULD YOU THINK THAT?
That's pretty harsh.
YOU JUST PRETEND TO UNDERSTAND US.
YOU UNDERESTIMATE YOUR STUDENTS. WE'RE NOT CHILDREN.
SHE'S NOT WET?!
I SEE... THE WATER IS...YOUR FRIEND.
For lack of a better term.

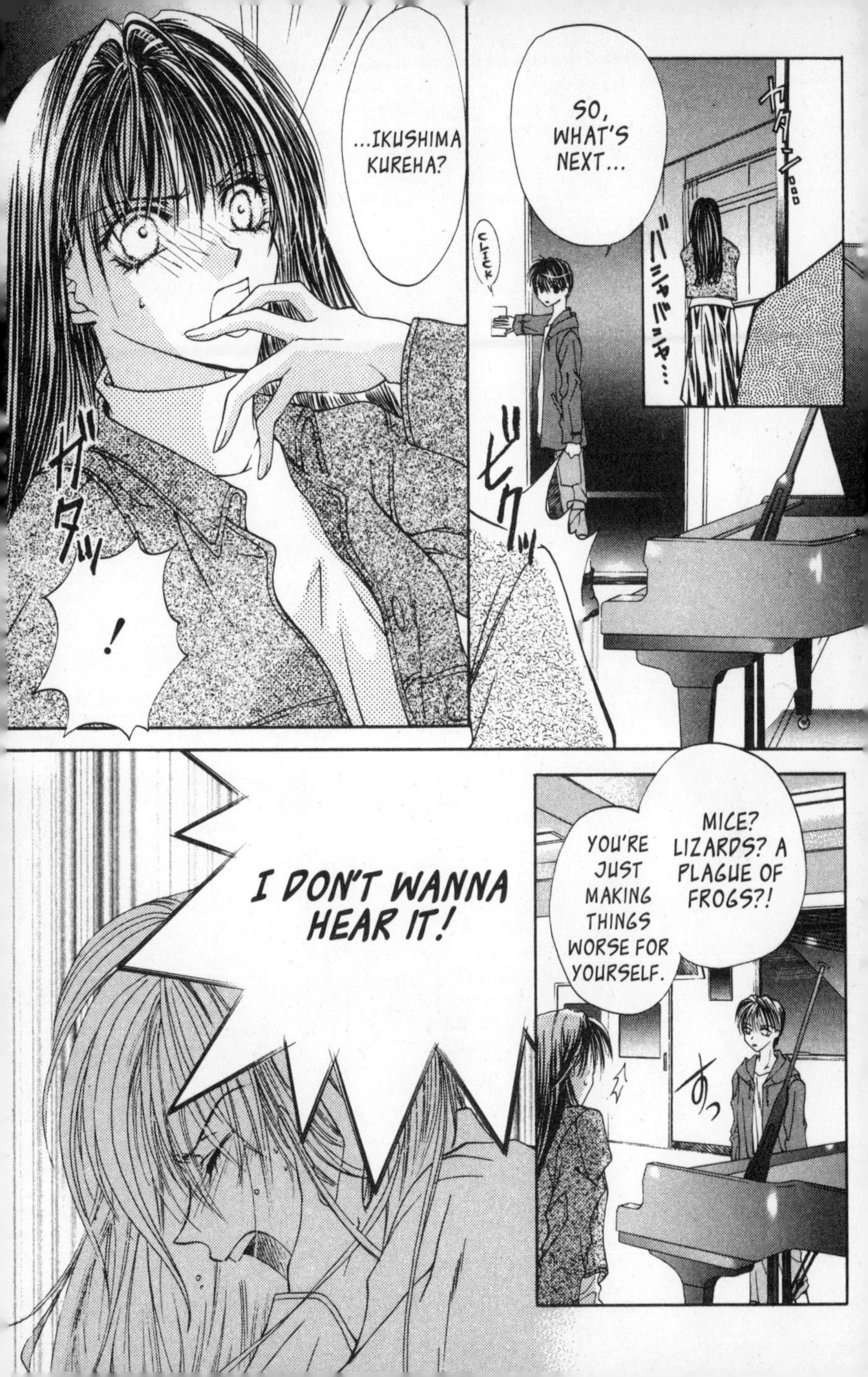
SO, WHAT'S NEXT...
CLICK
バシャバシャ…
ビクッ
...IKUSHIMA KUREHA?
ガタッ
!
MICE? LIZARDS? A PLAGUE OF FROGS?!
YOU'RE JUST MAKING THINGS WORSE FOR YOURSELF.
すっ
I DON'T WANNA HEAR IT!

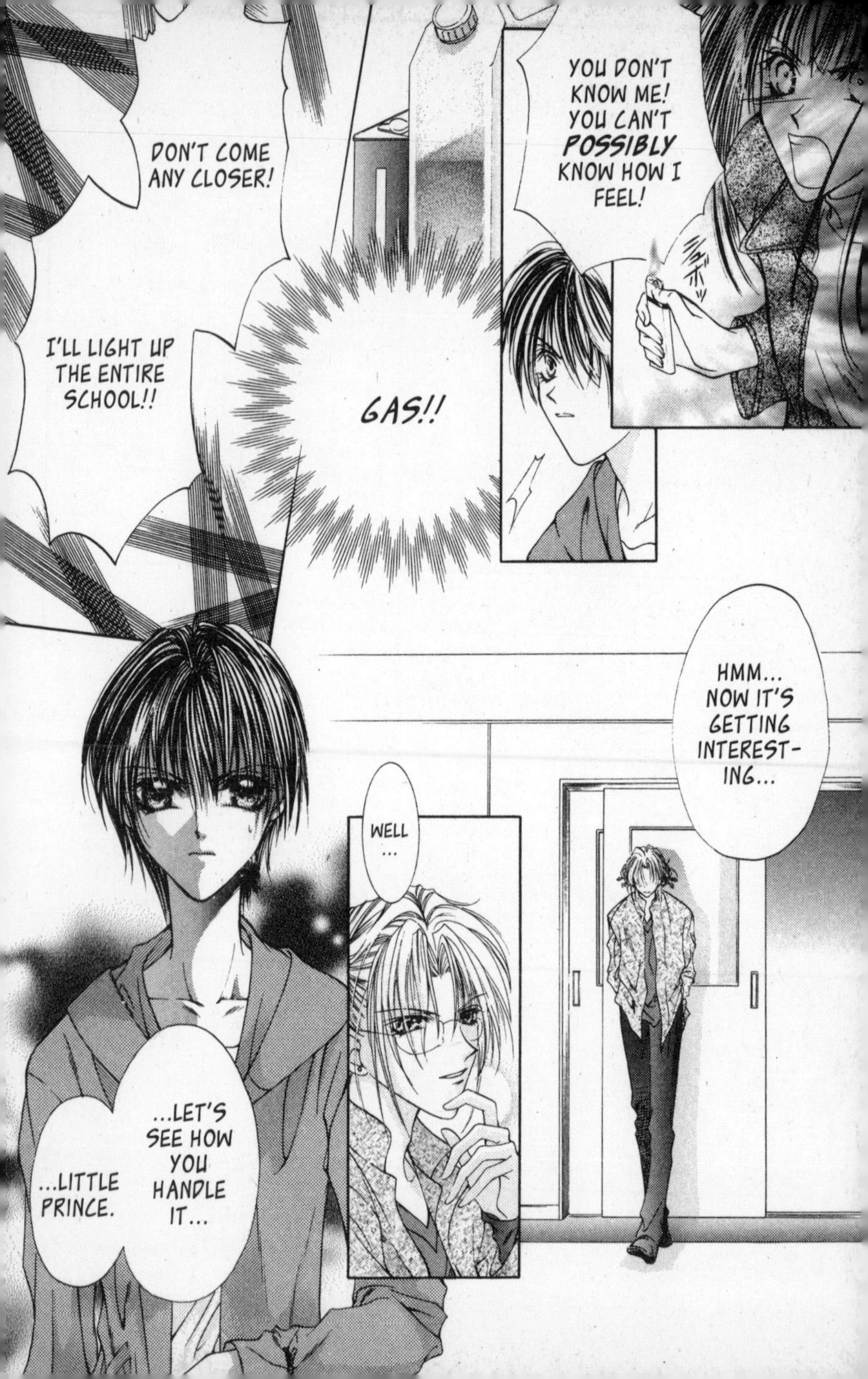
YOU DON'T KNOW ME! YOU CAN'T *POSSIBLY* KNOW HOW I FEEL!
DON'T COME ANY CLOSER!
I'LL LIGHT UP THE ENTIRE SCHOOL!!
GAS!!
HMM... NOW IT'S GETTING INTEREST-ING...
WELL...
...LET'S SEE HOW YOU HANDLE IT...
...LITTLE PRINCE.

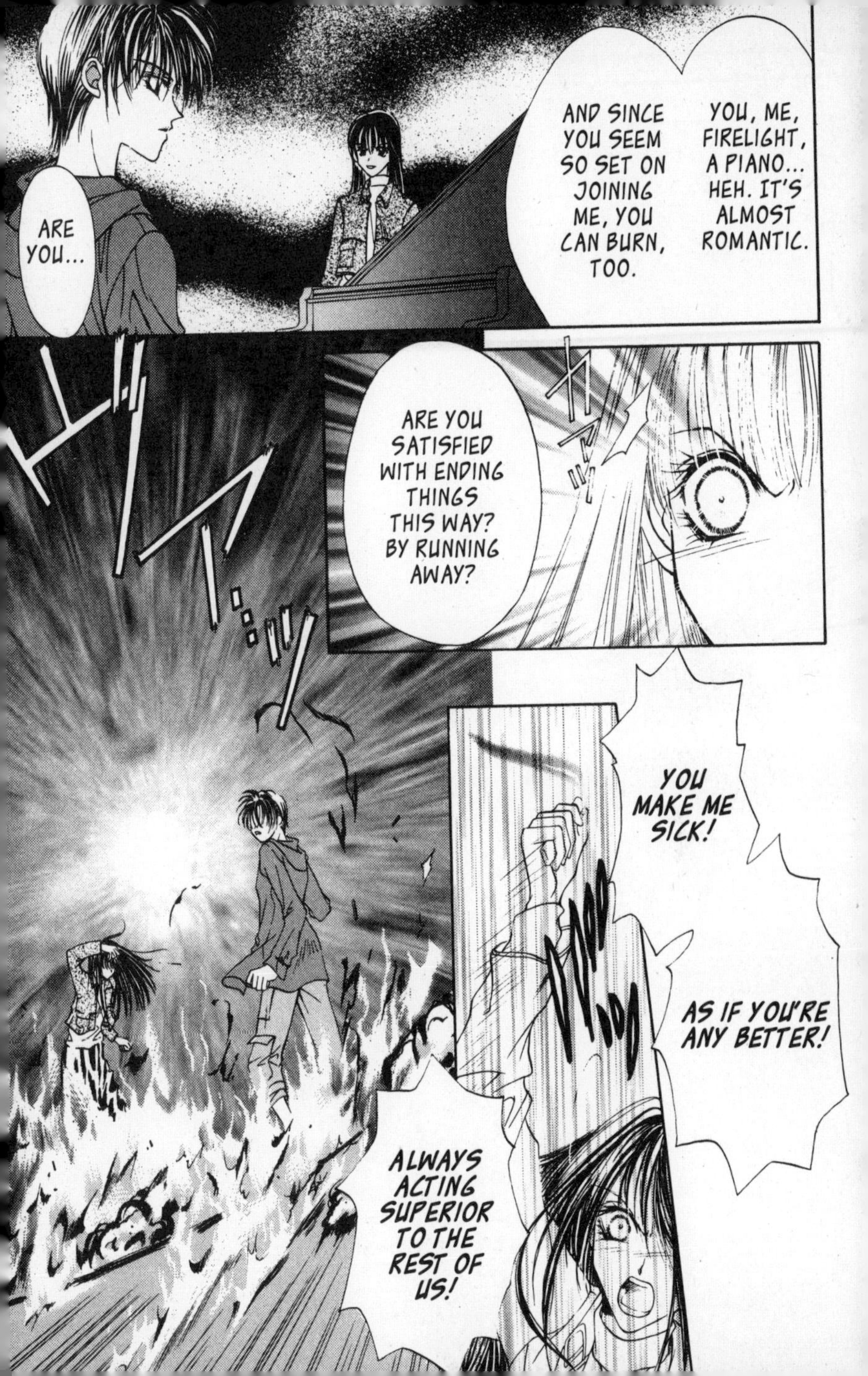
YOU, ME, FIRELIGHT, A PIANO... HEH. IT'S ALMOST ROMANTIC.
AND SINCE YOU SEEM SO SET ON JOINING ME, YOU CAN BURN, TOO.
ARE YOU...
ARE YOU SATISFIED WITH ENDING THINGS THIS WAY? BY RUNNING AWAY?
YOU MAKE ME SICK!
AS IF YOU'RE ANY BETTER!
ALWAYS ACTING SUPERIOR TO THE REST OF US!

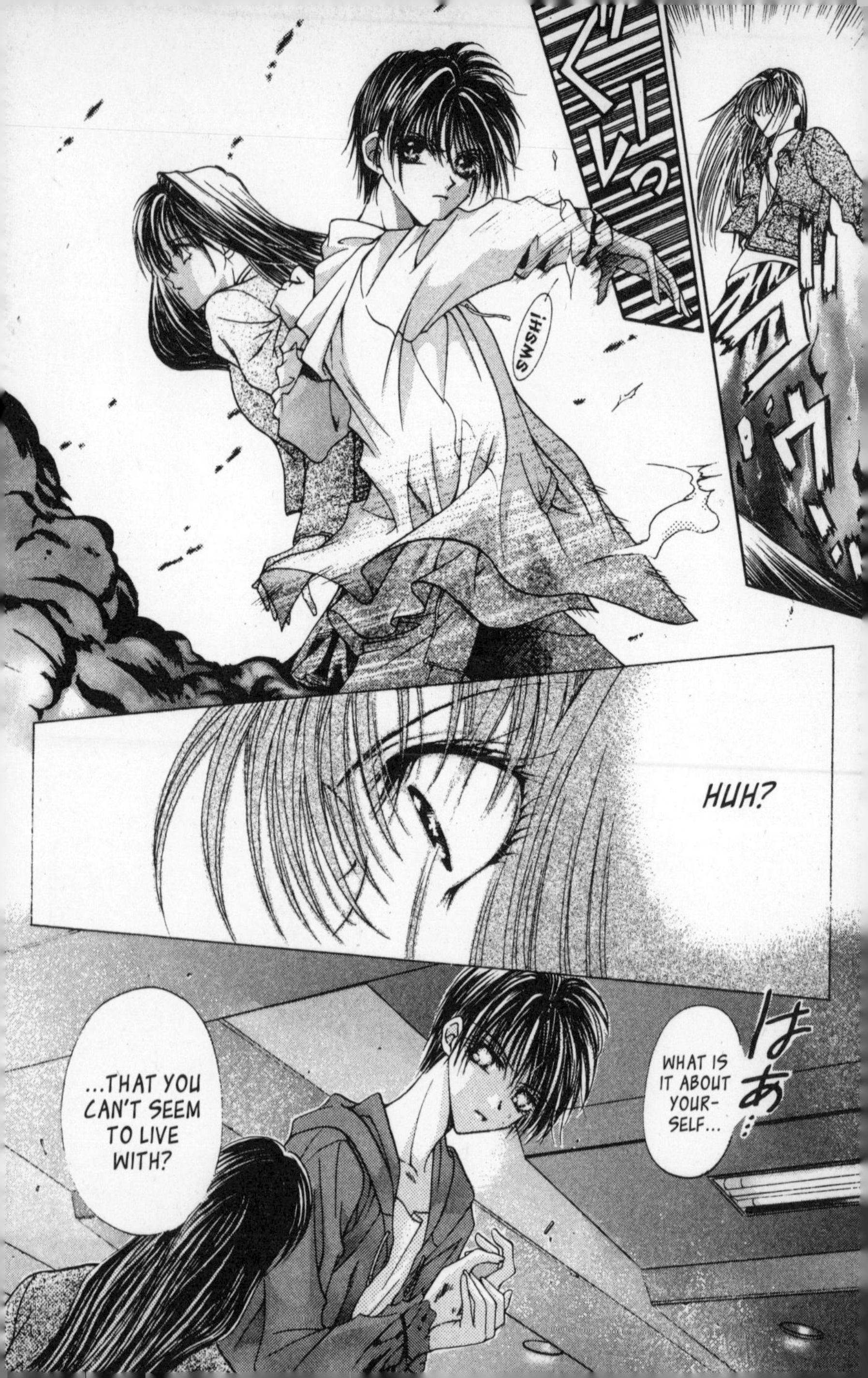
SWSH!
HUH?
はあ…
WHAT IS IT ABOUT YOUR-SELF...
...THAT YOU CAN'T SEEM TO LIVE WITH?

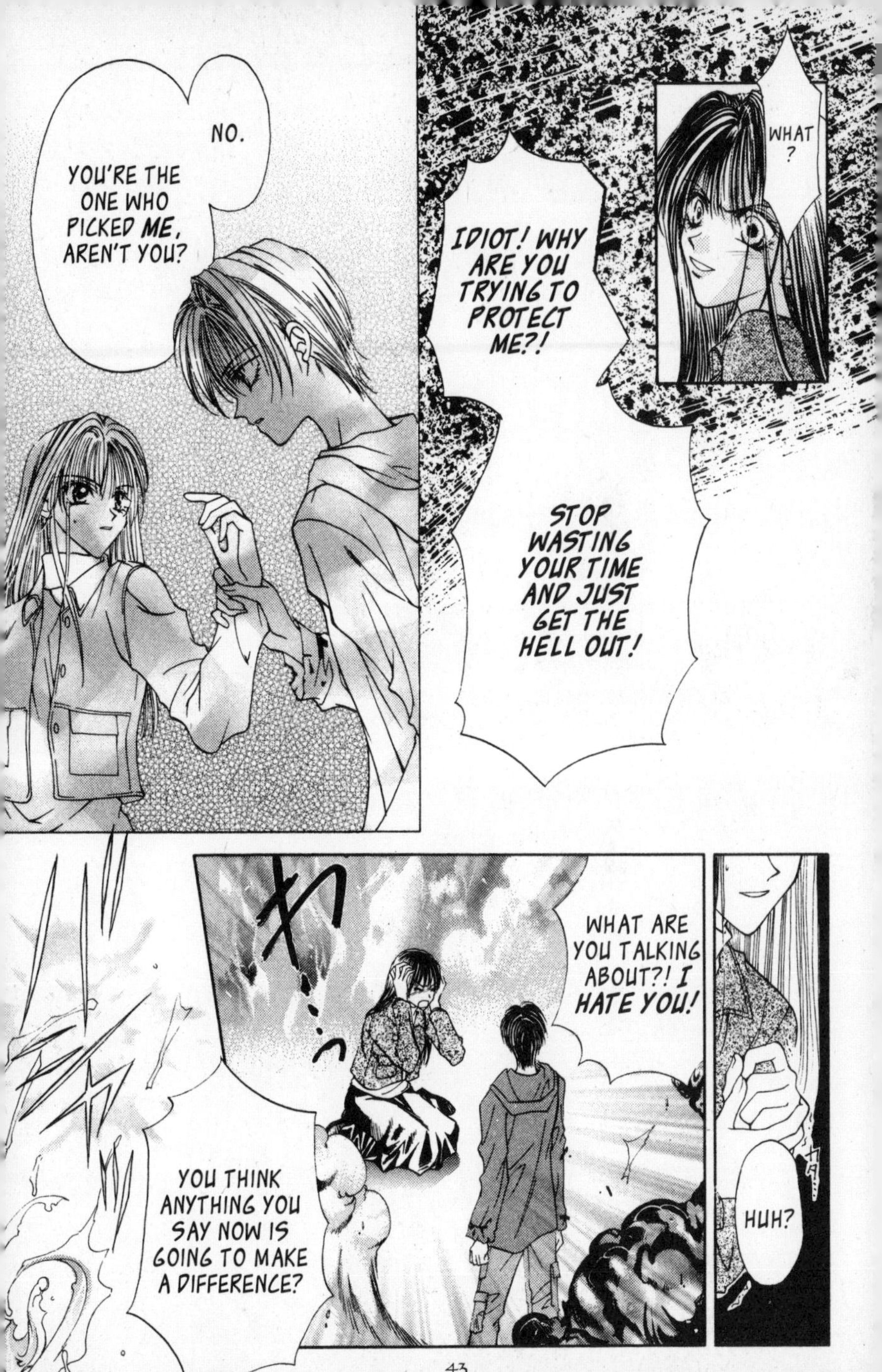
WHAT ?
IDIOT! WHY ARE YOU TRYING TO PROTECT ME?!
STOP WASTING YOUR TIME AND JUST GET THE HELL OUT!
NO.
YOU'RE THE ONE WHO PICKED ME, AREN'T YOU?
HUH?
WHAT ARE YOU TALKING ABOUT?! I HATE YOU!
YOU THINK ANYTHING YOU SAY NOW IS GOING TO MAKE A DIFFERENCE?

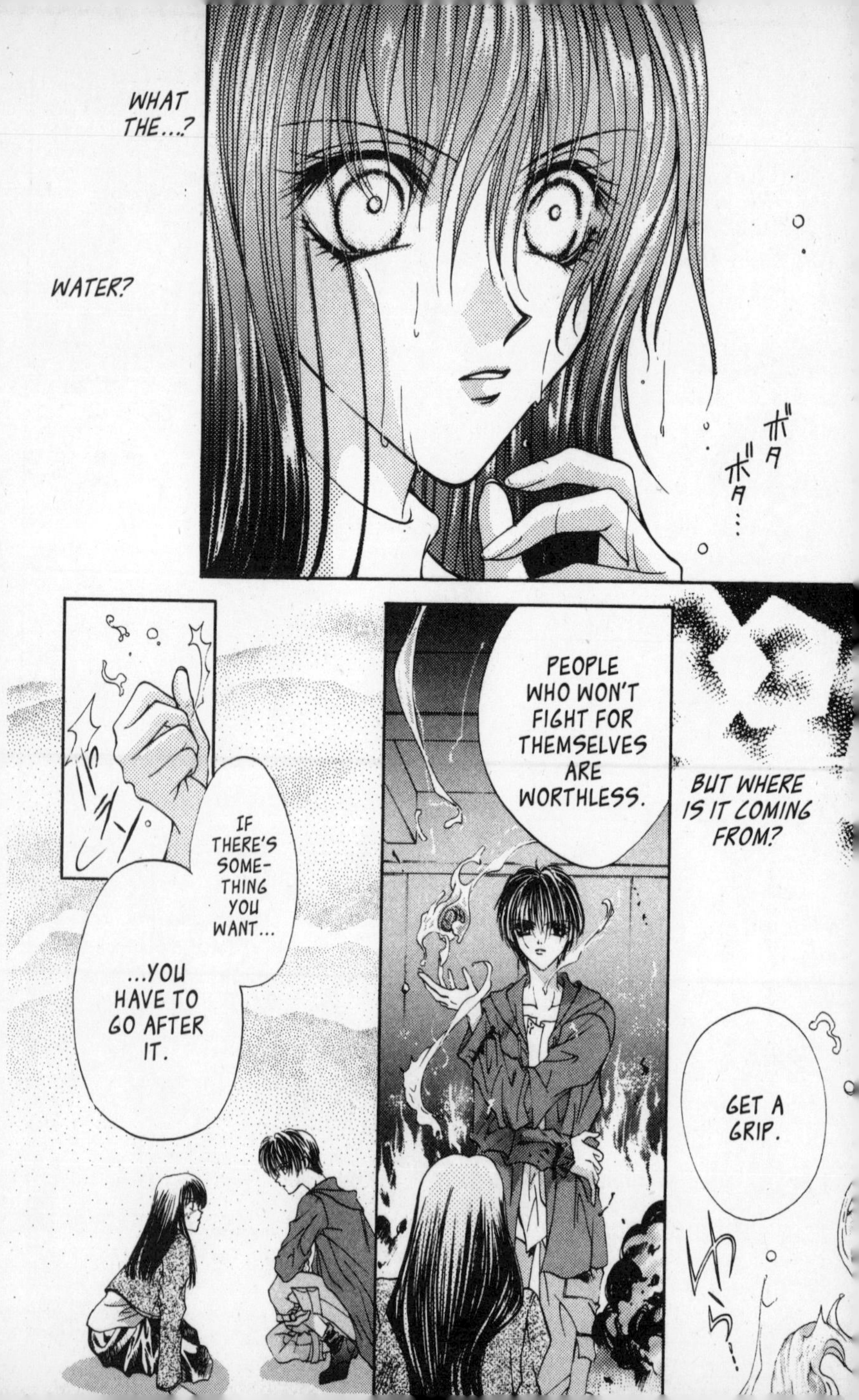
WHAT THE...?
WATER?
ボタボタ…
BUT WHERE IS IT COMING FROM?
GET A GRIP.
PEOPLE WHO WON'T FIGHT FOR THEMSELVES ARE WORTHLESS.
IF THERE'S SOME-THING YOU WANT...
...YOU HAVE TO GO AFTER IT.

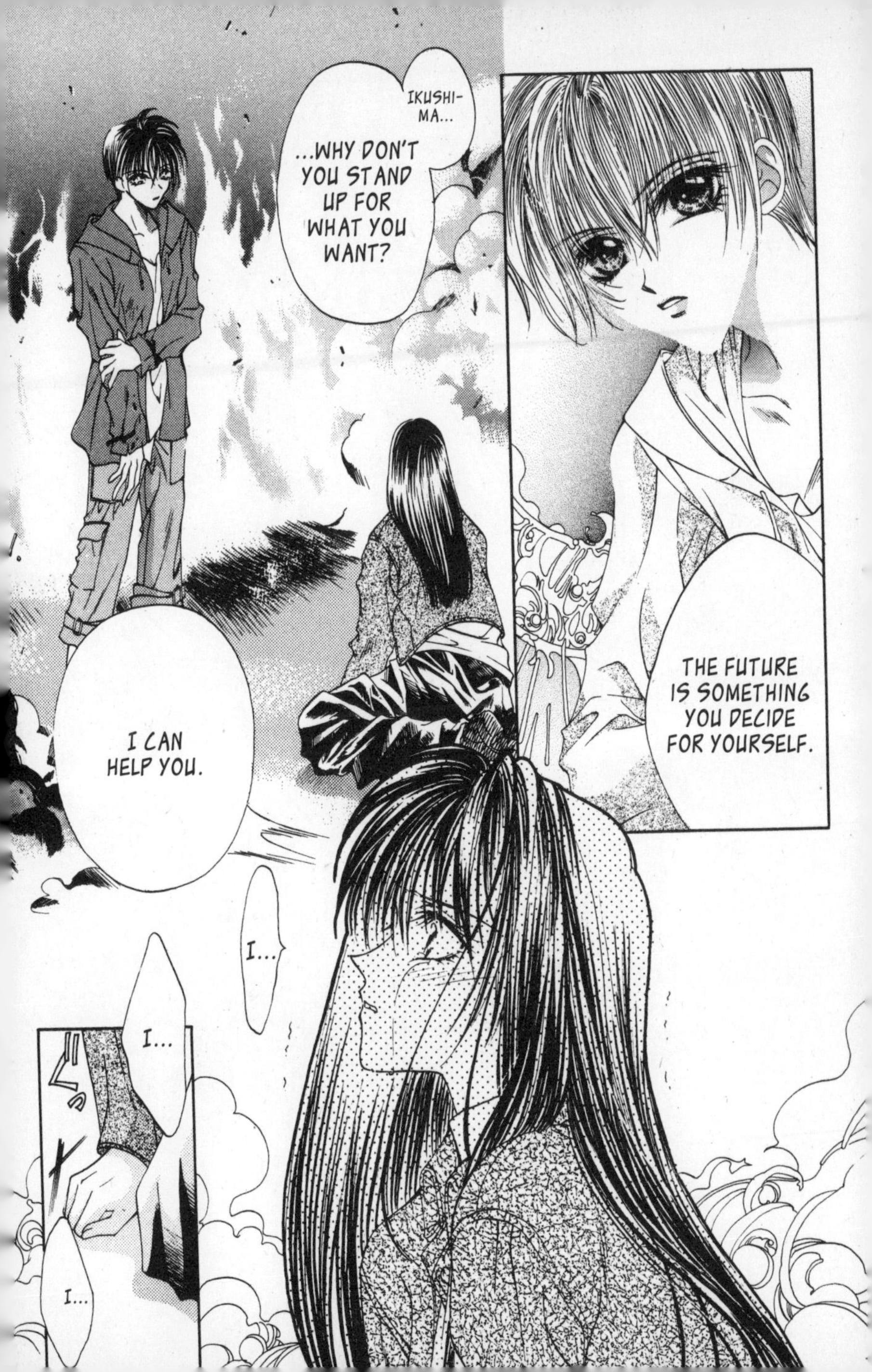
THE FUTURE IS SOMETHING YOU DECIDE FOR YOURSELF.
IKUSHIMA...
...WHY DON'T YOU STAND UP FOR WHAT YOU WANT?
I CAN HELP YOU.
I...
I...
I...

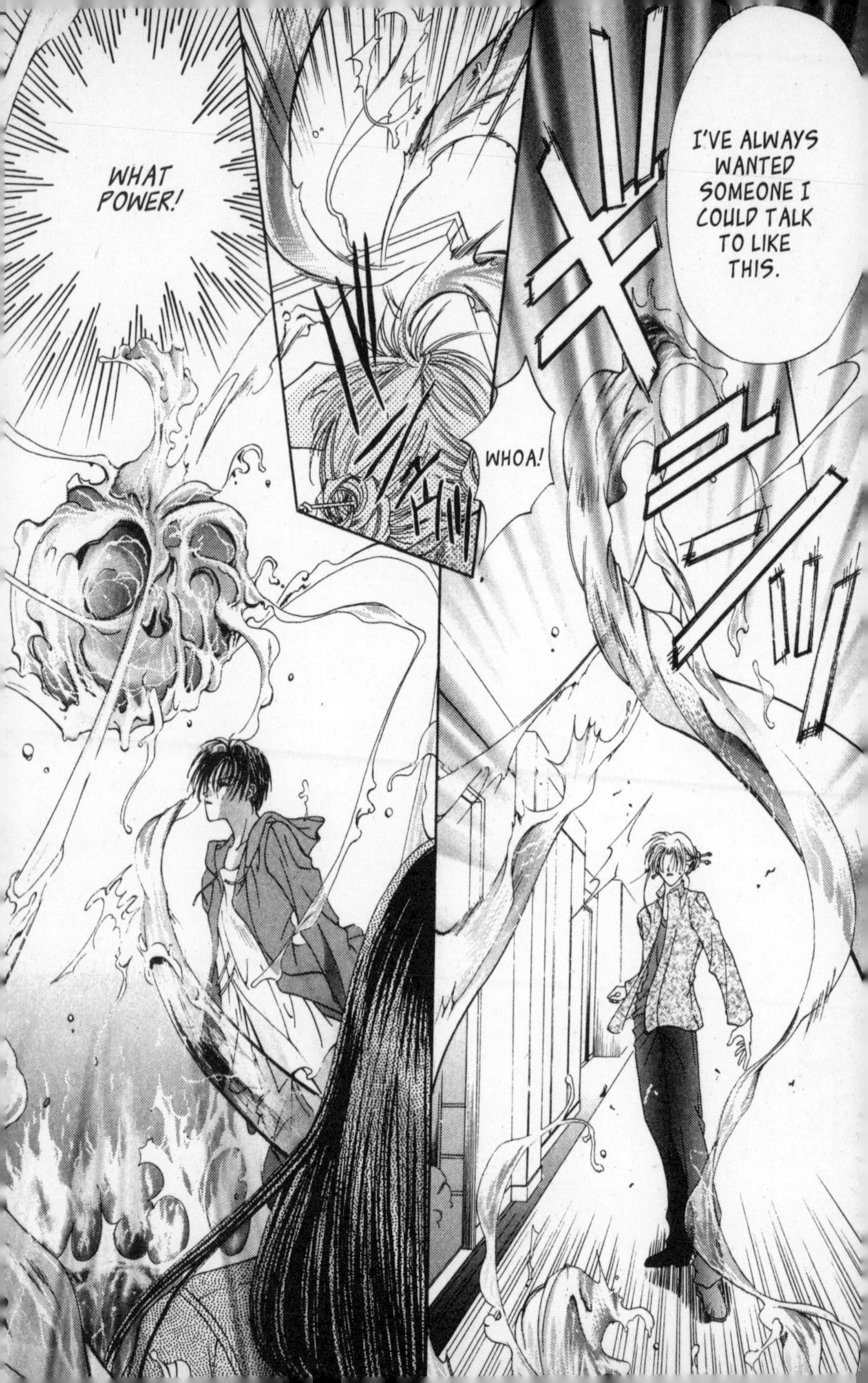
I'VE ALWAYS WANTED SOMEONE I COULD TALK TO LIKE THIS.
WHOA!
WHAT POWER!

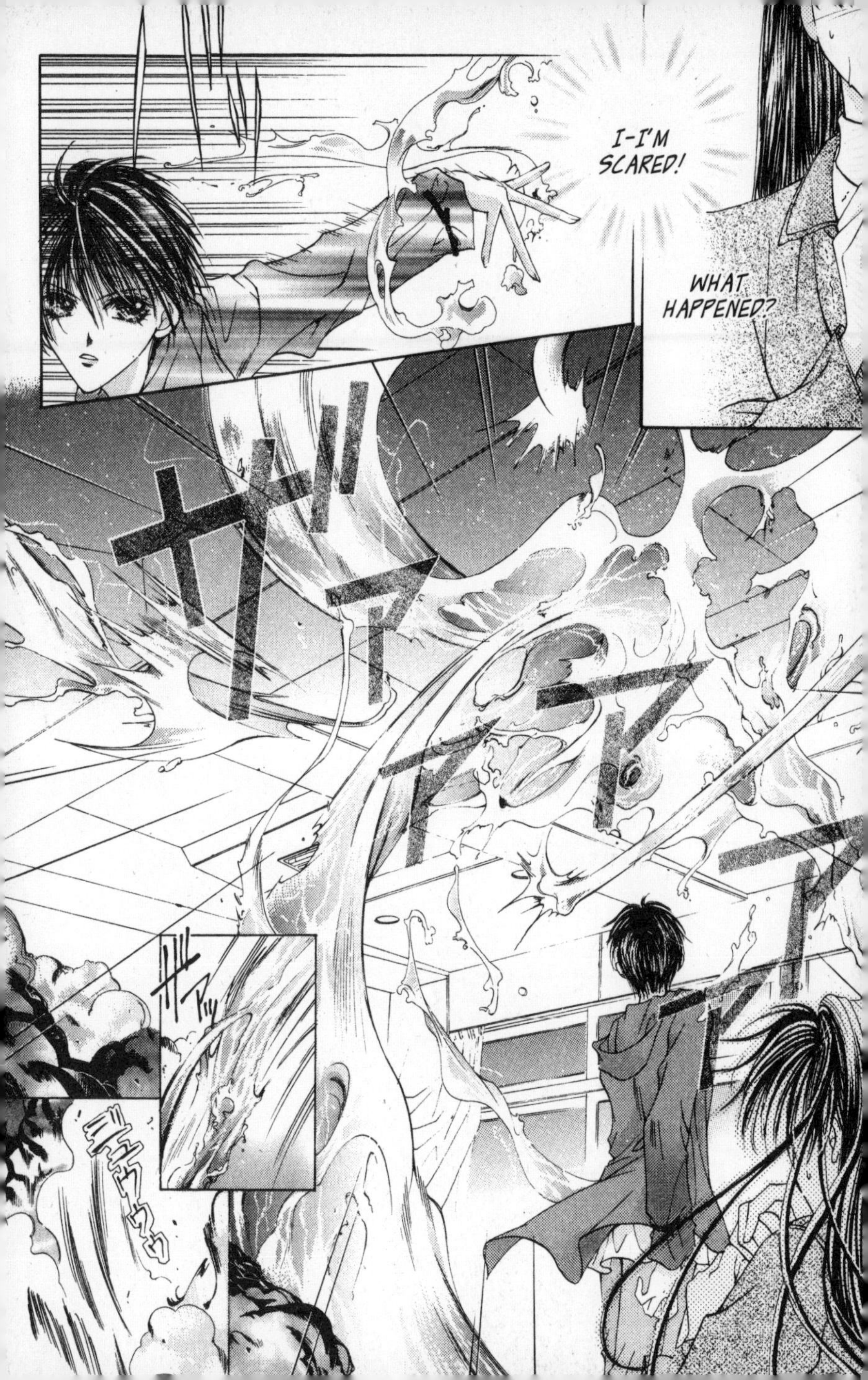
I-I'M SCARED!
WHAT HAPPENED?

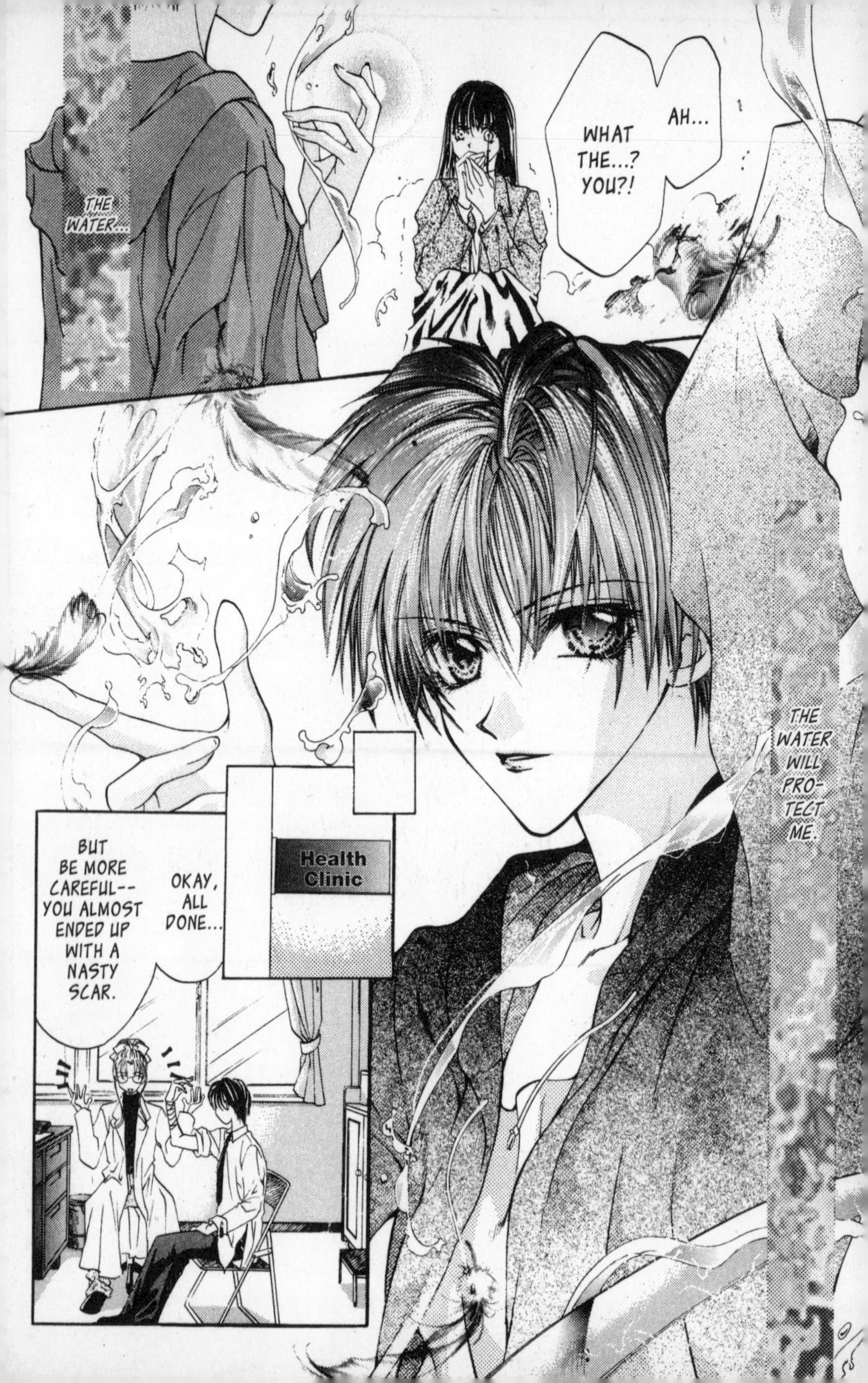
AH...
WHAT THE...? YOU?!
THE WATER...
THE WATER WILL PROTECT ME.
Health Clinic
OKAY, ALL DONE...
BUT BE MORE CAREFUL--YOU ALMOST ENDED UP WITH A NASTY SCAR.

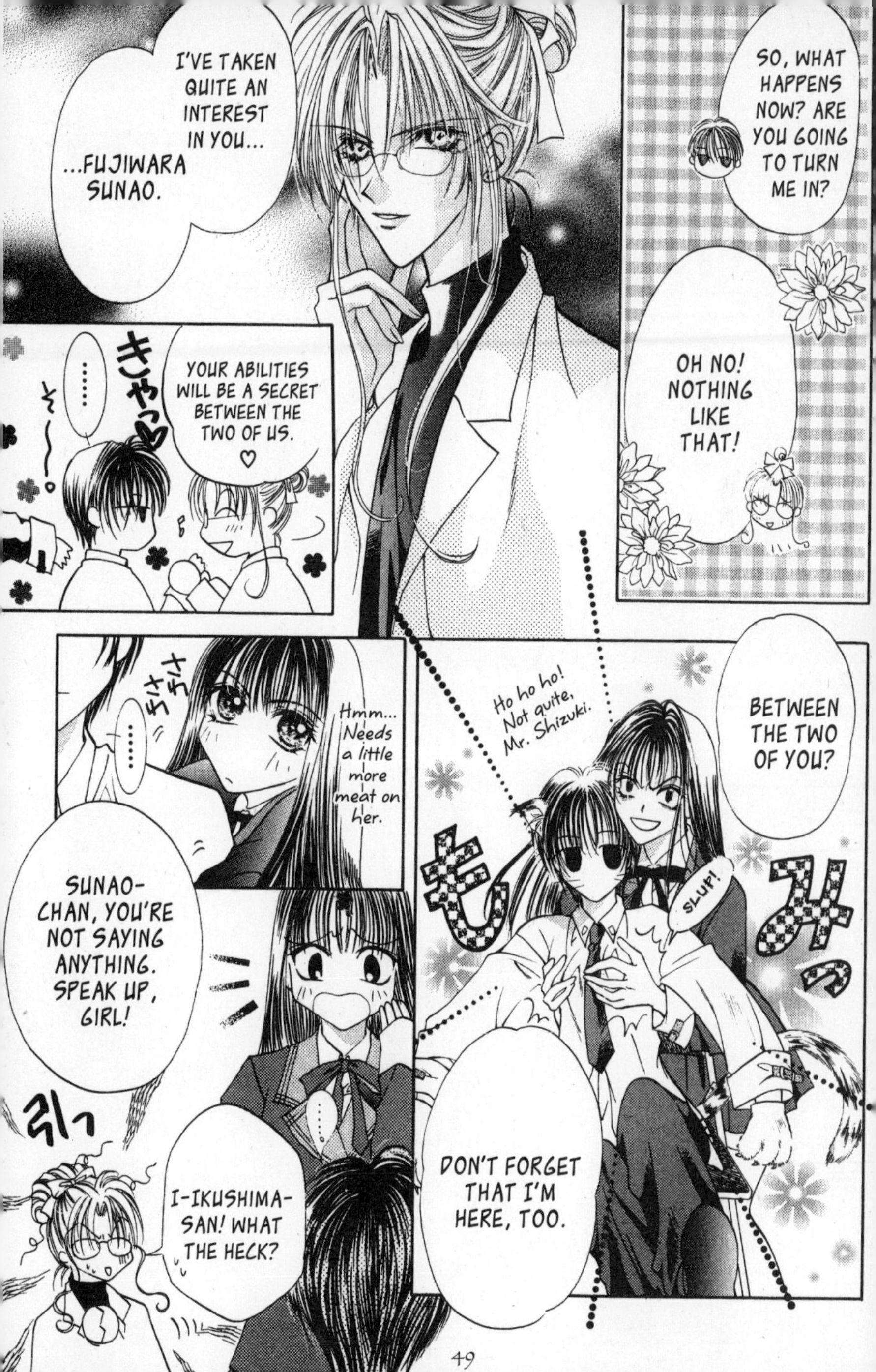
SO, WHAT HAPPENS NOW? ARE YOU GOING TO TURN ME IN?
OH NO! NOTHING LIKE THAT!
I'VE TAKEN QUITE AN INTEREST IN YOU...
...FUJIWARA SUNAO.
YOUR ABILITIES WILL BE A SECRET BETWEEN THE TWO OF US. ♡
きゃっ♡
......
そ〜〜。
BETWEEN THE TWO OF YOU?
Ho ho ho! Not quite, Mr. Shizuki.
もみっ
SLUP!
DON'T FORGET THAT I'M HERE, TOO.
さらさら
......
Hmm... Needs a little more meat on her.
SUNAO-CHAN, YOU'RE NOT SAYING ANYTHING. SPEAK UP, GIRL!
......
引っ
I-IKUSHIMA-SAN! WHAT THE HECK?

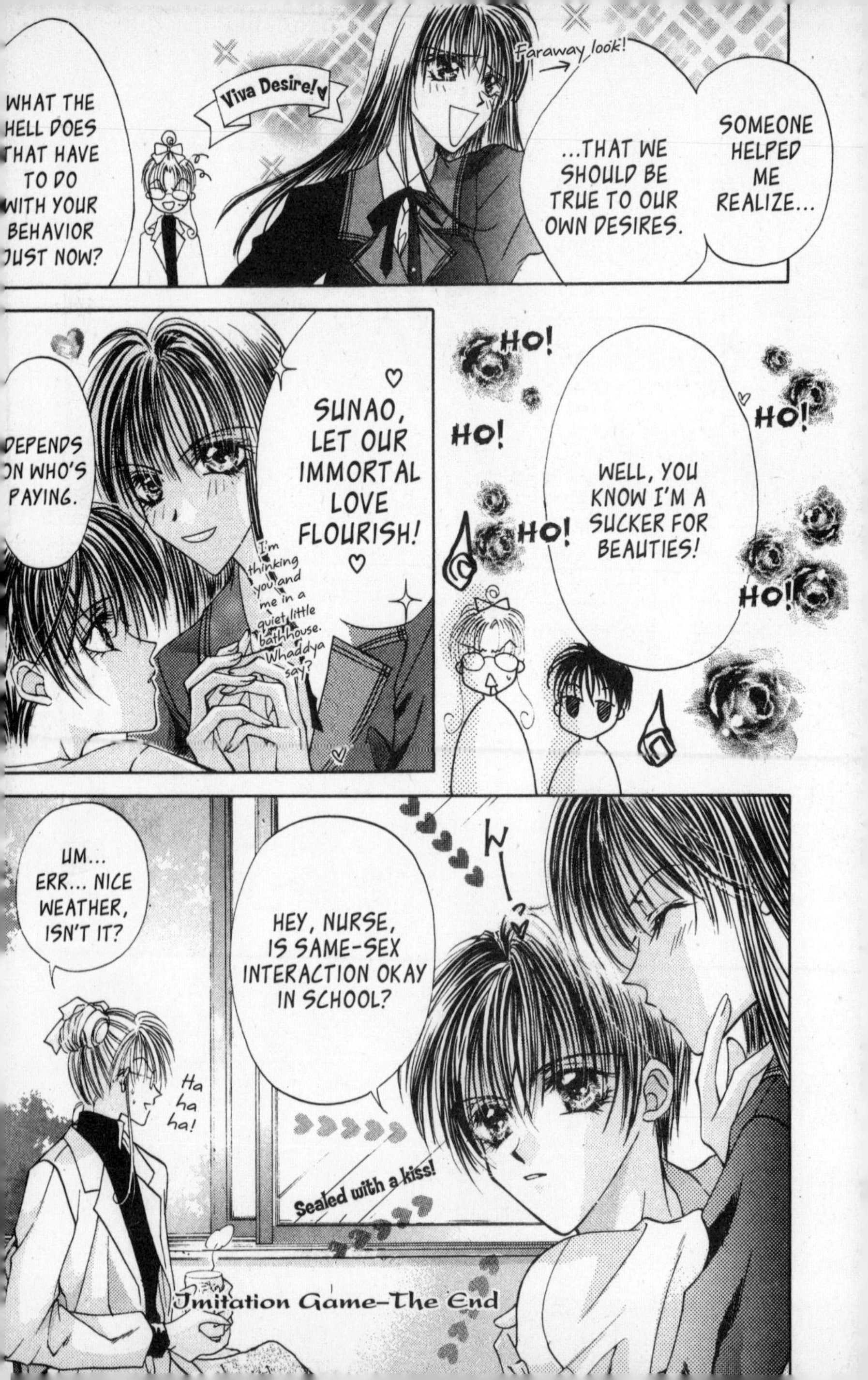
SOMEONE HELPED ME REALIZE...
...THAT WE SHOULD BE TRUE TO OUR OWN DESIRES.
Faraway look!
Viva Desire!♥
WHAT THE HELL DOES THAT HAVE TO DO WITH YOUR BEHAVIOR JUST NOW?
HO! HO! HO! HO! HO!
WELL, YOU KNOW I'M A SUCKER FOR BEAUTIES!
SUNAO, LET OUR IMMORTAL LOVE FLOURISH!
I'm thinking you and me in a quiet little bathhouse. Whaddya say?
DEPENDS ON WHO'S PAYING.
HEY, NURSE, IS SAME-SEX INTERACTION OKAY IN SCHOOL?
Sealed with a kiss!
UM... ERR... NICE WEATHER, ISN'T IT?
Ha ha ha!
Imitation Game–The End

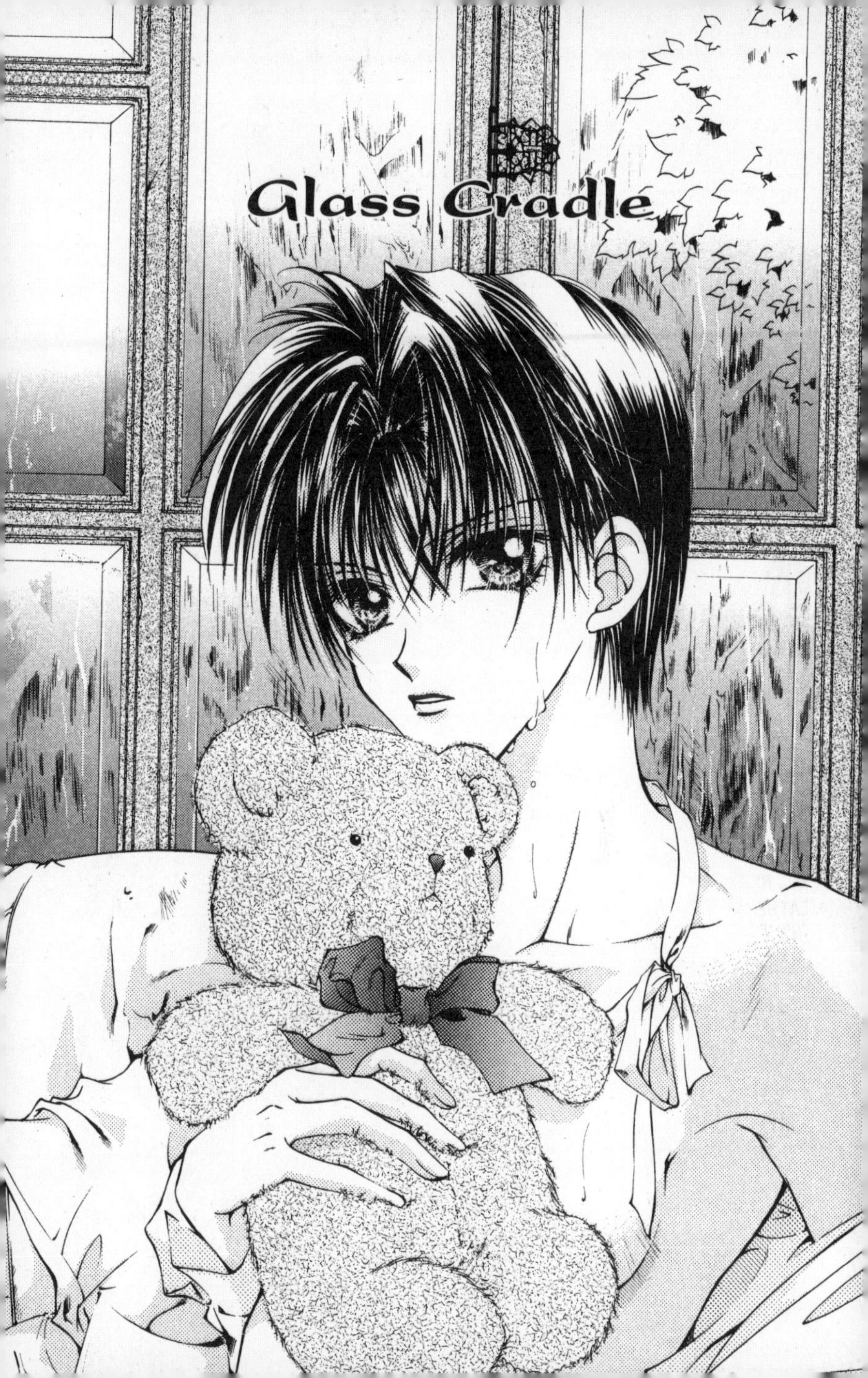
Glass Cradle

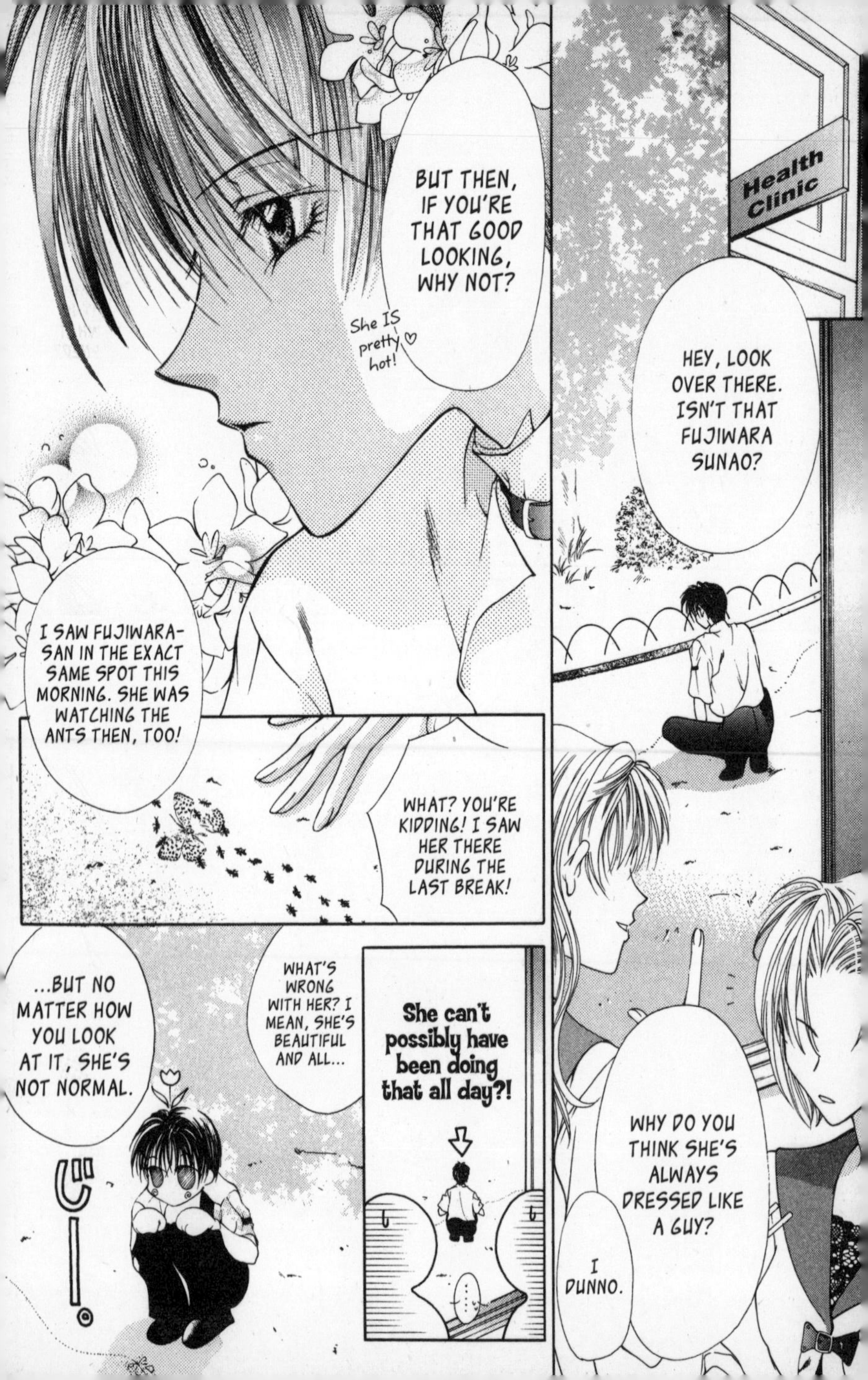
Health Clinic
HEY, LOOK OVER THERE. ISN'T THAT FUJIWARA SUNAO?
WHY DO YOU THINK SHE'S ALWAYS DRESSED LIKE A GUY?
I DUNNO.
BUT THEN, IF YOU'RE THAT GOOD LOOKING, WHY NOT?
She IS pretty hot! ♡
I SAW FUJIWARA-SAN IN THE EXACT SAME SPOT THIS MORNING. SHE WAS WATCHING THE ANTS THEN, TOO!
WHAT? YOU'RE KIDDING! I SAW HER THERE DURING THE LAST BREAK!
She can't possibly have been doing that all day?!
WHAT'S WRONG WITH HER? I MEAN, SHE'S BEAUTIFUL AND ALL...
...BUT NO MATTER HOW YOU LOOK AT IT, SHE'S NOT NORMAL.
じー!

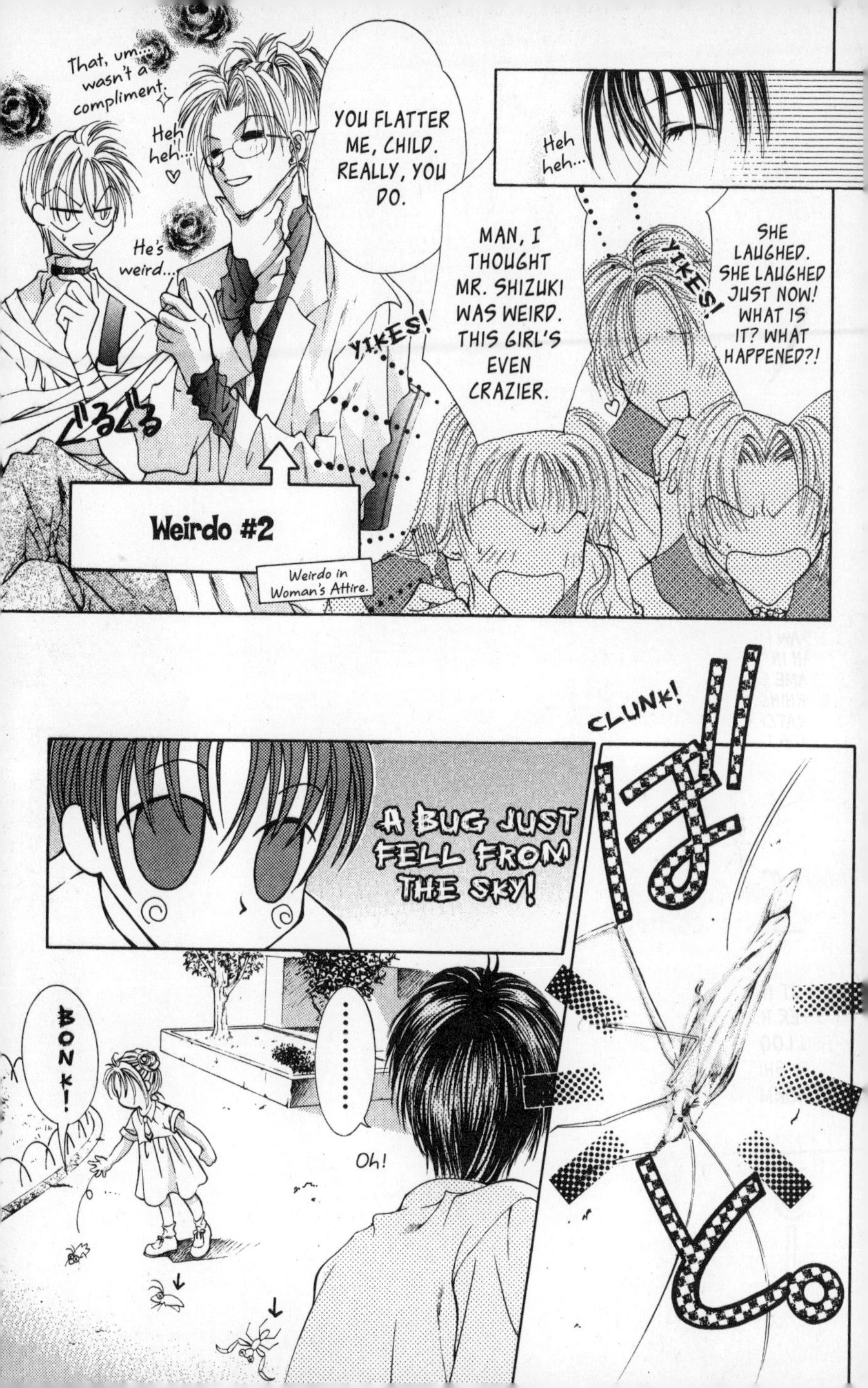
Heh heh...
SHE LAUGHED. SHE LAUGHED JUST NOW! WHAT IS IT? WHAT HAPPENED?!
YIKES!
MAN, I THOUGHT MR. SHIZUKI WAS WEIRD. THIS GIRL'S EVEN CRAZIER.
YOU FLATTER ME, CHILD. REALLY, YOU DO.
That, um... wasn't a compliment.
Heh heh...♡
He's weird...
YIKES!
ぐるぐる
Weirdo #2
Weirdo in Woman's Attire.
CLUNK!
ぽと。
A BUG JUST FELL FROM THE SKY!
......
Oh!
BONK!

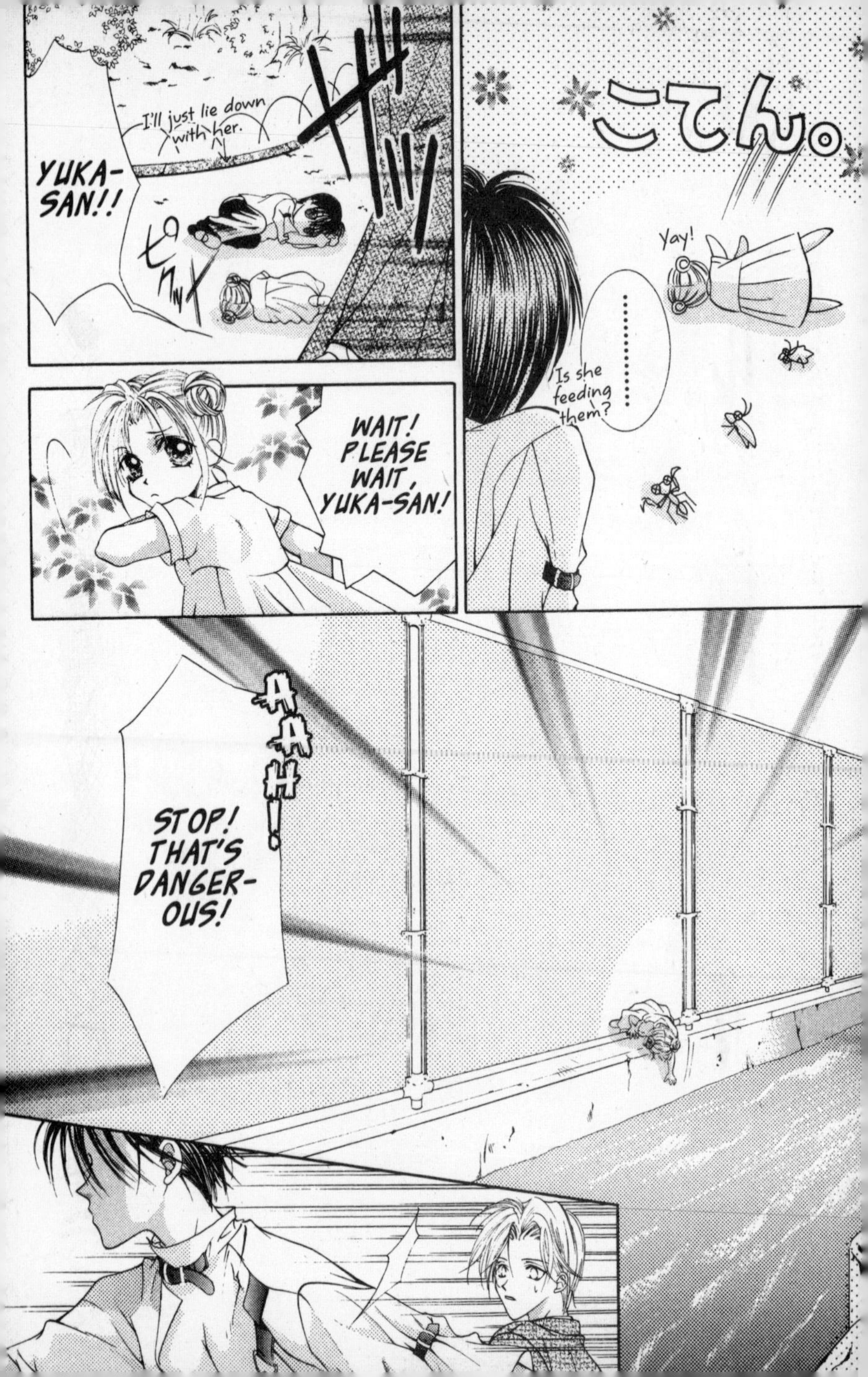
こてん。
Yay!
......
Is she feeding them?
I'll just lie down with her.
YUKA-SAN!!
WAIT! PLEASE WAIT, YUKA-SAN!
AAAH!
STOP! THAT'S DANGER-OUS!

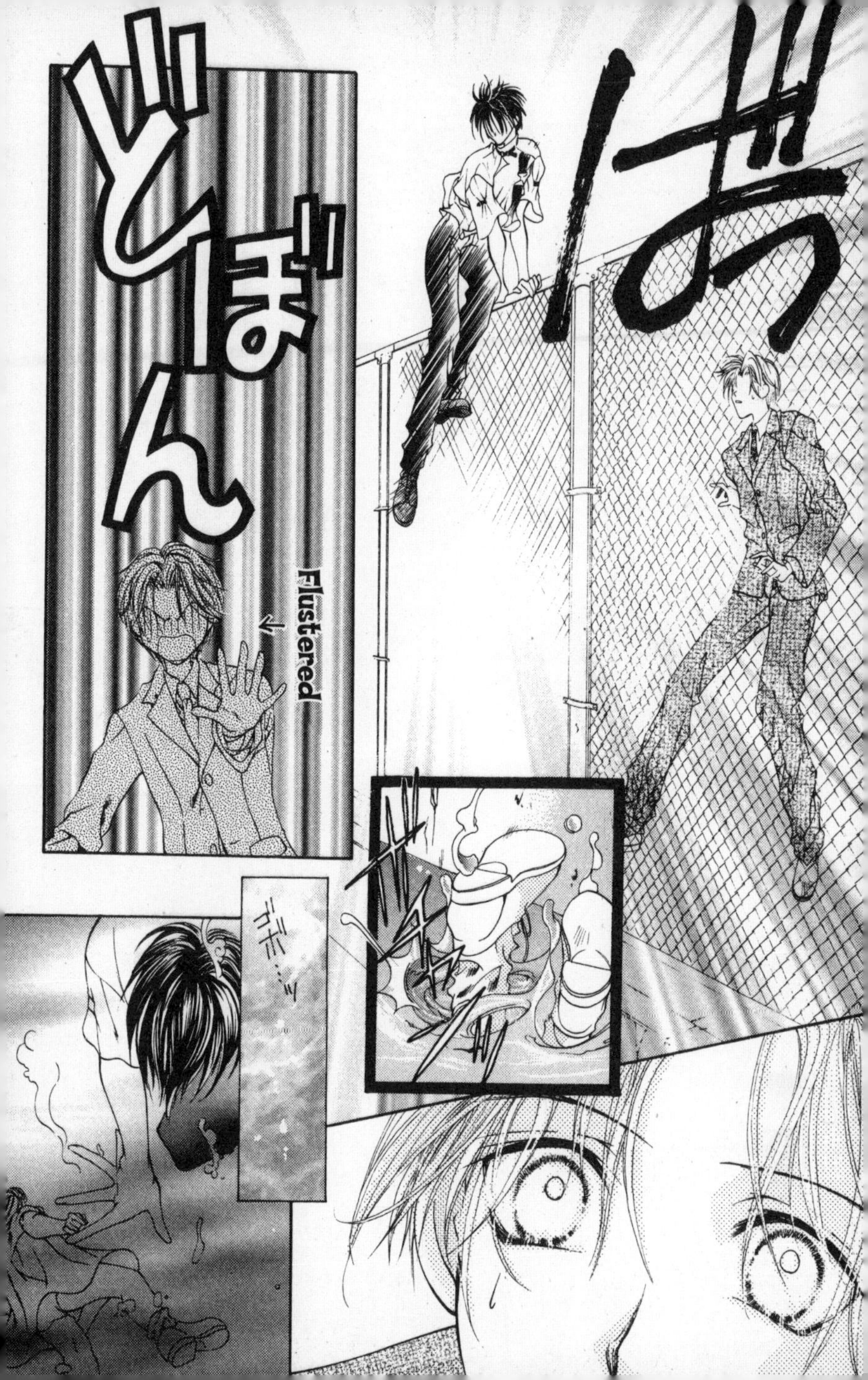
ばっ
どぼん
Flustered
ゴボ…ッ

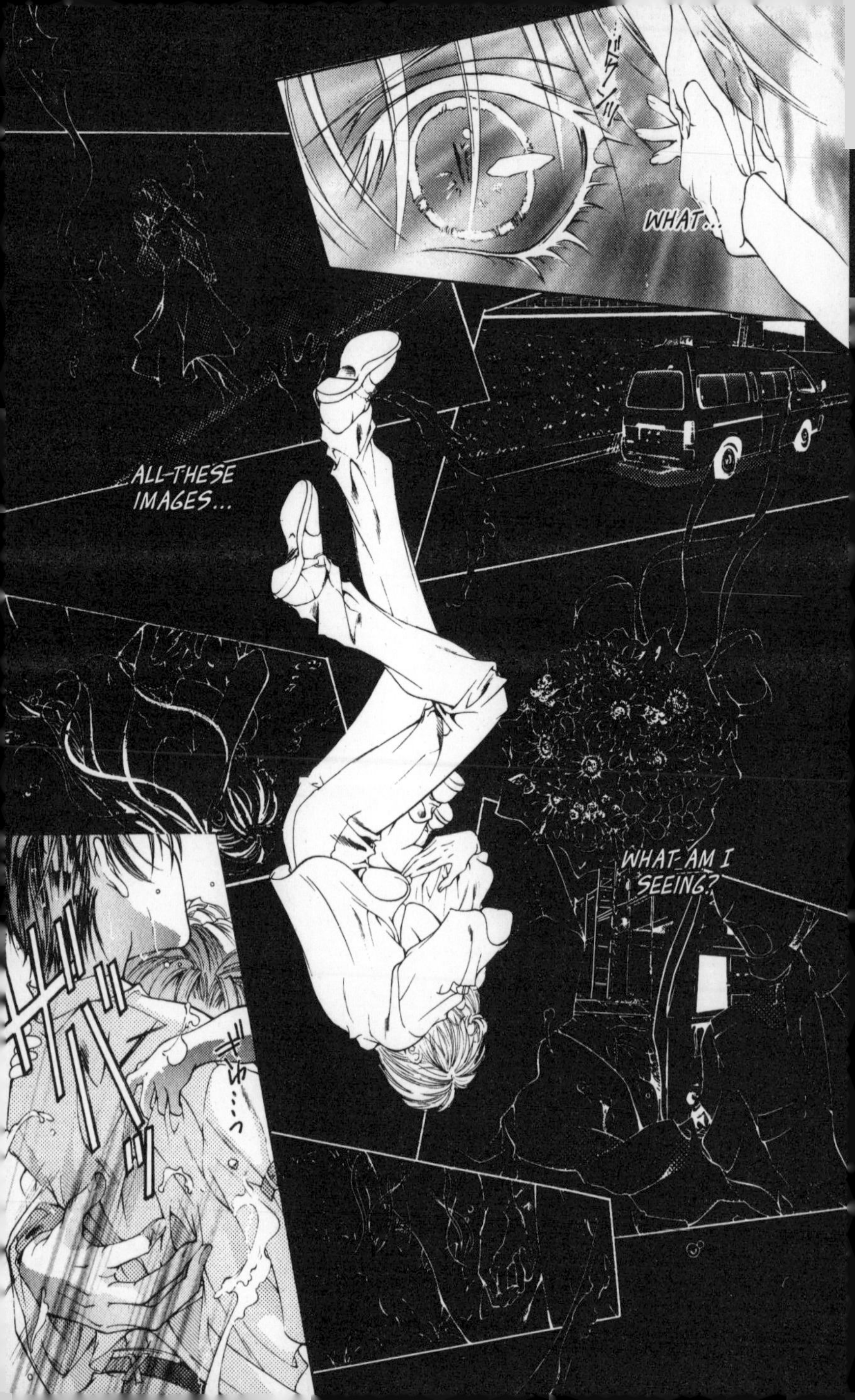
WHAT...
ALL THESE IMAGES...
WHAT AM I SEEING?

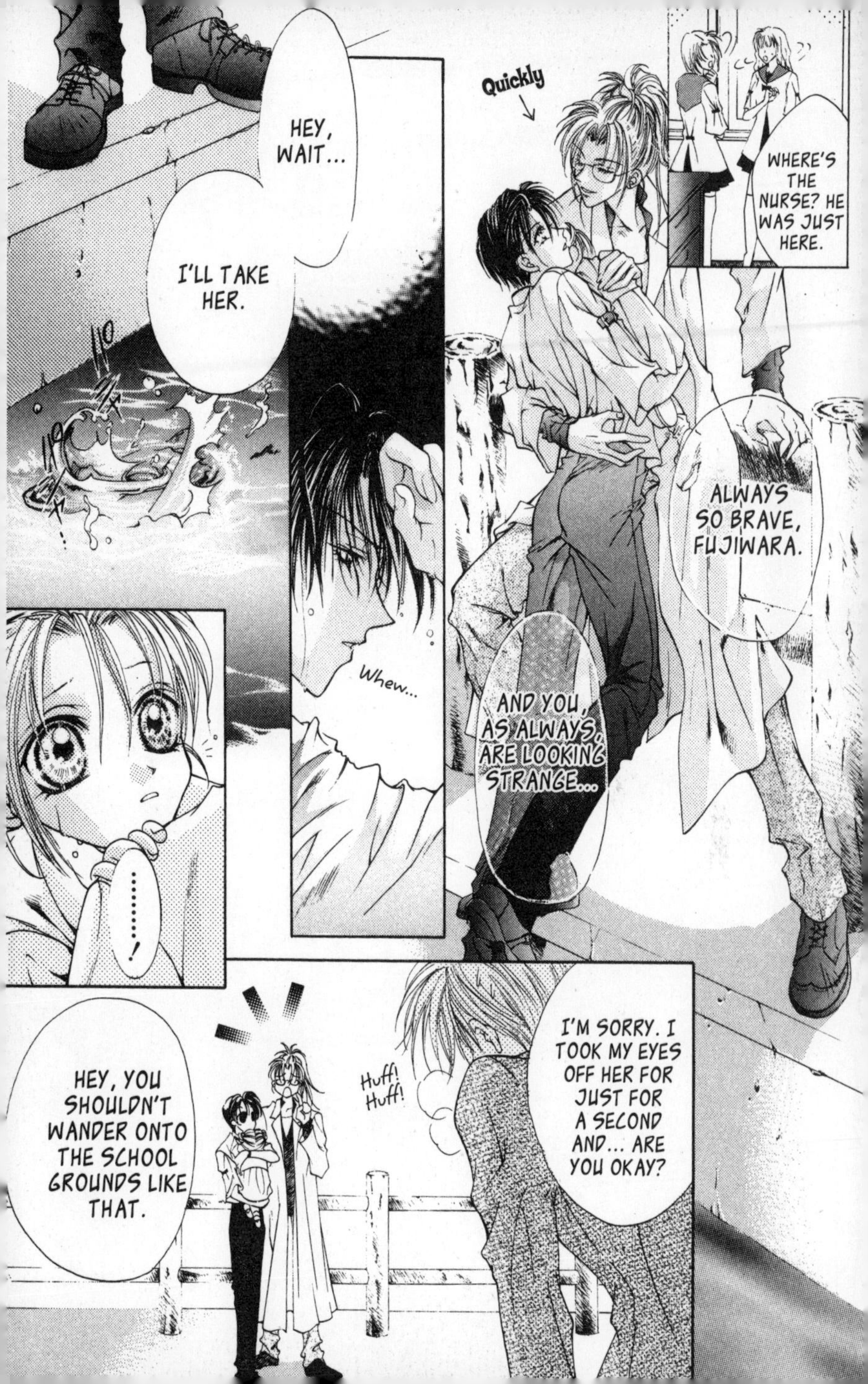
WHERE'S THE NURSE? HE WAS JUST HERE.
Quickly
ALWAYS SO BRAVE, FUJIWARA.
AND YOU, AS ALWAYS, ARE LOOKING STRANGE...
HEY, WAIT...
I'LL TAKE HER.
Whew...
......!
I'M SORRY. I TOOK MY EYES OFF HER FOR JUST FOR A SECOND AND... ARE YOU OKAY?
Huff! Huff!
HEY, YOU SHOULDN'T WANDER ONTO THE SCHOOL GROUNDS LIKE THAT.

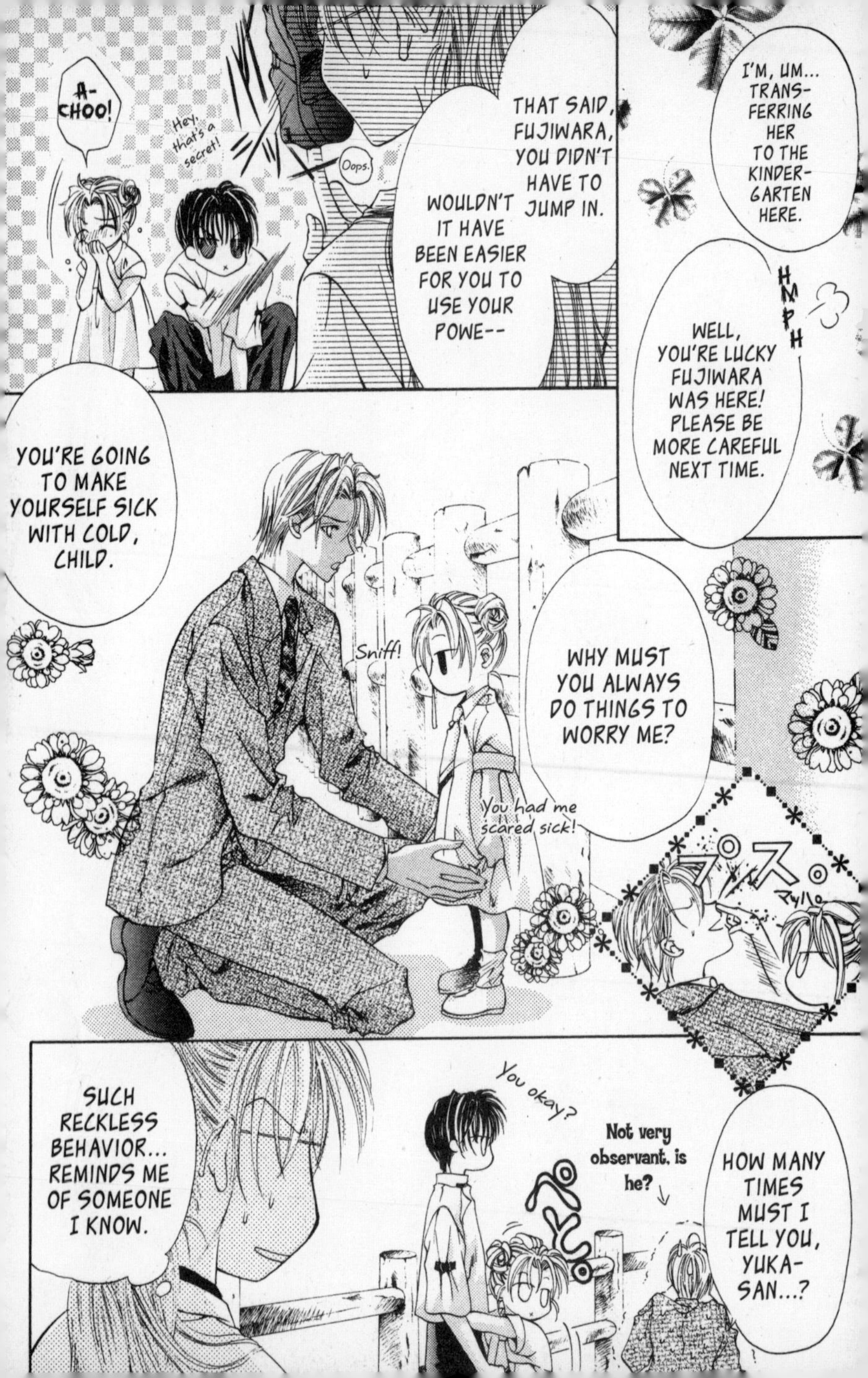
I'M, UM... TRANSFERRING HER TO THE KINDERGARTEN HERE.
HMPH
WELL, YOU'RE LUCKY FUJIWARA WAS HERE! PLEASE BE MORE CAREFUL NEXT TIME.
THAT SAID, FUJIWARA, YOU DIDN'T HAVE TO JUMP IN.
WOULDN'T IT HAVE BEEN EASIER FOR YOU TO USE YOUR POWE--
Oops.
Hey, that's a secret!
A-CHOO!
WHY MUST YOU ALWAYS DO THINGS TO WORRY ME?
You had me scared sick!
Sniff!
YOU'RE GOING TO MAKE YOURSELF SICK WITH COLD, CHILD.
HOW MANY TIMES MUST I TELL YOU, YUKA-SAN...?
Not very observant, is he?
You okay?
SUCH RECKLESS BEHAVIOR... REMINDS ME OF SOMEONE I KNOW.

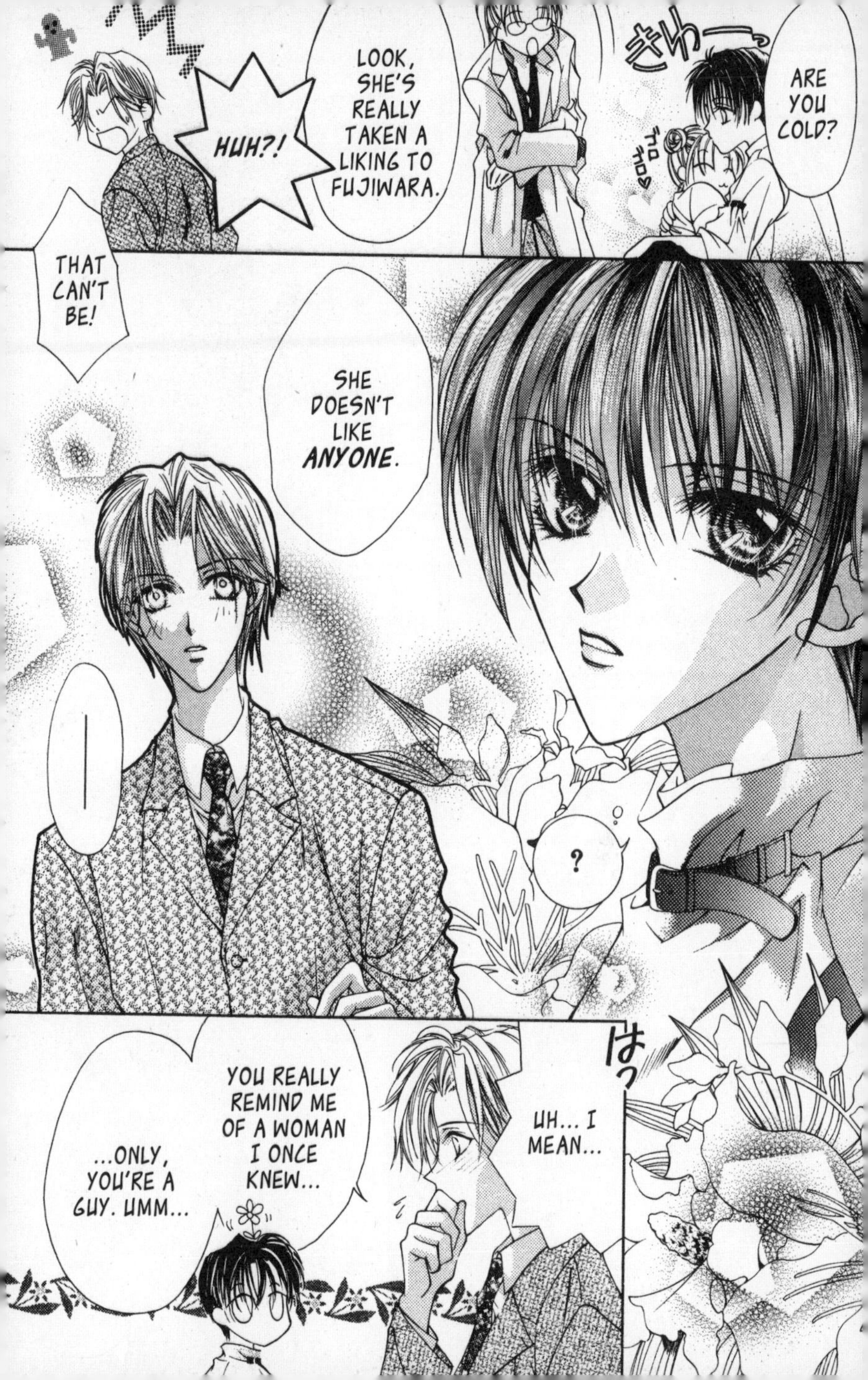
きゅーっ
ARE YOU COLD?
ゴロゴロ♥
LOOK, SHE'S REALLY TAKEN A LIKING TO FUJIWARA.
HUH?!
THAT CAN'T BE!
SHE DOESN'T LIKE **ANYONE**.
?
|
はっ
UH... I MEAN...
YOU REALLY REMIND ME OF A WOMAN I ONCE KNEW...
...ONLY, YOU'RE A GUY. UMM...

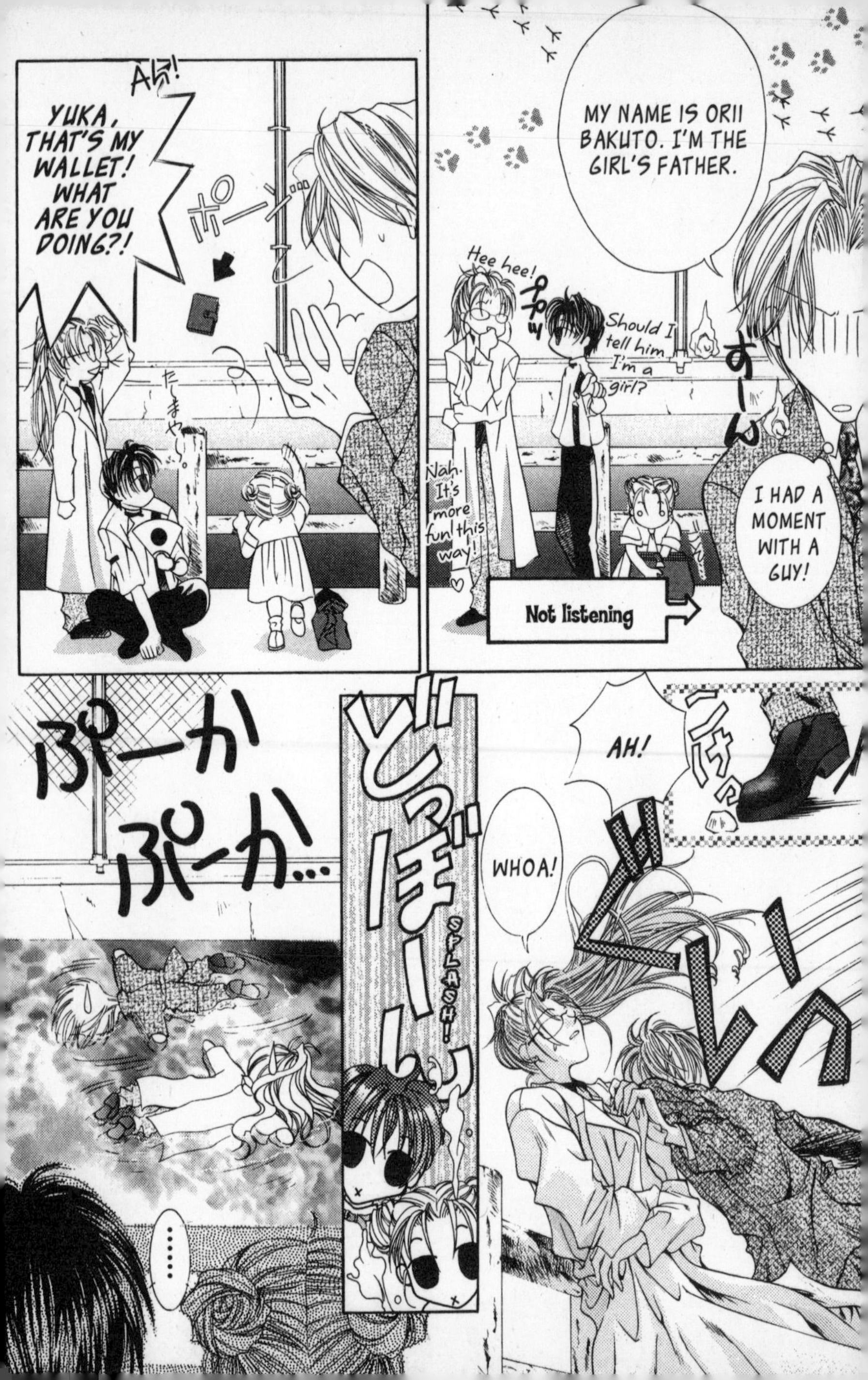

MY NAME IS ORII BAKUTO. I'M THE GIRL'S FATHER.
すーん
Should I tell him I'm a girl?
Hee hee!
ププッ
I HAD A MOMENT WITH A GUY!
Nah. It's more fun this way!
Not listening
Ah!
YUKA, THAT'S MY WALLET! WHAT ARE YOU DOING?!
ポーイ
たまやー。
こけっ
AH!
WHOA!
ぐいっ
どっぼーん
SPLASH!
ぷーか
ぷーか…
……

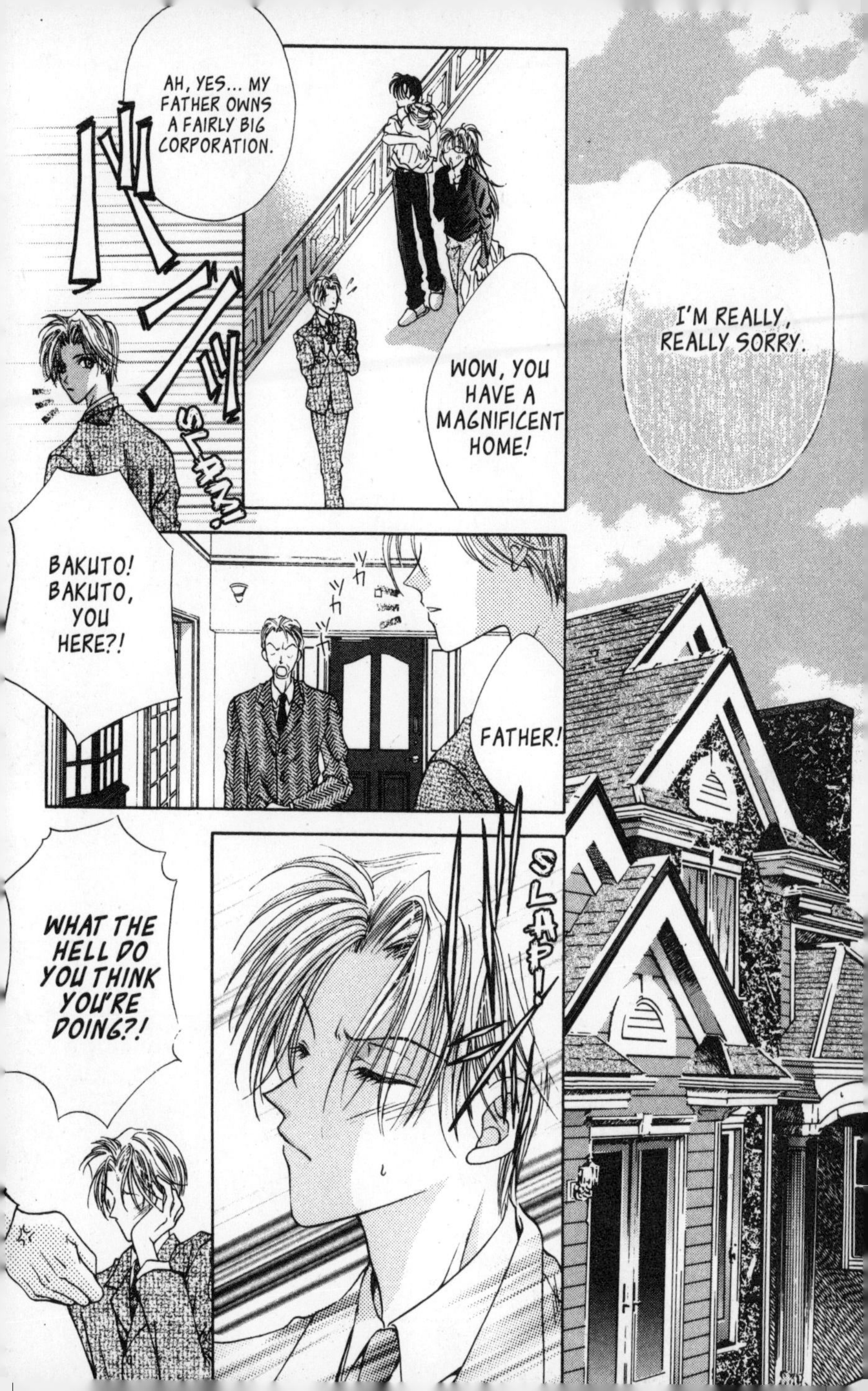
I'M REALLY, REALLY SORRY.
WOW, YOU HAVE A MAGNIFICENT HOME!
AH, YES... MY FATHER OWNS A FAIRLY BIG CORPORATION.
SLAM!
FATHER!
BAKUTO! BAKUTO, YOU HERE?!
SLAP!
WHAT THE HELL DO YOU THINK YOU'RE DOING?!

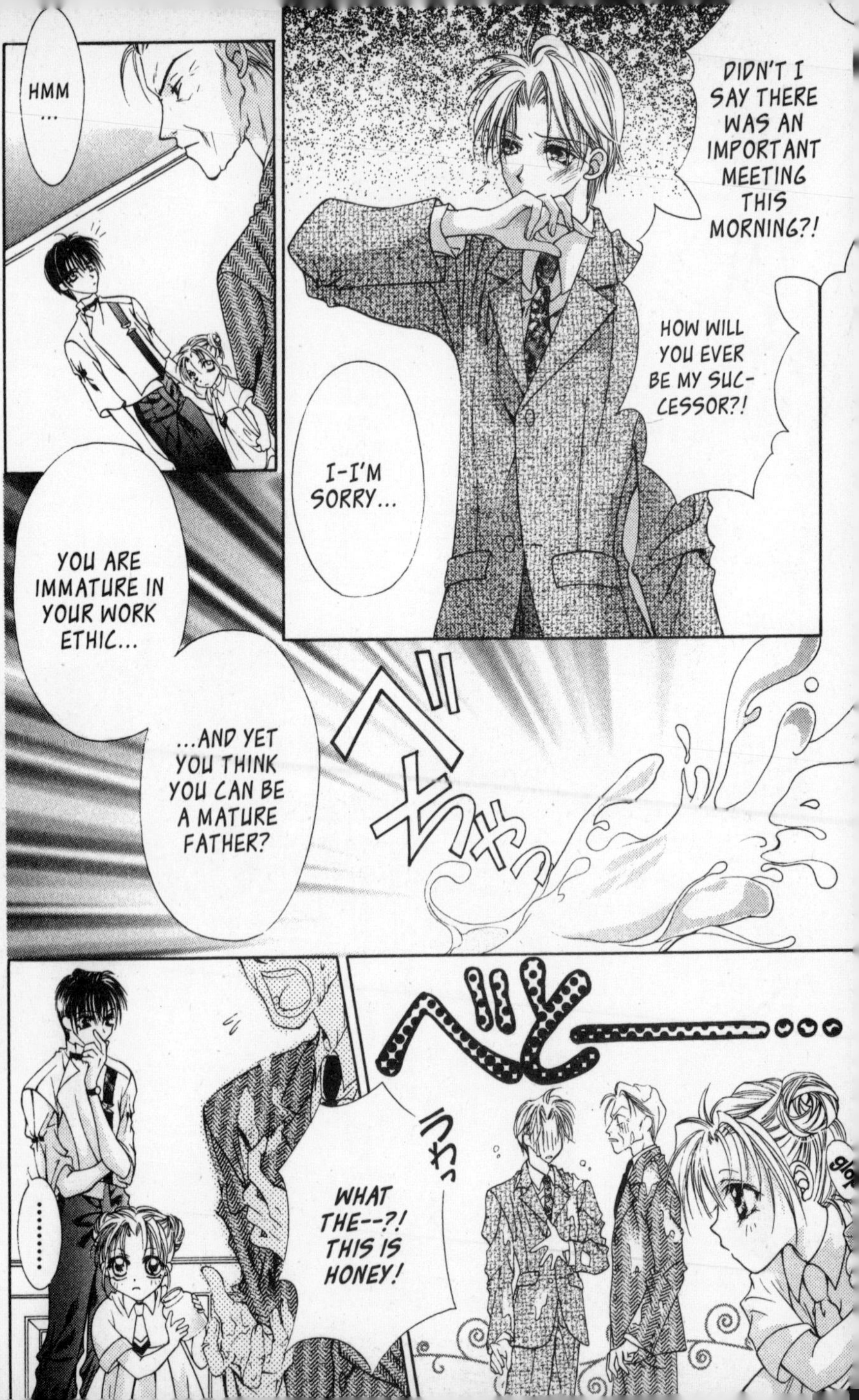
DIDN'T I SAY THERE WAS AN IMPORTANT MEETING THIS MORNING?!
HOW WILL YOU EVER BE MY SUC-CESSOR?!
I-I'M SORRY...
HMM...
YOU ARE IMMATURE IN YOUR WORK ETHIC...
...AND YET YOU THINK YOU CAN BE A MATURE FATHER?
べちゃっ
べと——
glop
うわっ
WHAT THE--?! THIS IS HONEY!
......

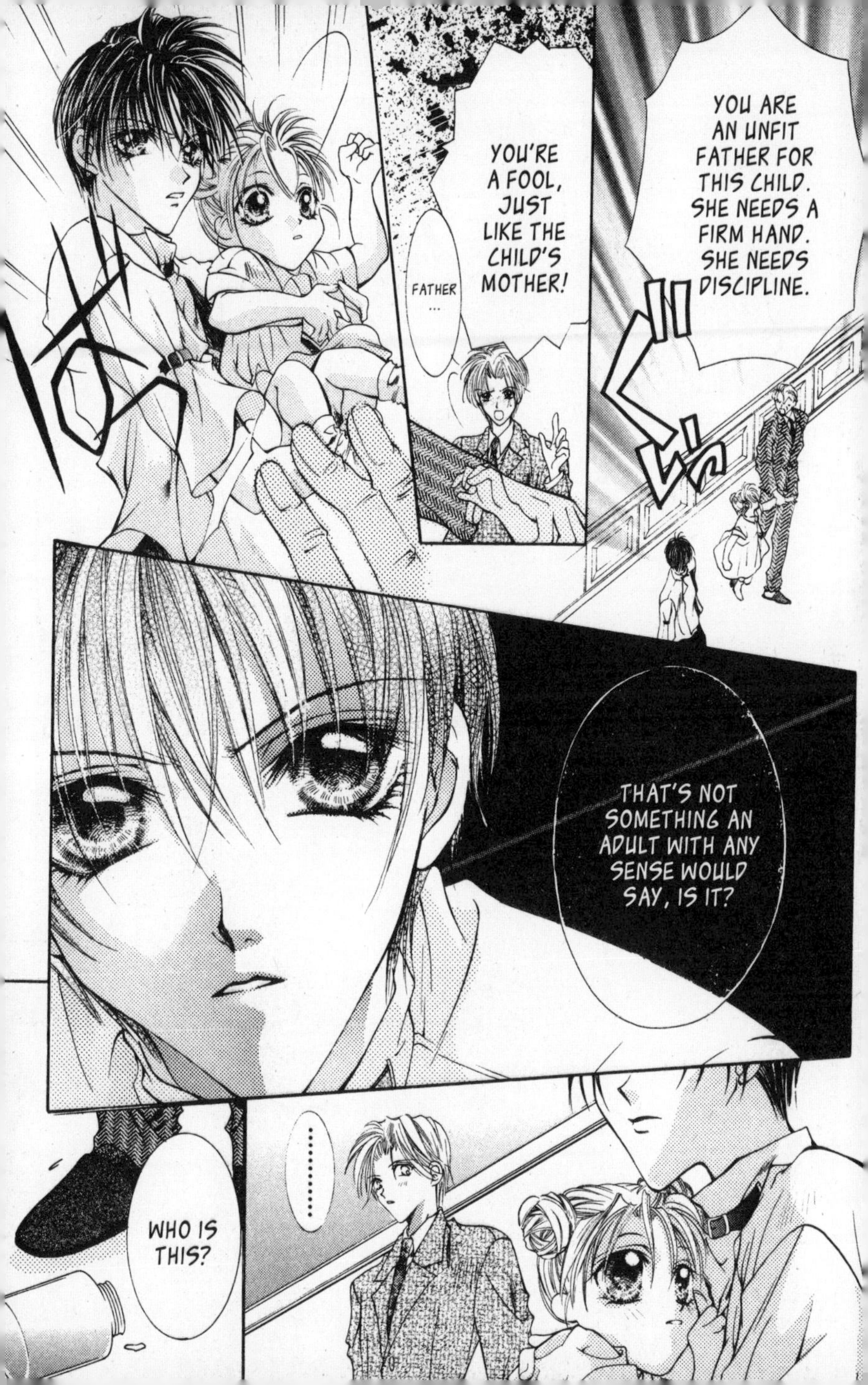
YOU ARE AN UNFIT FATHER FOR THIS CHILD. SHE NEEDS A FIRM HAND. SHE NEEDS DISCIPLINE.
YOU'RE A FOOL, JUST LIKE THE CHILD'S MOTHER!
FATHER ...
THAT'S NOT SOMETHING AN ADULT WITH ANY SENSE WOULD SAY, IS IT?
....
WHO IS THIS?

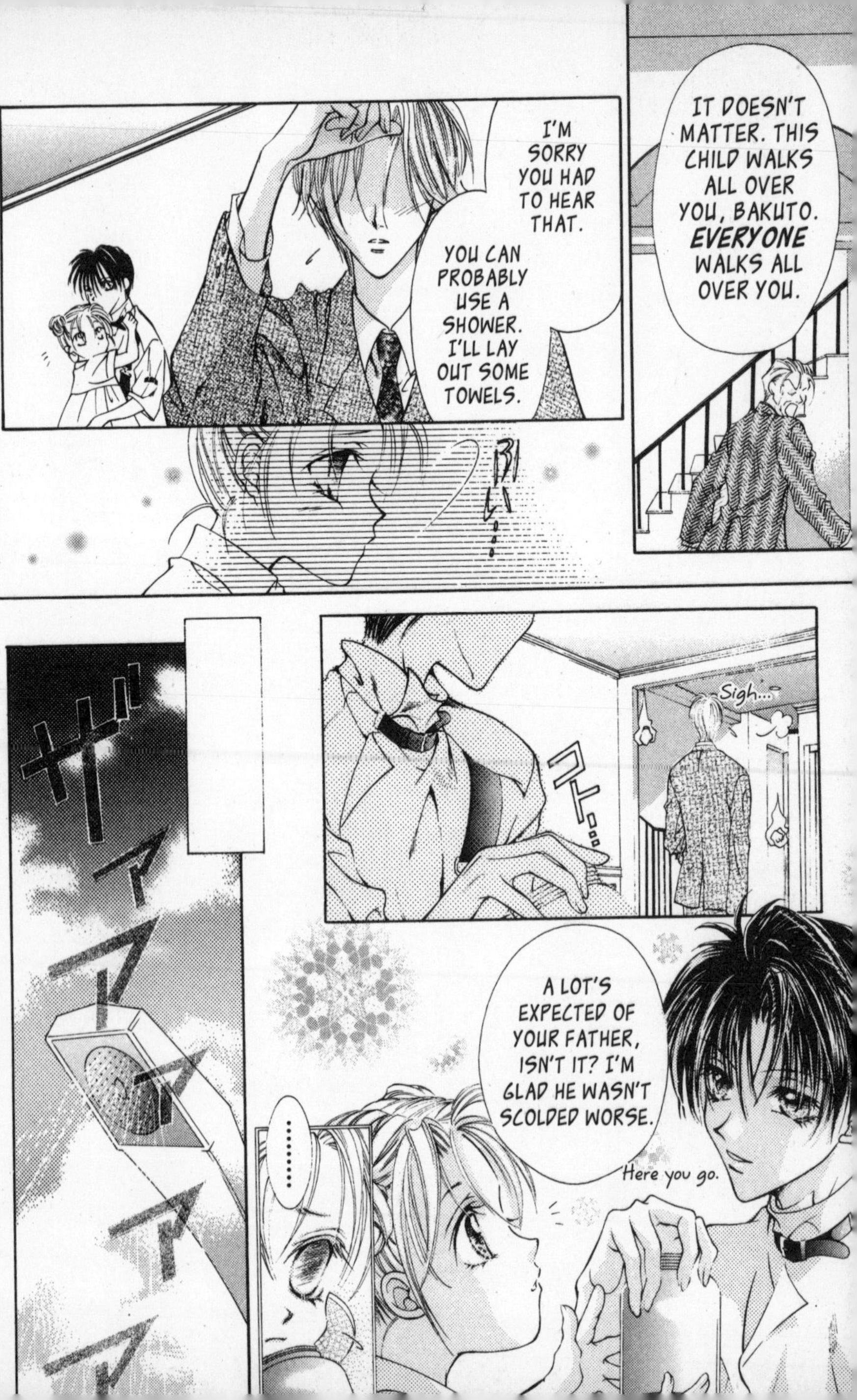

IT DOESN'T MATTER. THIS CHILD WALKS ALL OVER YOU, BAKUTO. **EVERYONE** WALKS ALL OVER YOU.
I'M SORRY YOU HAD TO HEAR THAT.
YOU CAN PROBABLY USE A SHOWER. I'LL LAY OUT SOME TOWELS.
Sigh...
A LOT'S EXPECTED OF YOUR FATHER, ISN'T IT? I'M GLAD HE WASN'T SCOLDED WORSE.
Here you go.
....

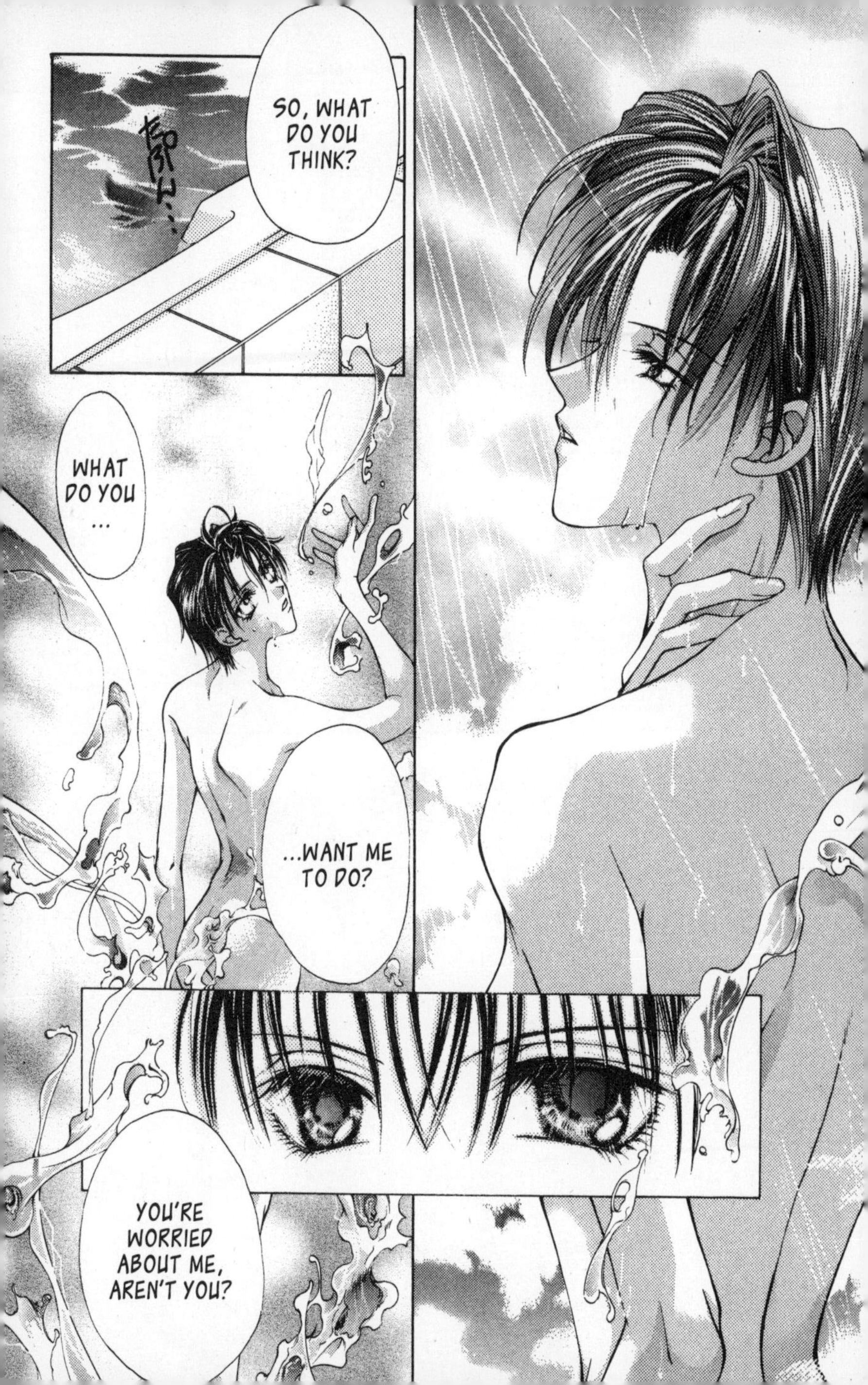
SO, WHAT DO YOU THINK?
たぷん…
WHAT DO YOU ...
...WANT ME TO DO?
YOU'RE WORRIED ABOUT ME, AREN'T YOU?

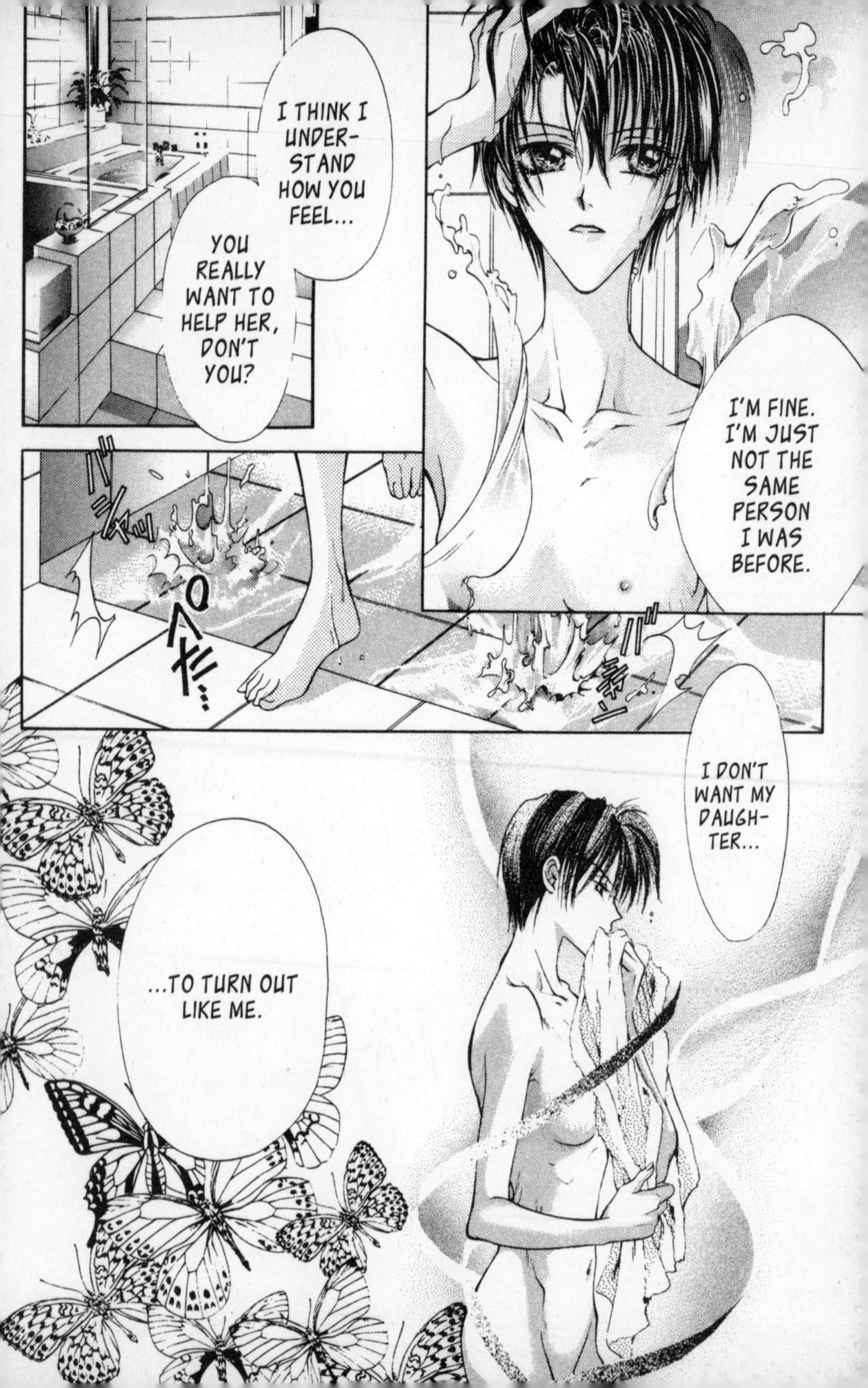
I'M FINE. I'M JUST NOT THE SAME PERSON I WAS BEFORE.
I THINK I UNDER-STAND HOW YOU FEEL...
YOU REALLY WANT TO HELP HER, DON'T YOU?
I DON'T WANT MY DAUGH-TER...
...TO TURN OUT LIKE ME.

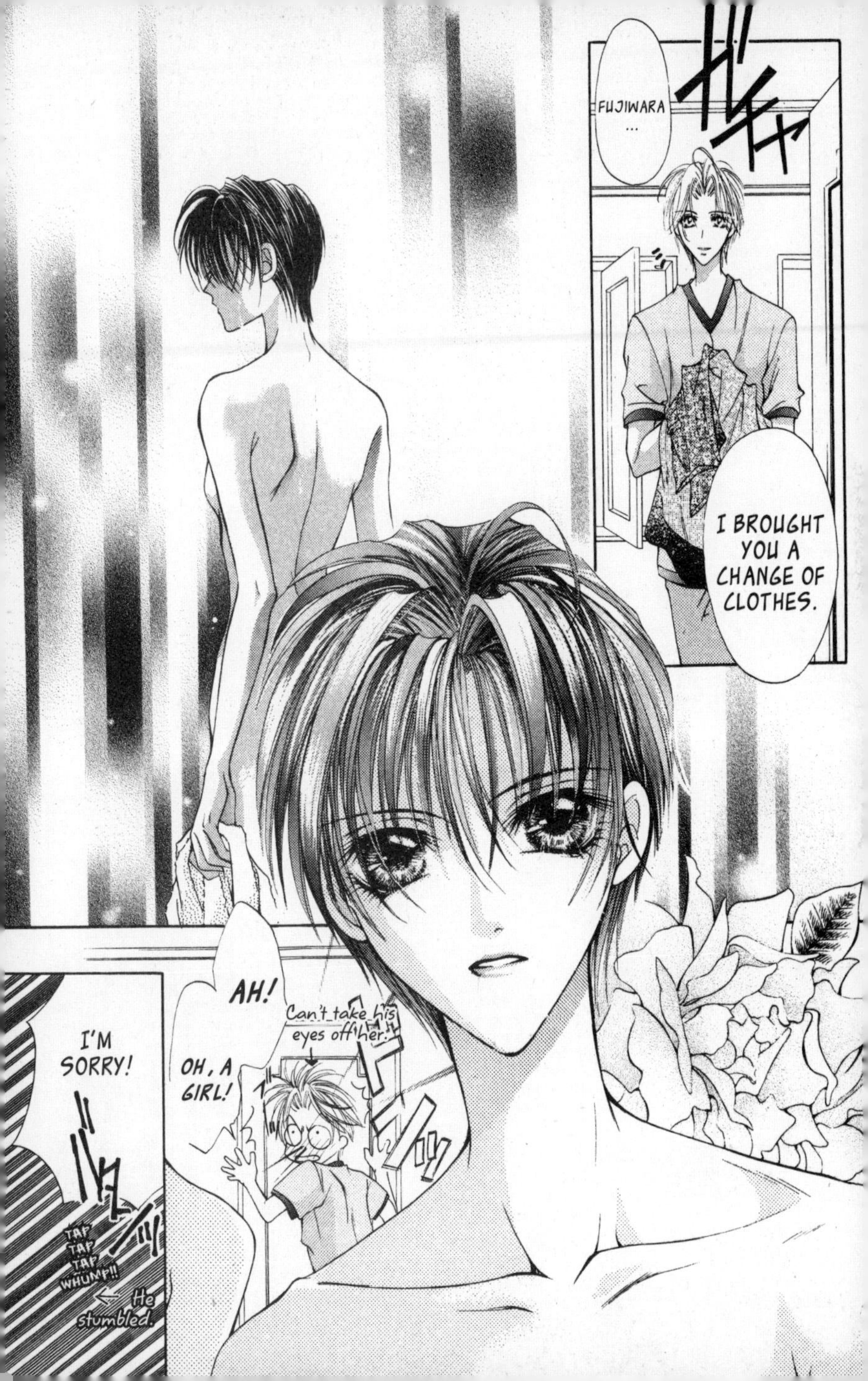
FUJIWARA ...
I BROUGHT YOU A CHANGE OF CLOTHES.
AH!
OH, A GIRL!
Can't take his eyes off her.
I'M SORRY!
TAP TAP TAP WHUMP!!
← He stumbled.

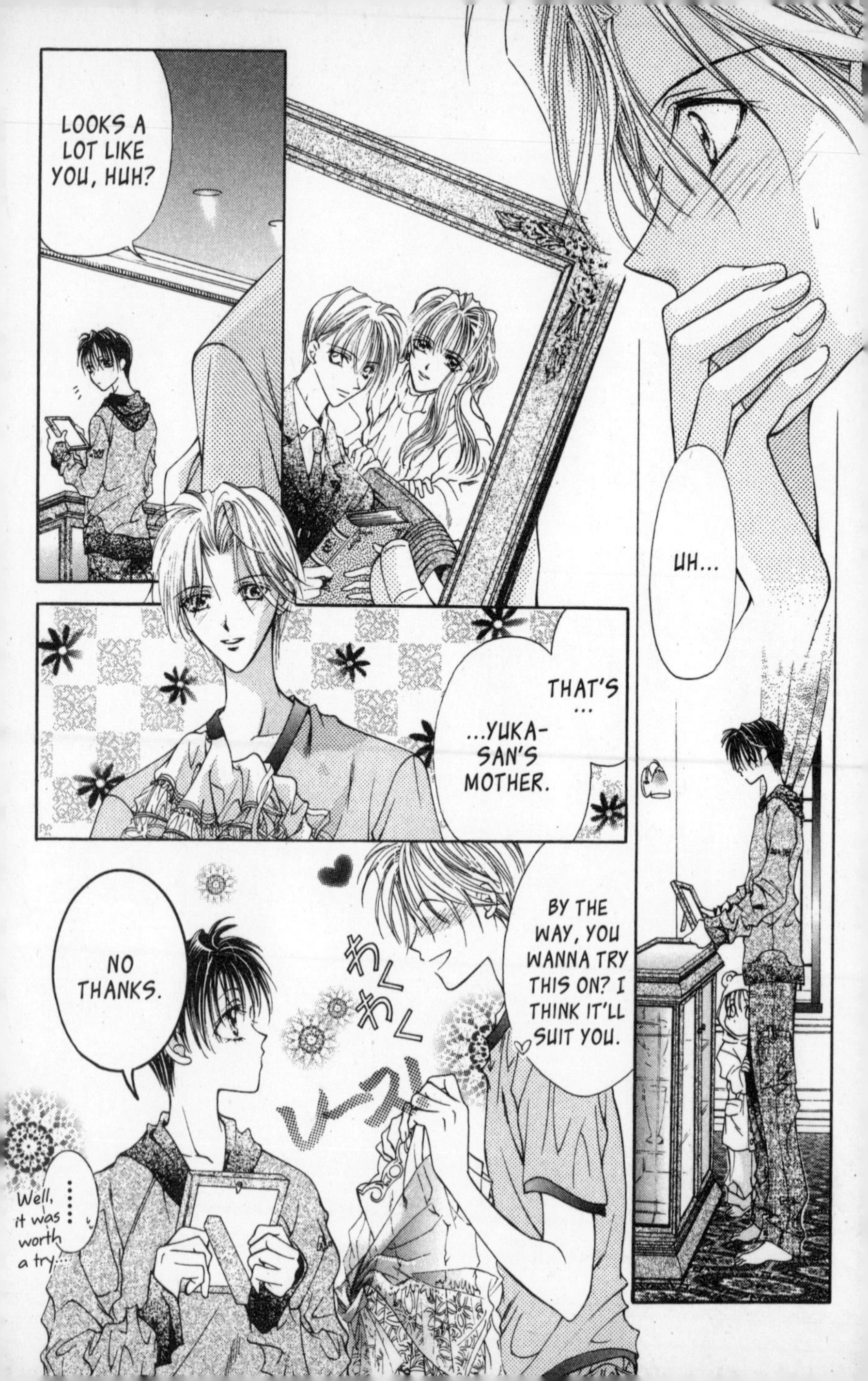
UH...
LOOKS A LOT LIKE YOU, HUH?
THAT'S... ...YUKA-SAN'S MOTHER.
BY THE WAY, YOU WANNA TRY THIS ON? I THINK IT'LL SUIT YOU.
わくわく
ソーッ
NO THANKS.
Well, it was worth a try......

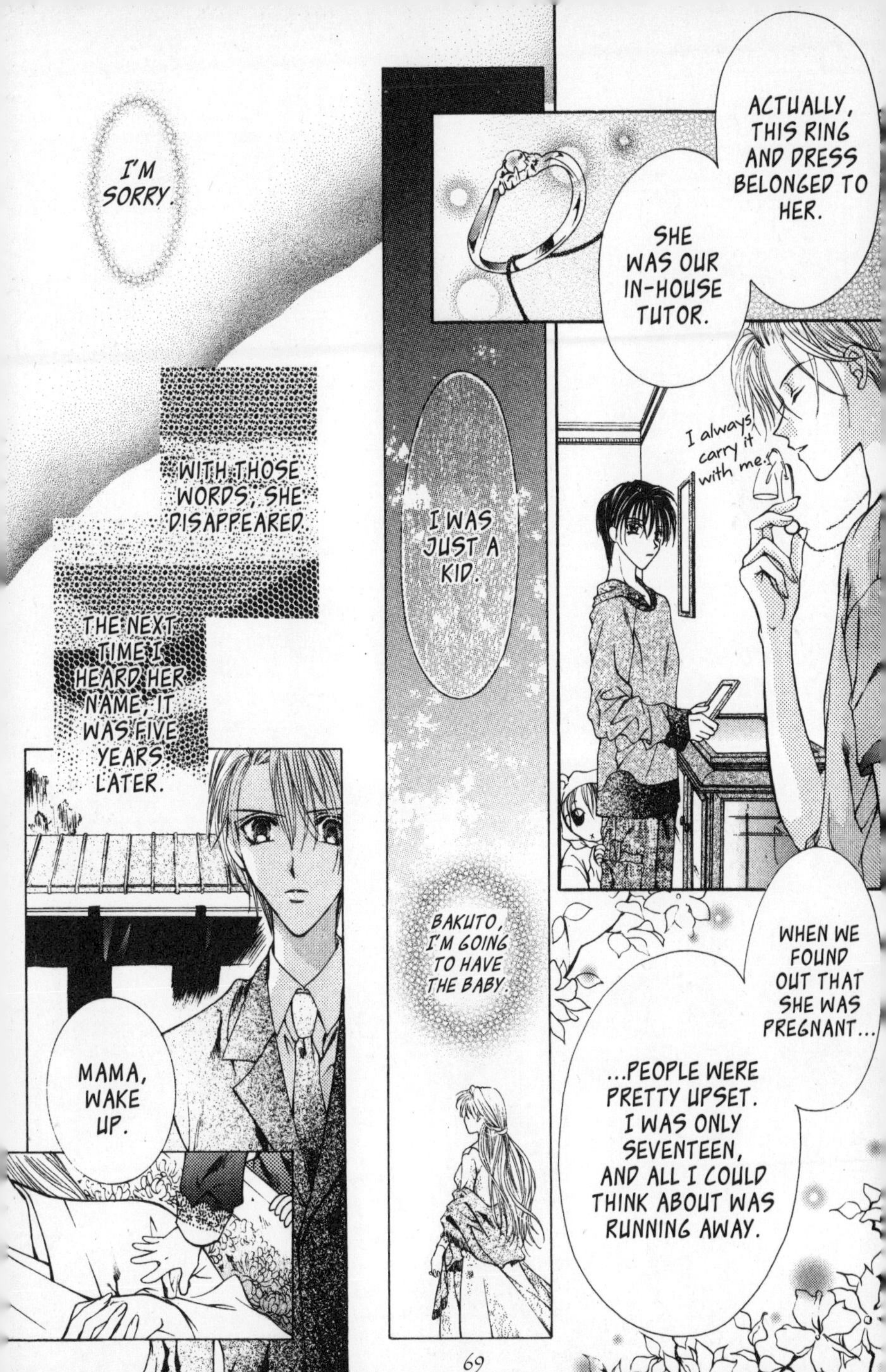
ACTUALLY, THIS RING AND DRESS BELONGED TO HER.
SHE WAS OUR IN-HOUSE TUTOR.
I always carry it with me.
WHEN WE FOUND OUT THAT SHE WAS PREGNANT...
...PEOPLE WERE PRETTY UPSET. I WAS ONLY SEVENTEEN, AND ALL I COULD THINK ABOUT WAS RUNNING AWAY.
I WAS JUST A KID.
BAKUTO, I'M GOING TO HAVE THE BABY.
I'M SORRY.
WITH THOSE WORDS, SHE DISAPPEARED.
THE NEXT TIME I HEARD HER NAME, IT WAS FIVE YEARS LATER.
MAMA, WAKE UP.

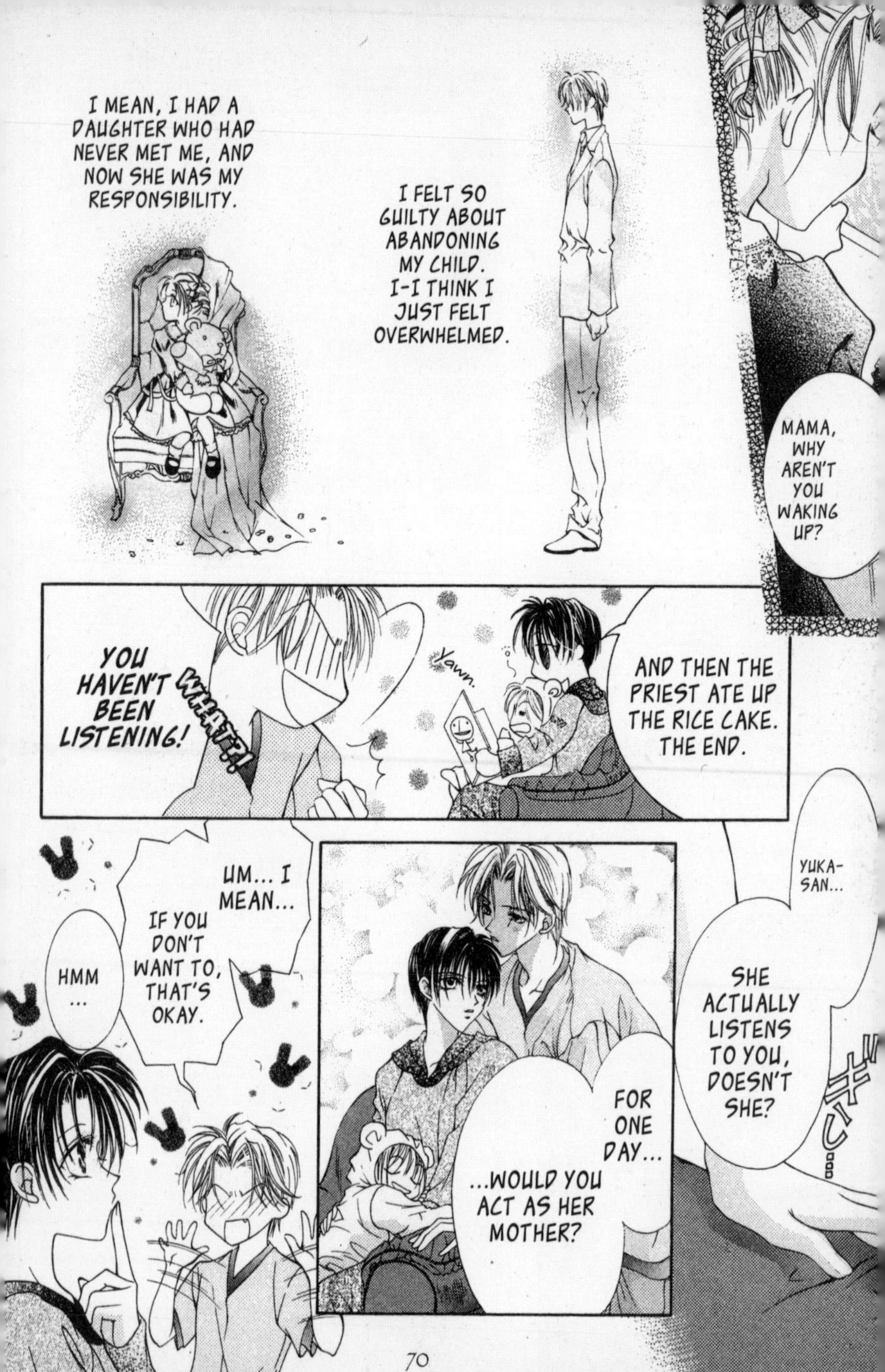
MAMA, WHY AREN'T YOU WAKING UP?
I FELT SO GUILTY ABOUT ABANDONING MY CHILD. I-I THINK I JUST FELT OVERWHELMED.
I MEAN, I HAD A DAUGHTER WHO HAD NEVER MET ME, AND NOW SHE WAS MY RESPONSIBILITY.
AND THEN THE PRIEST ATE UP THE RICE CAKE. THE END.
Yawn.
WHAT?!
YOU HAVEN'T BEEN LISTENING!
YUKA-SAN...
SHE ACTUALLY LISTENS TO YOU, DOESN'T SHE?
FOR ONE DAY...
...WOULD YOU ACT AS HER MOTHER?
UM... I MEAN...
IF YOU DON'T WANT TO, THAT'S OKAY.
HMM ...

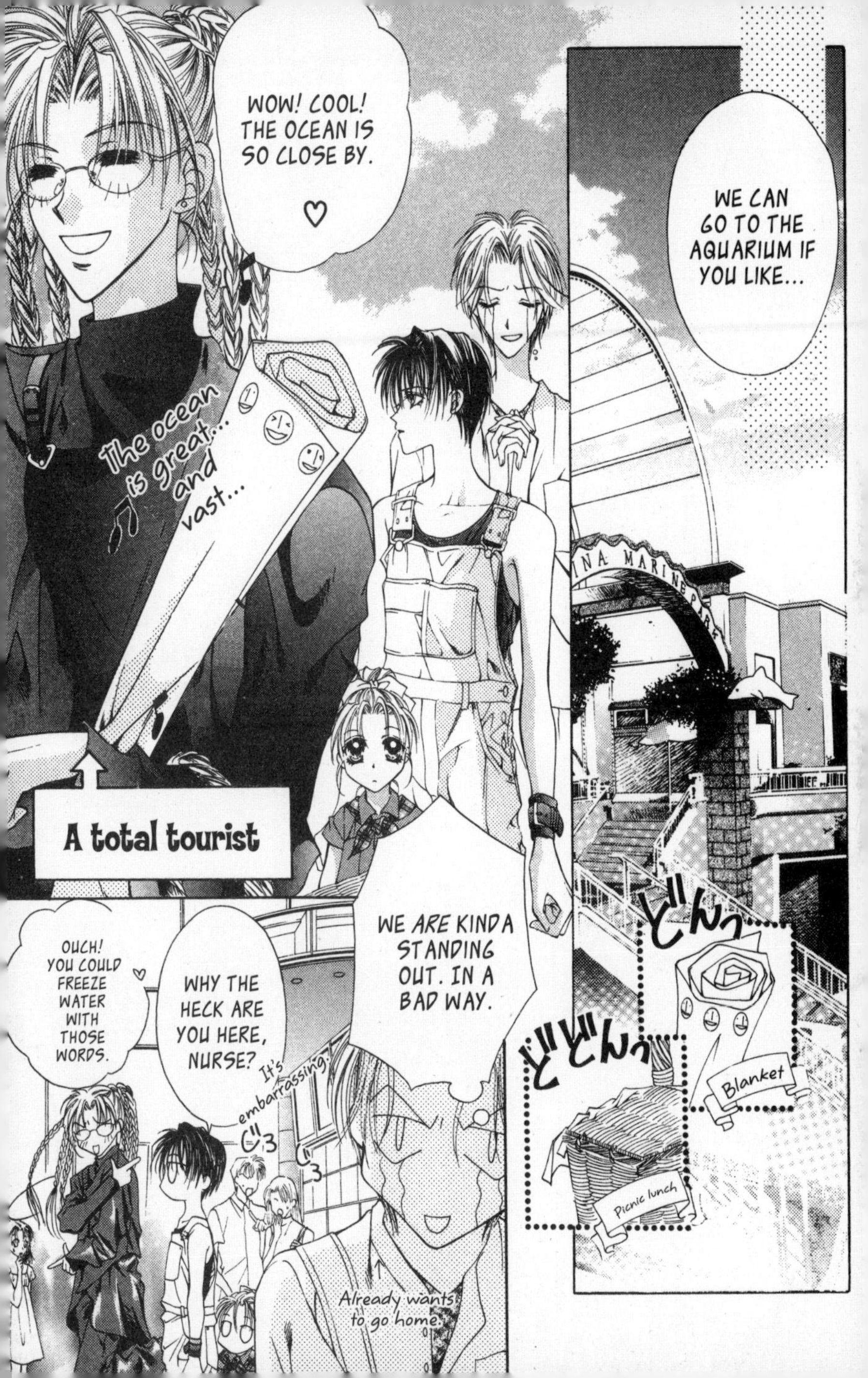
WE CAN GO TO THE AQUARIUM IF YOU LIKE...
WOW! COOL! THE OCEAN IS SO CLOSE BY. ♡
The ocean is great... and vast...
A total tourist
どんっ
Blanket
どどんっ
Picnic lunch
WE ARE KINDA STANDING OUT. IN A BAD WAY.
WHY THE HECK ARE YOU HERE, NURSE?
OUCH! YOU COULD FREEZE WATER WITH THOSE WORDS. ♡
It's embarrassing.
Already wants to go home.

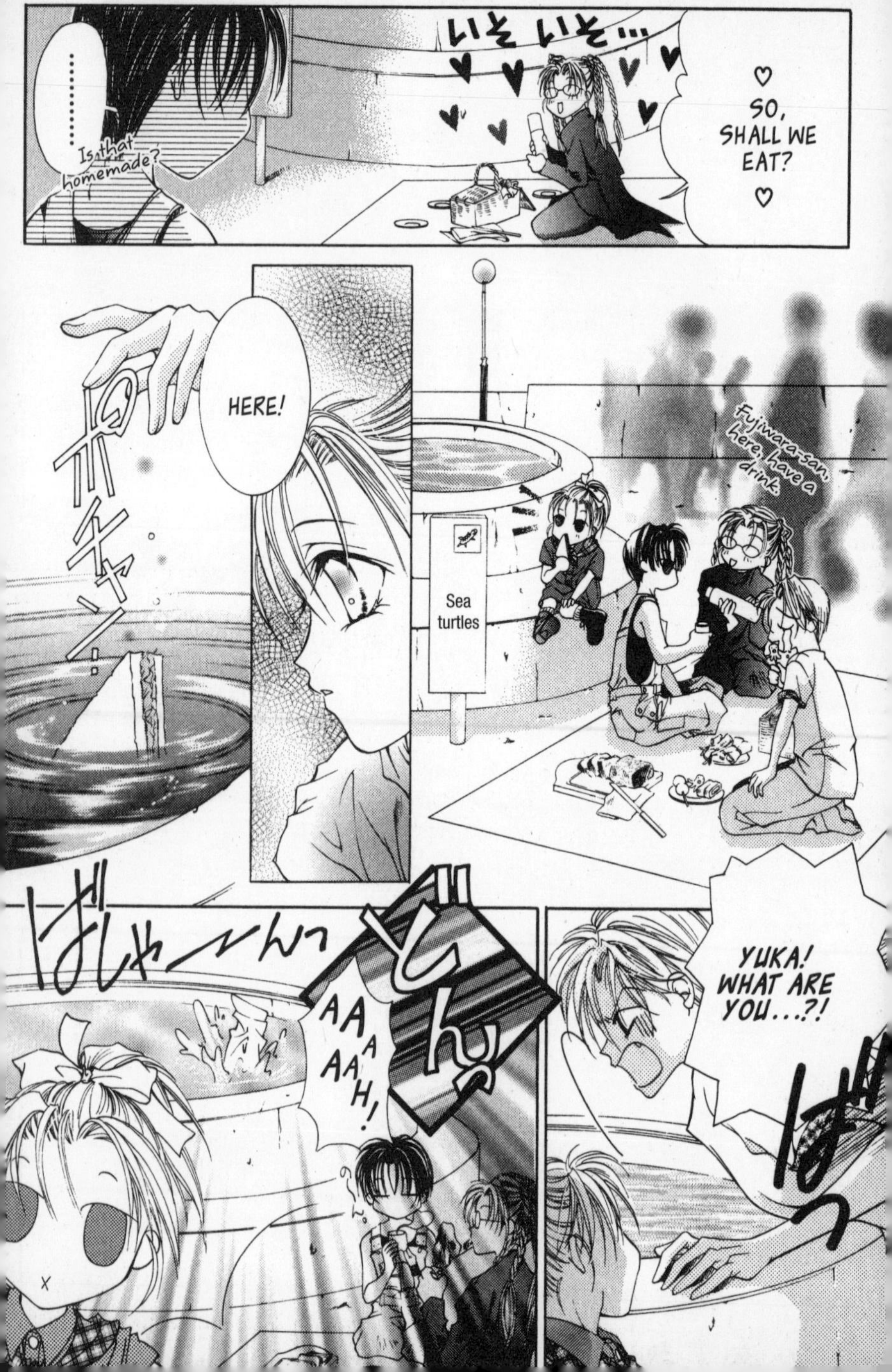
♡ SO, SHALL WE EAT? ♡
いそいそ…
……
Is that homemade?
Fujiwara-san, here, have a drink.
Sea turtles
HERE!
ポチャン!
YUKA! WHAT ARE YOU...?!
ぱっ
どんっ
AAAAAH!
ばしゃ〜んっ

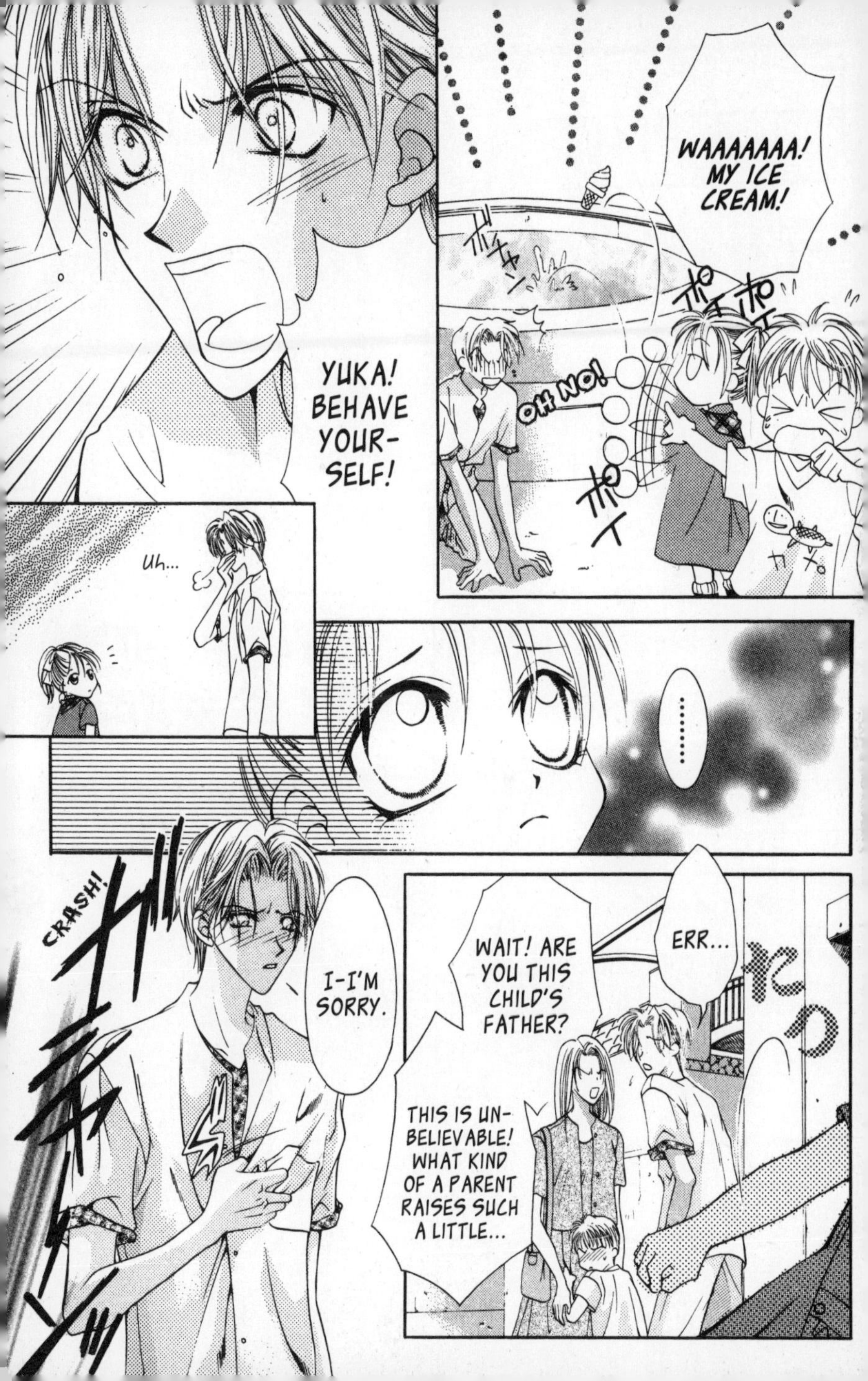
WAAAAAAA! MY ICE CREAM!
OH NO!
YUKA! BEHAVE YOUR-SELF!
Uh...
......
ERR...
WAIT! ARE YOU THIS CHILD'S FATHER?
THIS IS UN-BELIEVABLE! WHAT KIND OF A PARENT RAISES SUCH A LITTLE...
I-I'M SORRY.
CRASH!

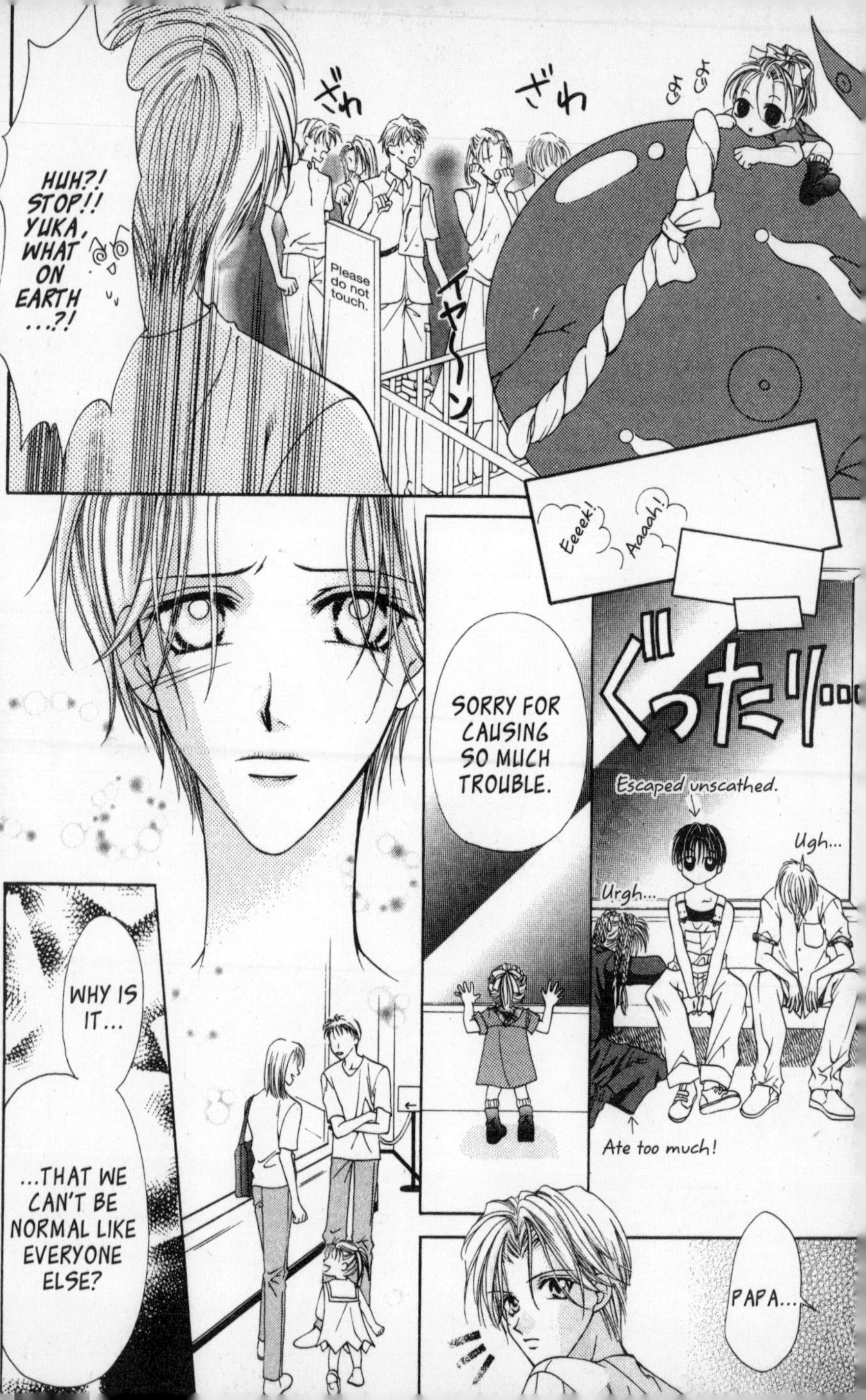
ざわ ざわ
Please do not touch.
イヤ〜ン
HUH?! STOP!! YUKA, WHAT ON EARTH...?!
Eeeek!
Aaaah!
ぐったり...
Escaped unscathed.
Ugh...
Urgh...
Ate too much!
SORRY FOR CAUSING SO MUCH TROUBLE.
PAPA...
WHY IS IT...
...THAT WE CAN'T BE NORMAL LIKE EVERYONE ELSE?

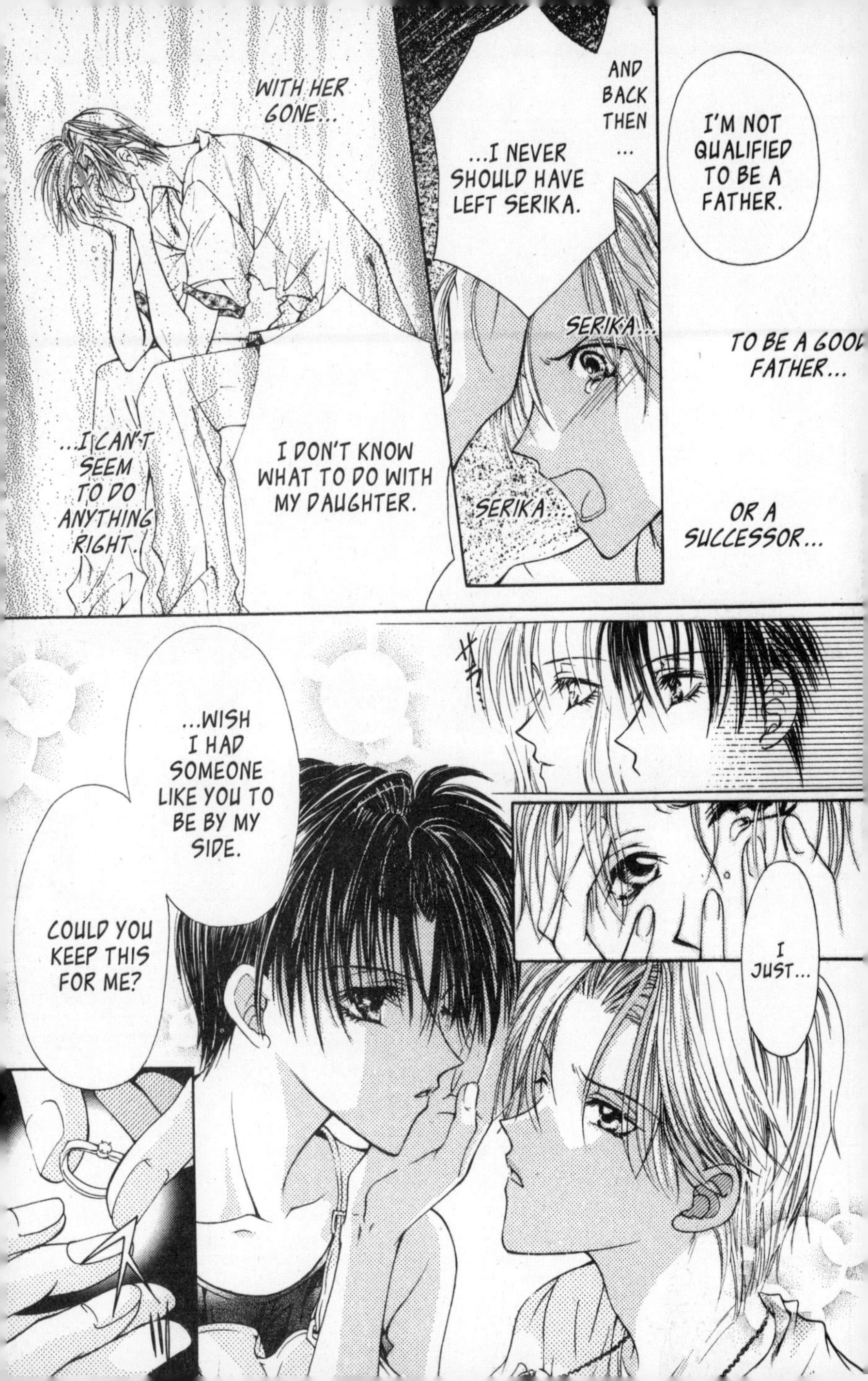
I'M NOT QUALIFIED TO BE A FATHER.
TO BE A GOOD FATHER...
OR A SUCCESSOR...
AND BACK THEN ...
...I NEVER SHOULD HAVE LEFT SERIKA.
SERIKA...
SERIKA
WITH HER GONE...
I DON'T KNOW WHAT TO DO WITH MY DAUGHTER.
...I CAN'T SEEM TO DO ANYTHING RIGHT.
I JUST...
...WISH I HAD SOMEONE LIKE YOU TO BE BY MY SIDE.
COULD YOU KEEP THIS FOR ME?

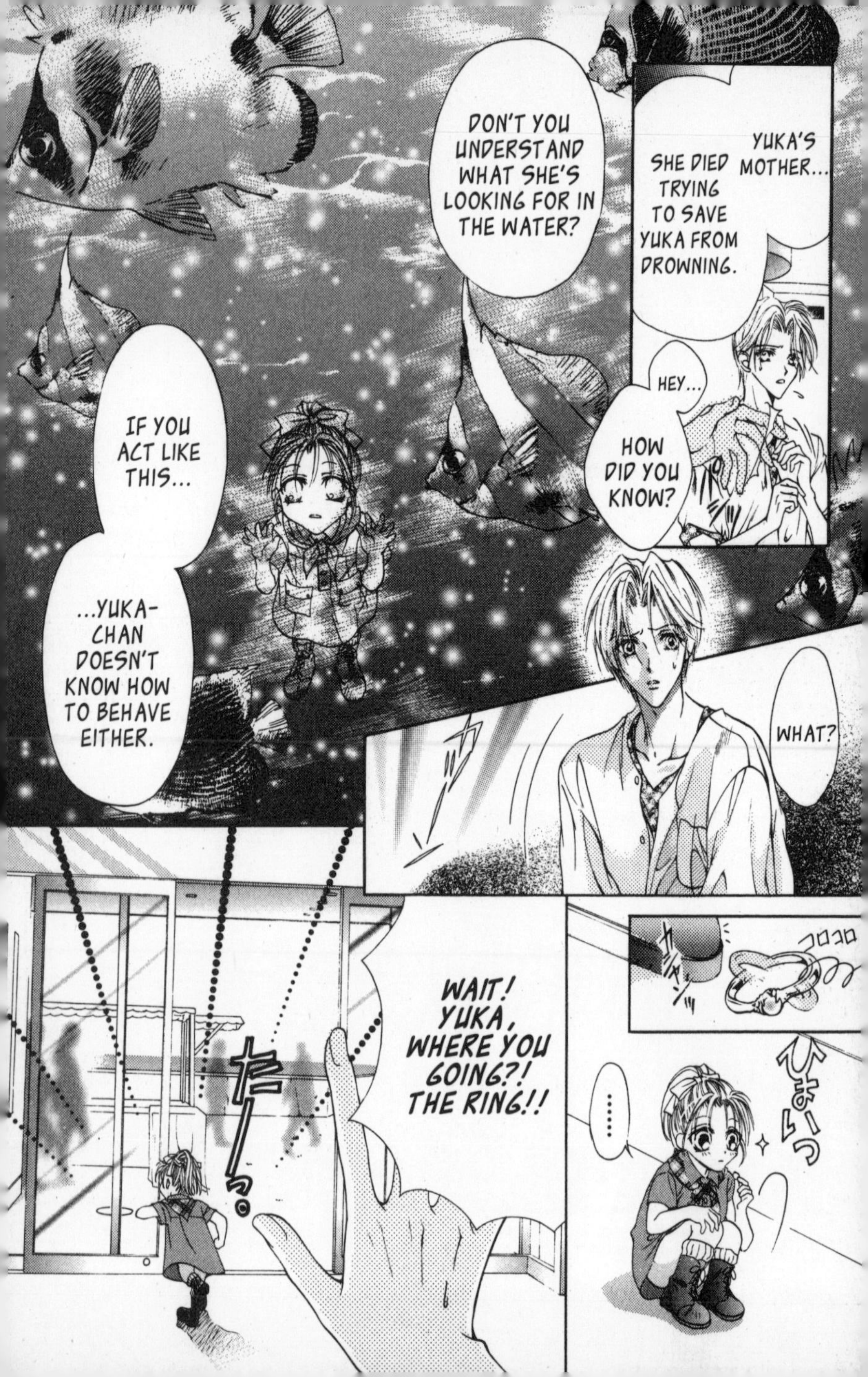
YUKA'S MOTHER...
SHE DIED TRYING TO SAVE YUKA FROM DROWNING.
HEY...
HOW DID YOU KNOW?
DON'T YOU UNDERSTAND WHAT SHE'S LOOKING FOR IN THE WATER?
IF YOU ACT LIKE THIS...
...YUKA-CHAN DOESN'T KNOW HOW TO BEHAVE EITHER.
WHAT?
コロコロ
......
WAIT! YUKA, WHERE YOU GOING?! THE RING!!

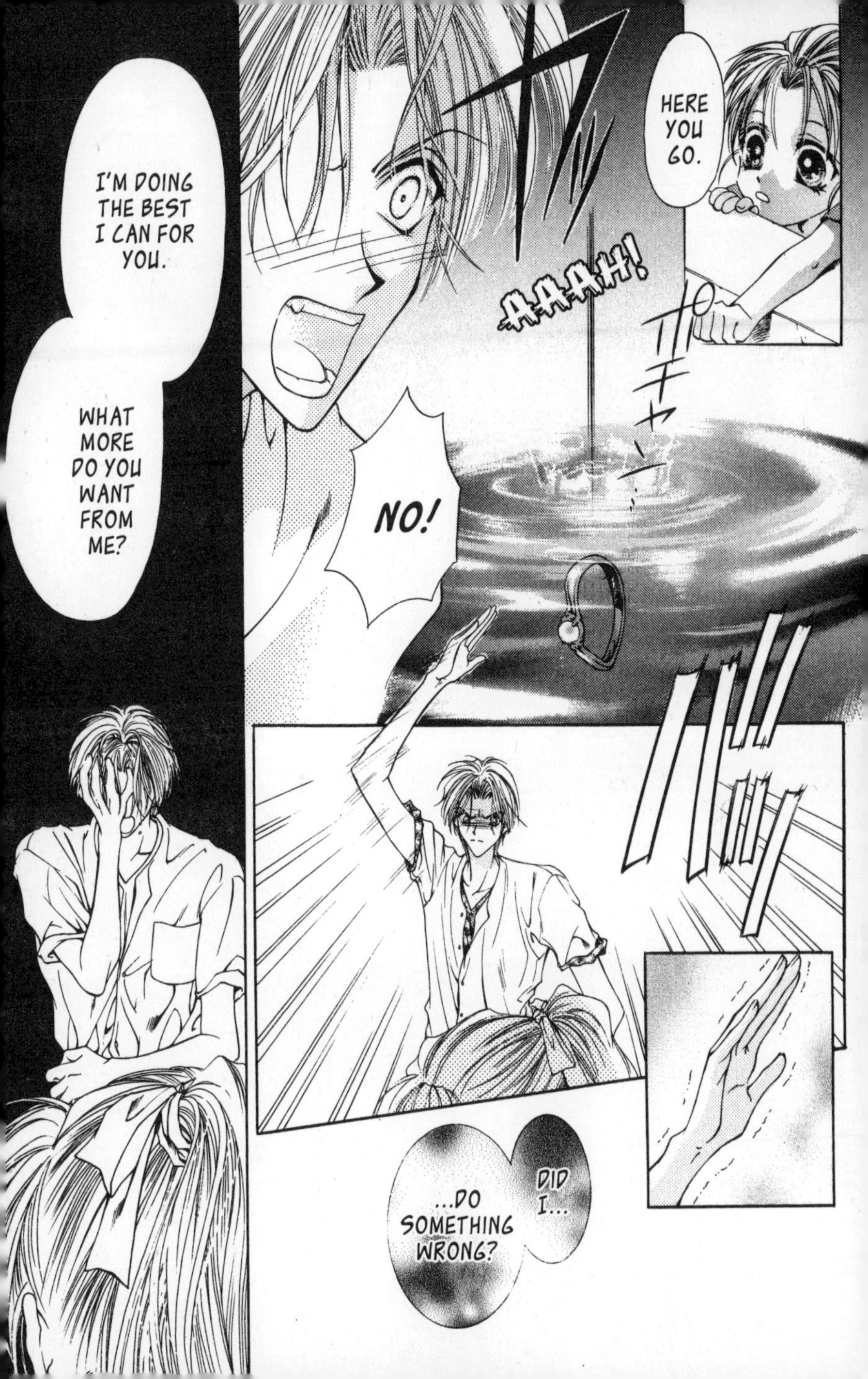
HERE YOU GO.
AAAAH!
NO!
DID I...
...DO SOMETHING WRONG?
I'M DOING THE BEST I CAN FOR YOU.
WHAT MORE DO YOU WANT FROM ME?

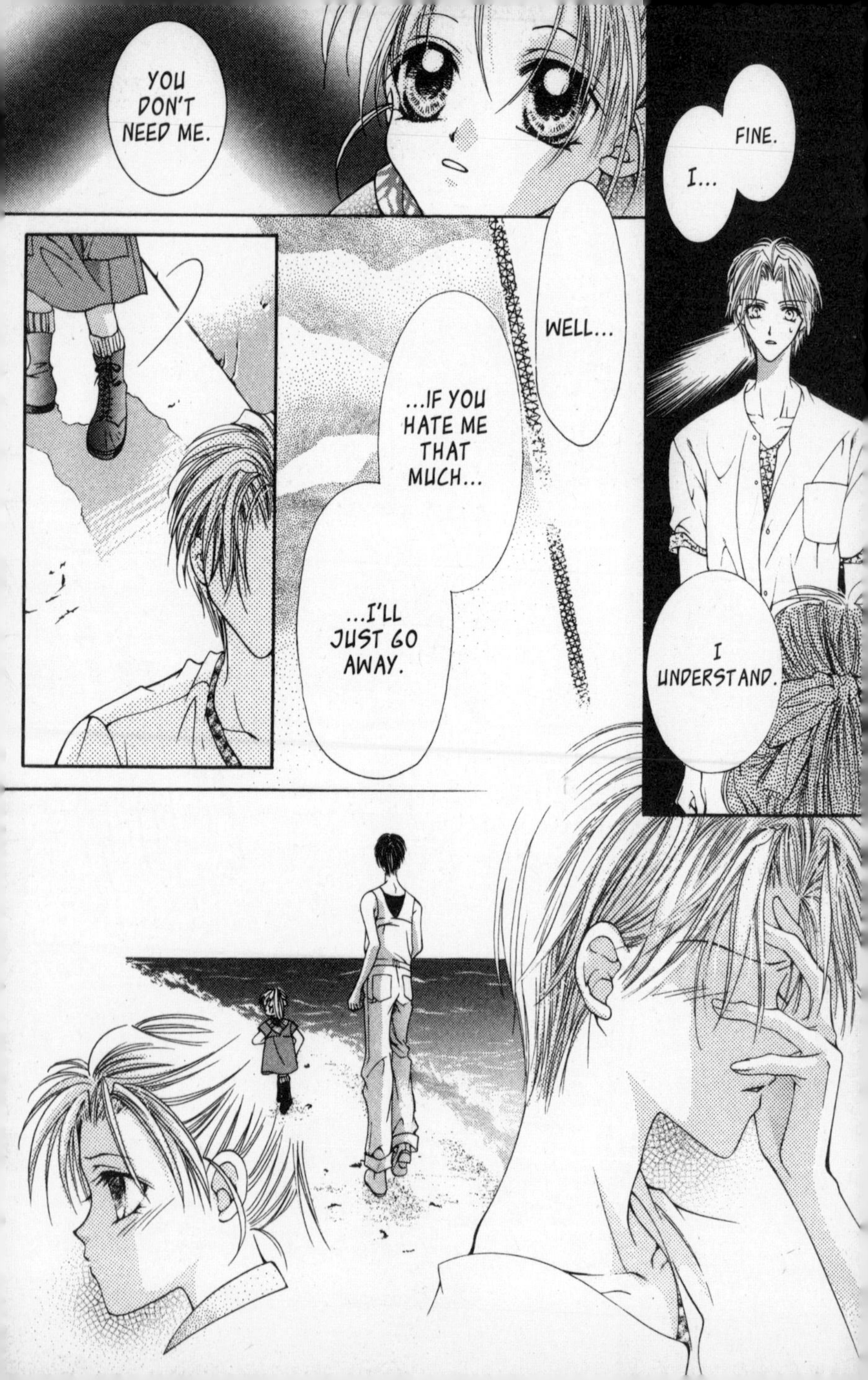
FINE. I...
I UNDERSTAND.
YOU DON'T NEED ME.
WELL...
...IF YOU HATE ME THAT MUCH...
...I'LL JUST GO AWAY.

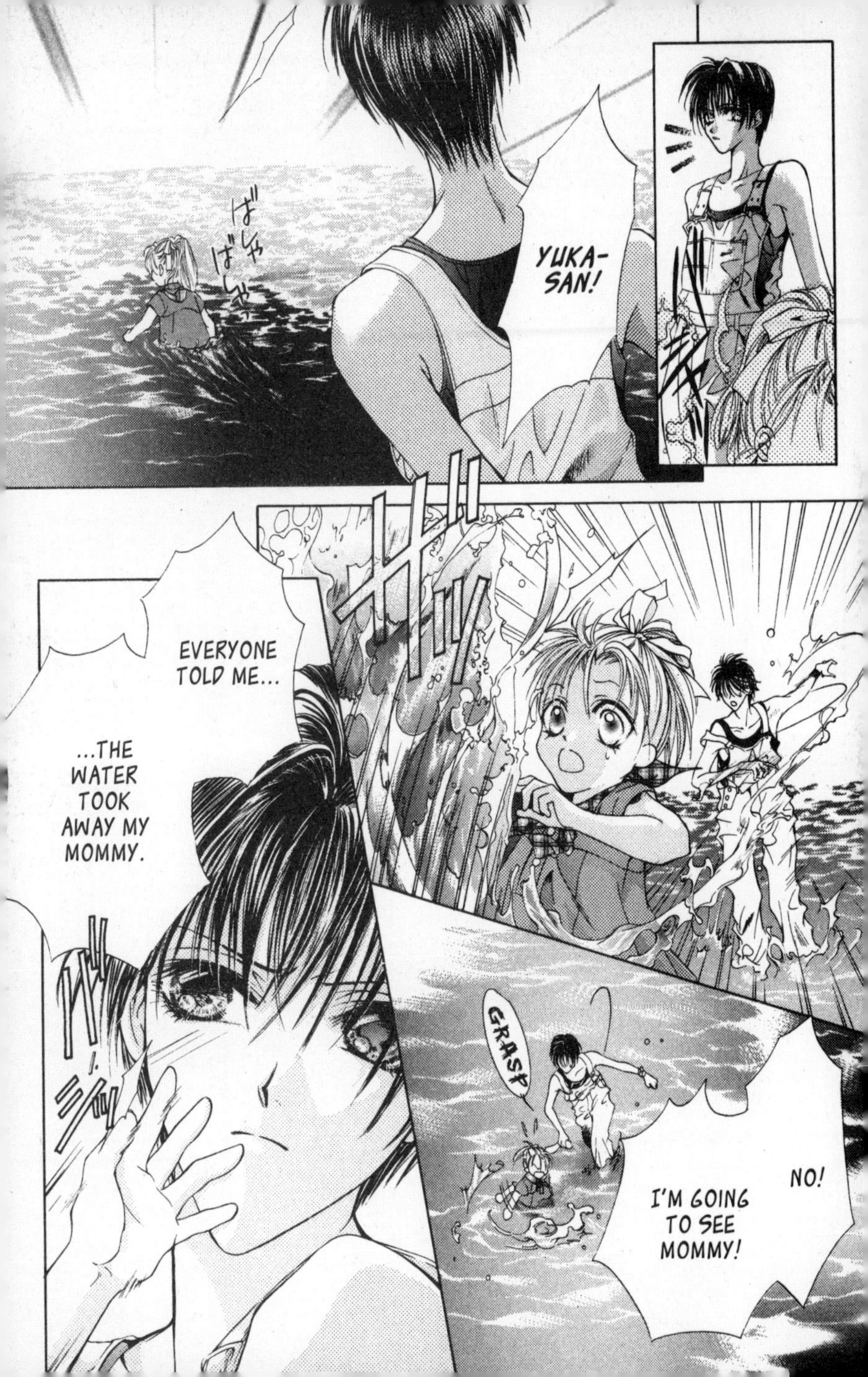
YUKA-SAN!
ばしゃばしゃ
GRASP
NO!
I'M GOING TO SEE MOMMY!
EVERYONE TOLD ME...
...THE WATER TOOK AWAY MY MOMMY.

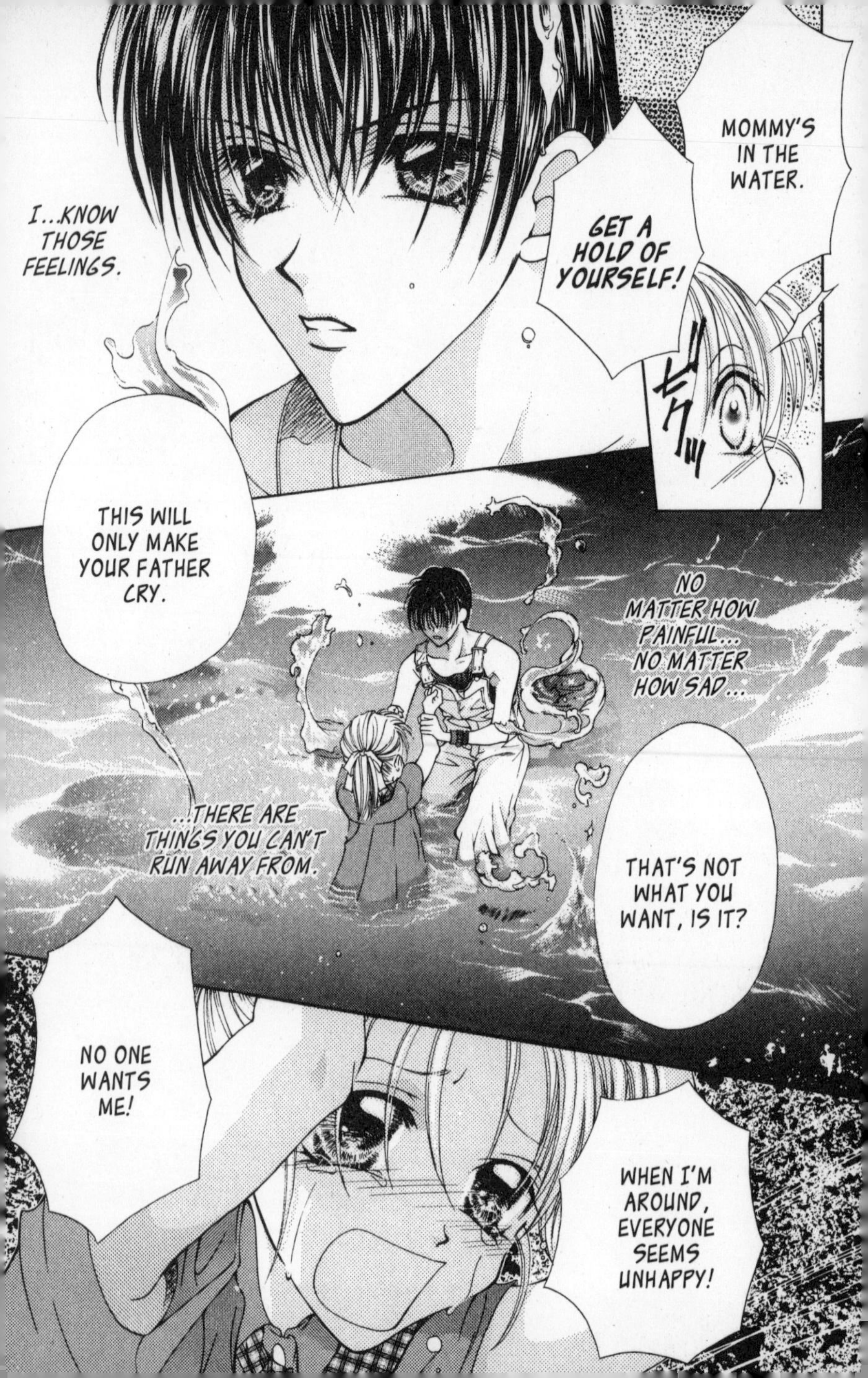
MOMMY'S IN THE WATER.
GET A HOLD OF YOURSELF!
I...KNOW THOSE FEELINGS.
THIS WILL ONLY MAKE YOUR FATHER CRY.
THAT'S NOT WHAT YOU WANT, IS IT?
NO MATTER HOW PAINFUL... NO MATTER HOW SAD...
...THERE ARE THINGS YOU CAN'T RUN AWAY FROM.
WHEN I'M AROUND, EVERYONE SEEMS UNHAPPY!
NO ONE WANTS ME!

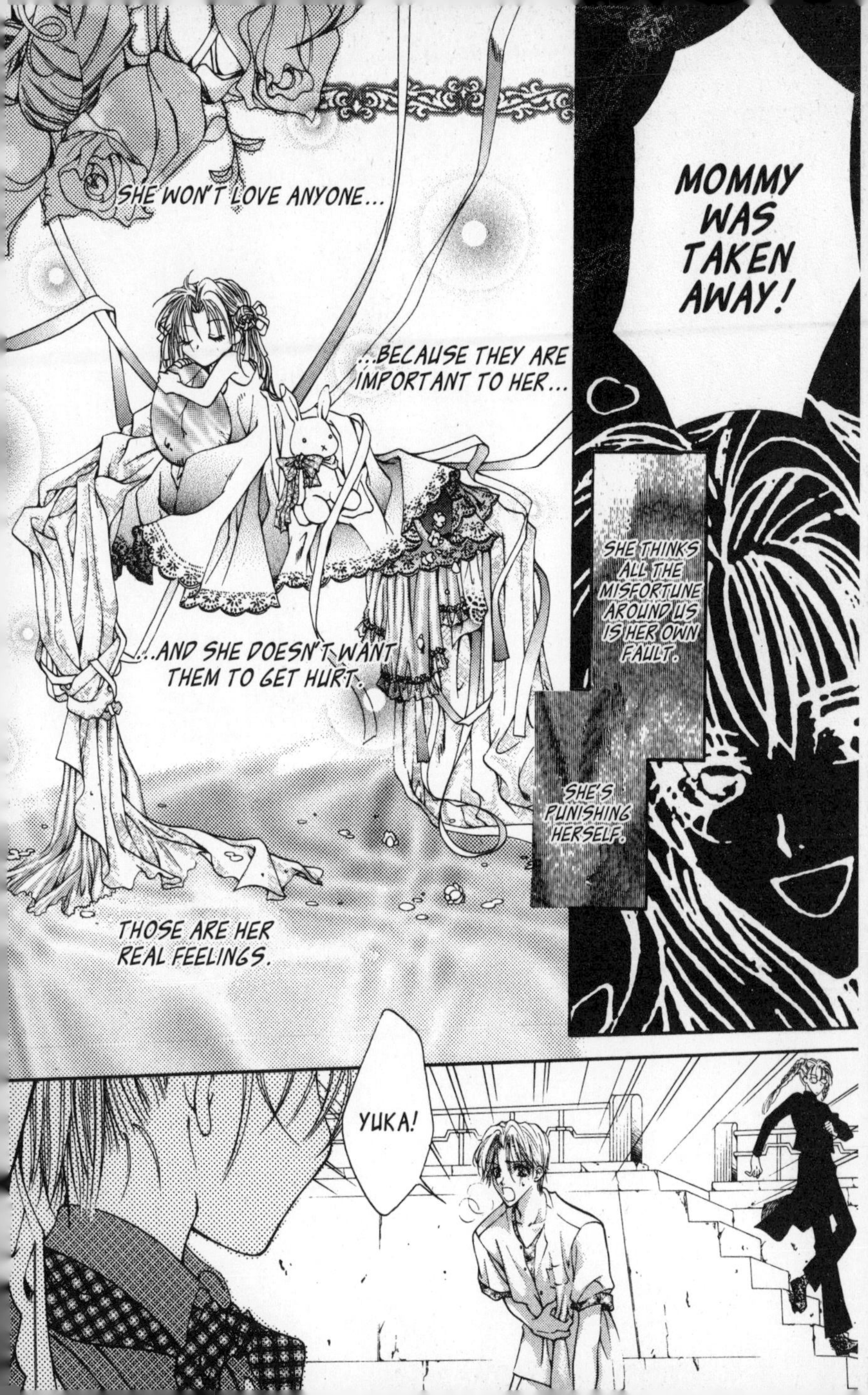
MOMMY WAS TAKEN AWAY!
SHE THINKS ALL THE MISFORTUNE AROUND US IS HER OWN FAULT.
SHE'S PUNISHING HERSELF.
SHE WON'T LOVE ANYONE...
...BECAUSE THEY ARE IMPORTANT TO HER...
...AND SHE DOESN'T WANT THEM TO GET HURT.
THOSE ARE HER REAL FEELINGS.
YUKA!

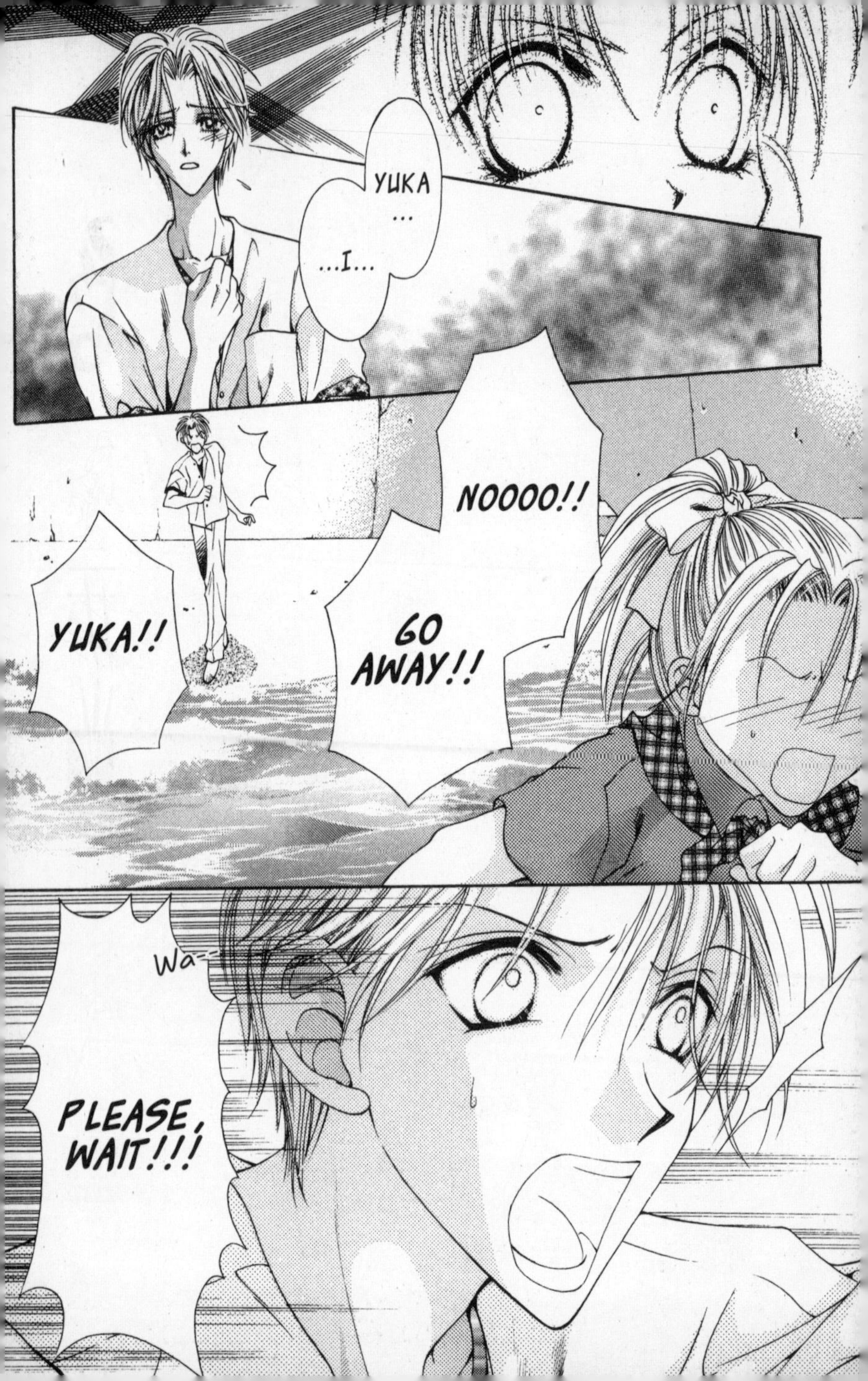
YUKA ... ...I...
NOOOO!!
GO AWAY!!
YUKA!!
Wa--
PLEASE, WAIT!!!

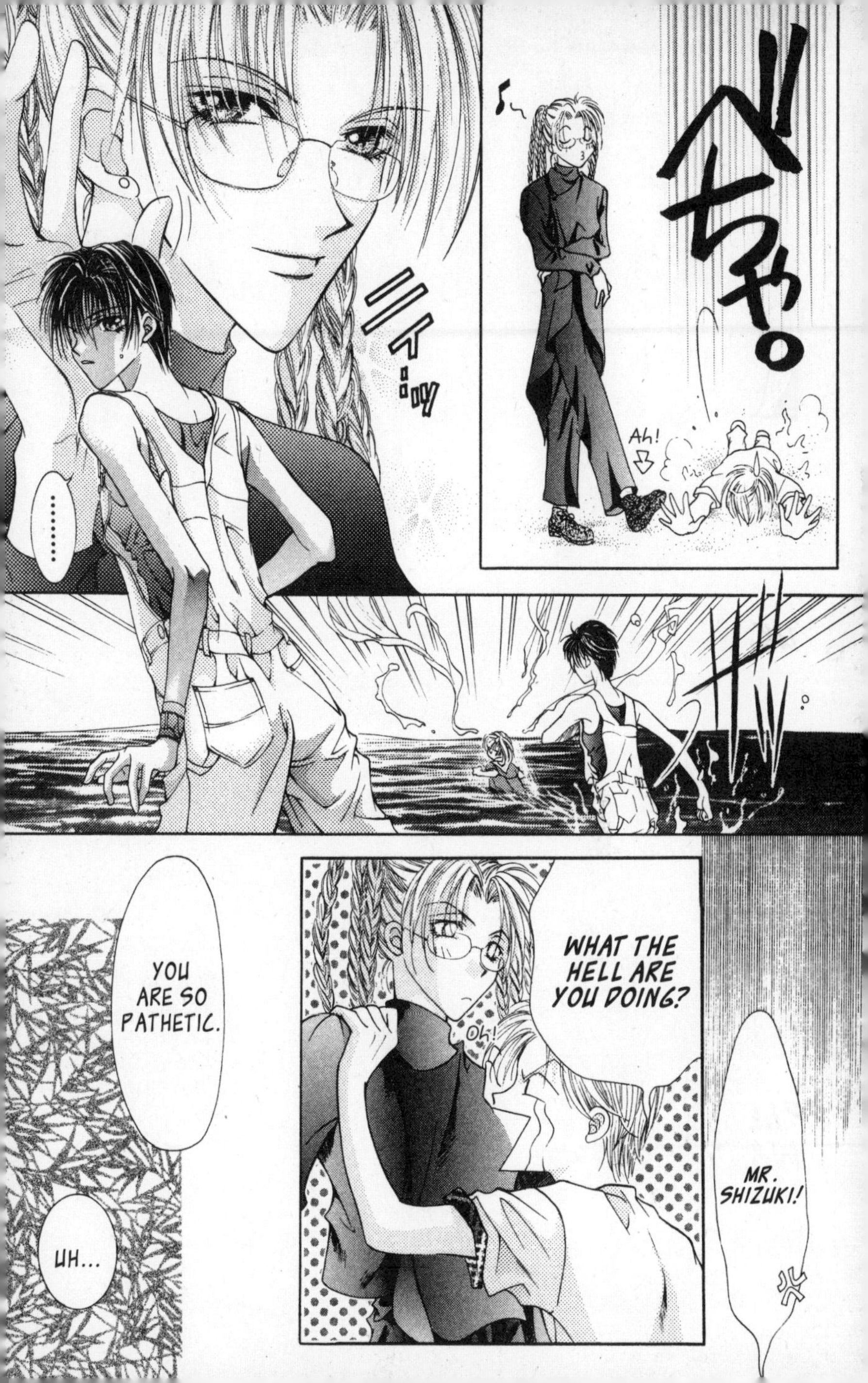
べちゃ。
AH!
......
WHAT THE HELL ARE YOU DOING?
MR. SHIZUKI!
OH!
YOU ARE SO PATHETIC.
UH...

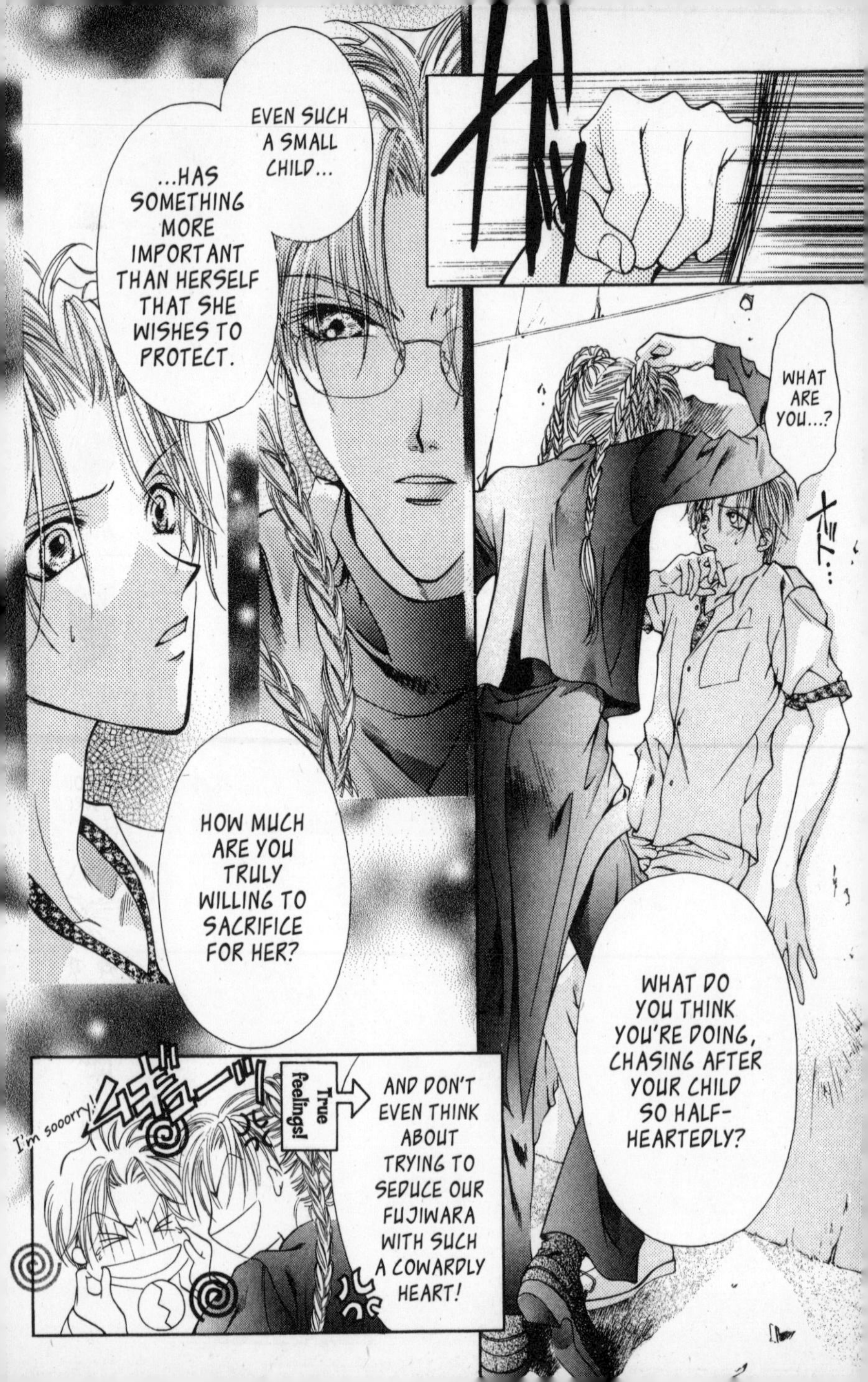

WHAT ARE YOU...?
WHAT DO YOU THINK YOU'RE DOING, CHASING AFTER YOUR CHILD SO HALF-HEARTEDLY?
EVEN SUCH A SMALL CHILD...
...HAS SOMETHING MORE IMPORTANT THAN HERSELF THAT SHE WISHES TO PROTECT.
HOW MUCH ARE YOU TRULY WILLING TO SACRIFICE FOR HER?
AND DON'T EVEN THINK ABOUT TRYING TO SEDUCE OUR FUJIWARA WITH SUCH A COWARDLY HEART!
True feelings!
I'm sooorry!

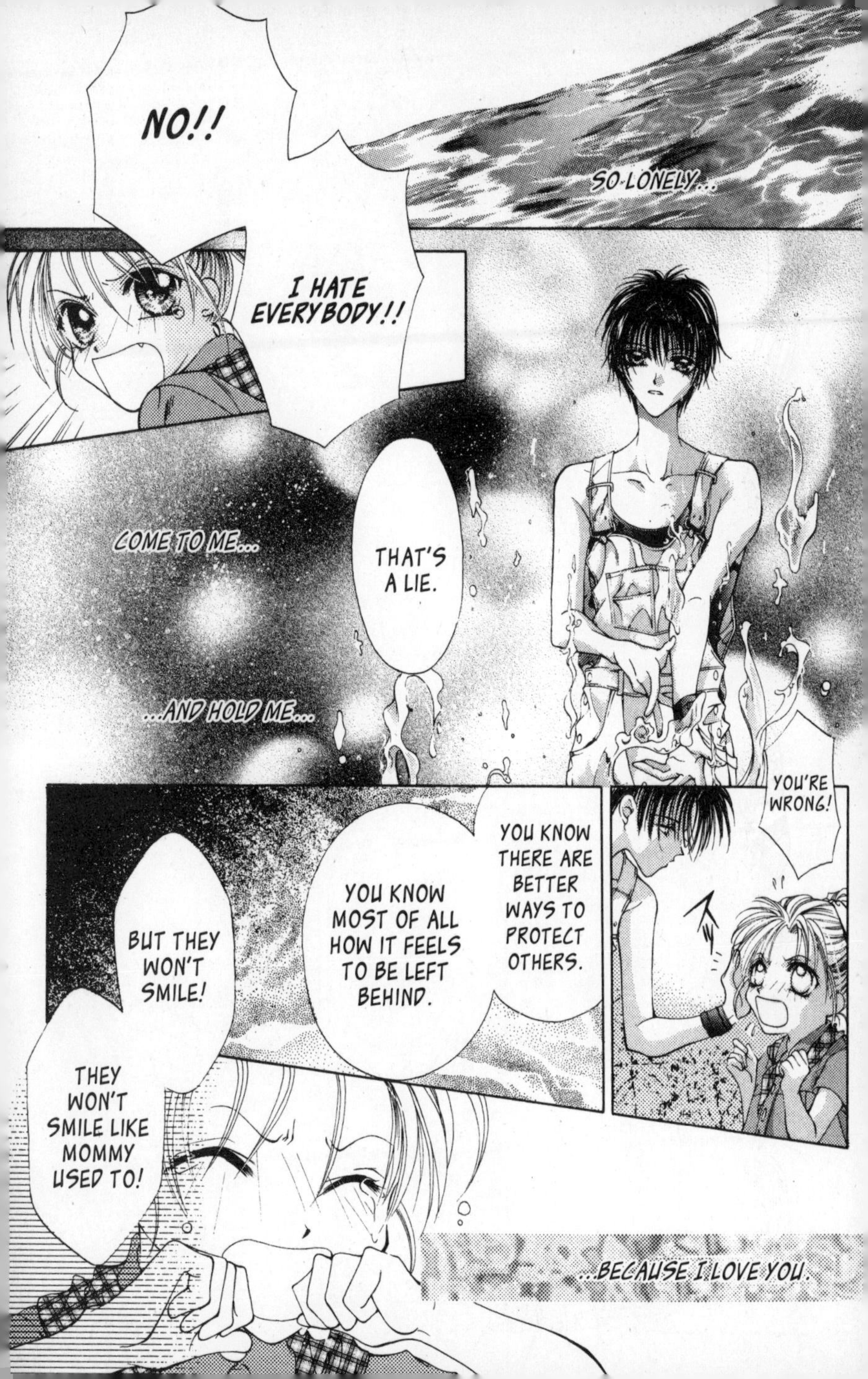
SO LONELY...
NO!!
I HATE EVERYBODY!!
COME TO ME...
THAT'S A LIE.
...AND HOLD ME...
YOU'RE WRONG!
YOU KNOW THERE ARE BETTER WAYS TO PROTECT OTHERS.
YOU KNOW MOST OF ALL HOW IT FEELS TO BE LEFT BEHIND.
BUT THEY WON'T SMILE!
THEY WON'T SMILE LIKE MOMMY USED TO!
...BECAUSE I LOVE YOU.

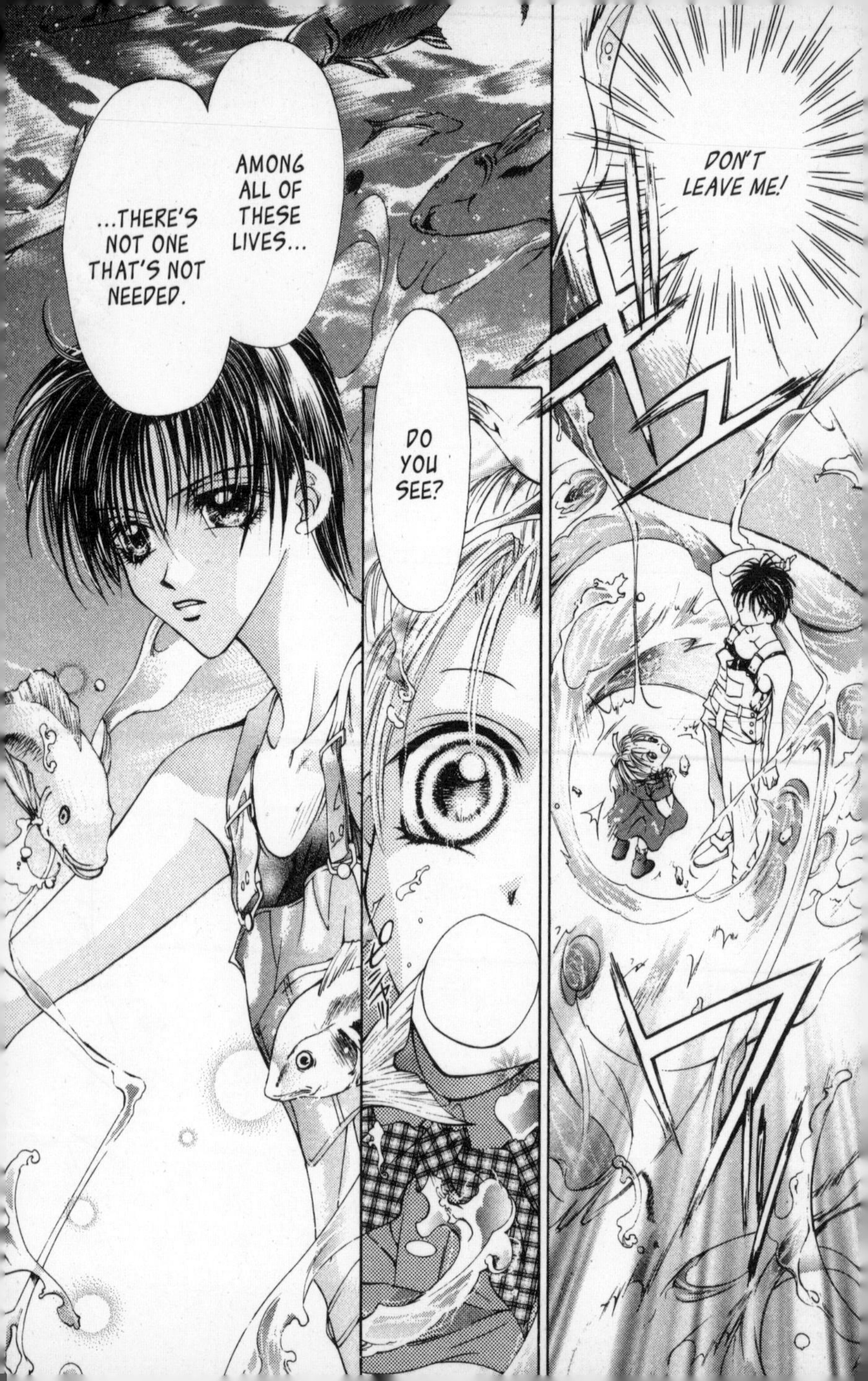
DON'T LEAVE ME!
AMONG ALL OF THESE LIVES...
...THERE'S NOT ONE THAT'S NOT NEEDED.
DO YOU SEE?

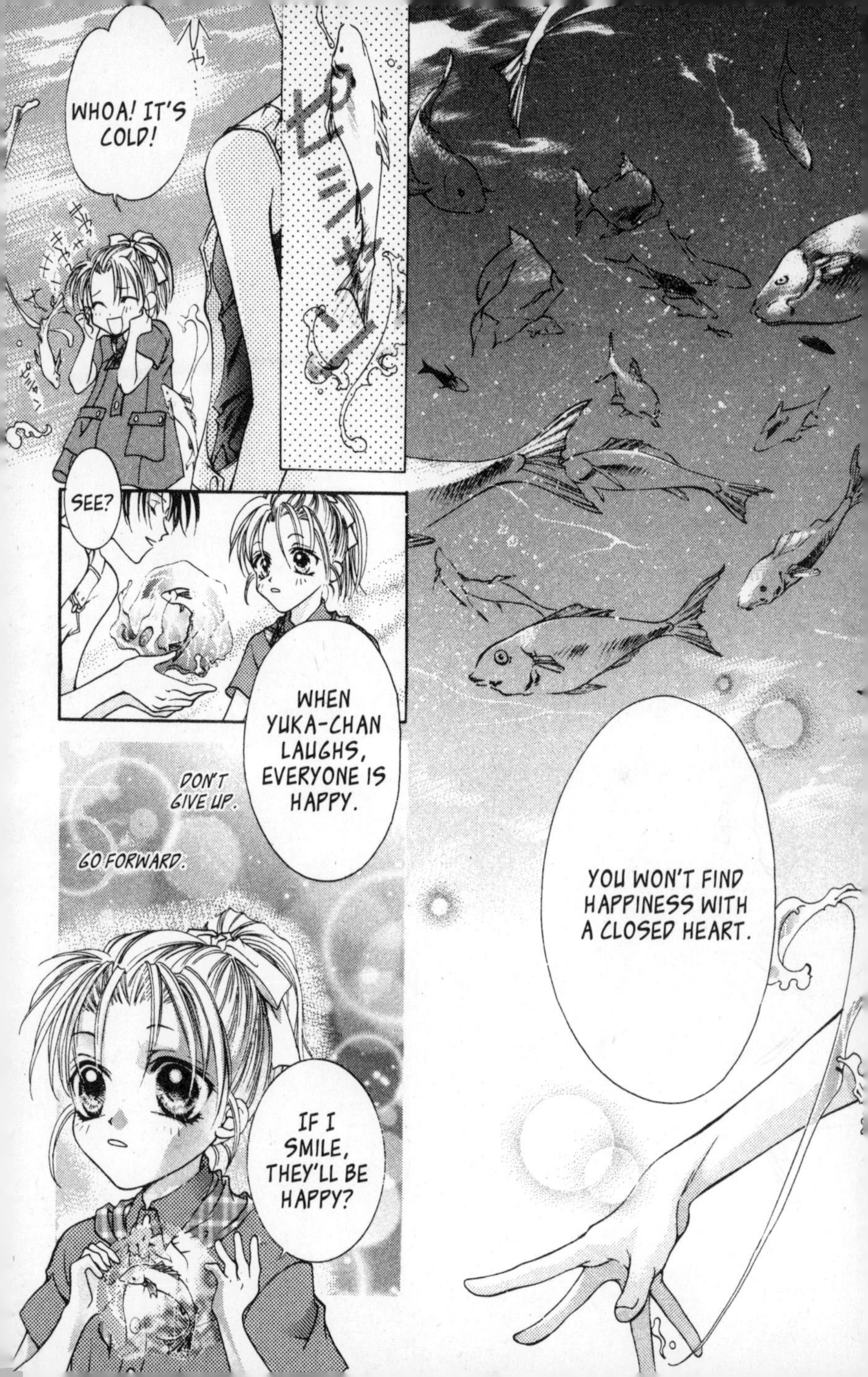
YOU WON'T FIND HAPPINESS WITH A CLOSED HEART.
WHOA! IT'S COLD!
SEE?
WHEN YUKA-CHAN LAUGHS, EVERYONE IS HAPPY.
DON'T GIVE UP.
GO FORWARD.
IF I SMILE, THEY'LL BE HAPPY?

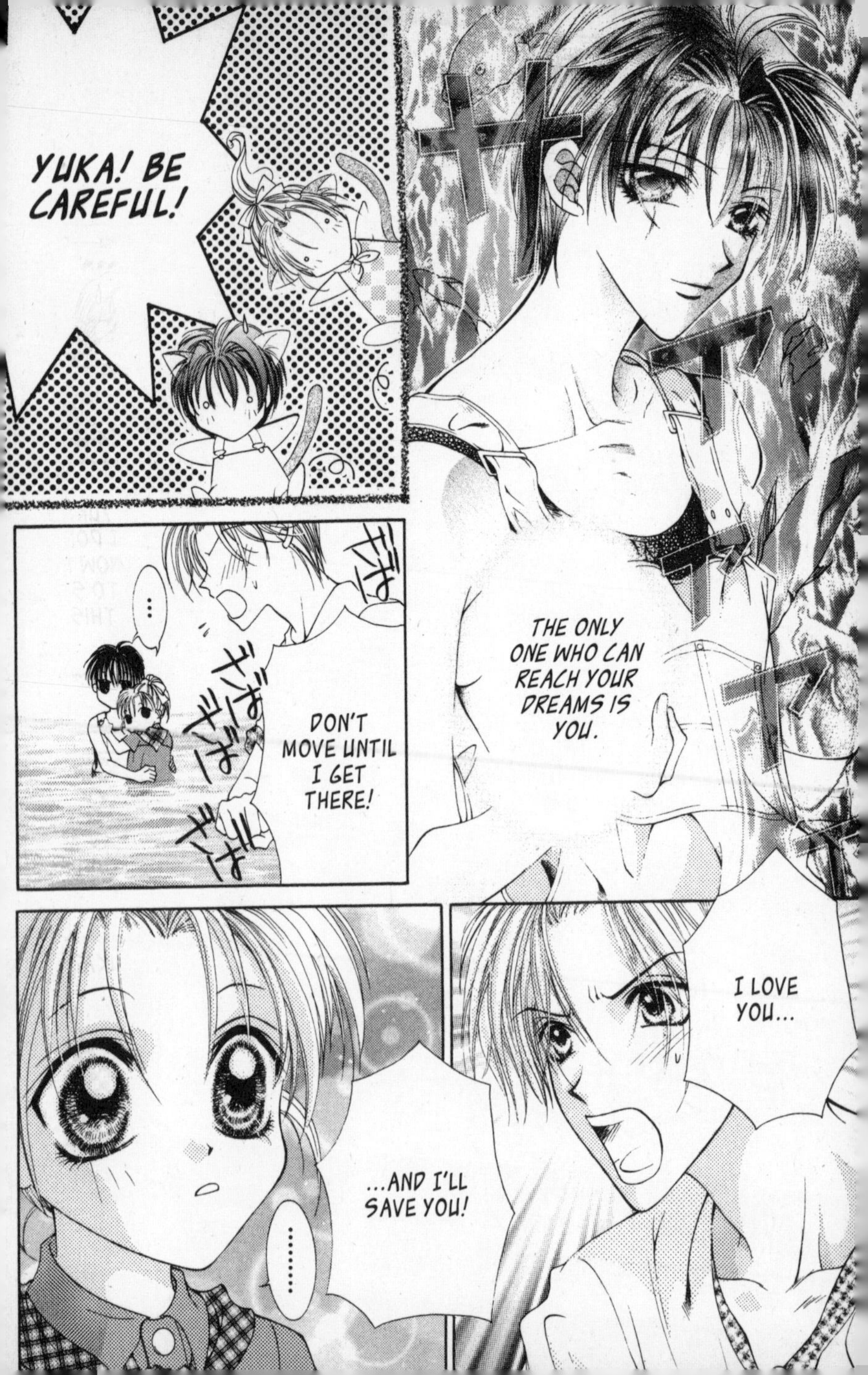
THE ONLY ONE WHO CAN REACH YOUR DREAMS IS YOU.
YUKA! BE CAREFUL!
DON'T MOVE UNTIL I GET THERE!
...
I LOVE YOU...
...AND I'LL SAVE YOU!
....

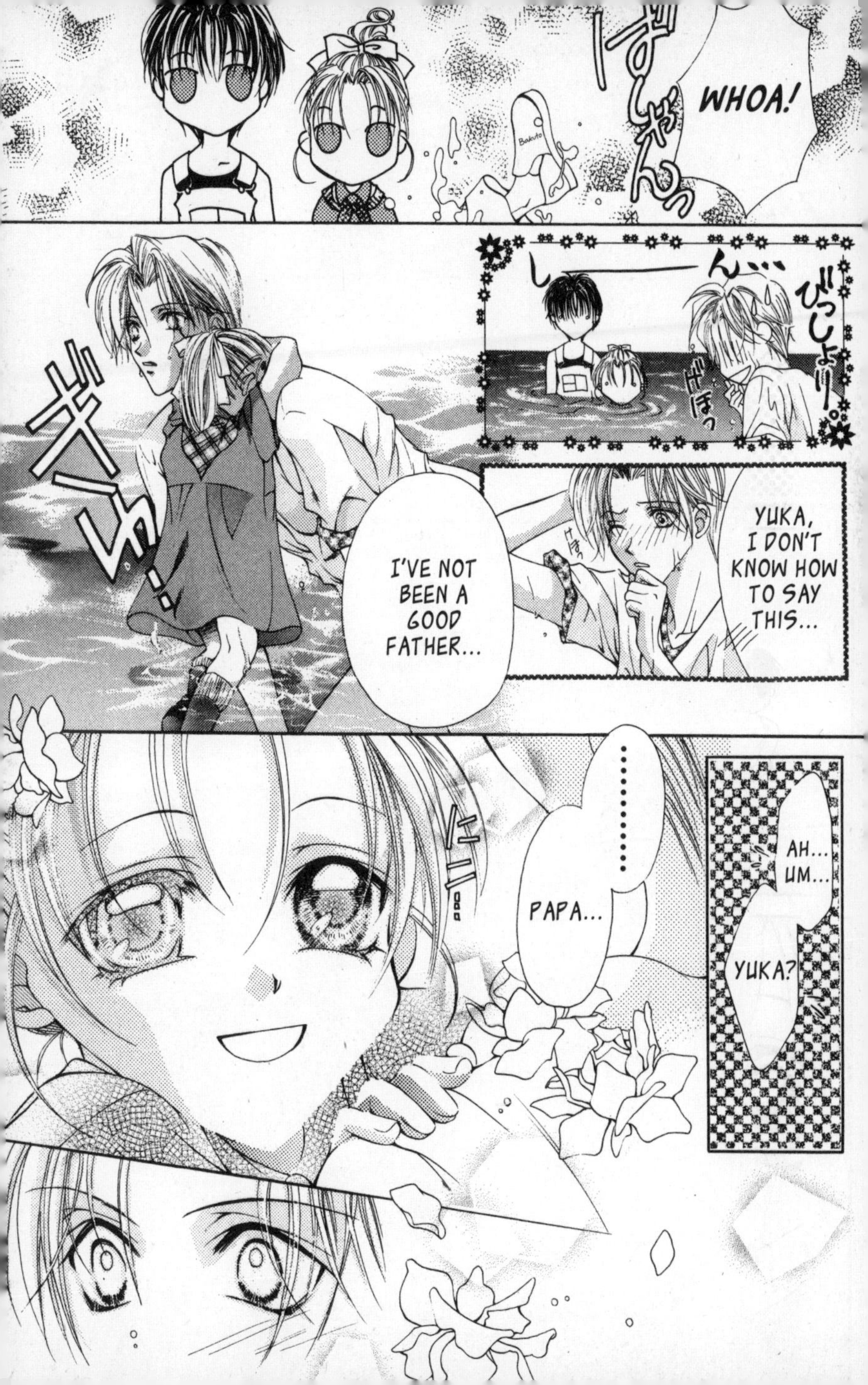
ずしゃんっ
WHOA!
しーーーーん…
びっしょり。
ごぼっ
YUKA, I DON'T KNOW HOW TO SAY THIS...
I'VE NOT BEEN A GOOD FATHER...
AH... UM...
YUKA?
......
PAPA...

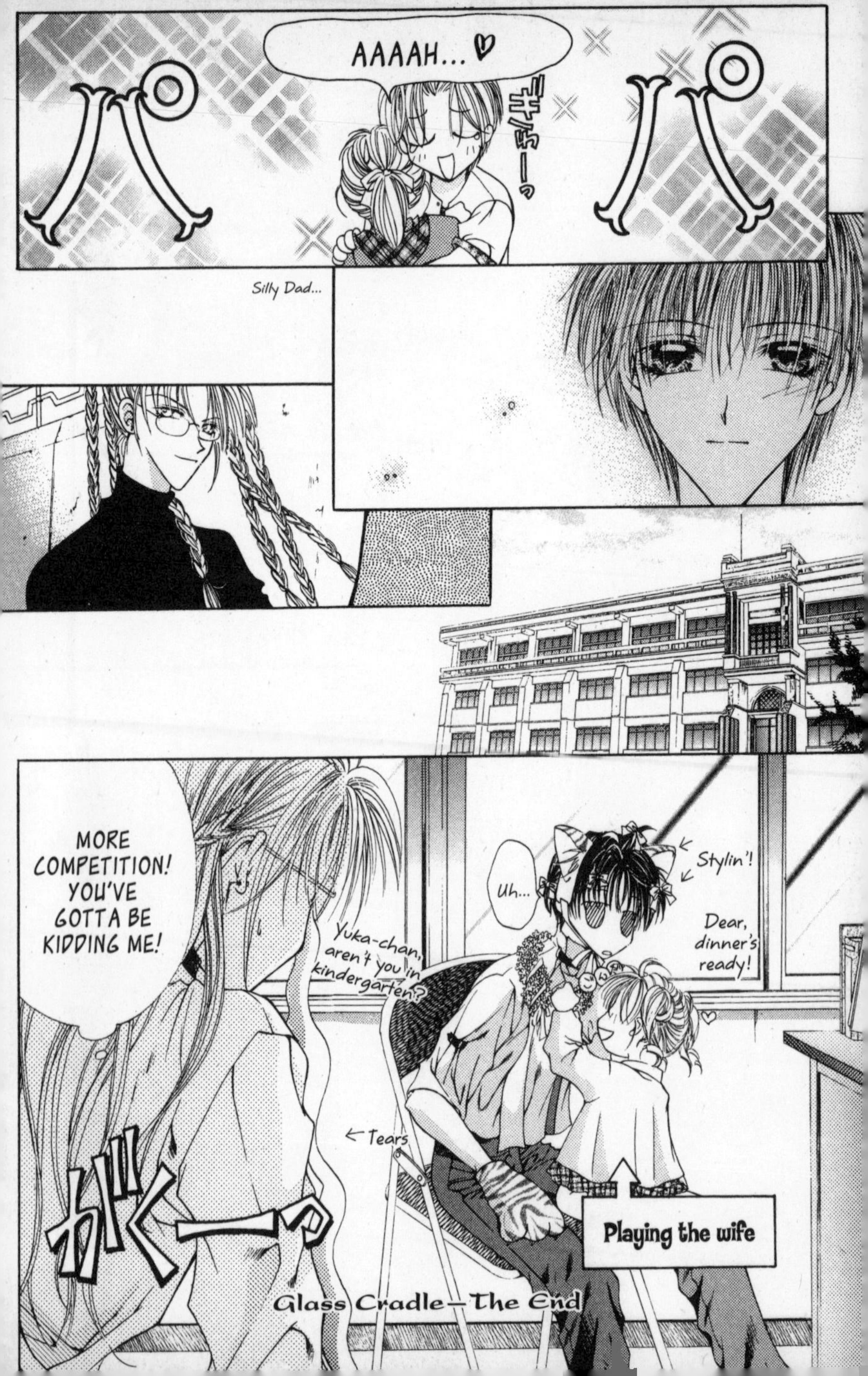
AAAAH...♥
パ
ギらーっ
パ
Silly Dad...
Stylin'!
Dear, dinner's ready!
Uh...
Playing the wife
Yuka-chan, aren't you in kindergarten?
← Tears
MORE COMPETITION! YOU'VE GOTTA BE KIDDING ME!
がくーっ
Glass Cradle—The End

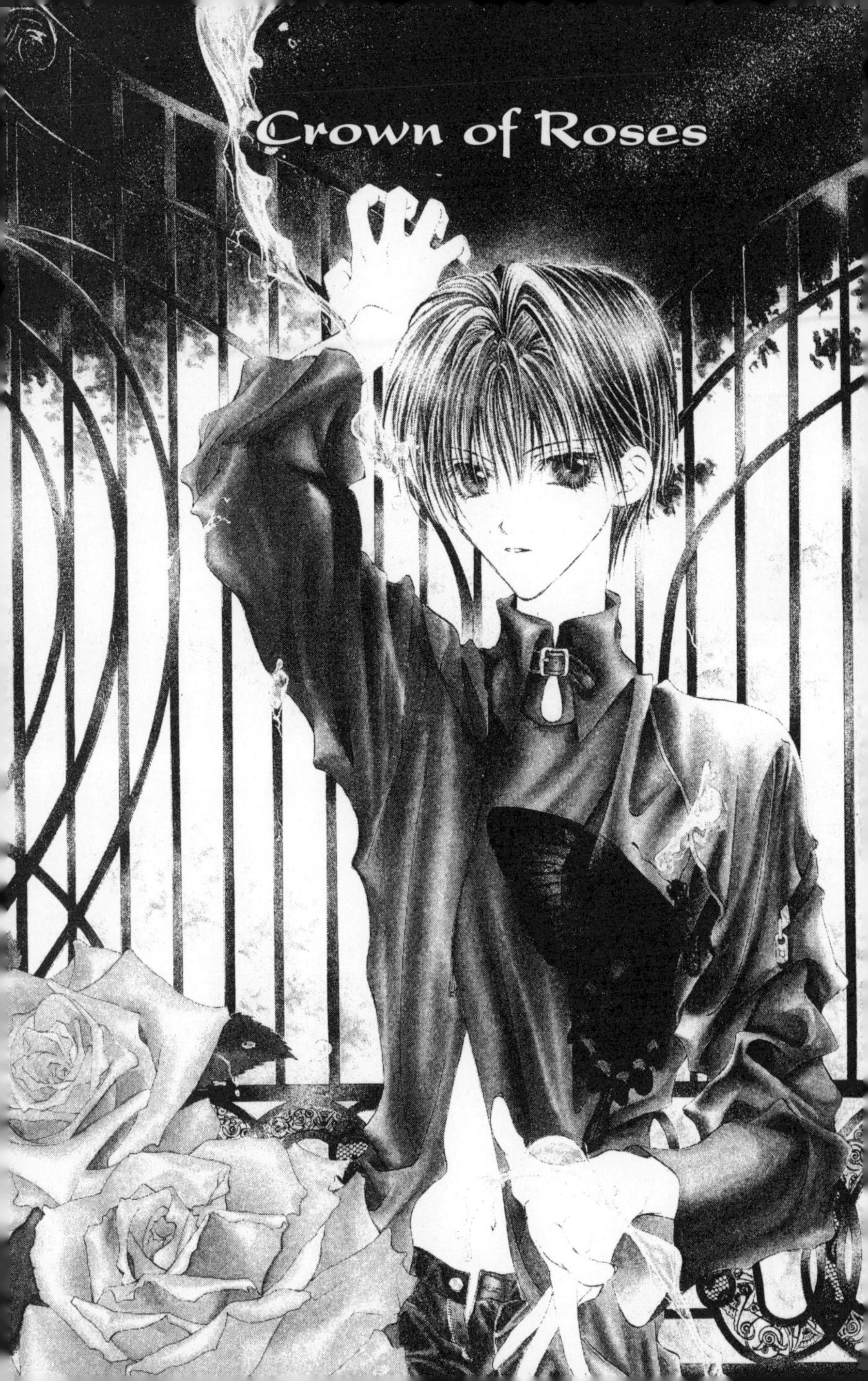
Crown of Roses

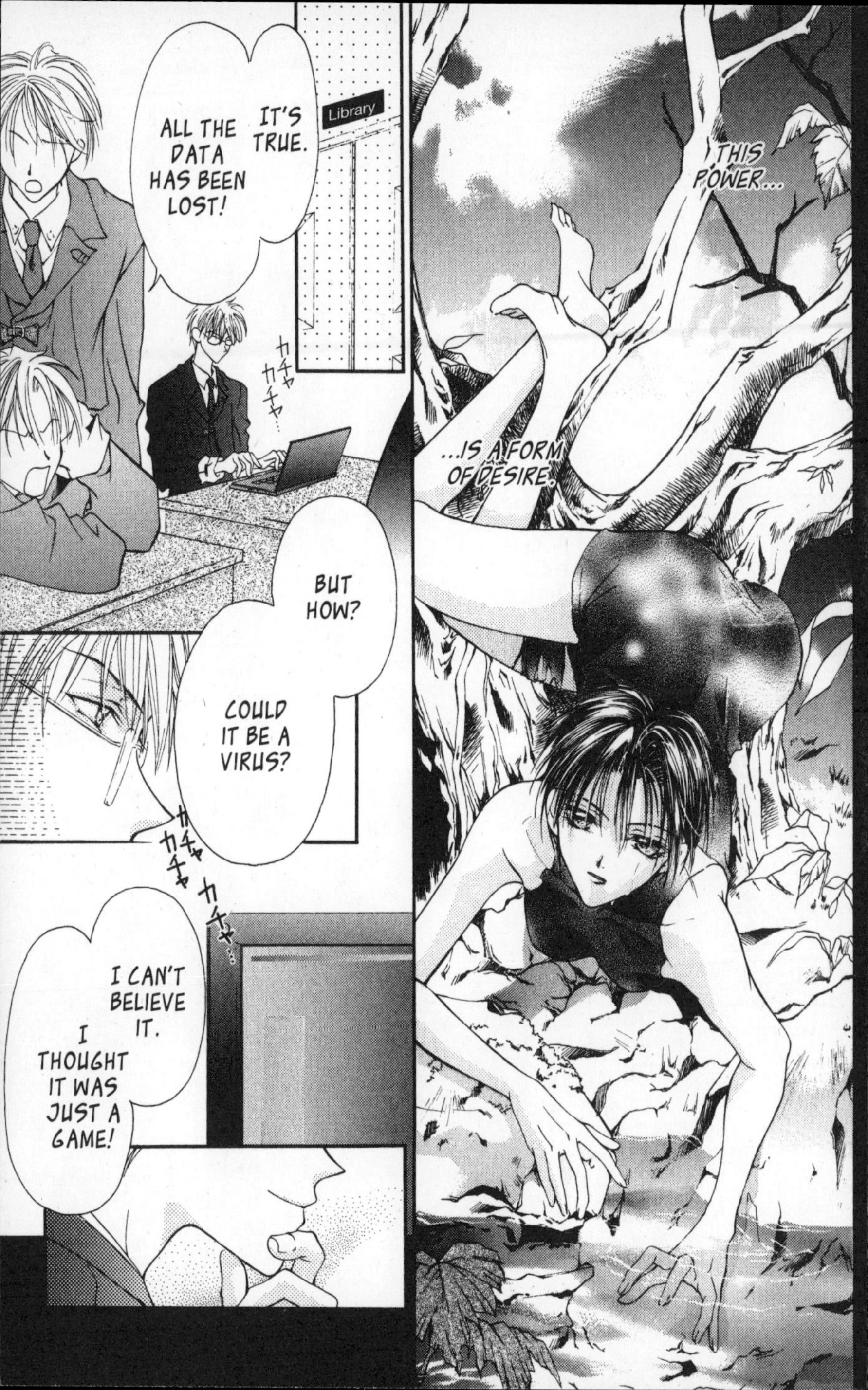
THIS POWER...
...IS A FORM OF DESIRE.
IT'S TRUE.
ALL THE DATA HAS BEEN LOST!
Library
カチャカチャ…
BUT HOW?
COULD IT BE A VIRUS?
カチャカチャ
カチャ…
I CAN'T BELIEVE IT.
I THOUGHT IT WAS JUST A GAME!

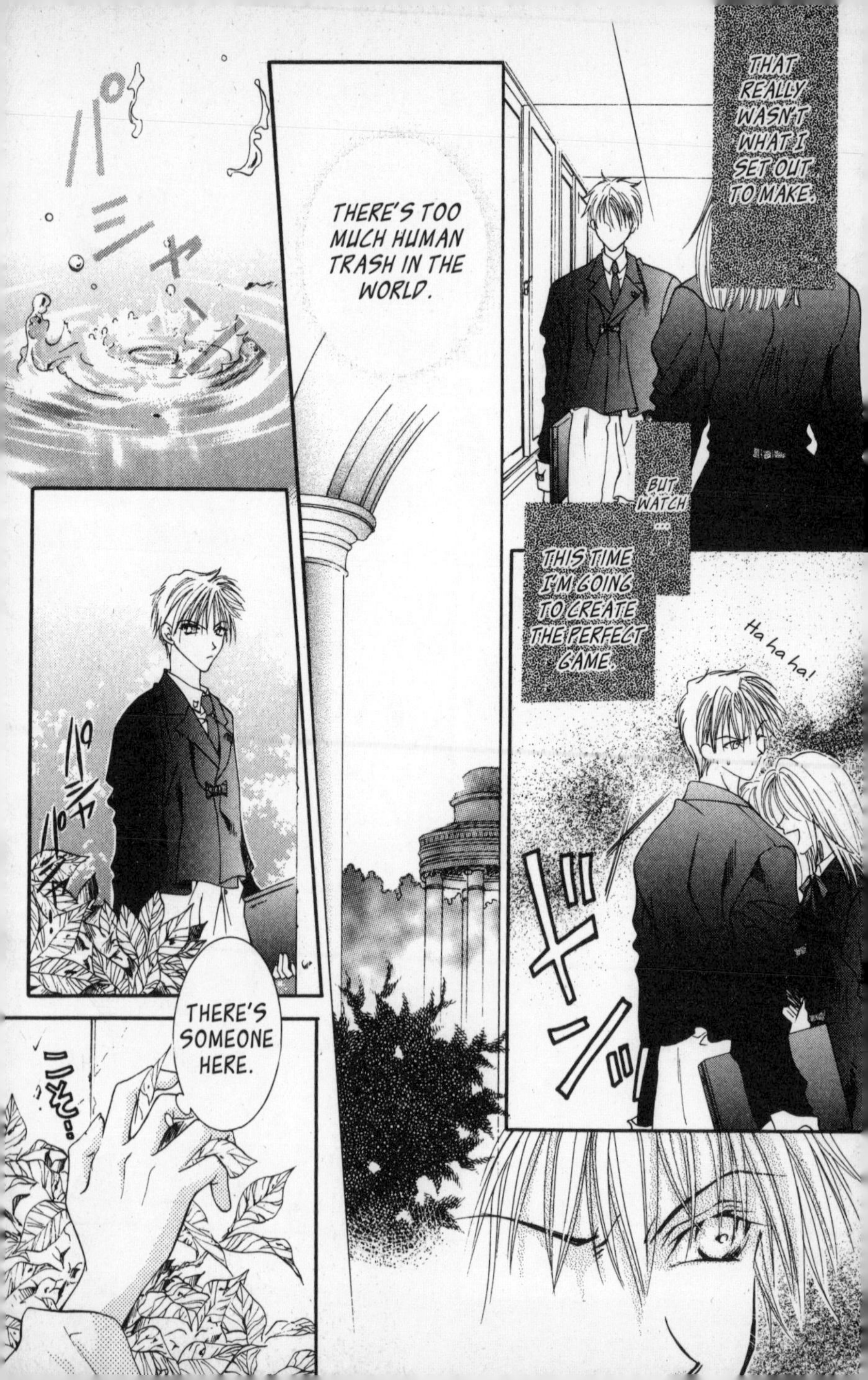
THAT REALLY WASN'T WHAT I SET OUT TO MAKE.
BUT WATCH...
THIS TIME I'M GOING TO CREATE THE PERFECT GAME.
Ha ha ha!
THERE'S TOO MUCH HUMAN TRASH IN THE WORLD.
パシャン
THERE'S SOMEONE HERE.

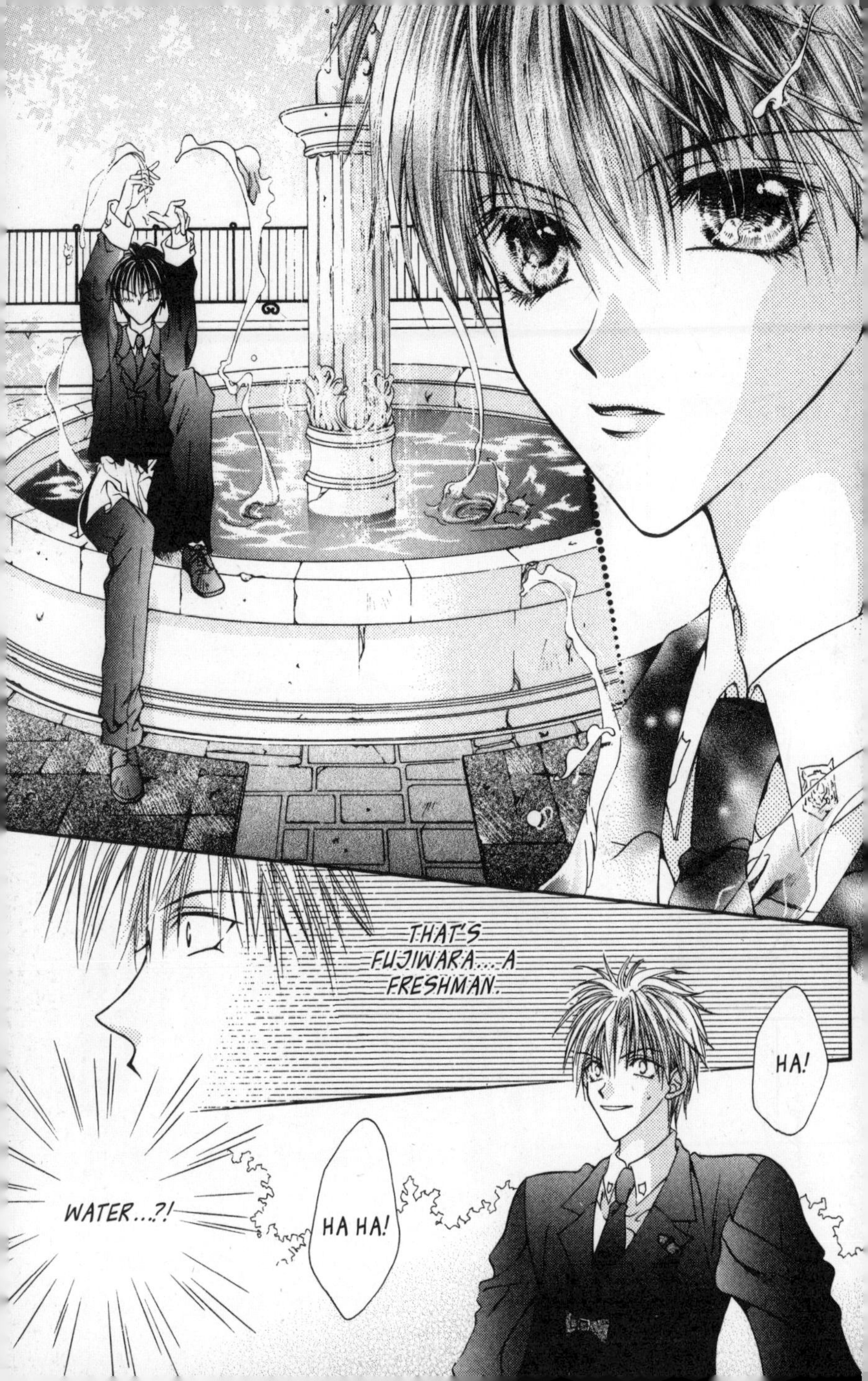
THAT'S FUJIWARA... A FRESHMAN.
HA!
HA HA!
WATER...?!

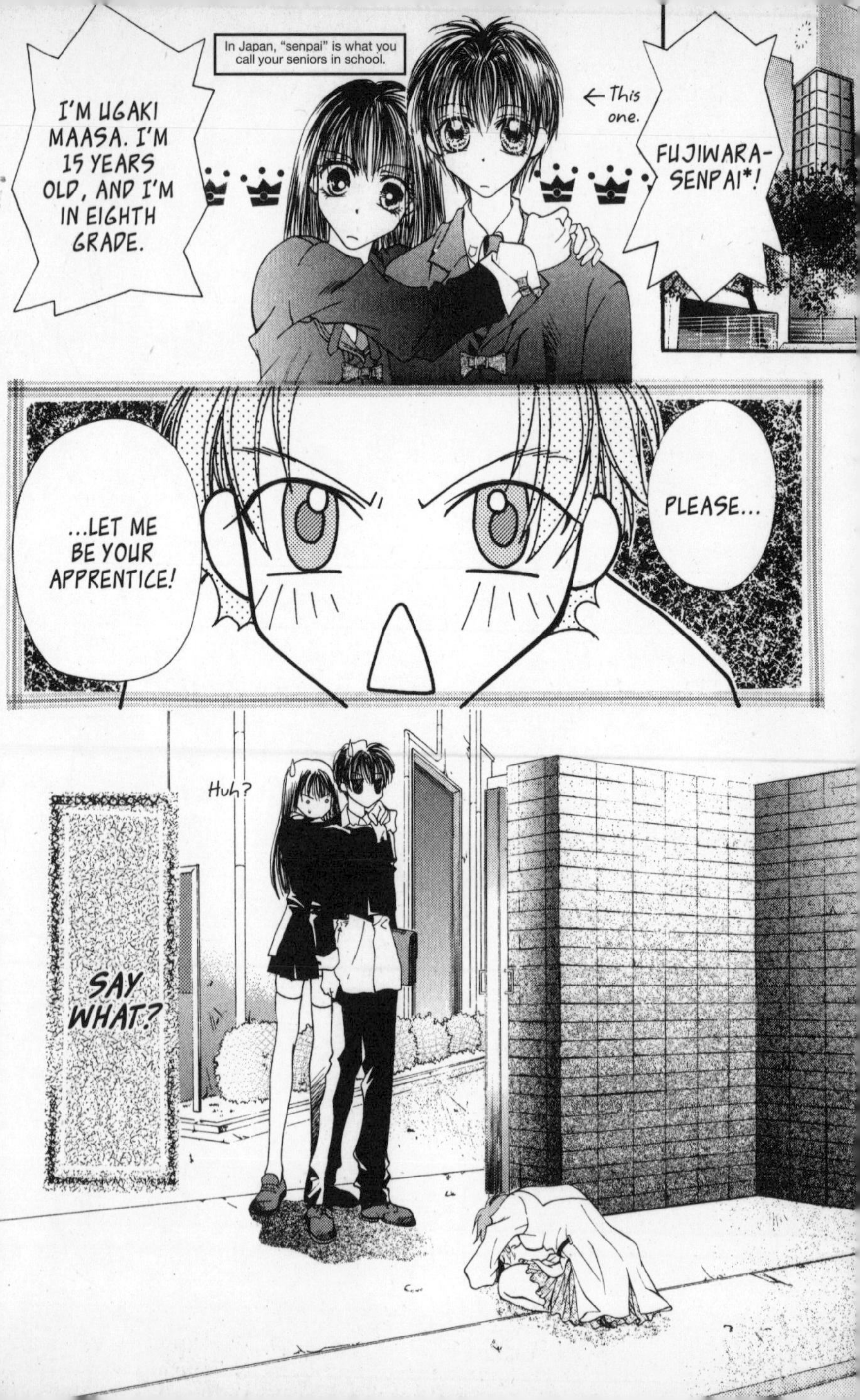
FUJIWARA-SENPAI*!
← This one.
I'M UGAKI MAASA. I'M 15 YEARS OLD, AND I'M IN EIGHTH GRADE.
PLEASE...
...LET ME BE YOUR APPRENTICE!
Huh?
SAY WHAT?
In Japan, "senpai" is what you call your seniors in school.

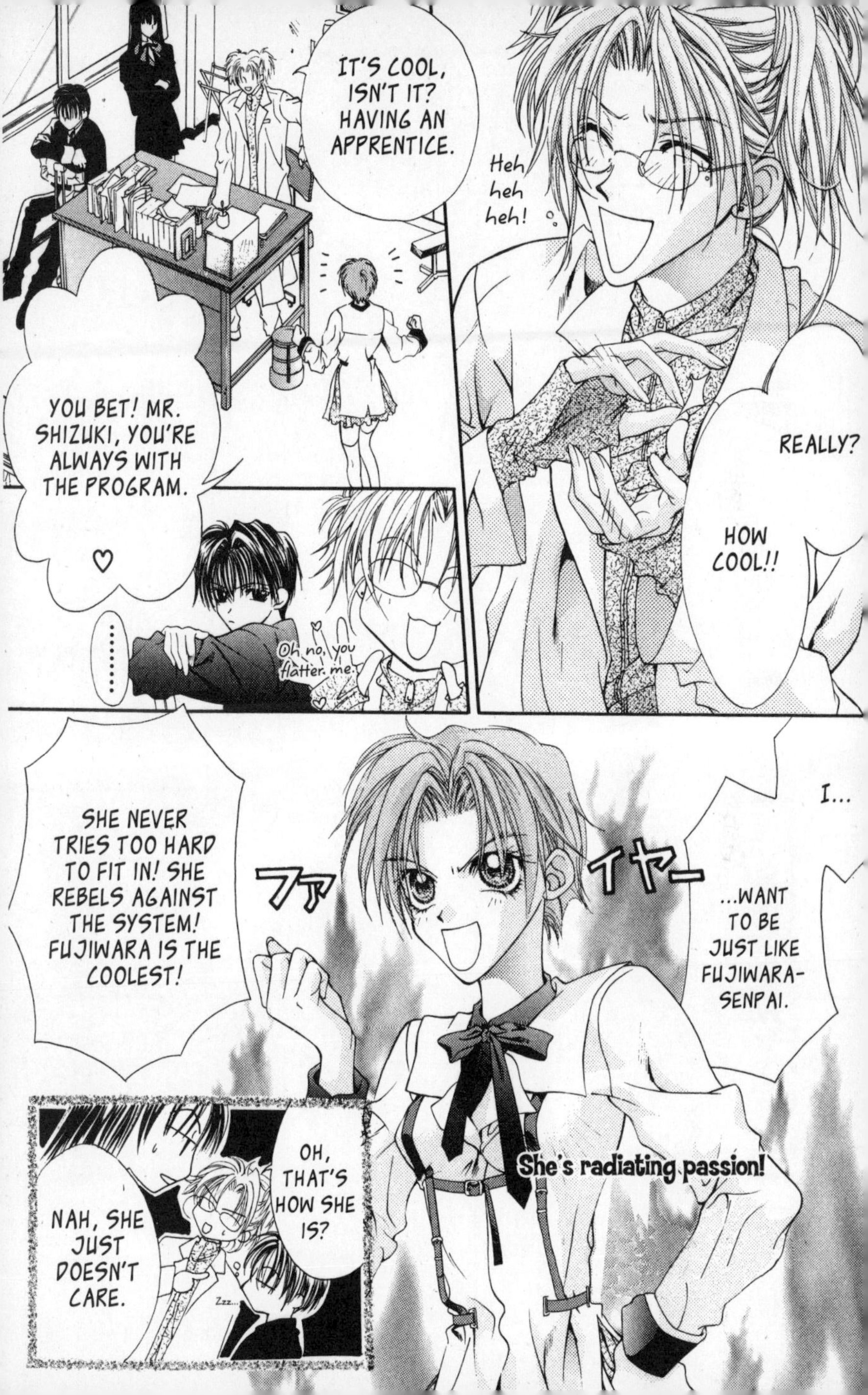

Heh heh heh!
REALLY?
HOW COOL!!
IT'S COOL, ISN'T IT? HAVING AN APPRENTICE.
YOU BET! MR. SHIZUKI, YOU'RE ALWAYS WITH THE PROGRAM.
♡
Oh no, you flatter me.
......
I...
...WANT TO BE JUST LIKE FUJIWARA-SENPAI.
ファイヤー
She's radiating passion!
SHE NEVER TRIES TOO HARD TO FIT IN! SHE REBELS AGAINST THE SYSTEM! FUJIWARA IS THE COOLEST!
OH, THAT'S HOW SHE IS?
NAH, SHE JUST DOESN'T CARE.
Zzz...

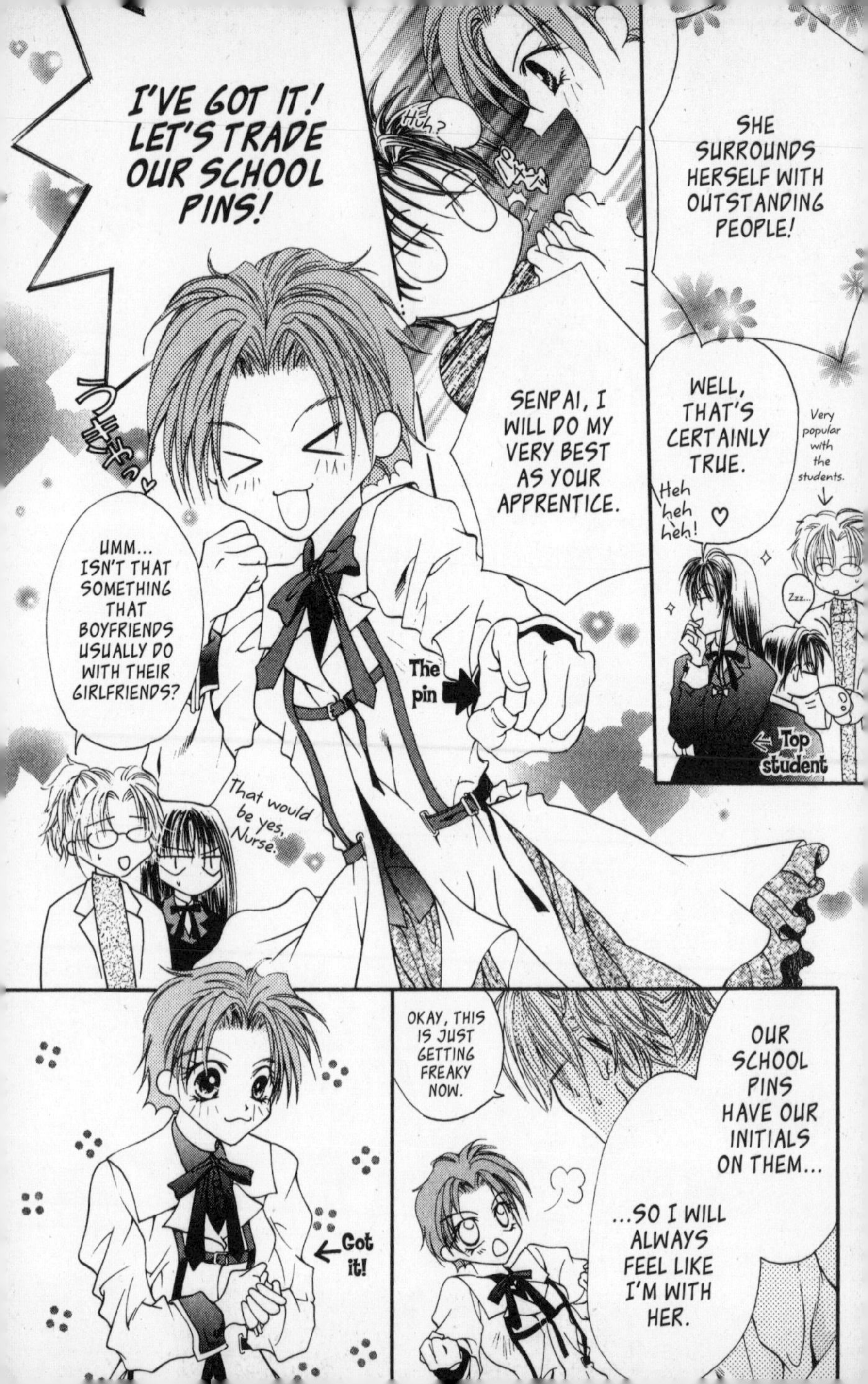
SHE SURROUNDS HERSELF WITH OUTSTANDING PEOPLE!
WELL, THAT'S CERTAINLY TRUE.
Heh heh heh! ♡
Very popular with the students.
Zzz...
Top student
Huh?
SENPAI, I WILL DO MY VERY BEST AS YOUR APPRENTICE.
I'VE GOT IT! LET'S TRADE OUR SCHOOL PINS!
The pin
UMM... ISN'T THAT SOMETHING THAT BOYFRIENDS USUALLY DO WITH THEIR GIRLFRIENDS?
That would be yes, Nurse.
OUR SCHOOL PINS HAVE OUR INITIALS ON THEM...
...SO I WILL ALWAYS FEEL LIKE I'M WITH HER.
OKAY, THIS IS JUST GETTING FREAKY NOW.
Got it!

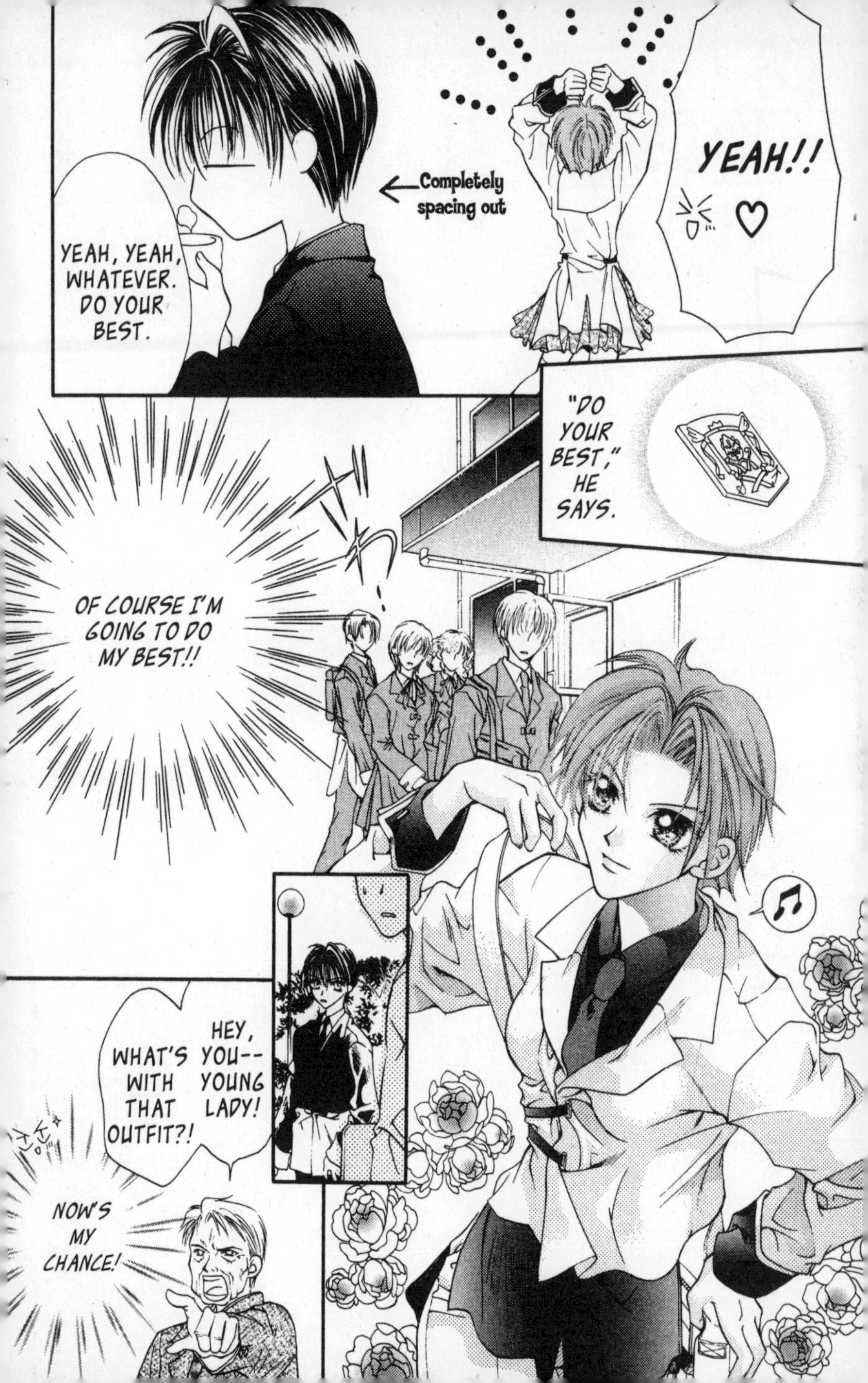
YEAH!! ♥
Completely spacing out
YEAH, YEAH, WHATEVER. DO YOUR BEST.
"DO YOUR BEST," HE SAYS.
OF COURSE I'M GOING TO DO MY BEST!!
HEY, YOU-- YOUNG LADY!
WHAT'S WITH THAT OUTFIT?!
NOW'S MY CHANCE!

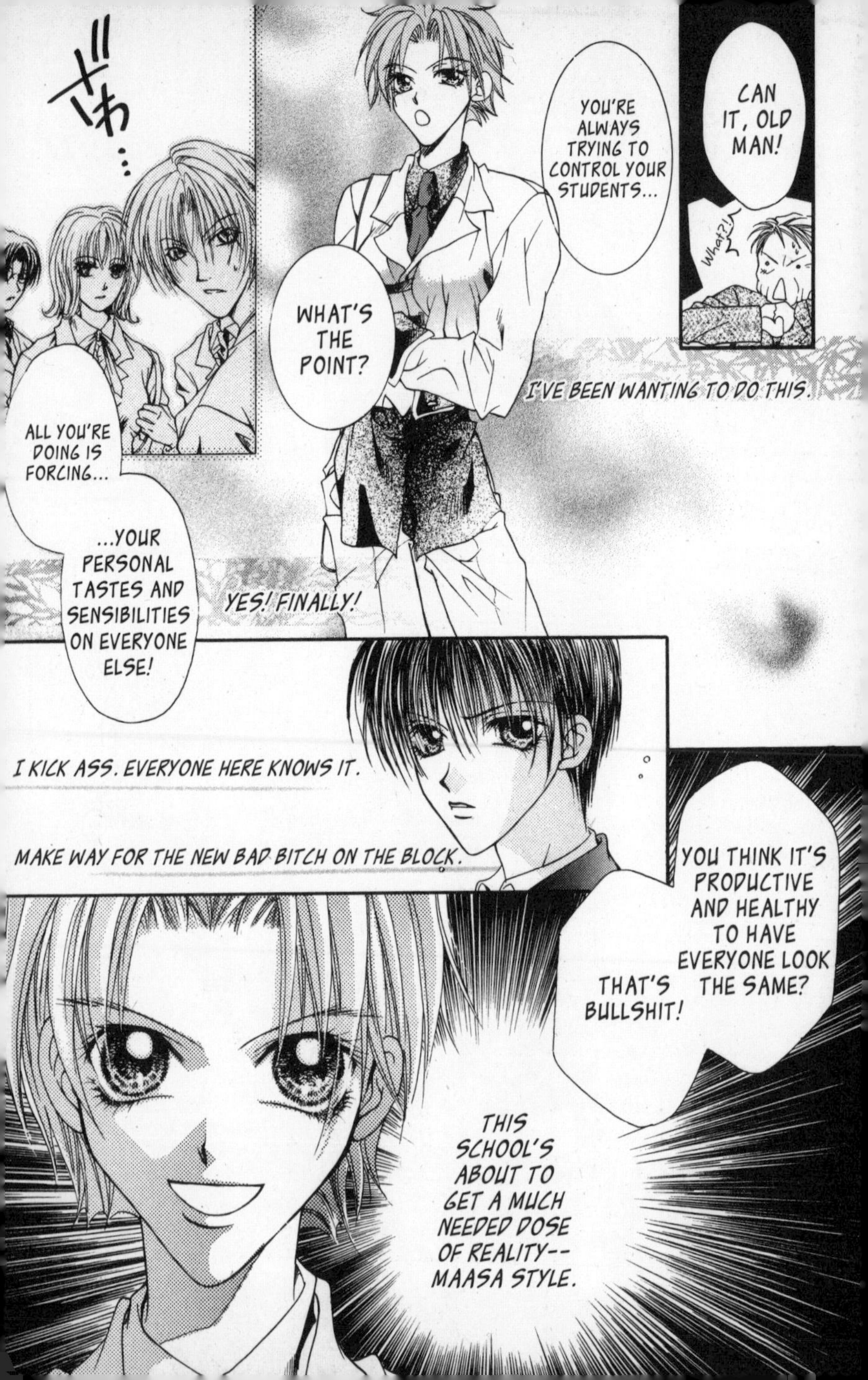
CAN IT, OLD MAN!
What?!
YOU'RE ALWAYS TRYING TO CONTROL YOUR STUDENTS...
WHAT'S THE POINT?
I'VE BEEN WANTING TO DO THIS.
ざわ…
ALL YOU'RE DOING IS FORCING...
...YOUR PERSONAL TASTES AND SENSIBILITIES ON EVERYONE ELSE!
YES! FINALLY!
I KICK ASS. EVERYONE HERE KNOWS IT.
MAKE WAY FOR THE NEW BAD BITCH ON THE BLOCK.
YOU THINK IT'S PRODUCTIVE AND HEALTHY TO HAVE EVERYONE LOOK THE SAME?
THAT'S BULLSHIT!
THIS SCHOOL'S ABOUT TO GET A MUCH NEEDED DOSE OF REALITY-- MAASA STYLE.

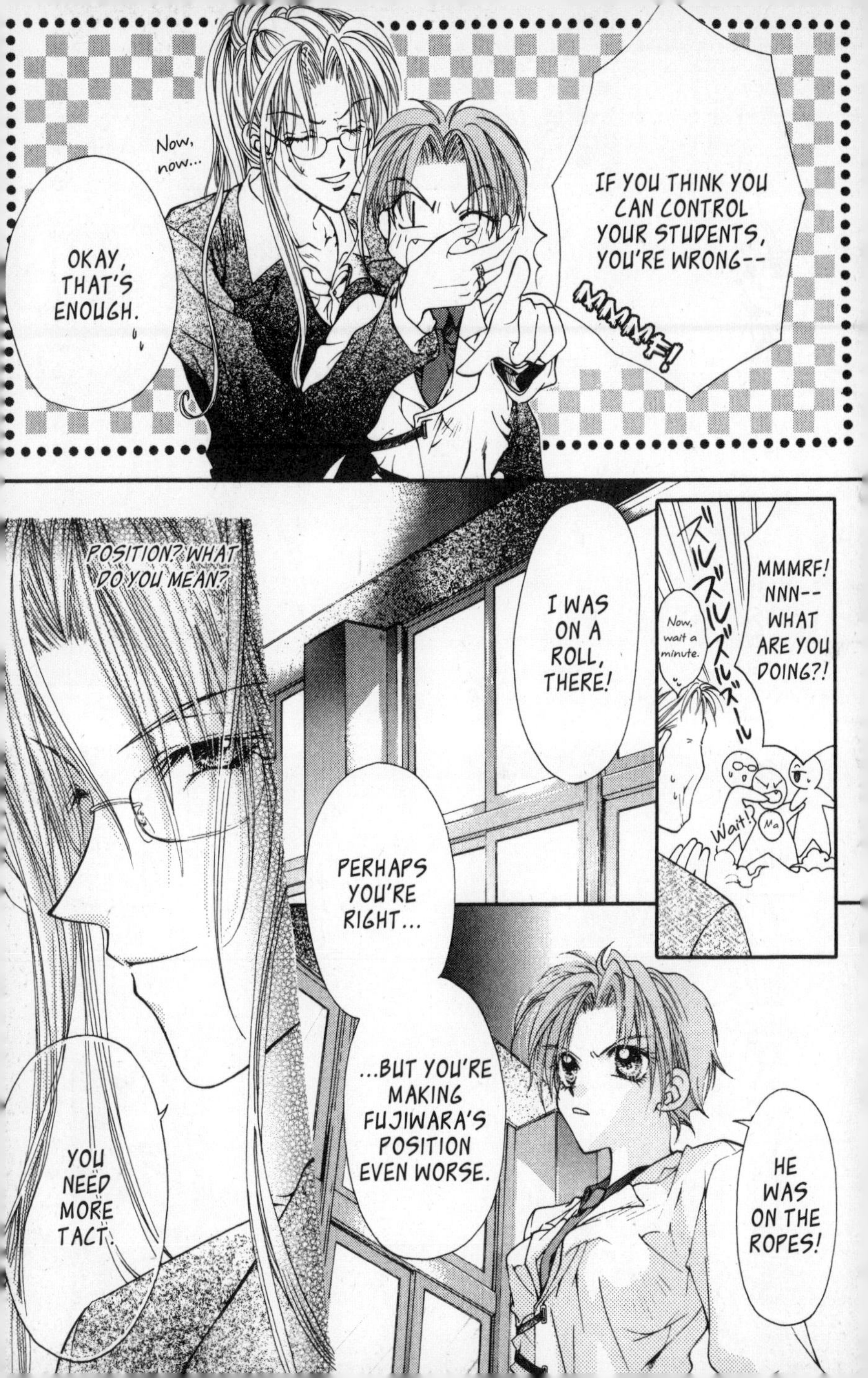
IF YOU THINK YOU CAN CONTROL YOUR STUDENTS, YOU'RE WRONG--
MMMF!
Now, now...
OKAY, THAT'S ENOUGH.
MMMRF! NNN--WHAT ARE YOU DOING?!
ズルズルズルズルズール
Now, wait a minute.
Wait!
Ma
I WAS ON A ROLL, THERE!
HE WAS ON THE ROPES!
PERHAPS YOU'RE RIGHT...
...BUT YOU'RE MAKING FUJIWARA'S POSITION EVEN WORSE.
POSITION? WHAT DO YOU MEAN?
YOU NEED MORE TACT.

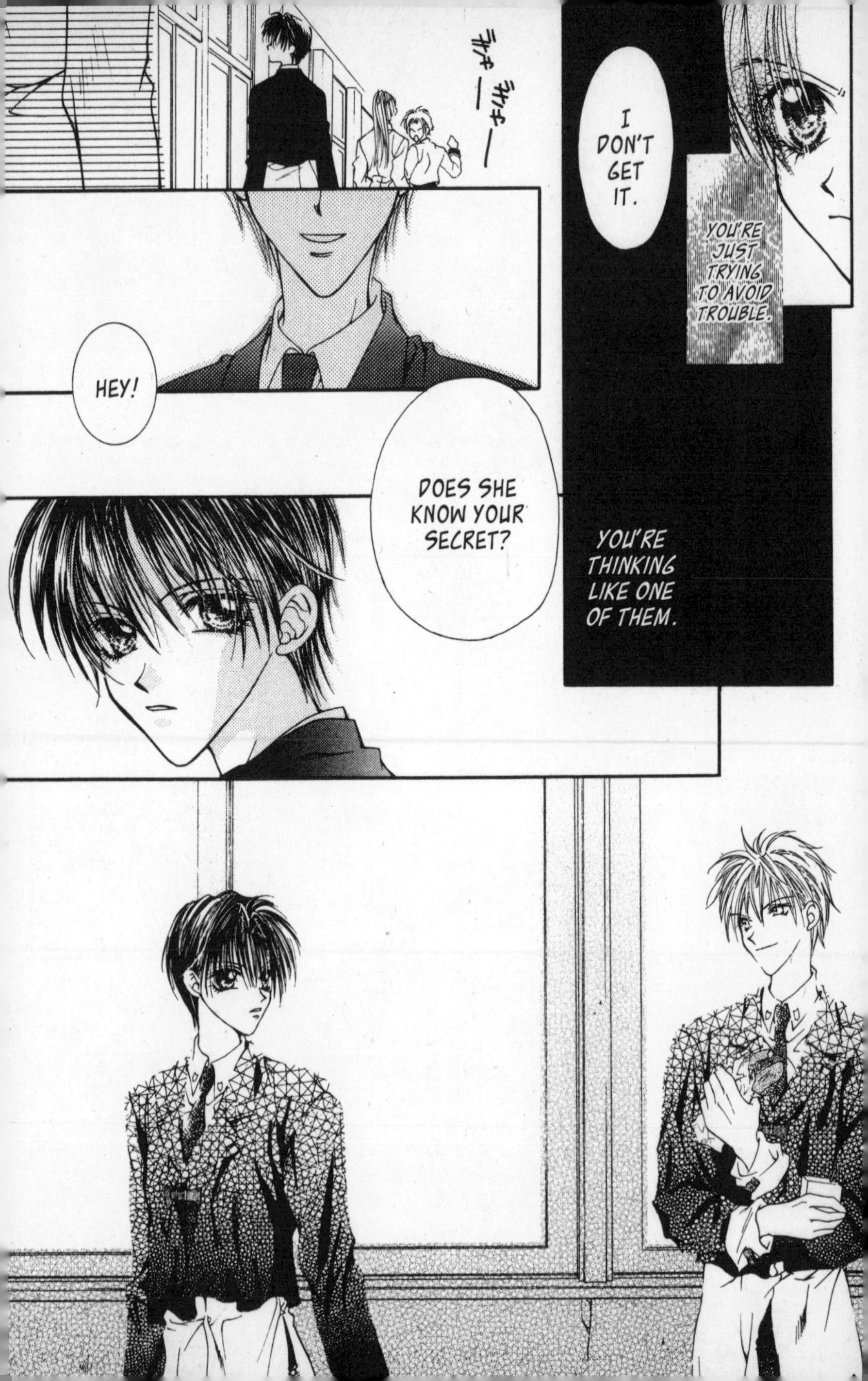
I DON'T GET IT.
YOU'RE JUST TRYING TO AVOID TROUBLE.
YOU'RE THINKING LIKE ONE OF THEM.
ギャー ギャー
HEY!
DOES SHE KNOW YOUR SECRET?

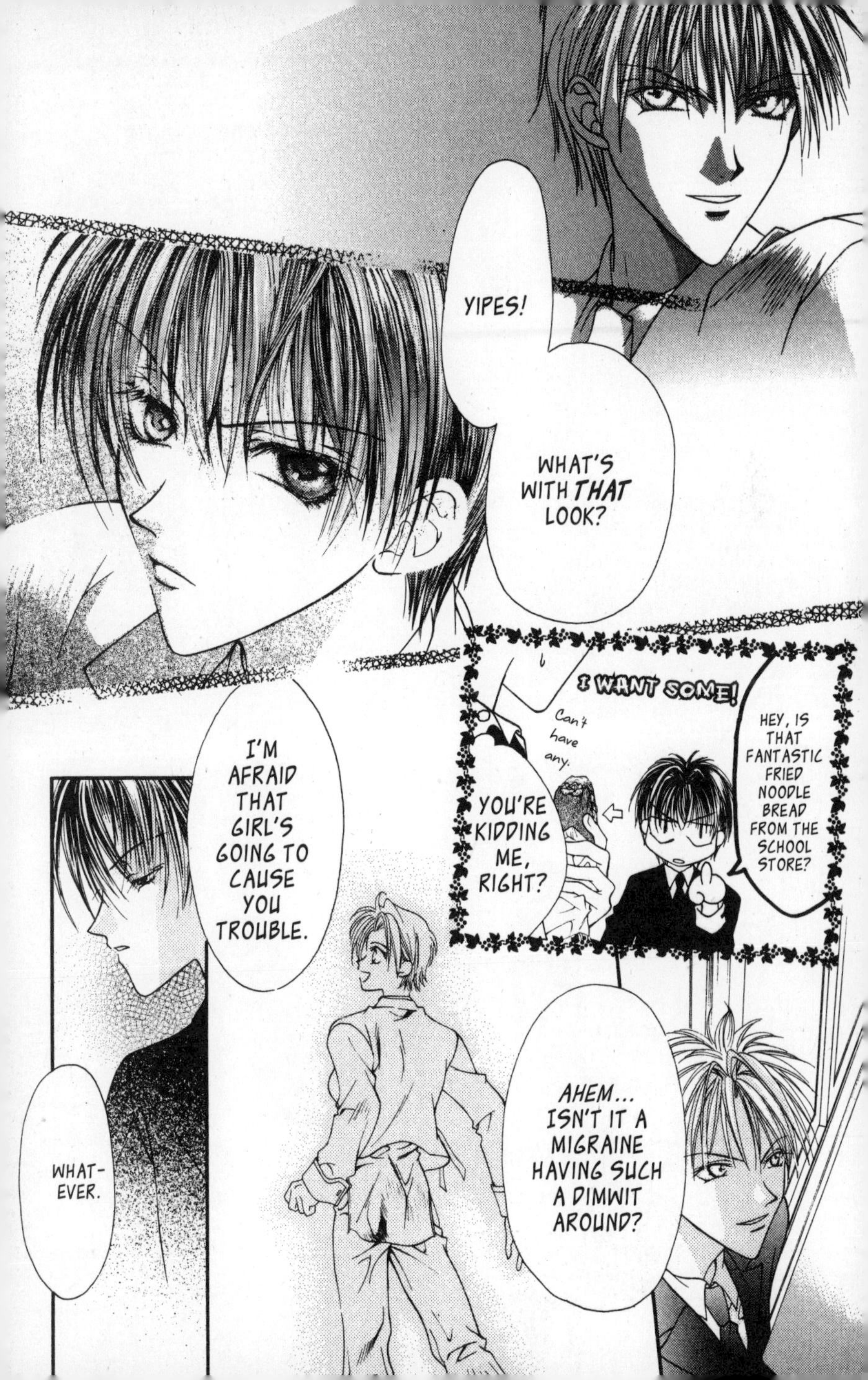
YIPES!
WHAT'S WITH *THAT* LOOK?
I WANT SOME!
HEY, IS THAT FANTASTIC FRIED NOODLE BREAD FROM THE SCHOOL STORE?
Can't have any.
YOU'RE KIDDING ME, RIGHT?
AHEM... ISN'T IT A MIGRAINE HAVING SUCH A DIMWIT AROUND?
I'M AFRAID THAT GIRL'S GOING TO CAUSE YOU TROUBLE.
WHAT-EVER.

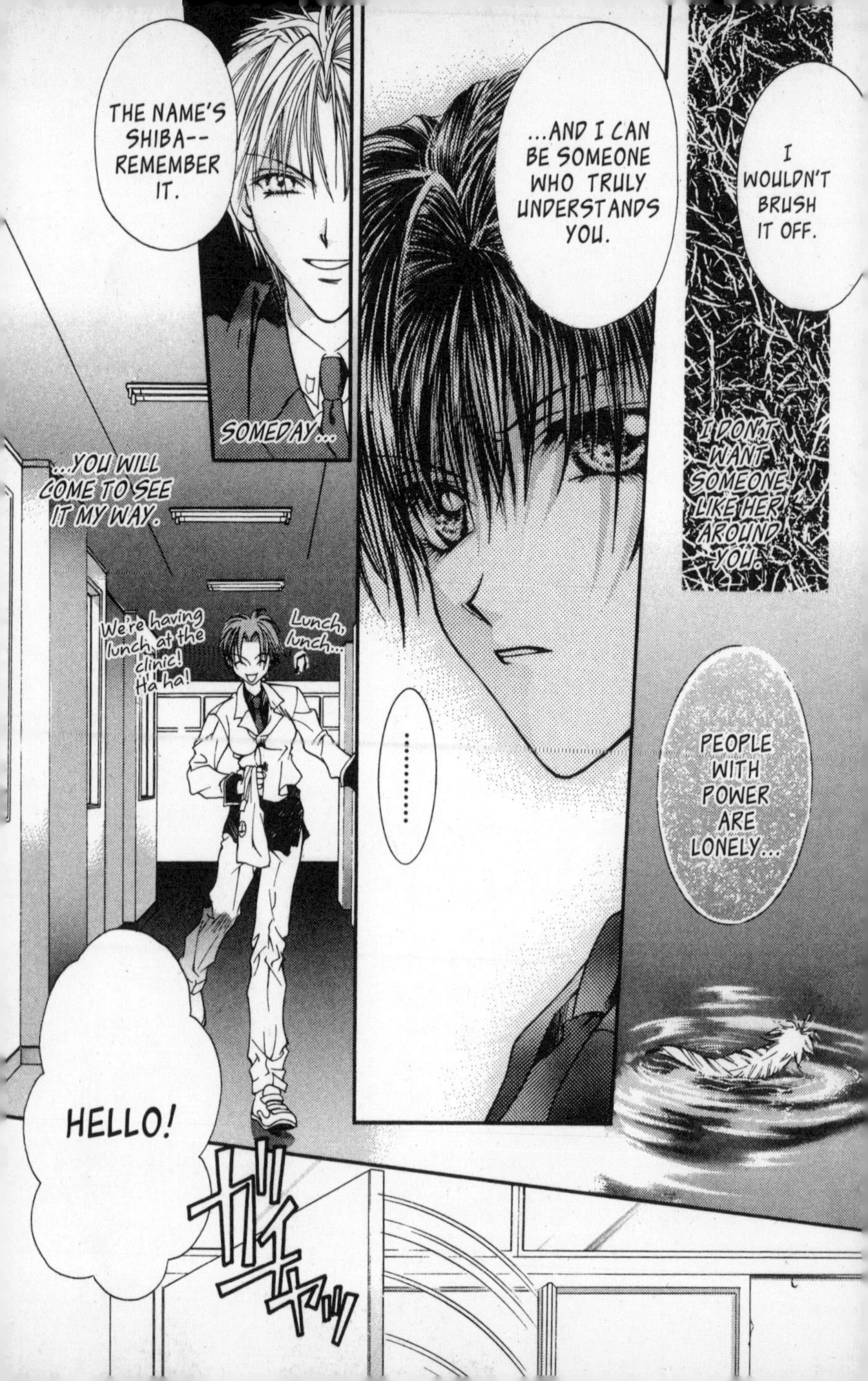
I WOULDN'T BRUSH IT OFF.
I DON'T WANT SOMEONE LIKE HER AROUND YOU.
...AND I CAN BE SOMEONE WHO TRULY UNDERSTANDS YOU.
PEOPLE WITH POWER ARE LONELY...
......
THE NAME'S SHIBA--REMEMBER IT.
SOMEDAY...
...YOU WILL COME TO SEE IT MY WAY.
Lunch, lunch...
We're having lunch at the clinic! Ha ha!
HELLO!
ガチャッ

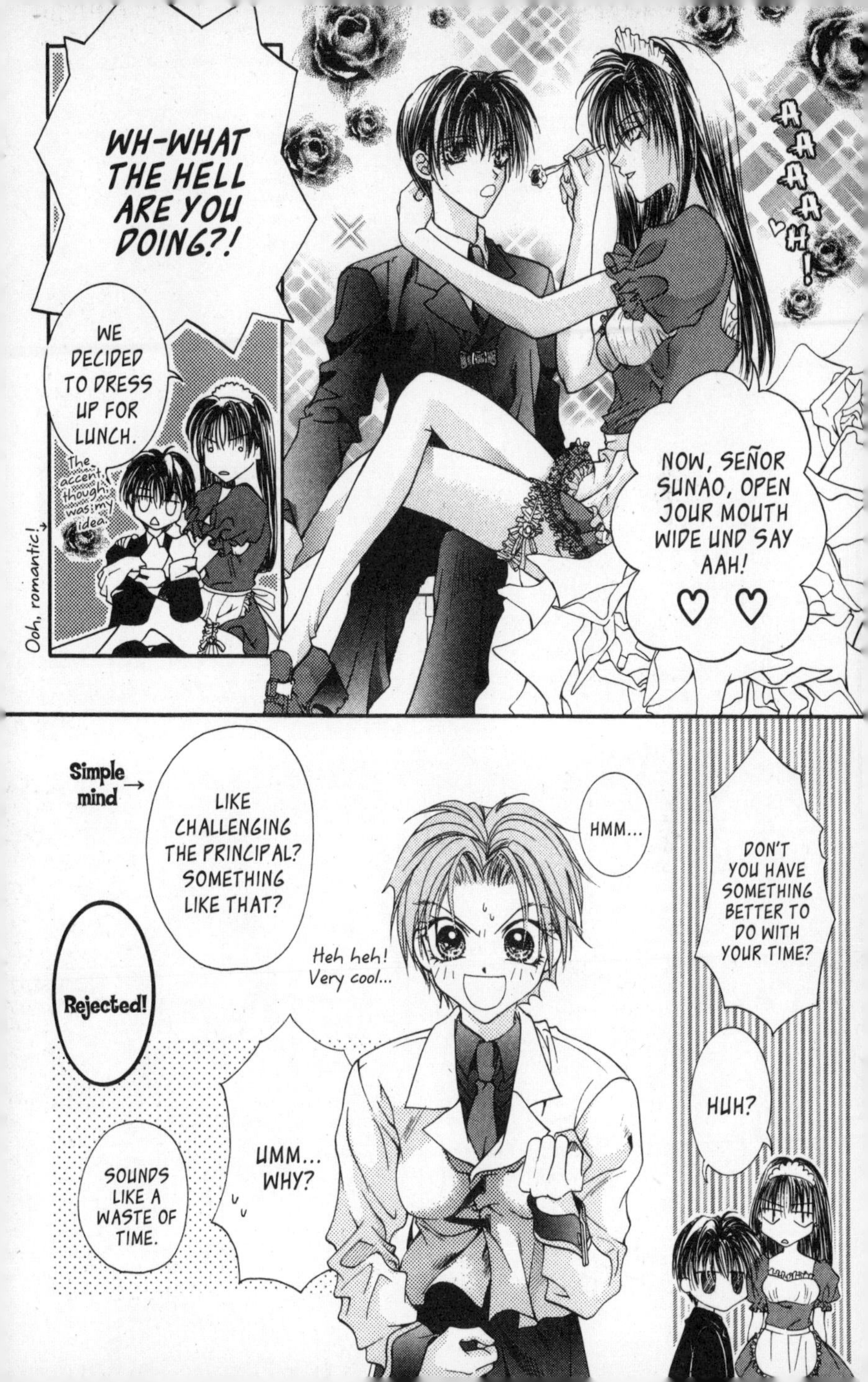
AAAAAH♥!
WH-WHAT THE HELL ARE YOU DOING?!
NOW, SEÑOR SUNAO, OPEN JOUR MOUTH WIDE UND SAY AAH! ♡ ♡
WE DECIDED TO DRESS UP FOR LUNCH.
The accent, though, was my idea.
Ooh, romantic!
DON'T YOU HAVE SOMETHING BETTER TO DO WITH YOUR TIME?
HUH?
HMM...
LIKE CHALLENGING THE PRINCIPAL? SOMETHING LIKE THAT?
Heh heh! Very cool...
UMM... WHY?
SOUNDS LIKE A WASTE OF TIME.
Simple mind
Rejected!

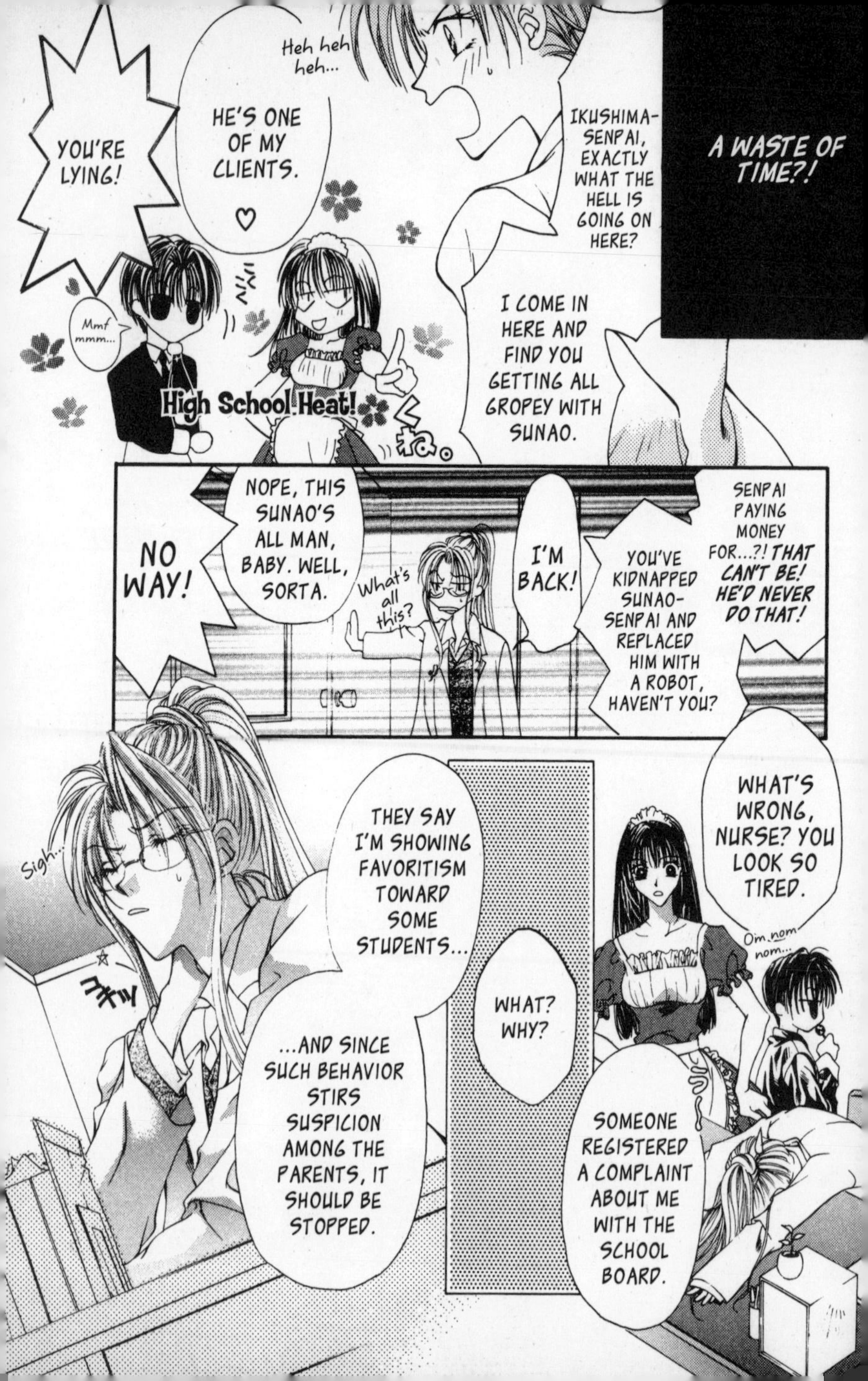
A WASTE OF TIME?!
IKUSHIMA-SENPAI, EXACTLY WHAT THE HELL IS GOING ON HERE?
I COME IN HERE AND FIND YOU GETTING ALL GROPEY WITH SUNAO.
Heh heh heh...
HE'S ONE OF MY CLIENTS. ♡
YOU'RE LYING!
Mmf mmm...
High School Heat!
SENPAI PAYING MONEY FOR...?! THAT CAN'T BE! HE'D NEVER DO THAT!
YOU'VE KIDNAPPED SUNAO-SENPAI AND REPLACED HIM WITH A ROBOT, HAVEN'T YOU?
I'M BACK!
What's all this?
NOPE, THIS SUNAO'S ALL MAN, BABY. WELL, SORTA.
NO WAY!
WHAT'S WRONG, NURSE? YOU LOOK SO TIRED.
Om nom nom...
SOMEONE REGISTERED A COMPLAINT ABOUT ME WITH THE SCHOOL BOARD.
WHAT? WHY?
THEY SAY I'M SHOWING FAVORITISM TOWARD SOME STUDENTS...
...AND SINCE SUCH BEHAVIOR STIRS SUSPICION AMONG THE PARENTS, IT SHOULD BE STOPPED.
Sigh...

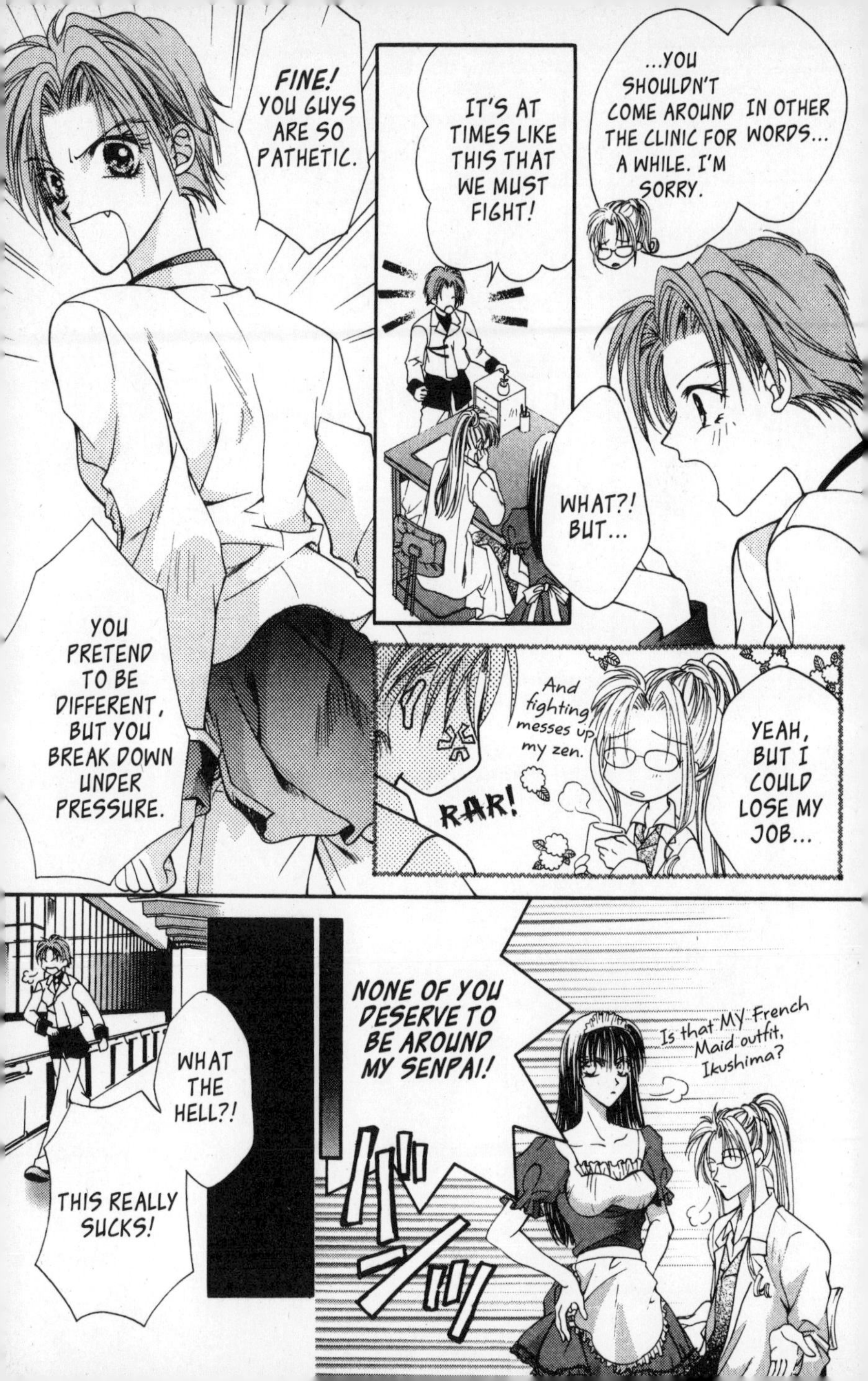
IN OTHER WORDS...
...YOU SHOULDN'T COME AROUND THE CLINIC FOR A WHILE. I'M SORRY.
WHAT?! BUT...
IT'S AT TIMES LIKE THIS THAT WE MUST FIGHT!
YEAH, BUT I COULD LOSE MY JOB...
And fighting messes up my zen.
RAR!
FINE! YOU GUYS ARE SO PATHETIC.
YOU PRETEND TO BE DIFFERENT, BUT YOU BREAK DOWN UNDER PRESSURE.
NONE OF YOU DESERVE TO BE AROUND MY SENPAI!
Is that My French Maid outfit, Ikushima?
WHAT THE HELL?!
THIS REALLY SUCKS!

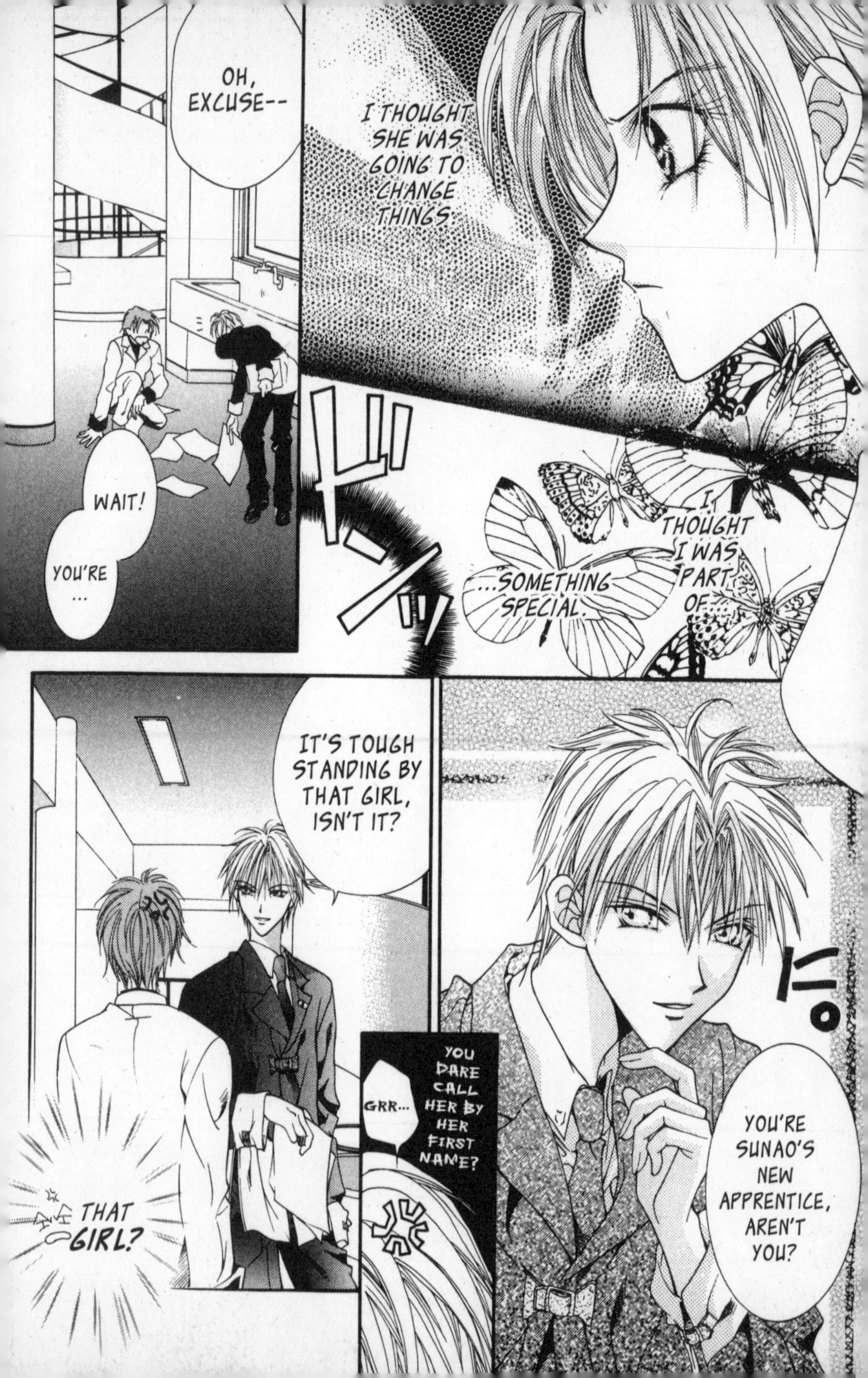
I THOUGHT SHE WAS GOING TO CHANGE THINGS.
I THOUGHT I WAS PART OF
...SOMETHING SPECIAL.
OH, EXCUSE--
WAIT!
YOU'RE ...
YOU'RE SUNAO'S NEW APPRENTICE, AREN'T YOU?
YOU DARE CALL HER BY HER FIRST NAME?
GRR...
IT'S TOUGH STANDING BY THAT GIRL, ISN'T IT?
THAT GIRL?

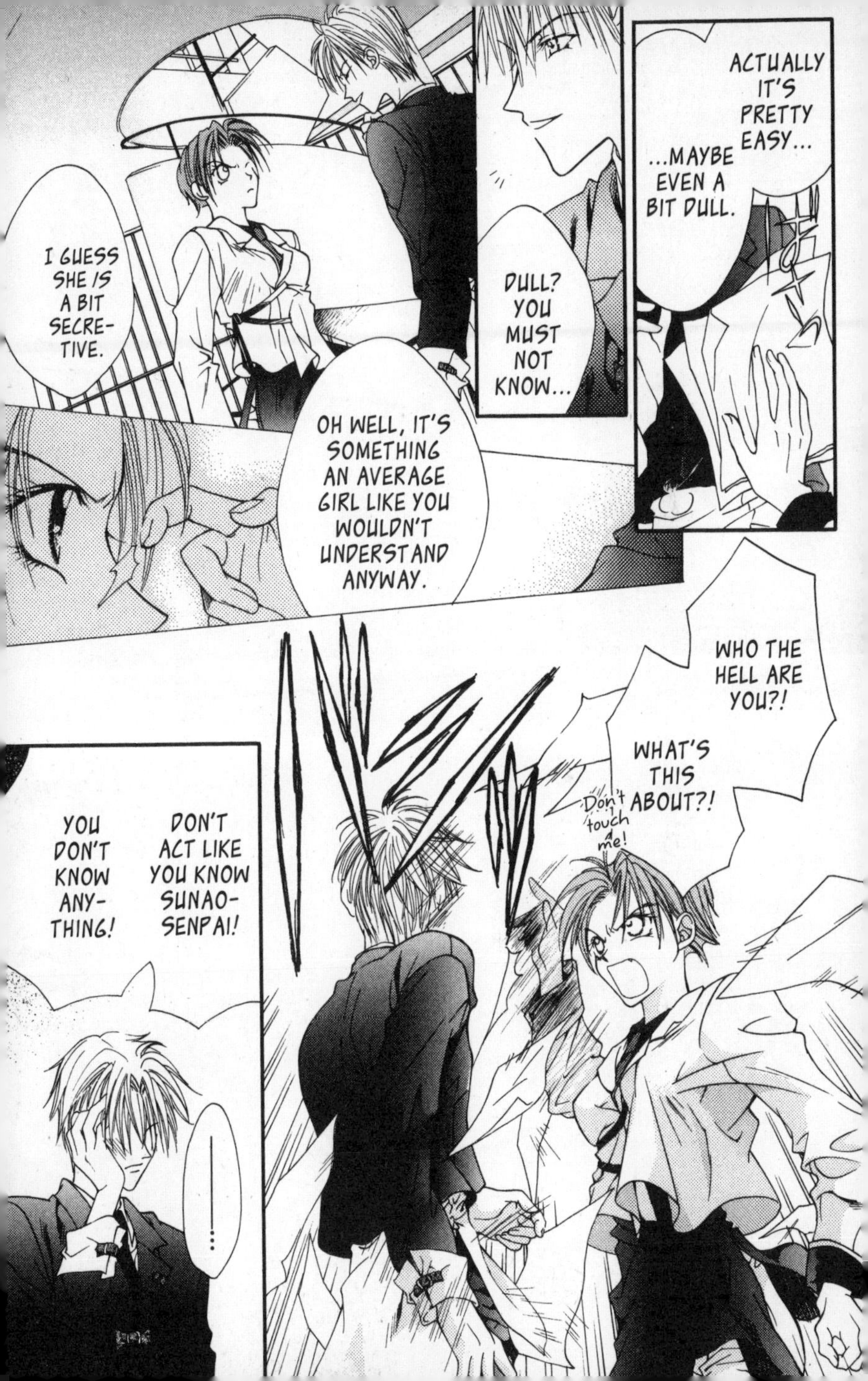
ACTUALLY IT'S PRETTY EASY...
...MAYBE EVEN A BIT DULL.
DULL? YOU MUST NOT KNOW...
I GUESS SHE IS A BIT SECRE-TIVE.
OH WELL, IT'S SOMETHING AN AVERAGE GIRL LIKE YOU WOULDN'T UNDERSTAND ANYWAY.
WHO THE HELL ARE YOU?!
WHAT'S THIS ABOUT?!
Don't touch me!
DON'T ACT LIKE YOU KNOW SUNAO-SENPAI!
YOU DON'T KNOW ANY-THING!
......

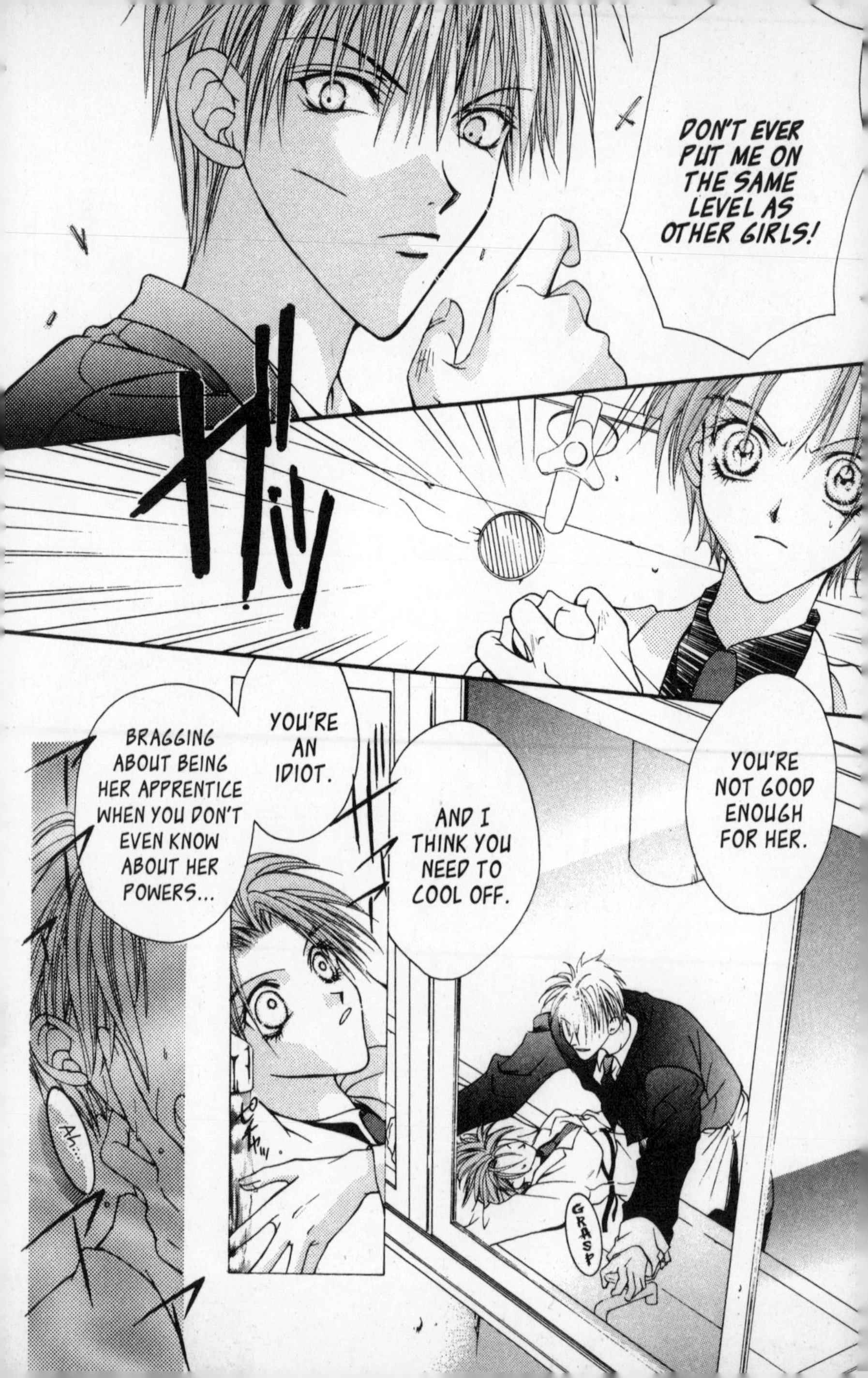
DON'T EVER PUT ME ON THE SAME LEVEL AS OTHER GIRLS!
YOU'RE NOT GOOD ENOUGH FOR HER.
GRASP
AND I THINK YOU NEED TO COOL OFF.
YOU'RE AN IDIOT.
BRAGGING ABOUT BEING HER APPRENTICE WHEN YOU DON'T EVEN KNOW ABOUT HER POWERS...
Ah...

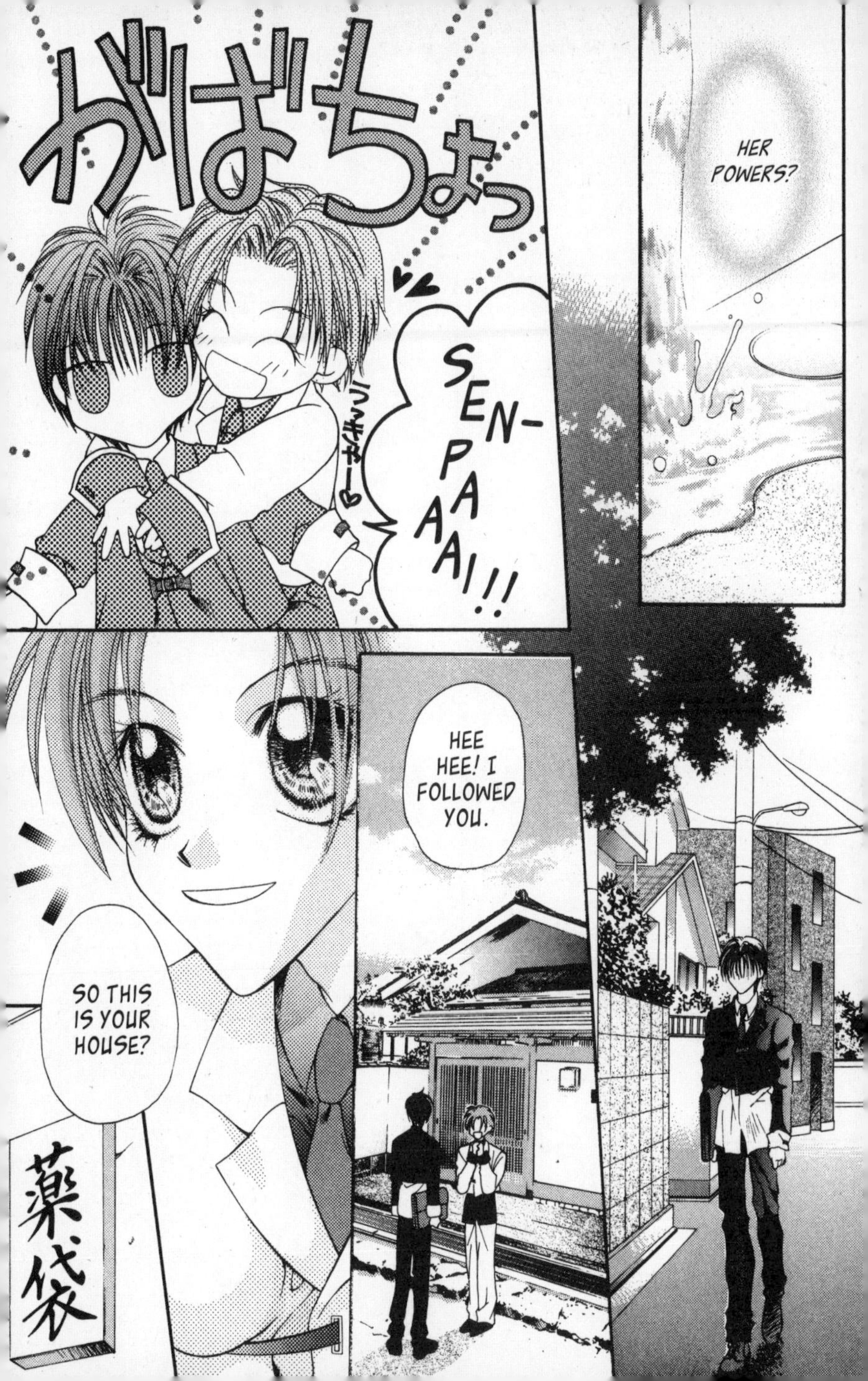
HER POWERS?
がばちょっ
SEN-PAAAAI!!!
HEE HEE! I FOLLOWED YOU.
SO THIS IS YOUR HOUSE?
薬袋

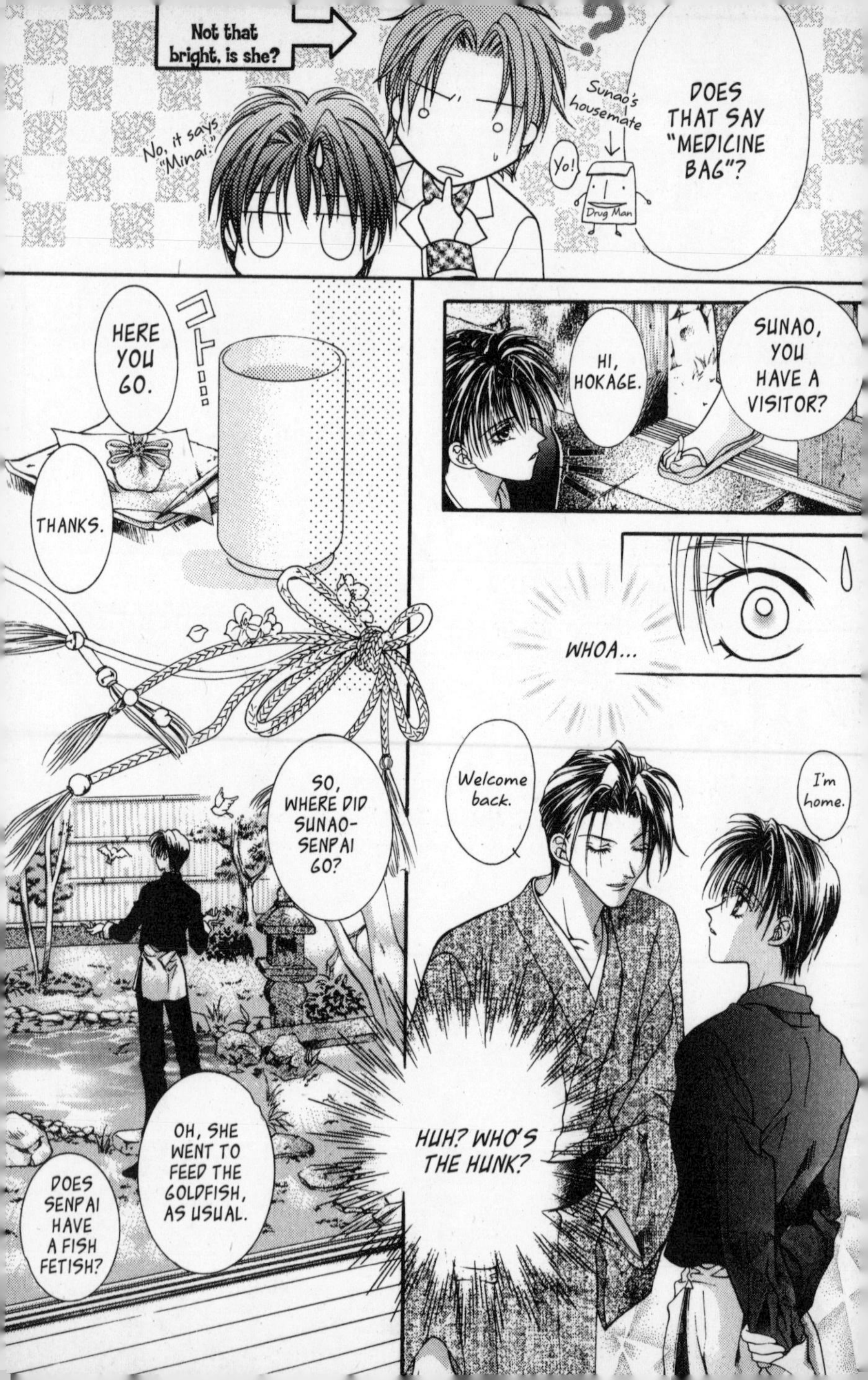
DOES THAT SAY "MEDICINE BAG"?
Sunao's housemate
Yo!
Drug Man
No, it says "Minai."
Not that bright, is she?
SUNAO, YOU HAVE A VISITOR?
HI, HOKAGE.
WHOA...
I'm home.
Welcome back.
HUH? WHO'S THE HUNK?
HERE YOU GO.
THANKS.
SO, WHERE DID SUNAO-SENPAI GO?
OH, SHE WENT TO FEED THE GOLDFISH, AS USUAL.
DOES SENPAI HAVE A FISH FETISH?

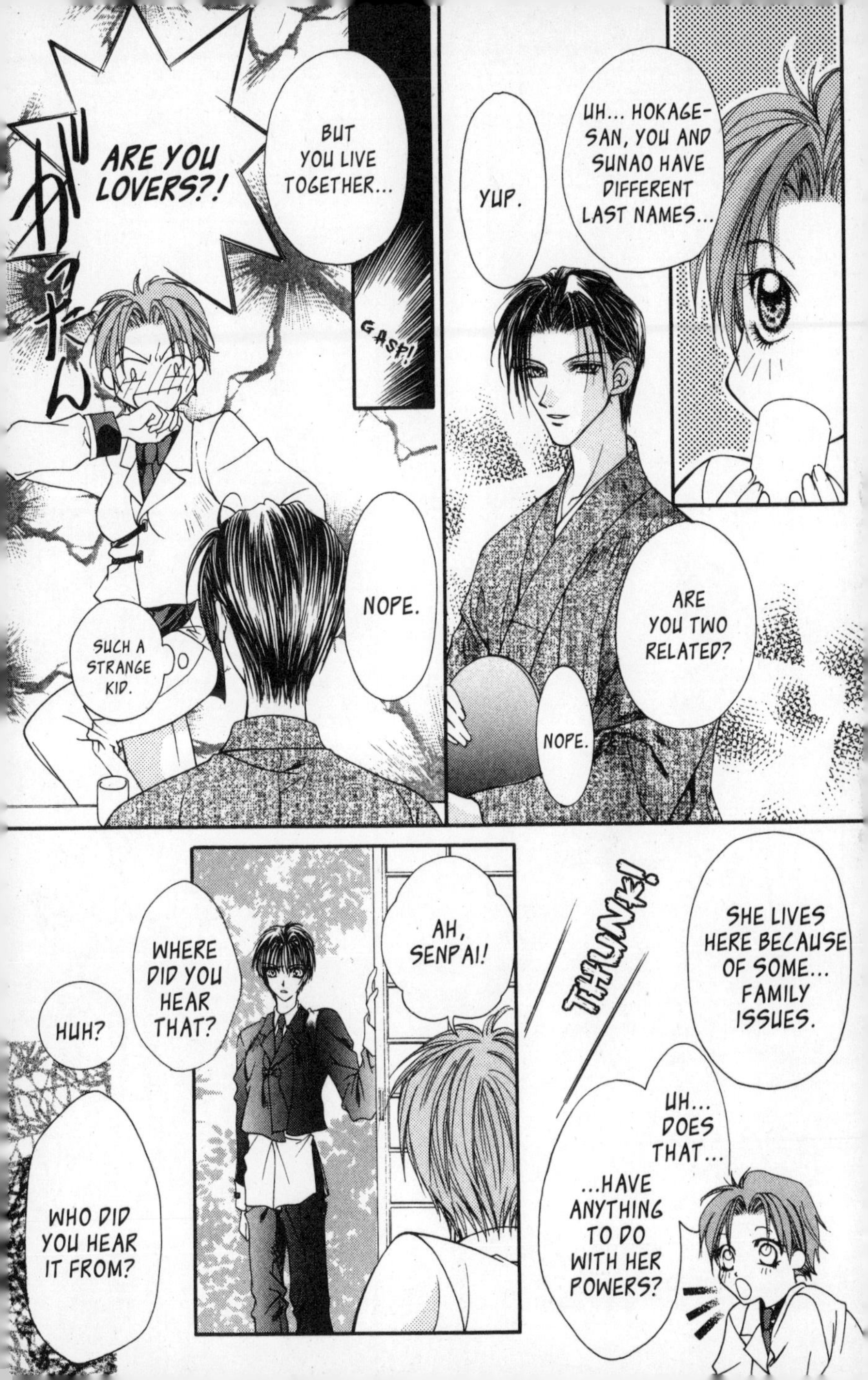
UH... HOKAGE-SAN, YOU AND SUNAO HAVE DIFFERENT LAST NAMES...
YUP.
ARE YOU TWO RELATED?
NOPE.
BUT YOU LIVE TOGETHER...
GASP!
ARE YOU LOVERS?!
NOPE.
SUCH A STRANGE KID.
SHE LIVES HERE BECAUSE OF SOME... FAMILY ISSUES.
UH... DOES THAT...
...HAVE ANYTHING TO DO WITH HER POWERS?
THUNK!
AH, SENPAI!
WHERE DID YOU HEAR THAT?
HUH?
WHO DID YOU HEAR IT FROM?

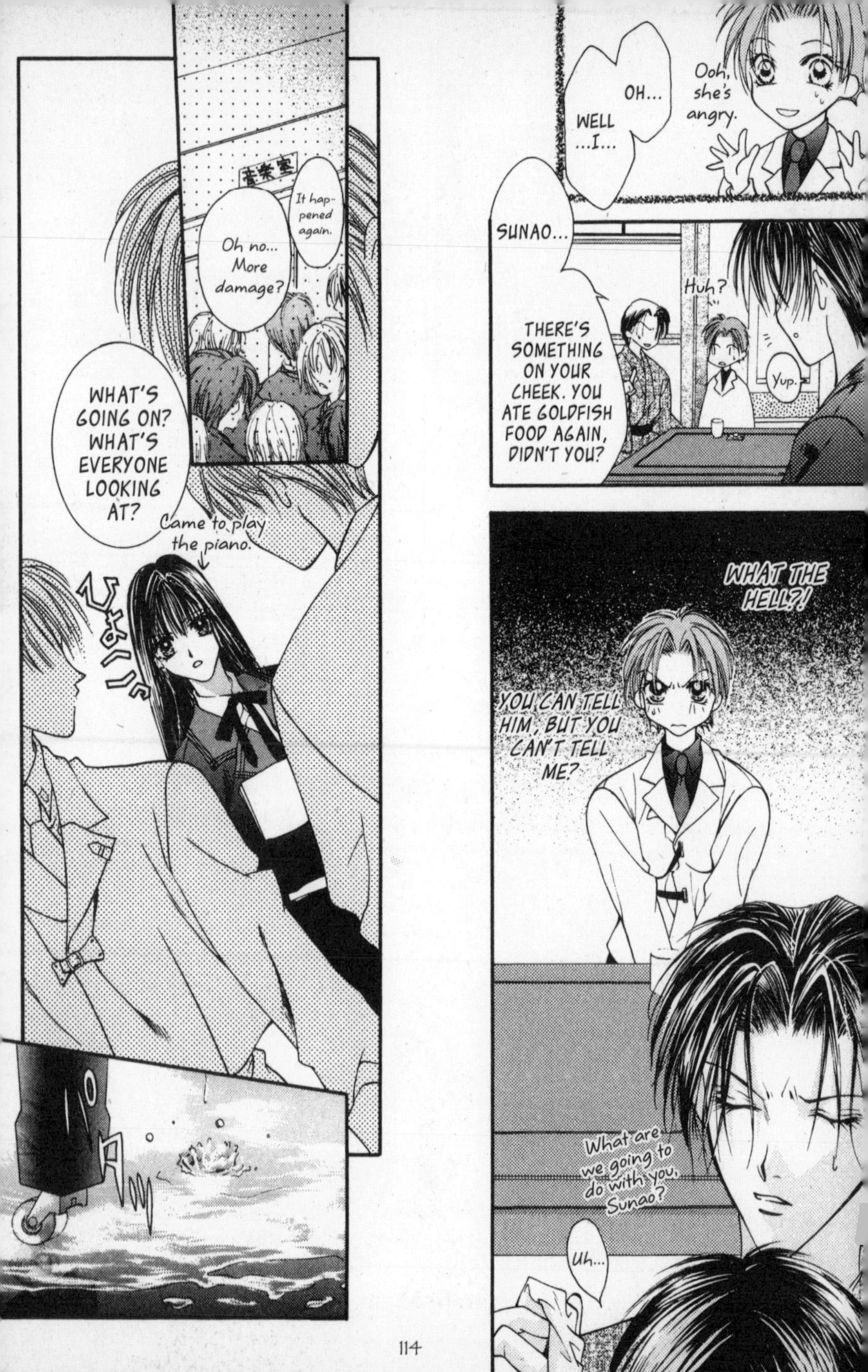
Ooh, she's angry.
OH... WELL ...I...
SUNAO... THERE'S SOMETHING ON YOUR CHEEK. YOU ATE GOLDFISH FOOD AGAIN, DIDN'T YOU?
Huh?
Yup.
WHAT THE HELL?!
YOU CAN TELL HIM, BUT YOU CAN'T TELL ME?
What are we going to do with you, Sunao?
Uh...
音楽室
It hap-pened again.
Oh no... More damage?
WHAT'S GOING ON? WHAT'S EVERYONE LOOKING AT?
Came to play the piano.

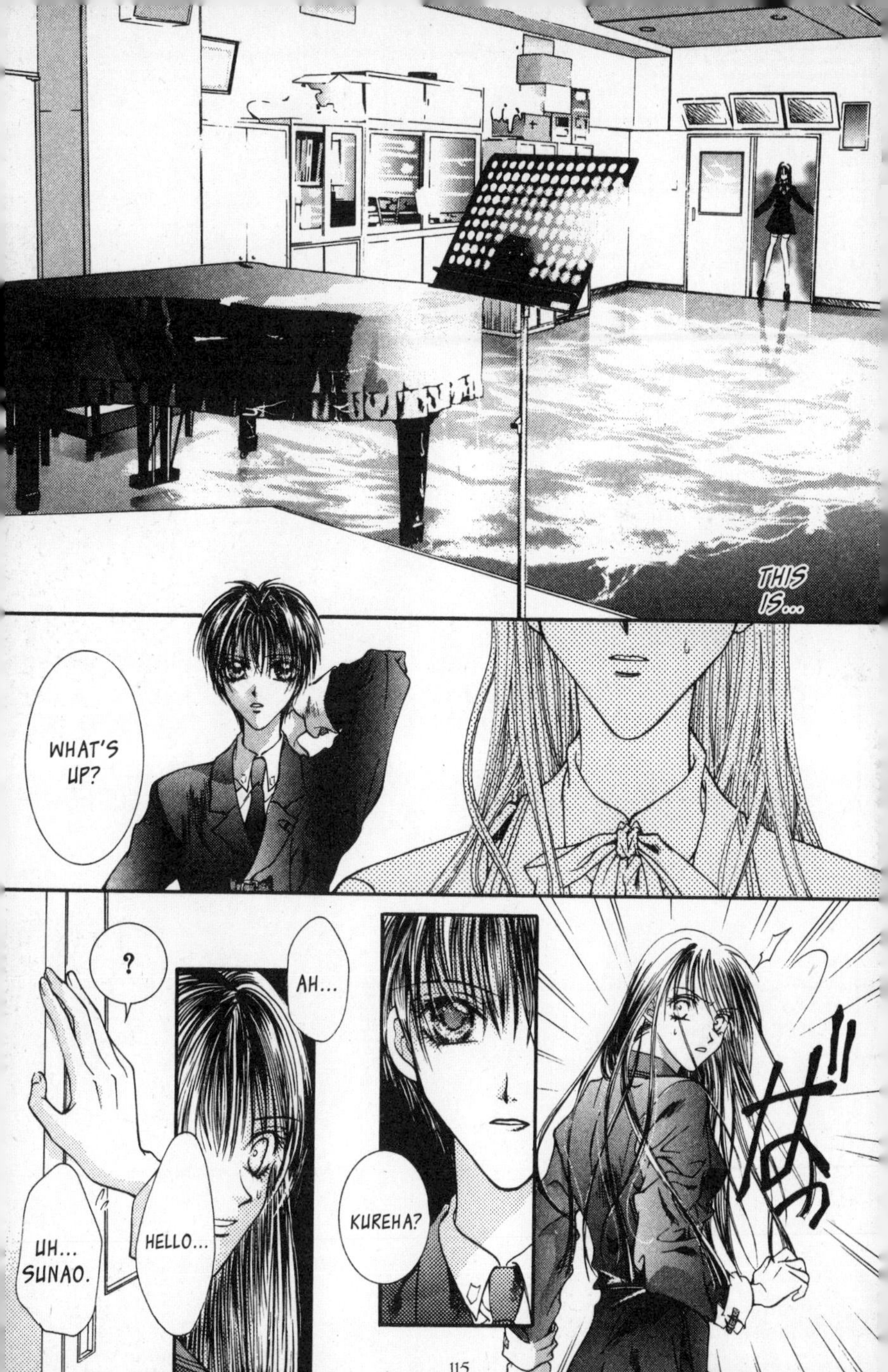
THIS IS...
WHAT'S UP?
AH...
KUREHA?
?
HELLO...
UH... SUNAO.

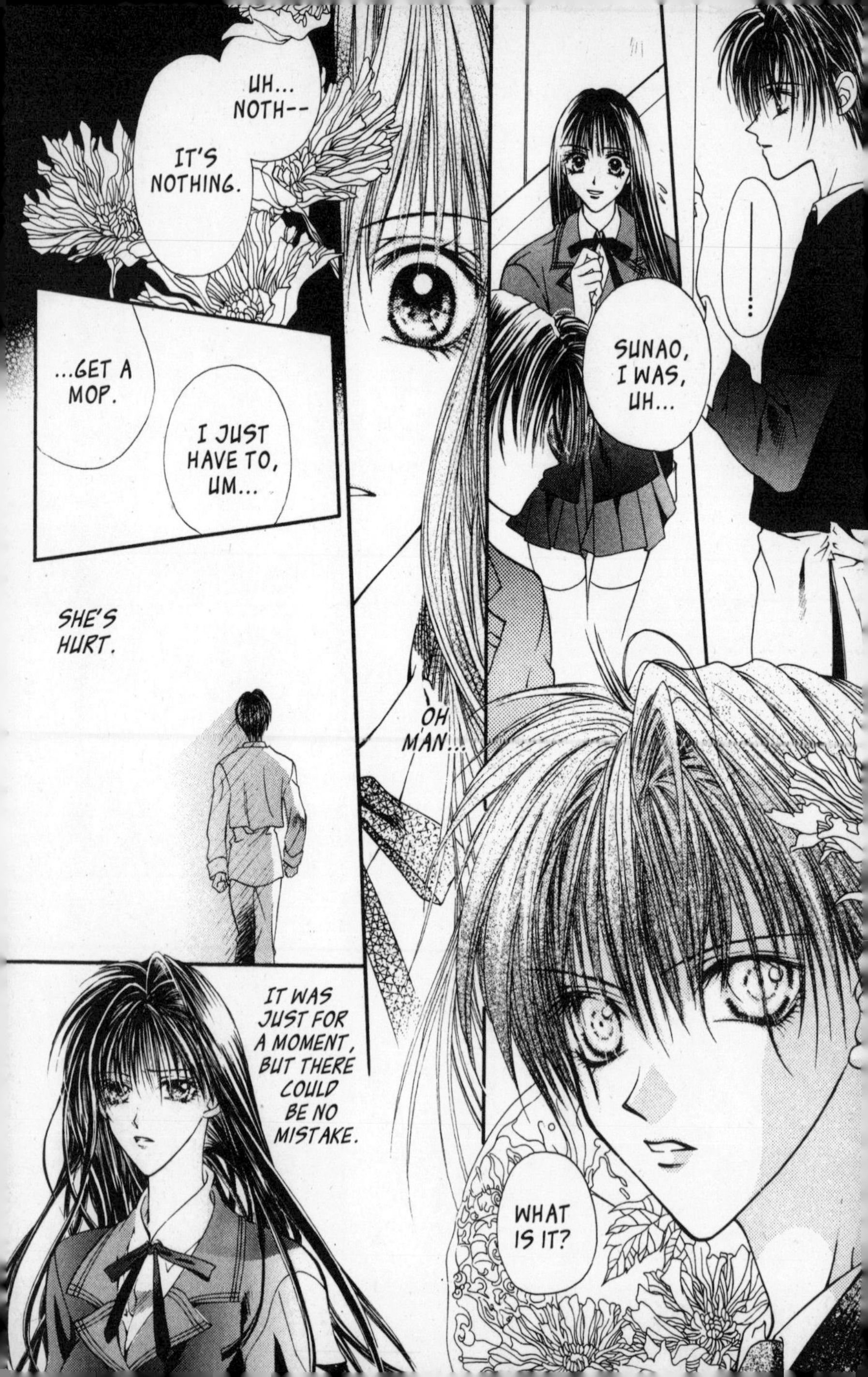
......
SUNAO, I WAS, UH...
WHAT IS IT?
OH MAN...
UH... NOTH--
IT'S NOTHING.
I JUST HAVE TO, UM...
...GET A MOP.
SHE'S HURT.
IT WAS JUST FOR A MOMENT, BUT THERE COULD BE NO MISTAKE.

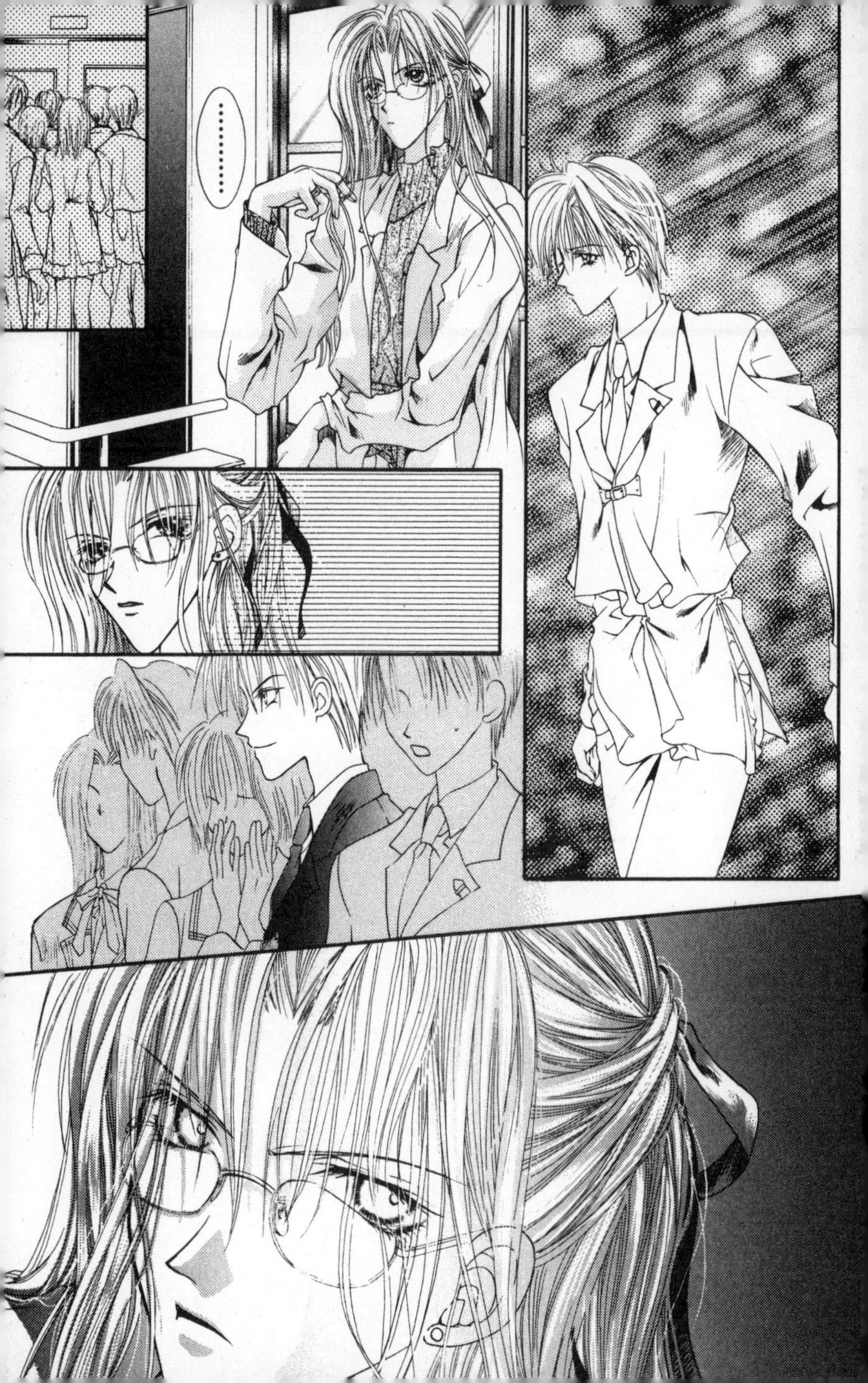
......

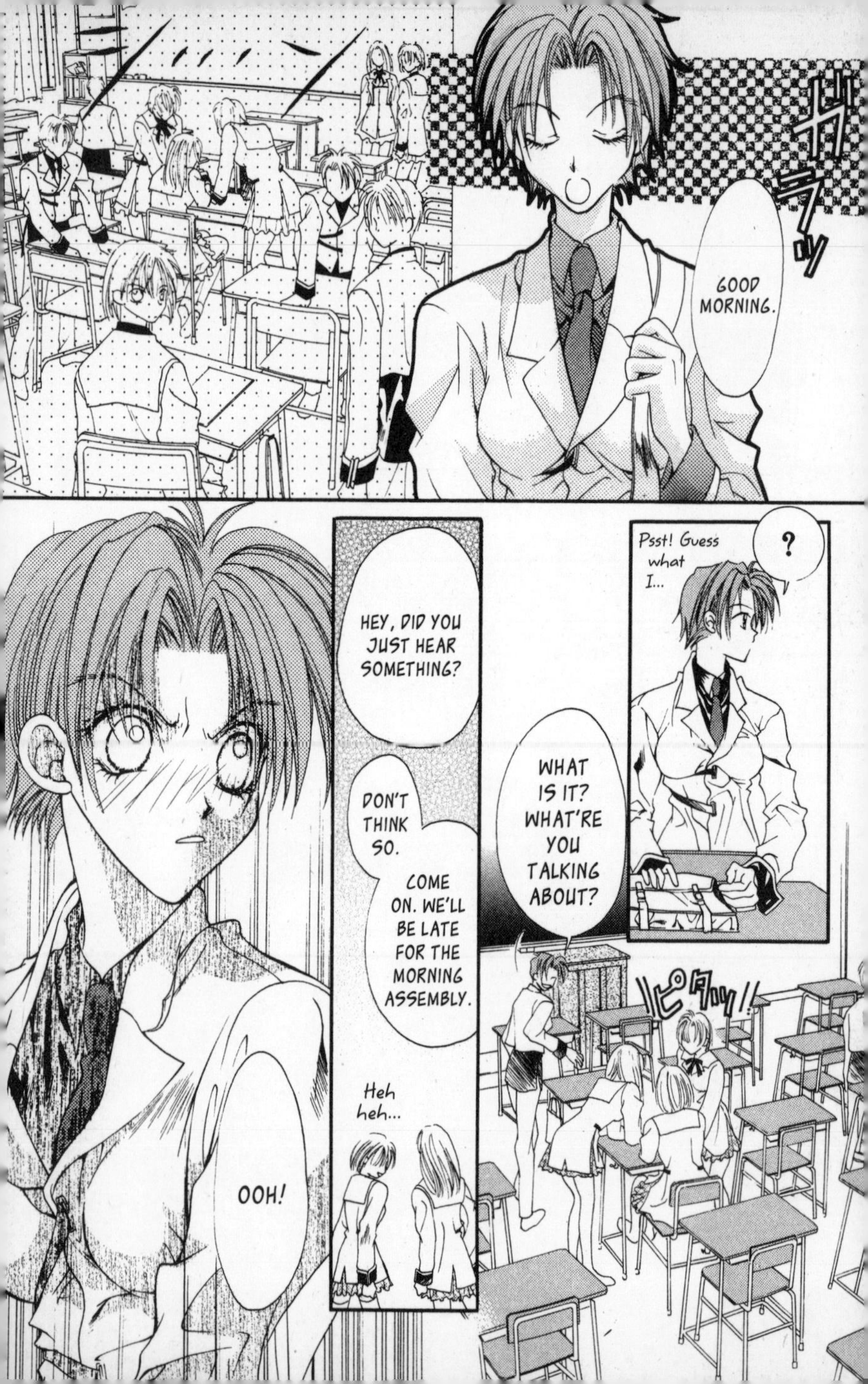
ガラッ
GOOD MORNING.
Psst! Guess what I...
?
WHAT IS IT? WHAT'RE YOU TALKING ABOUT?
ピタッ!!
HEY, DID YOU JUST HEAR SOMETHING?
DON'T THINK SO.
COME ON. WE'LL BE LATE FOR THE MORNING ASSEMBLY.
Heh heh...
OOH!

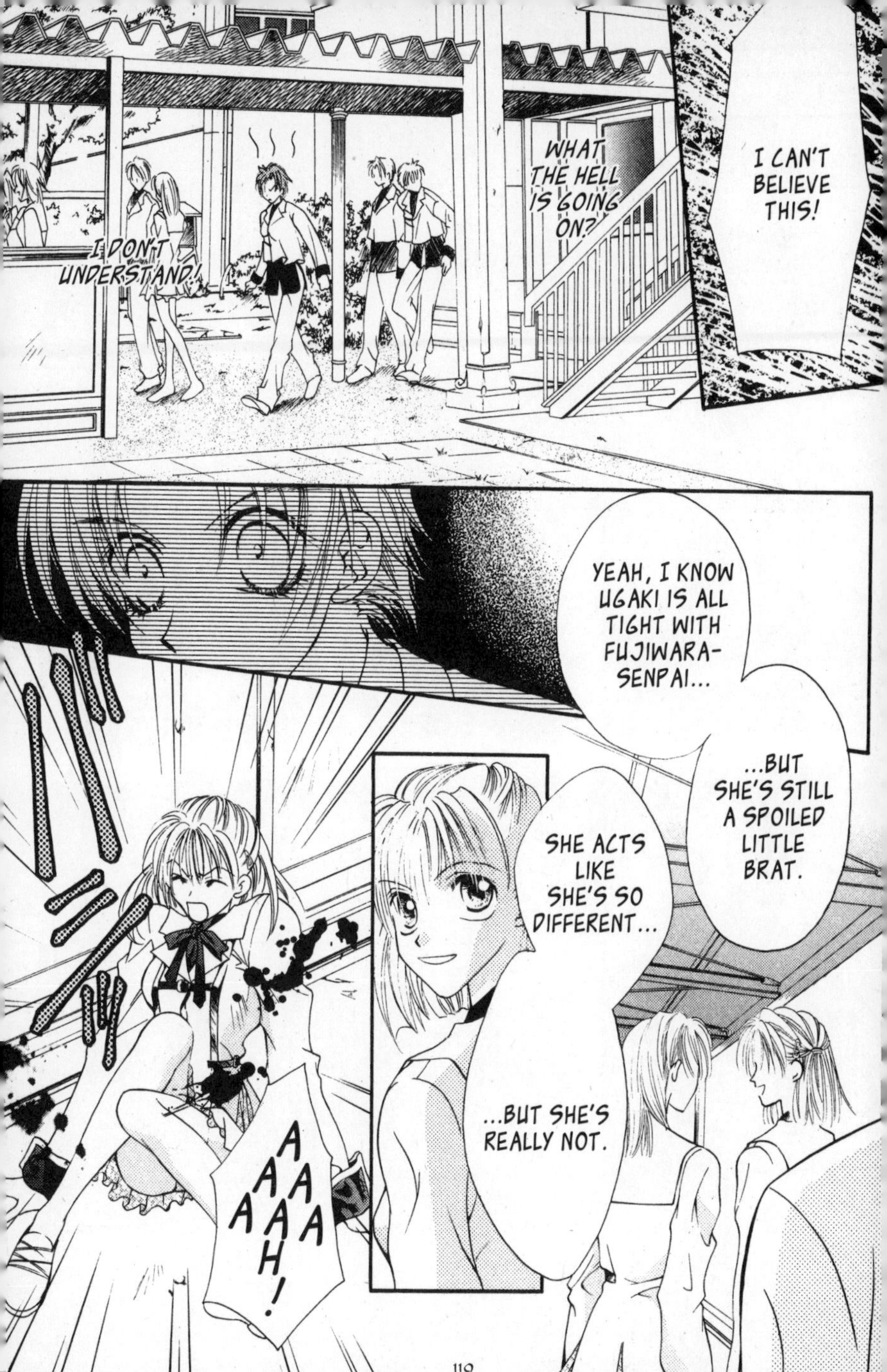
I CAN'T BELIEVE THIS!
WHAT THE HELL IS GOING ON?
I DON'T UNDERSTAND!
YEAH, I KNOW UGAKI IS ALL TIGHT WITH FUJIWARA-SENPAI...
...BUT SHE'S STILL A SPOILED LITTLE BRAT.
SHE ACTS LIKE SHE'S SO DIFFERENT...
...BUT SHE'S REALLY NOT.
AAAAAAAH!

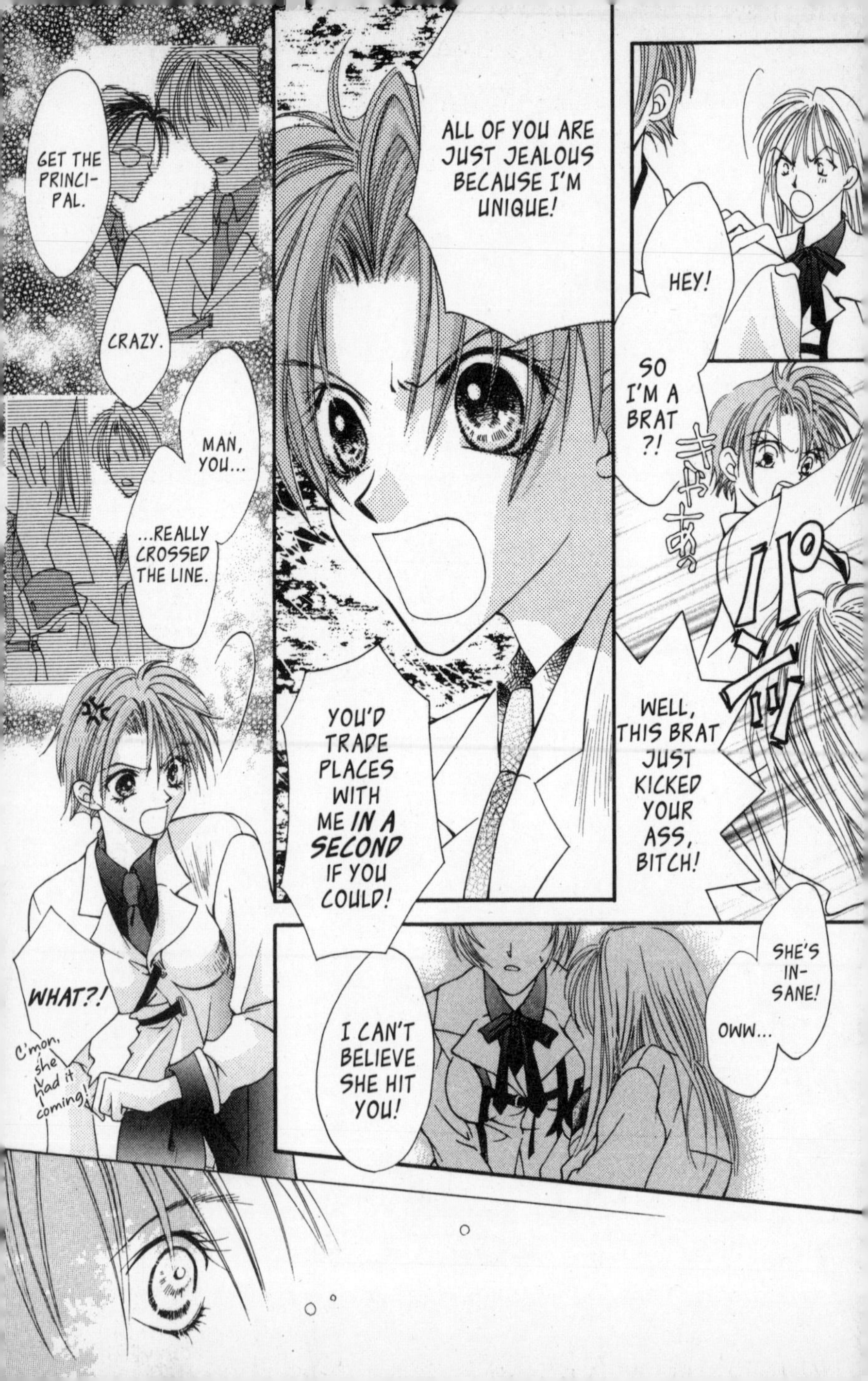
HEY!
SO I'M A BRAT ?!
WELL, THIS BRAT JUST KICKED YOUR ASS, BITCH!
ALL OF YOU ARE JUST JEALOUS BECAUSE I'M UNIQUE!
YOU'D TRADE PLACES WITH ME ***IN A SECOND*** IF YOU COULD!
GET THE PRINCI-PAL.
CRAZY.
MAN, YOU...
...REALLY CROSSED THE LINE.
WHAT?!
C'mon, she had it coming!
SHE'S IN-SANE!
OWW...
I CAN'T BELIEVE SHE HIT YOU!

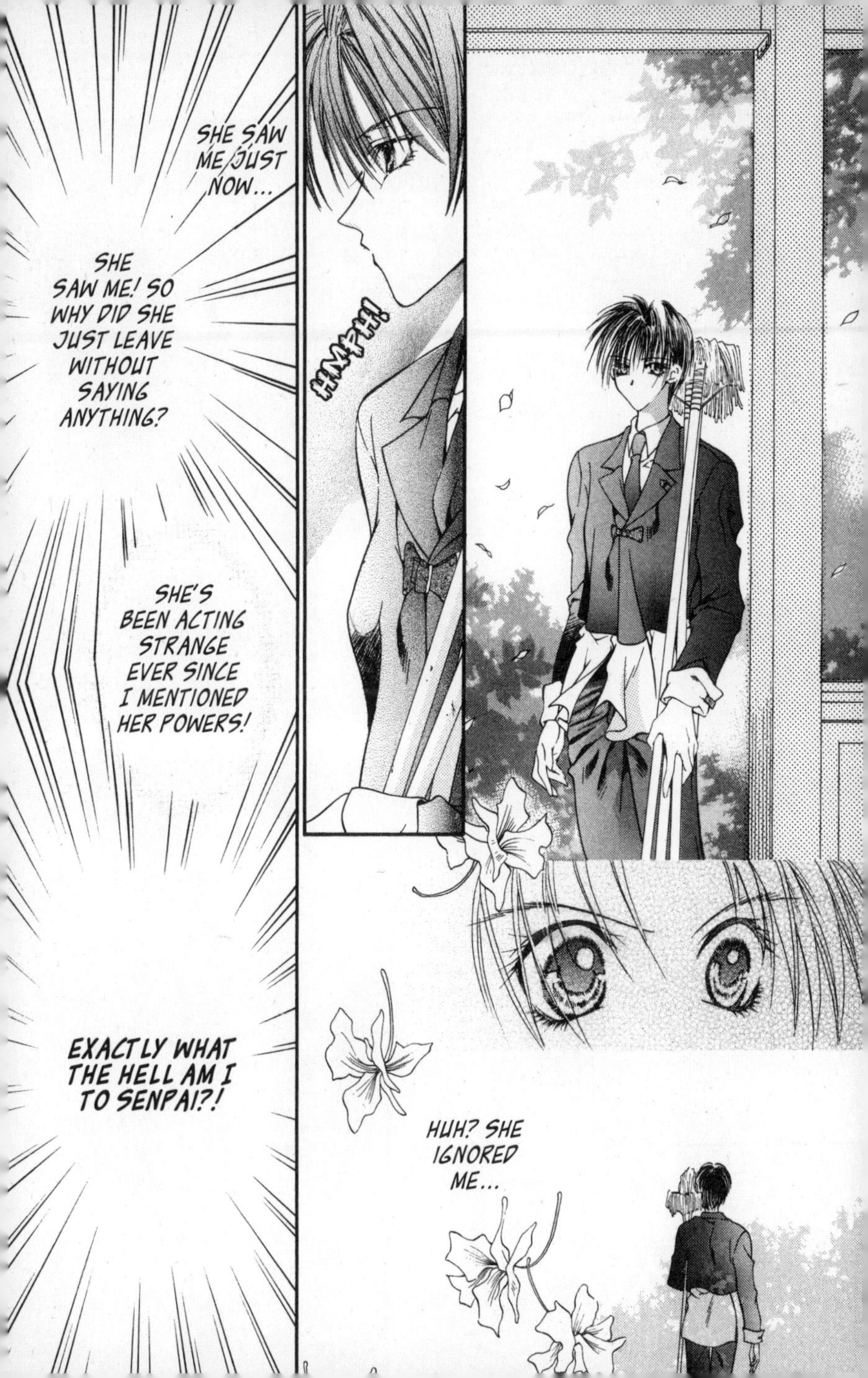
HMPH!
HUH? SHE IGNORED ME...
SHE SAW ME JUST NOW...
SHE SAW ME! SO WHY DID SHE JUST LEAVE WITHOUT SAYING ANYTHING?
SHE'S BEEN ACTING STRANGE EVER SINCE I MENTIONED HER POWERS!
EXACTLY WHAT THE HELL AM I TO SENPAI?!

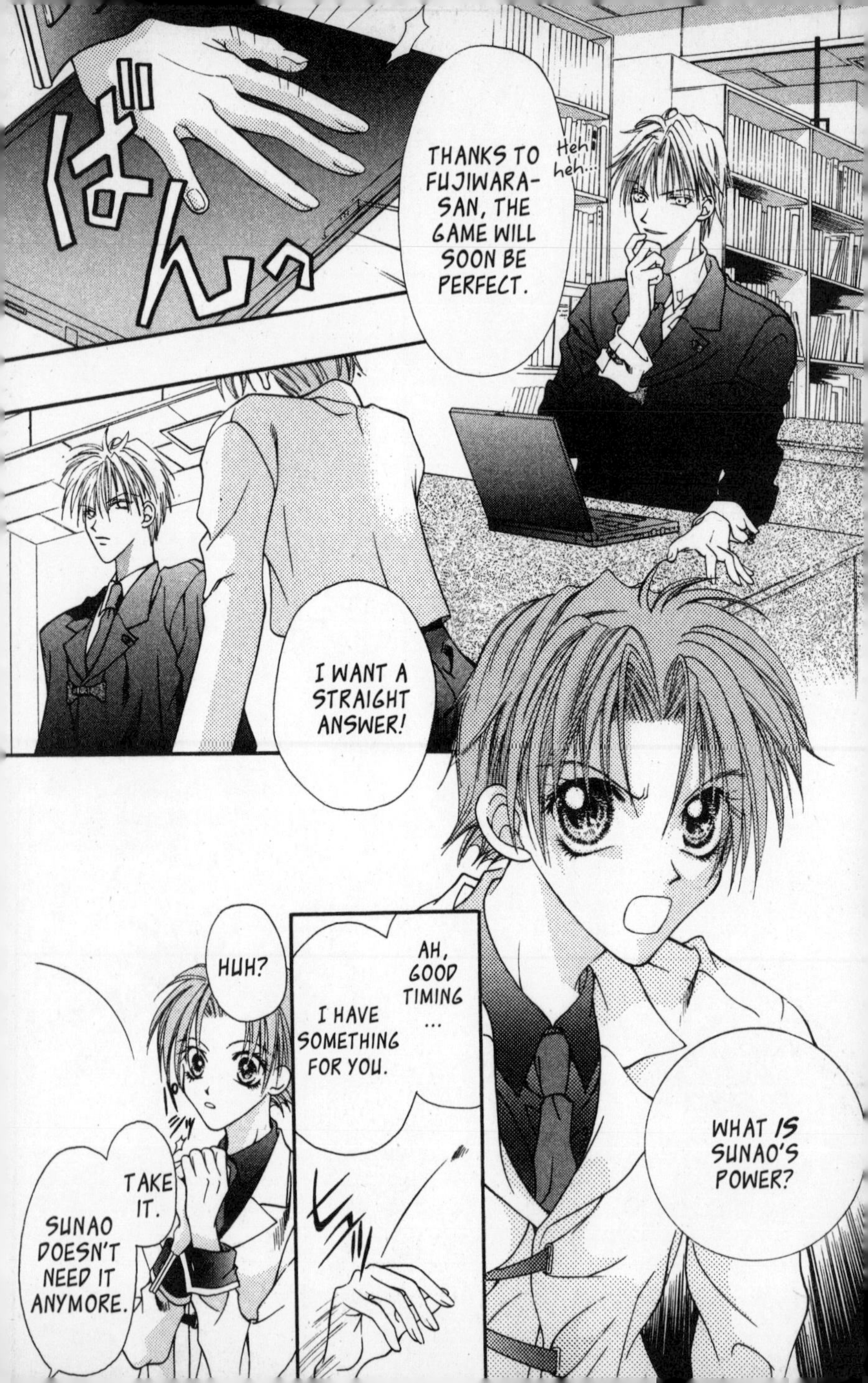
Heh heh...
THANKS TO FUJIWARA-SAN, THE GAME WILL SOON BE PERFECT.
ばんっ
I WANT A STRAIGHT ANSWER!
WHAT *IS* SUNAO'S POWER?
AH, GOOD TIMING...
I HAVE SOMETHING FOR YOU.
HUH?
TAKE IT.
SUNAO DOESN'T NEED IT ANYMORE.

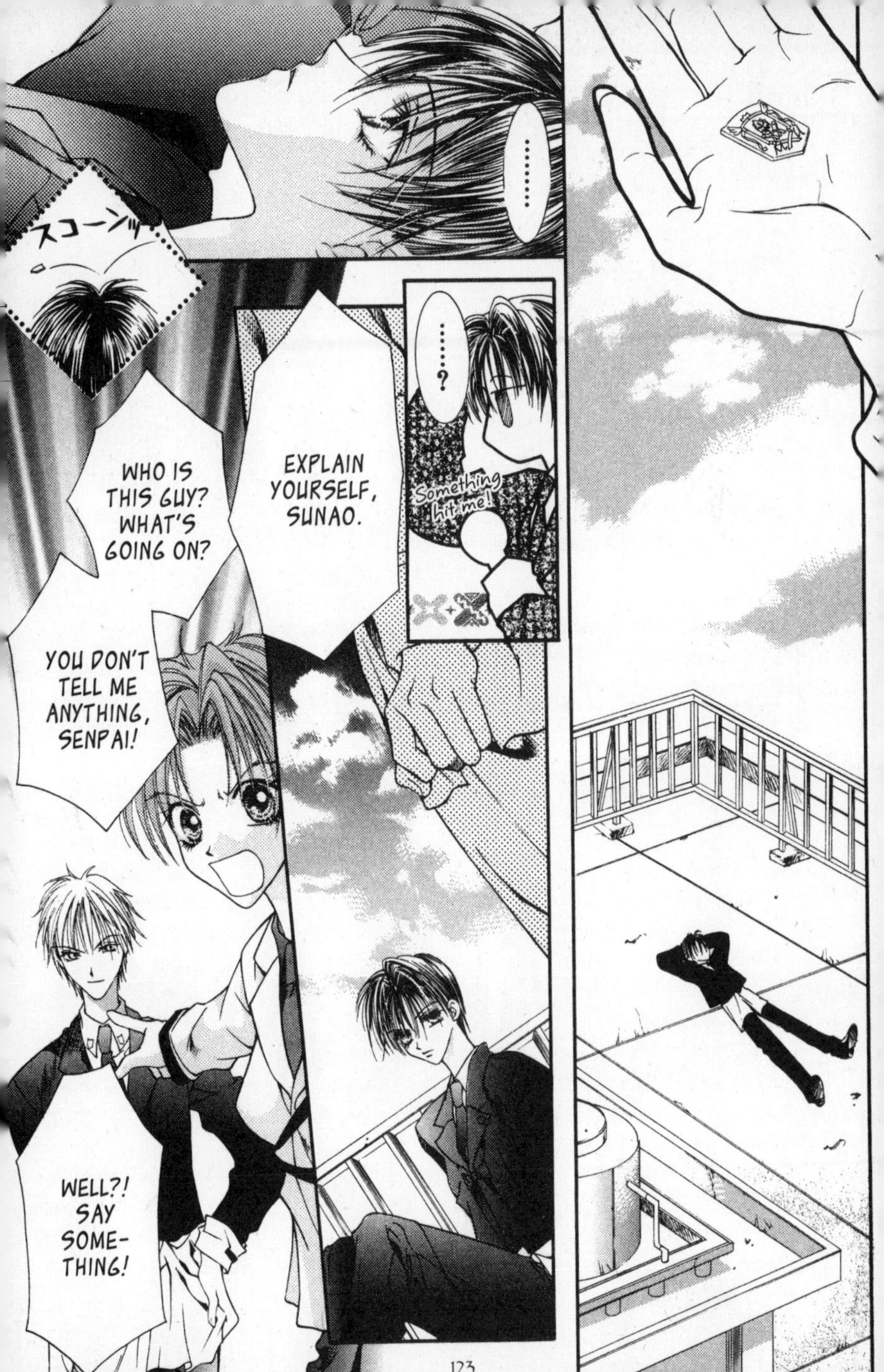
......
スコーンッ
......?
Something hit me!
EXPLAIN YOURSELF, SUNAO.
WHO IS THIS GUY? WHAT'S GOING ON?
YOU DON'T TELL ME ANYTHING, SENPAI!
WELL?! SAY SOME-THING!

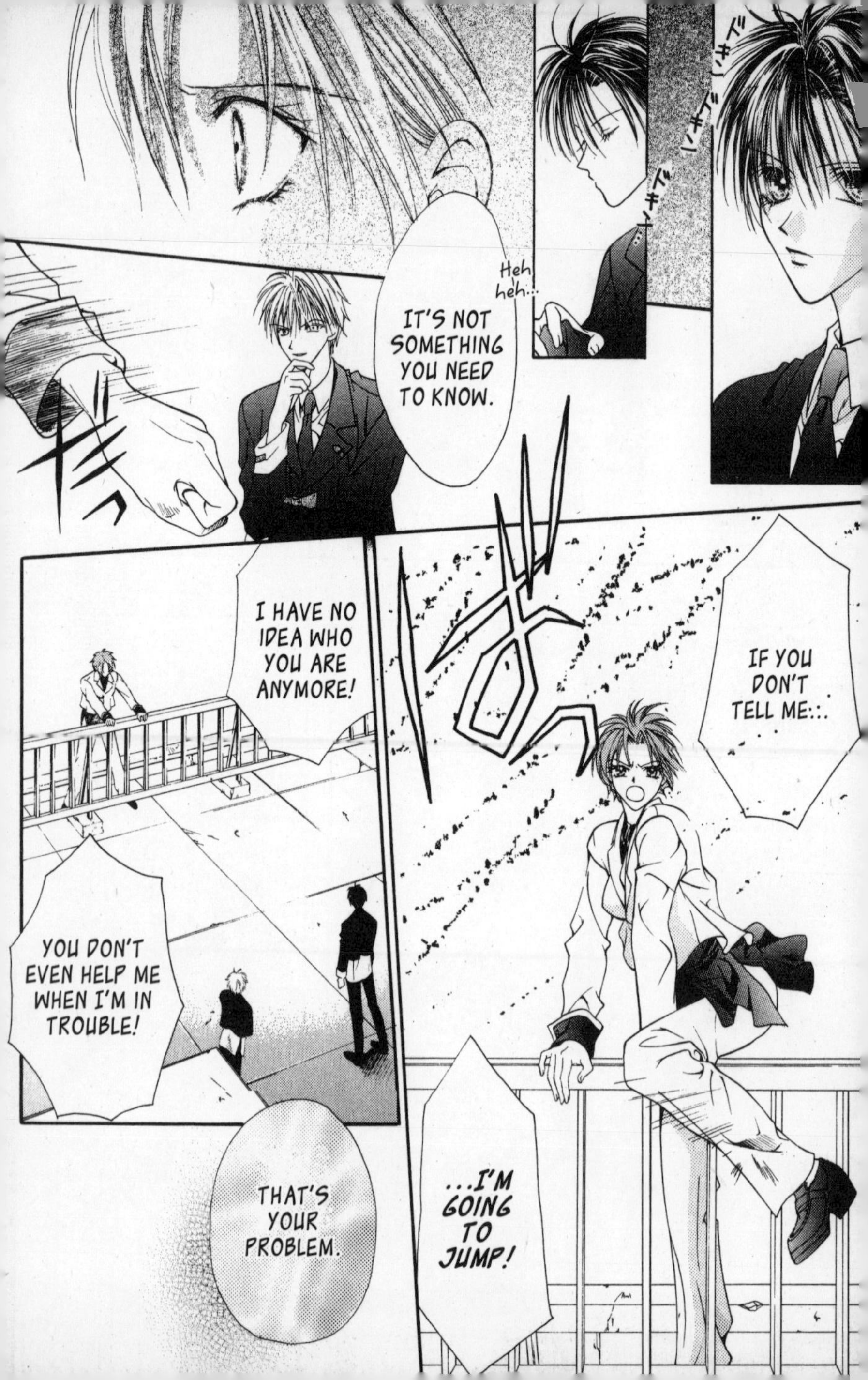

Heh heh...
IT'S NOT SOMETHING YOU NEED TO KNOW.
IF YOU DON'T TELL ME...
...I'M GOING TO JUMP!
I HAVE NO IDEA WHO YOU ARE ANYMORE!
YOU DON'T EVEN HELP ME WHEN I'M IN TROUBLE!
THAT'S YOUR PROBLEM.

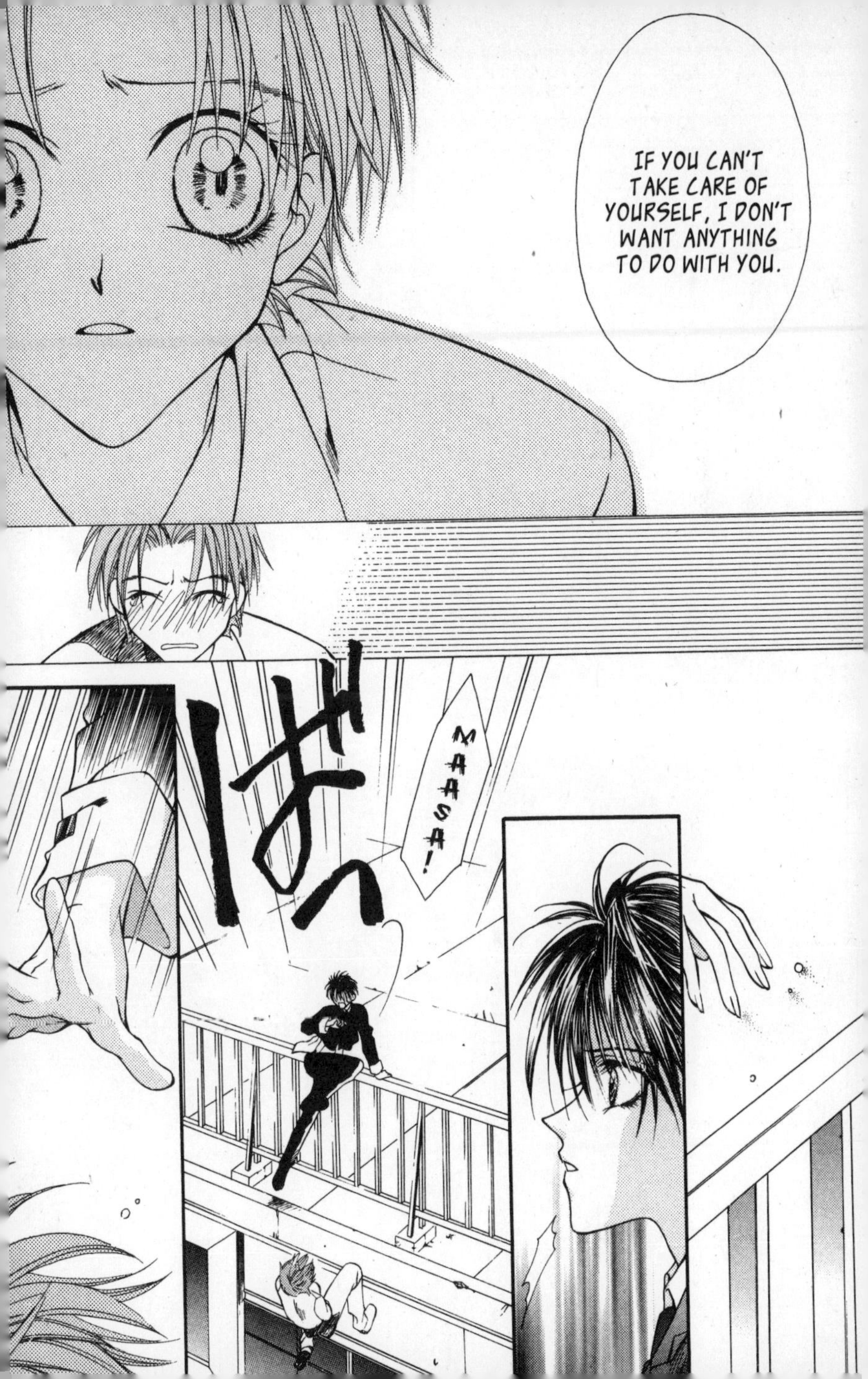
IF YOU CAN'T TAKE CARE OF YOURSELF, I DON'T WANT ANYTHING TO DO WITH YOU.
MAASA!

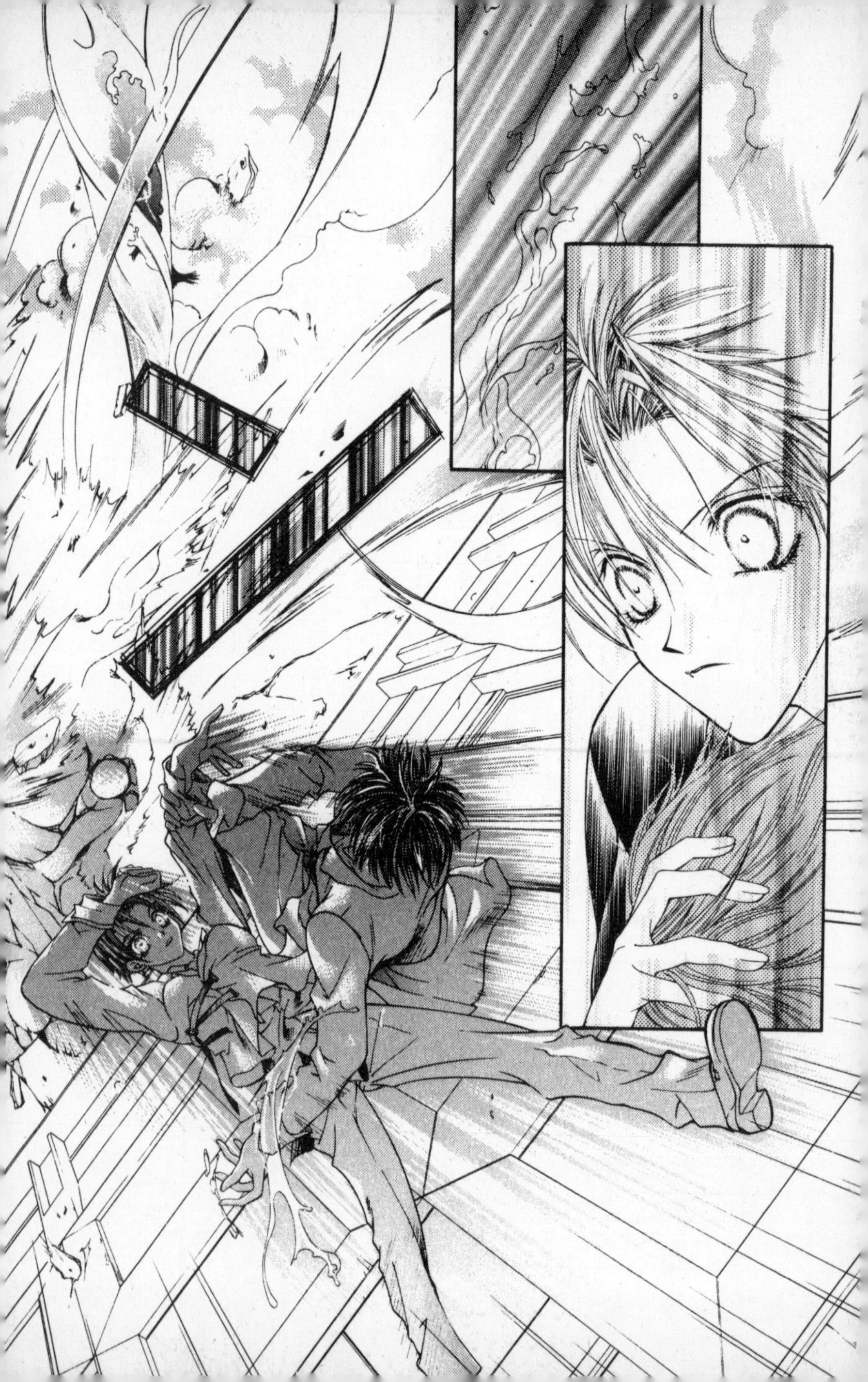

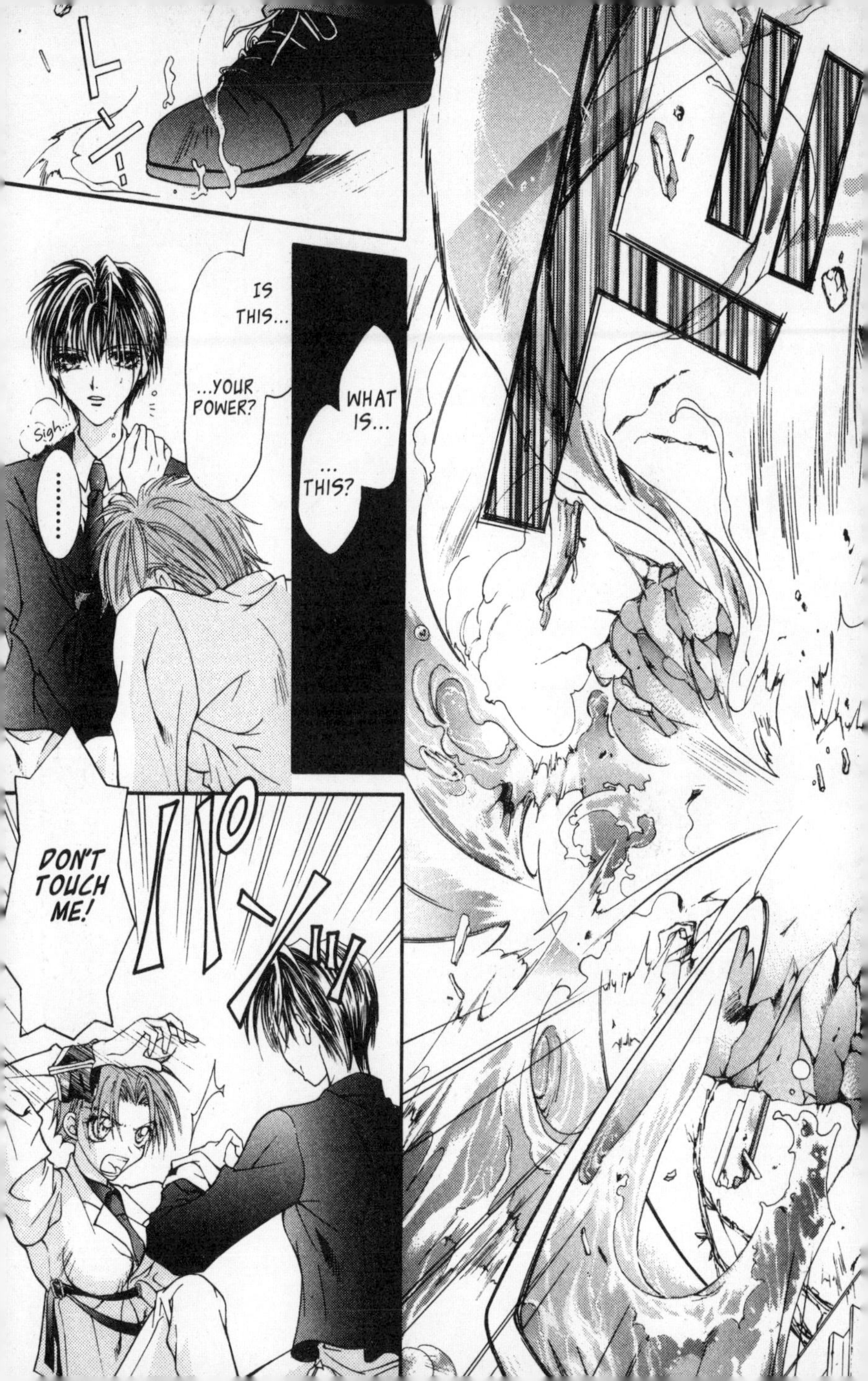
WHAT IS... ...THIS?
IS THIS... ...YOUR POWER?
Sigh...
....
DON'T TOUCH ME!

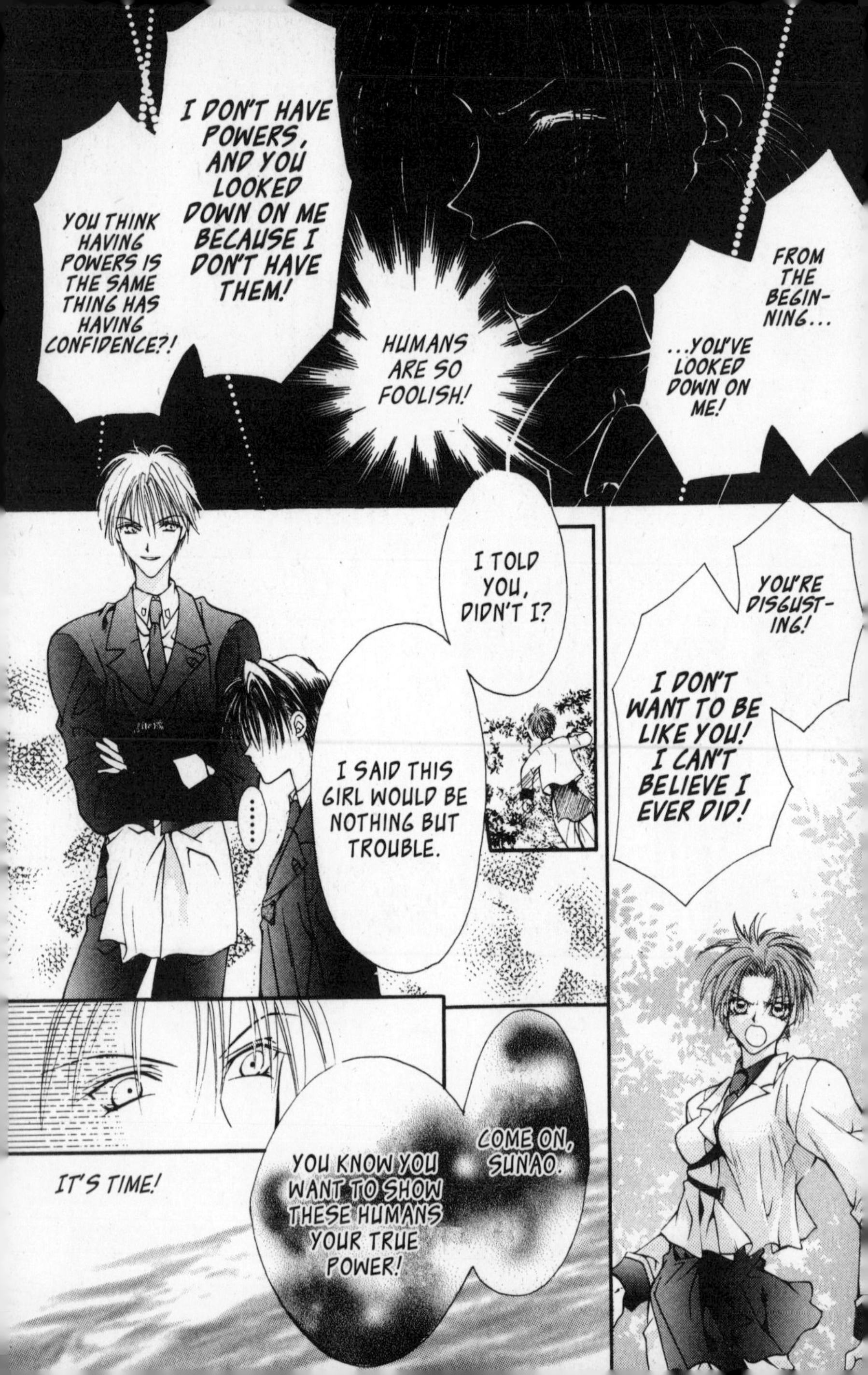
FROM THE BEGINNING...
...YOU'VE LOOKED DOWN ON ME!
HUMANS ARE SO FOOLISH!
I DON'T HAVE POWERS, AND YOU LOOKED DOWN ON ME BECAUSE I DON'T HAVE THEM!
YOU THINK HAVING POWERS IS THE SAME THING HAS HAVING CONFIDENCE?!
YOU'RE DISGUSTING!
I DON'T WANT TO BE LIKE YOU! I CAN'T BELIEVE I EVER DID!
I TOLD YOU, DIDN'T I?
I SAID THIS GIRL WOULD BE NOTHING BUT TROUBLE.
......
COME ON, SUNAO.
YOU KNOW YOU WANT TO SHOW THESE HUMANS YOUR TRUE POWER!
IT'S TIME!

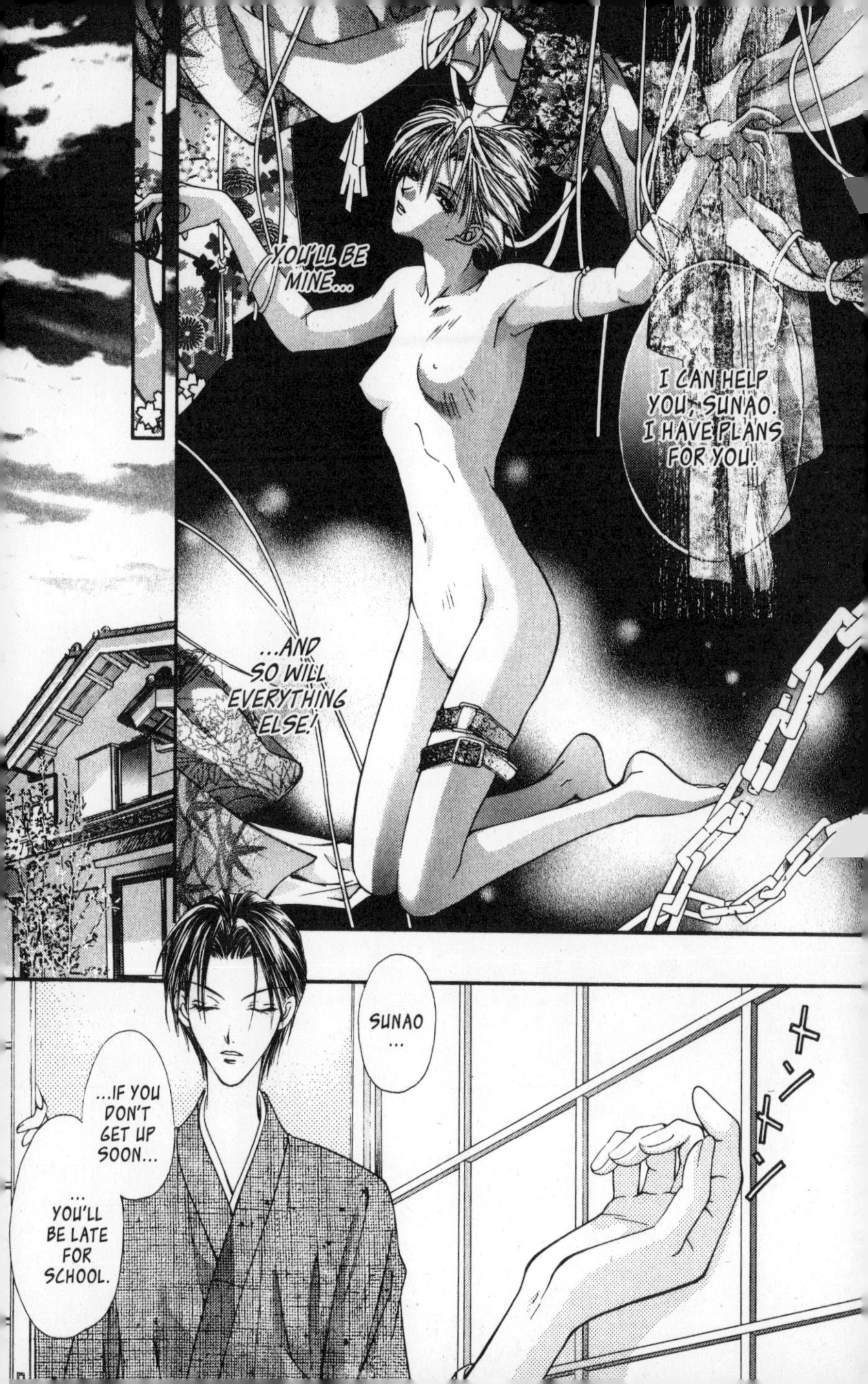
I CAN HELP YOU, SUNAO. I HAVE PLANS FOR YOU!
YOU'LL BE MINE...
...AND SO WILL EVERYTHING ELSE!
SUNAO ...
...IF YOU DON'T GET UP SOON...
... YOU'LL BE LATE FOR SCHOOL.

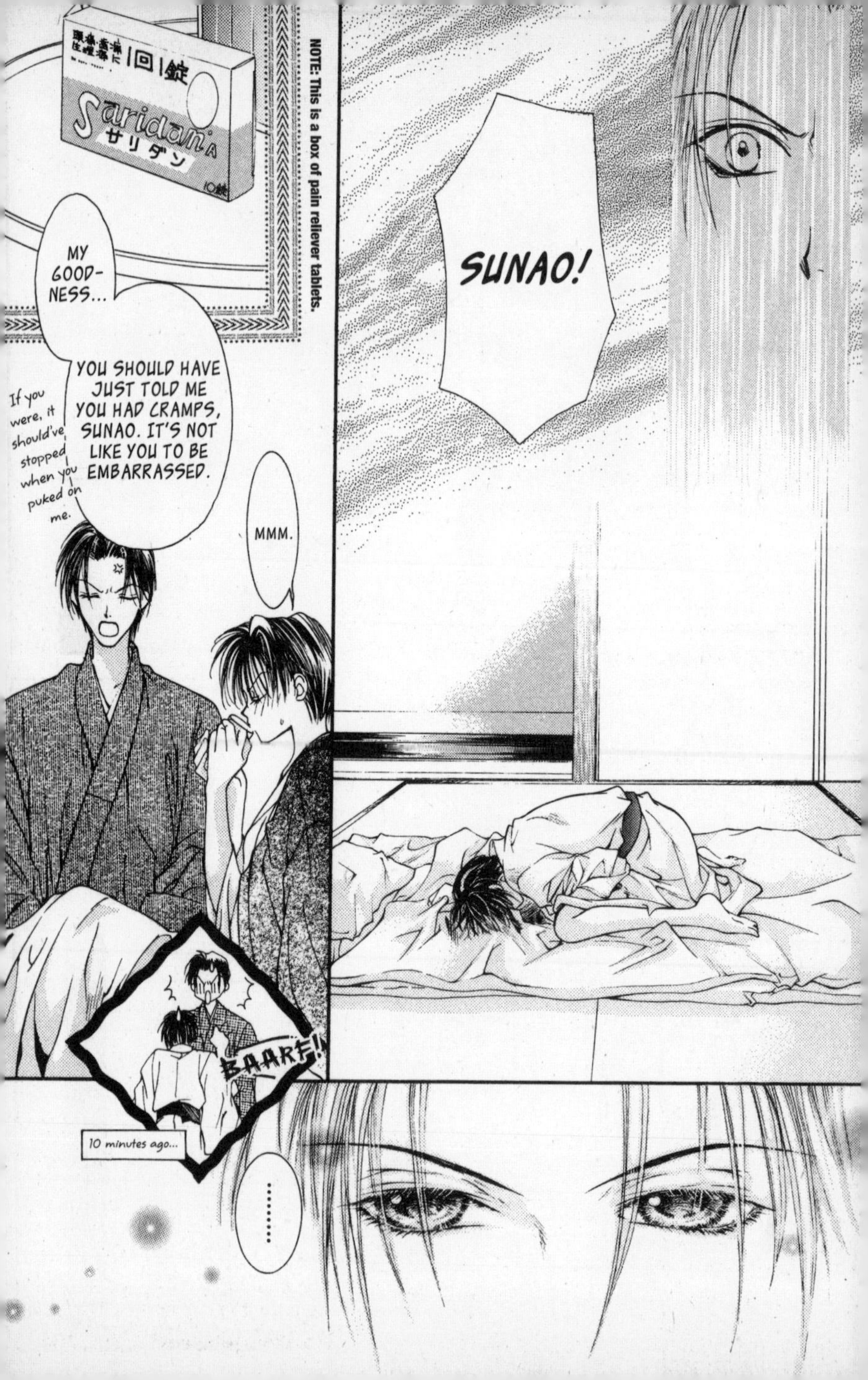
SUNAO!
NOTE: This is a box of pain reliever tablets.
1回1錠
Saridan A
サリダン
MY GOODNESS...
YOU SHOULD HAVE JUST TOLD ME YOU HAD CRAMPS, SUNAO. IT'S NOT LIKE YOU TO BE EMBARRASSED.
If you were, it should've stopped when you puked on me.
MMM.
10 minutes ago...
BAARF!
....

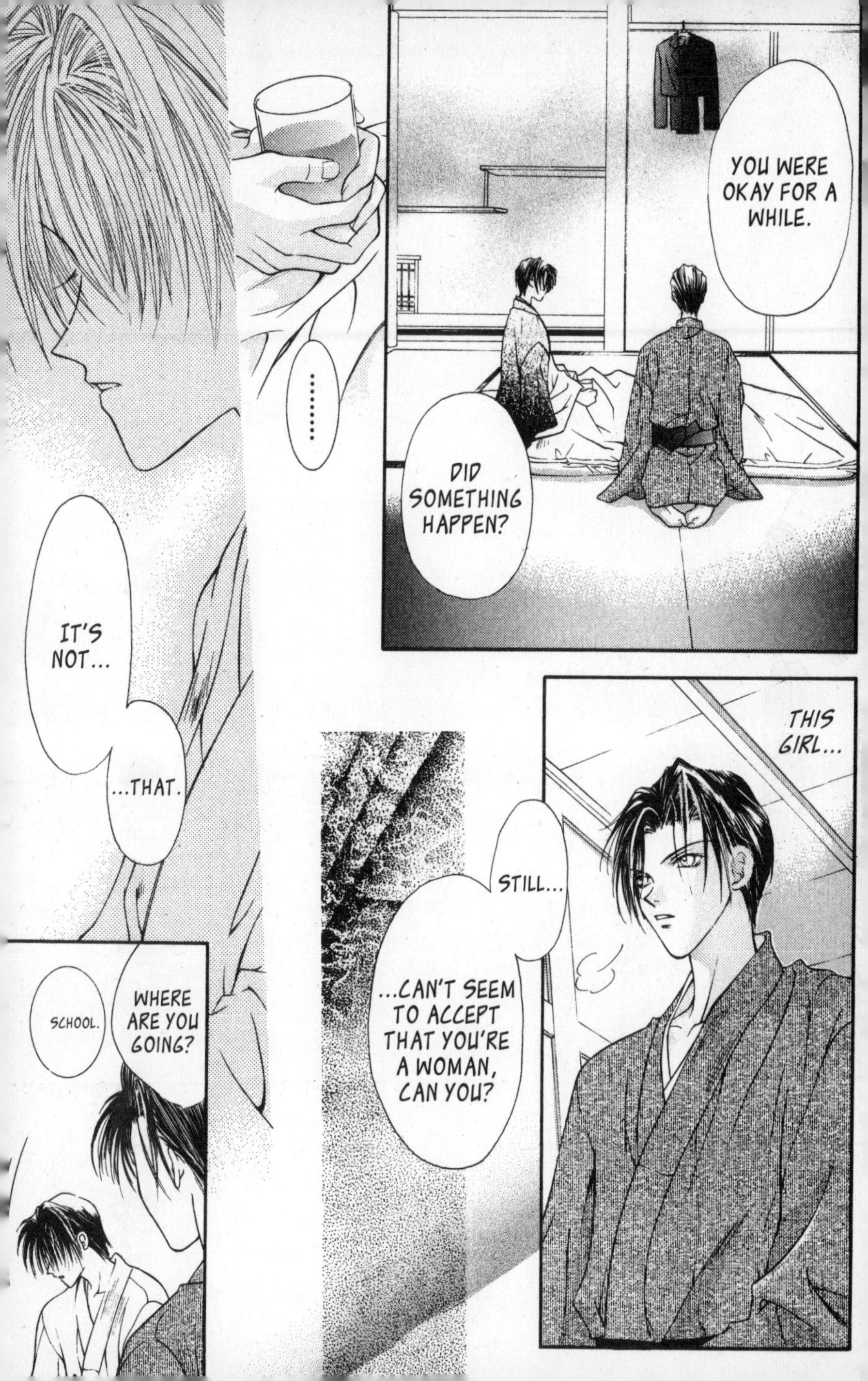

YOU WERE OKAY FOR A WHILE.
DID SOMETHING HAPPEN?
......
IT'S NOT...
...THAT.
THIS GIRL...
STILL...
...CAN'T SEEM TO ACCEPT THAT YOU'RE A WOMAN, CAN YOU?
WHERE ARE YOU GOING?
SCHOOL.

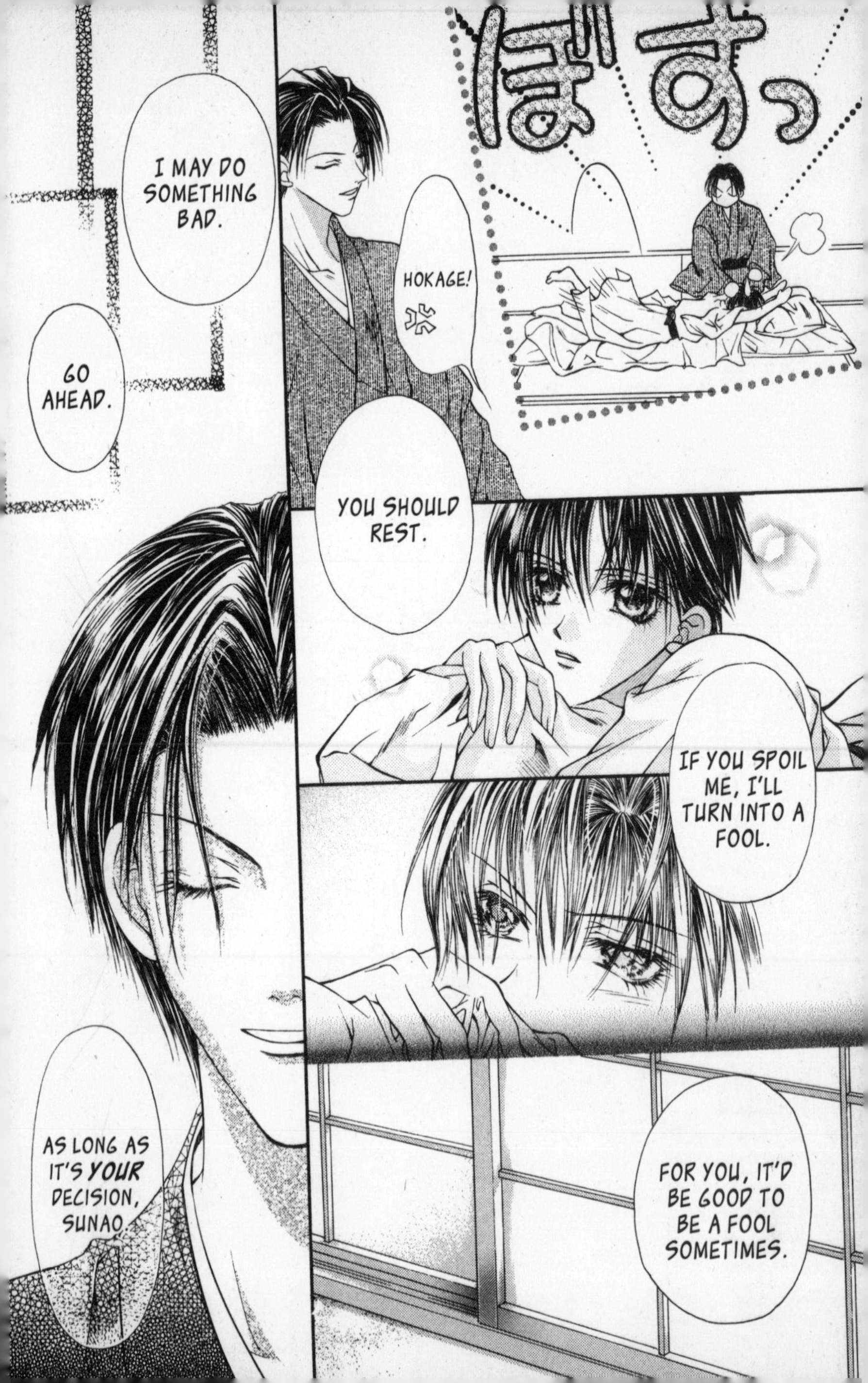
ぼすっ
HOKAGE!
YOU SHOULD REST.
IF YOU SPOIL ME, I'LL TURN INTO A FOOL.
FOR YOU, IT'D BE GOOD TO BE A FOOL SOMETIMES.
I MAY DO SOMETHING BAD.
GO AHEAD.
AS LONG AS IT'S *YOUR* DECISION, SUNAO.

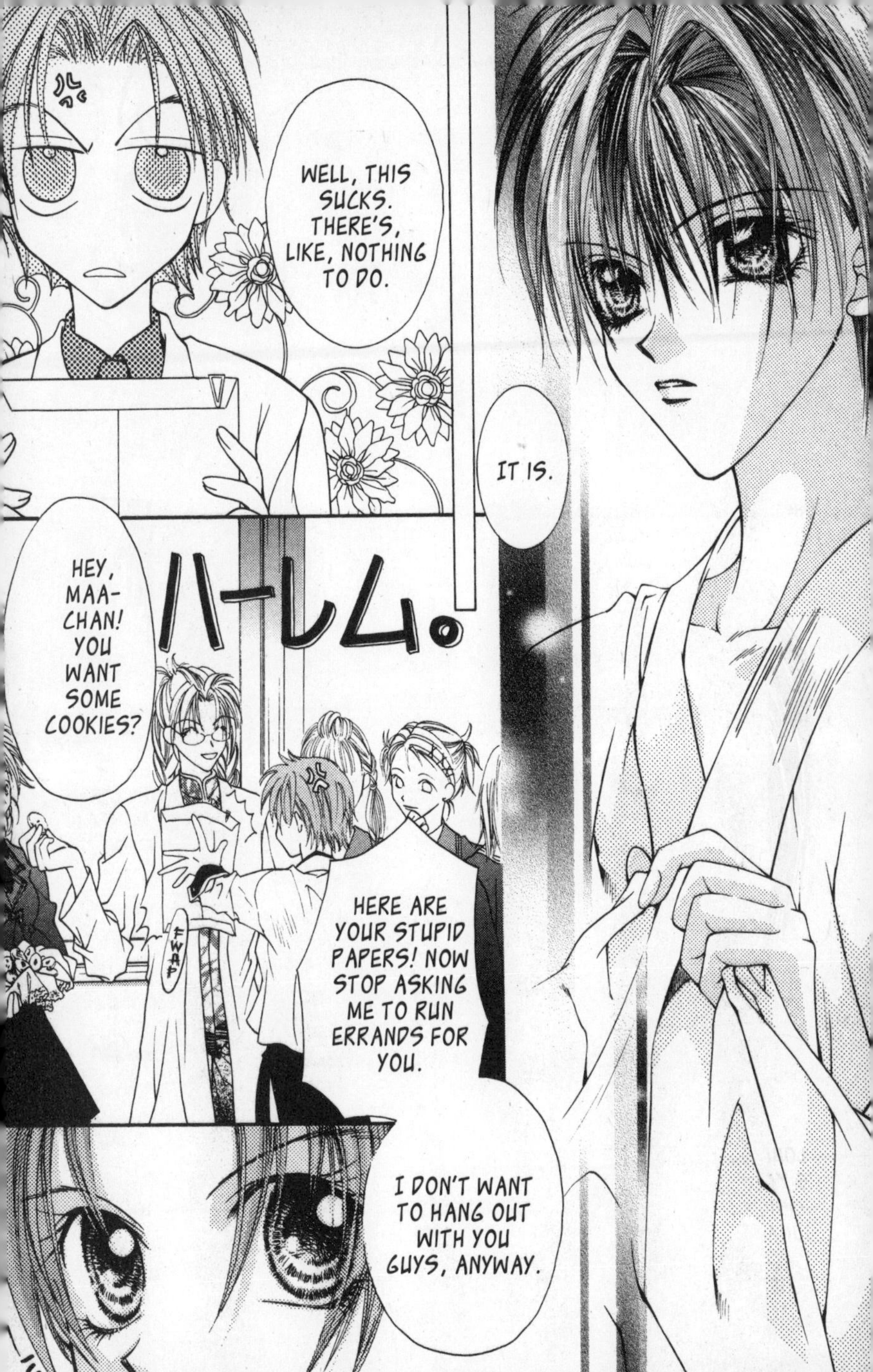
IT IS.
WELL, THIS SUCKS. THERE'S, LIKE, NOTHING TO DO.
ハーレム。
HEY, MAA-CHAN! YOU WANT SOME COOKIES?
HERE ARE YOUR STUPID PAPERS! NOW STOP ASKING ME TO RUN ERRANDS FOR YOU.
FWAP
I DON'T WANT TO HANG OUT WITH YOU GUYS, ANYWAY.

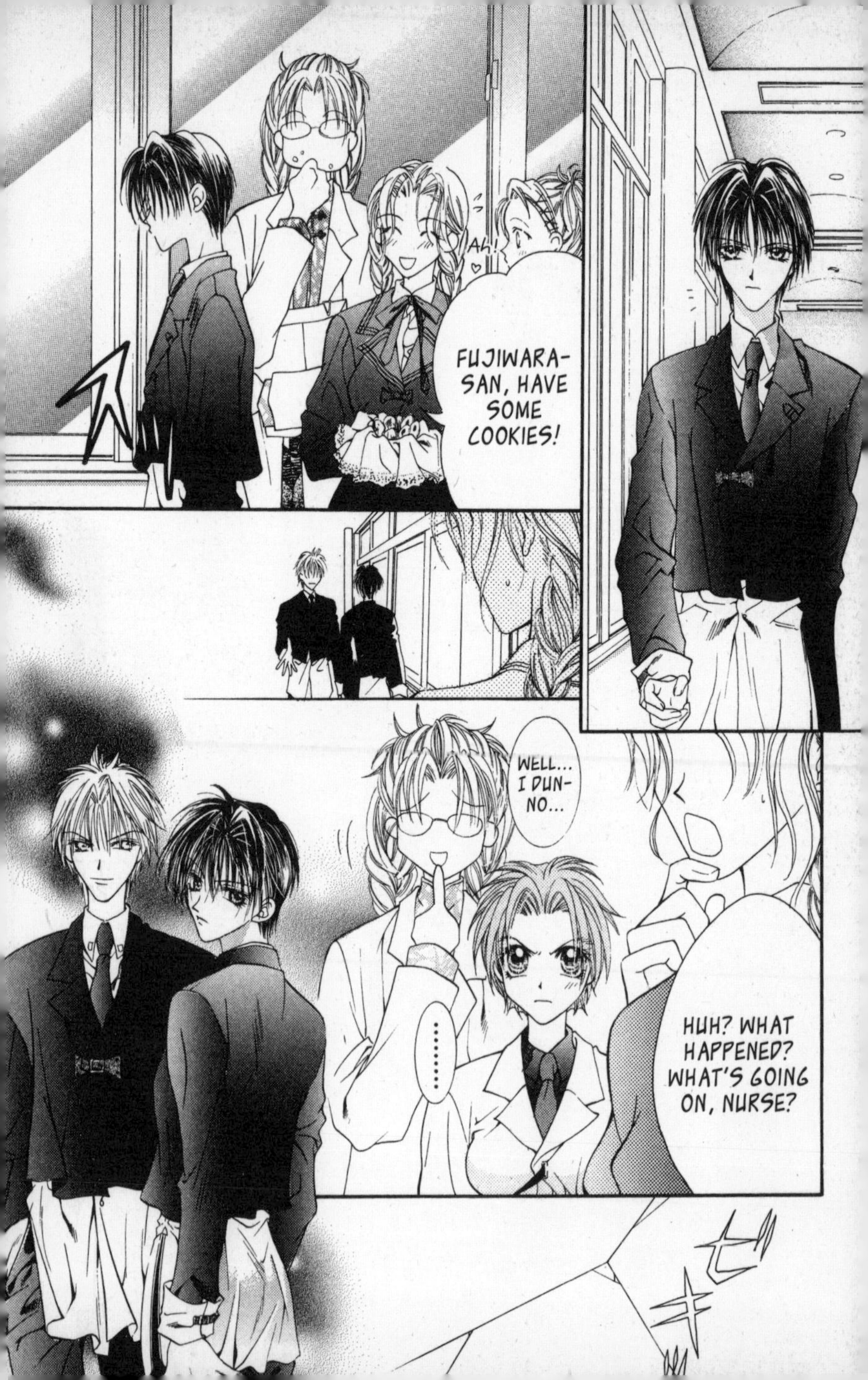

Ah!
FUJIWARA-SAN, HAVE SOME COOKIES!
HUH? WHAT HAPPENED? WHAT'S GOING ON, NURSE?
WELL... I DUNNO...
....

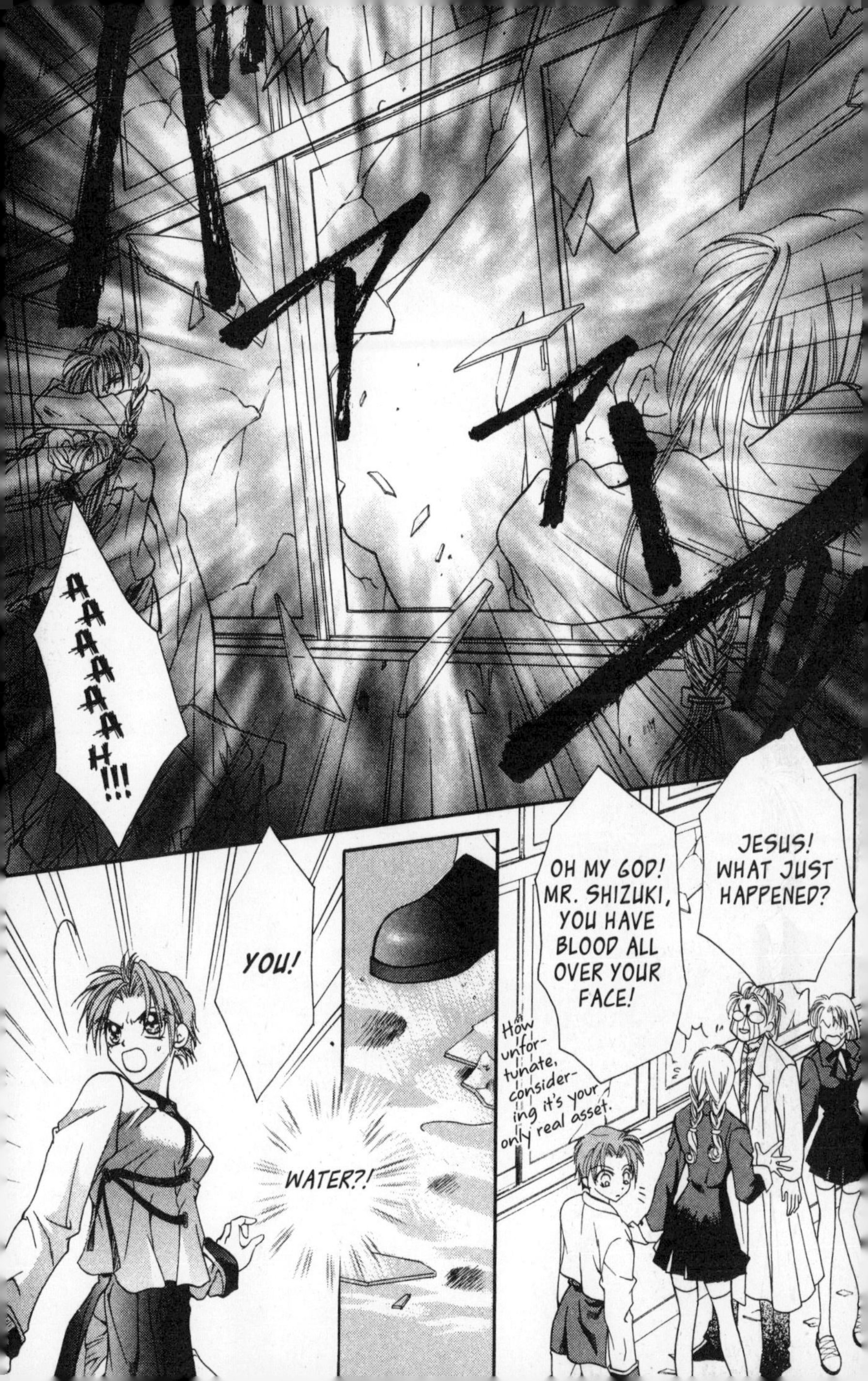
AAAAAAH!!!
JESUS! WHAT JUST HAPPENED?
OH MY GOD! MR. SHIZUKI, YOU HAVE BLOOD ALL OVER YOUR FACE!
How unfor-tunate, consider-ing it's your only real asset.
YOU!
WATER?!

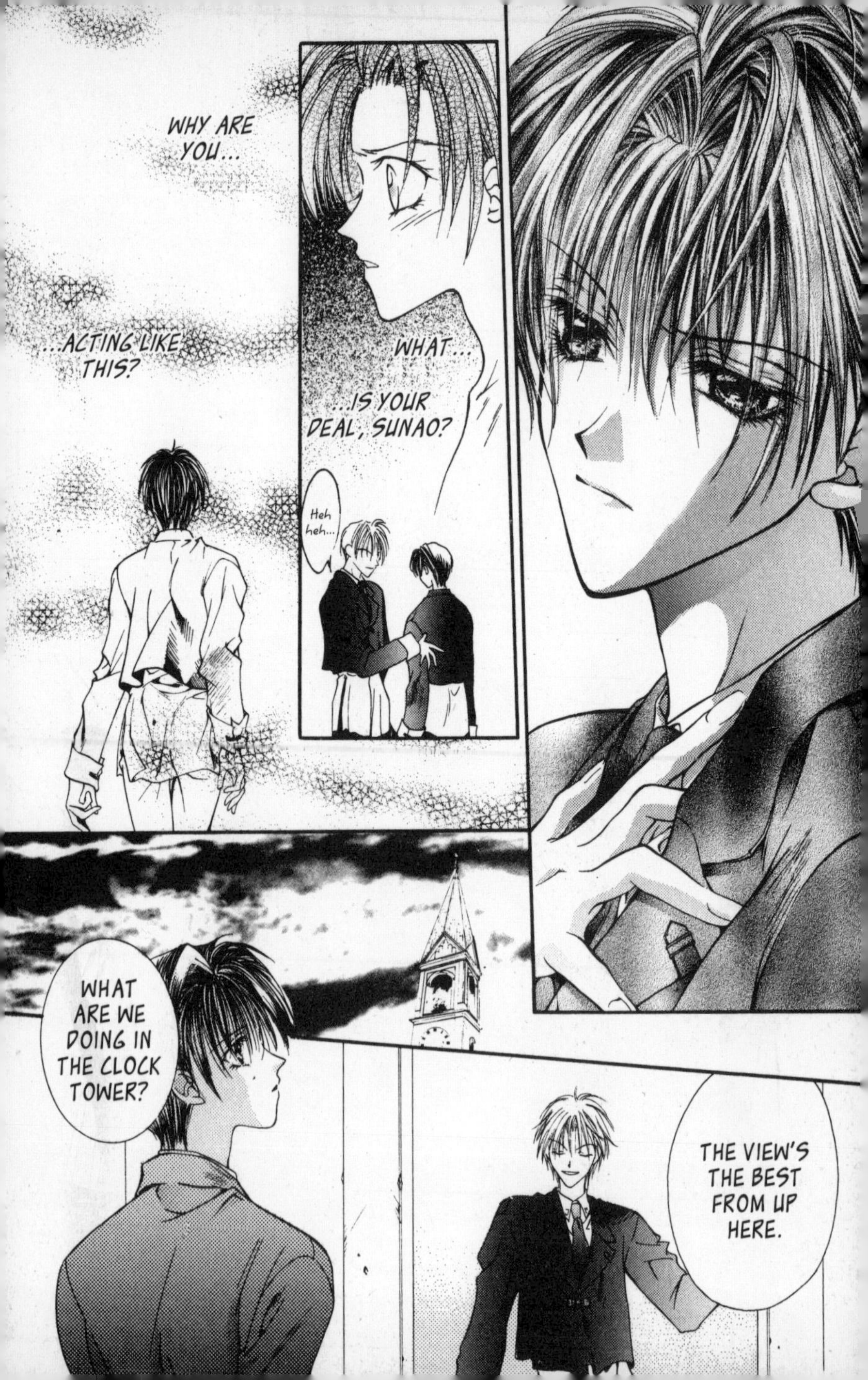
WHAT...
...IS YOUR DEAL, SUNAO?
Heh heh...
WHY ARE YOU...
...ACTING LIKE THIS?
WHAT ARE WE DOING IN THE CLOCK TOWER?
THE VIEW'S THE BEST FROM UP HERE.

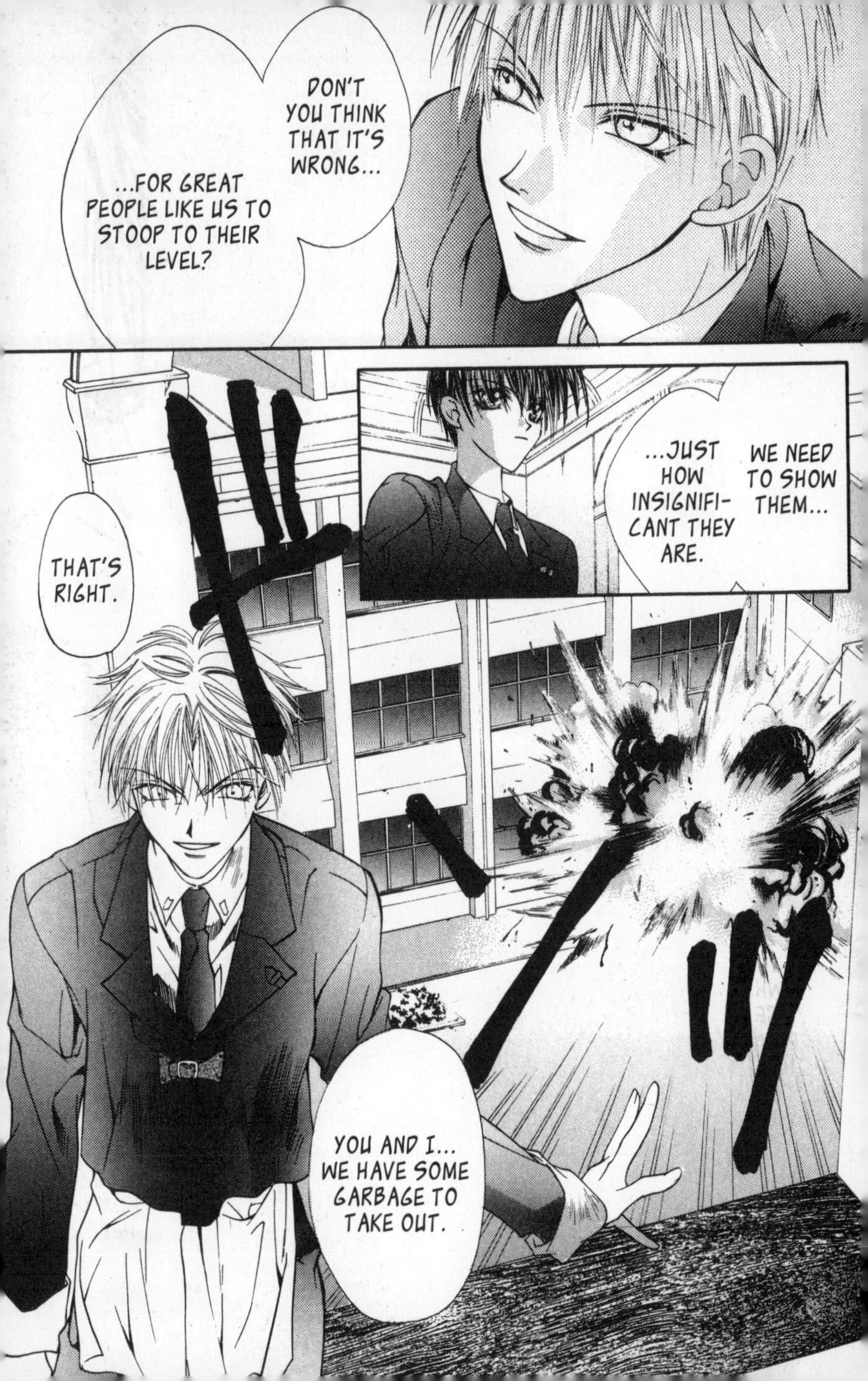
DON'T YOU THINK THAT IT'S WRONG...
...FOR GREAT PEOPLE LIKE US TO STOOP TO THEIR LEVEL?
WE NEED TO SHOW THEM...
...JUST HOW INSIGNIFI-CANT THEY ARE.
THAT'S RIGHT.
YOU AND I... WE HAVE SOME GARBAGE TO TAKE OUT.

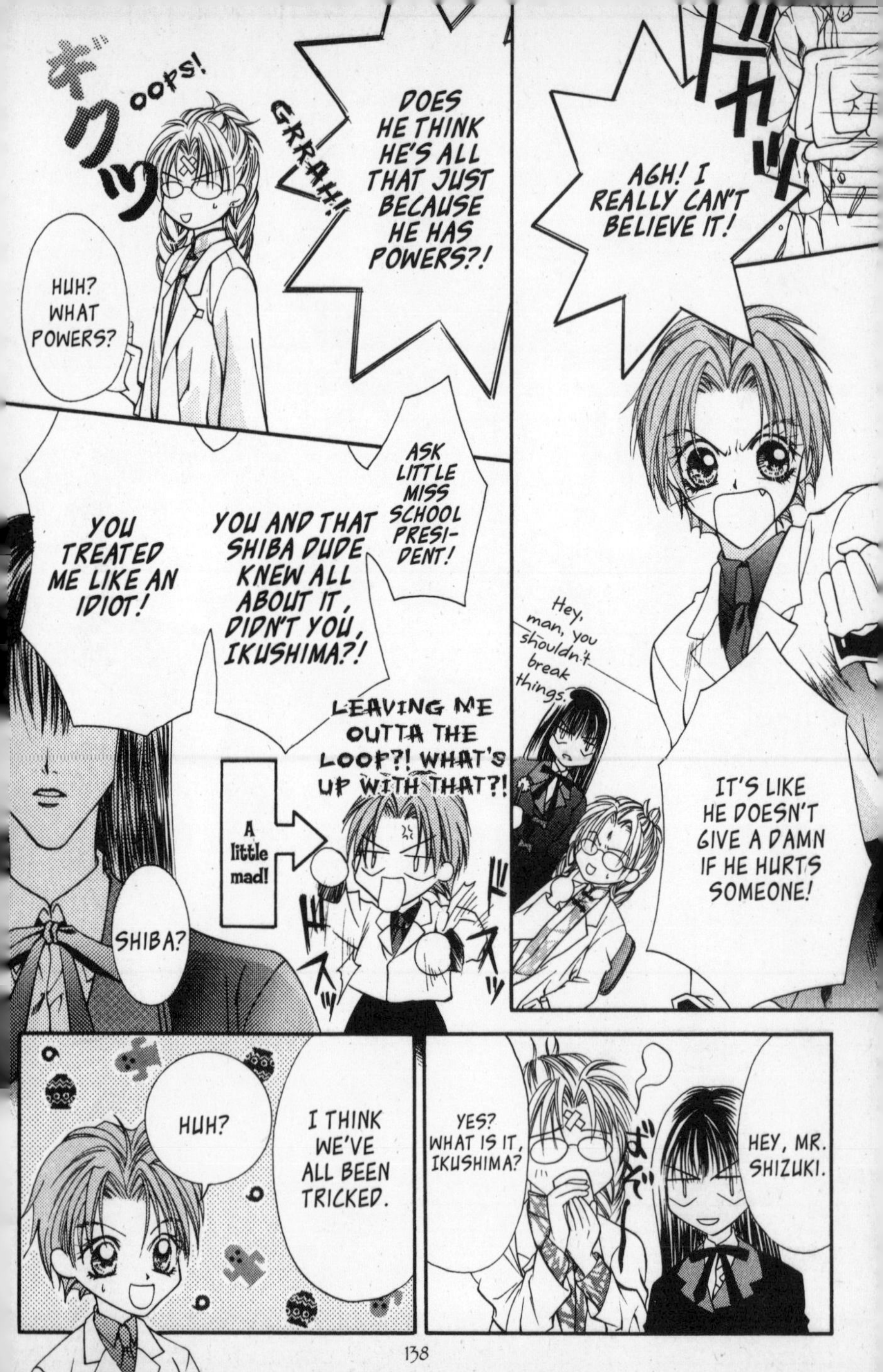
AGH! I REALLY CAN'T BELIEVE IT!
IT'S LIKE HE DOESN'T GIVE A DAMN IF HE HURTS SOMEONE!
Hey, man, you shouldn't break things.
DOES HE THINK HE'S ALL THAT JUST BECAUSE HE HAS POWERS?!
GRRAH!!
OOPS!
HUH? WHAT POWERS?
ASK LITTLE MISS SCHOOL PRESIDENT!
YOU AND THAT SHIBA DUDE KNEW ALL ABOUT IT, DIDN'T YOU, IKUSHIMA?!
YOU TREATED ME LIKE AN IDIOT!
LEAVING ME OUTTA THE LOOP?! WHAT'S UP WITH THAT?!
A little mad!
SHIBA?
HEY, MR. SHIZUKI.
YES? WHAT IS IT, IKUSHIMA?
I THINK WE'VE ALL BEEN TRICKED.
HUH?

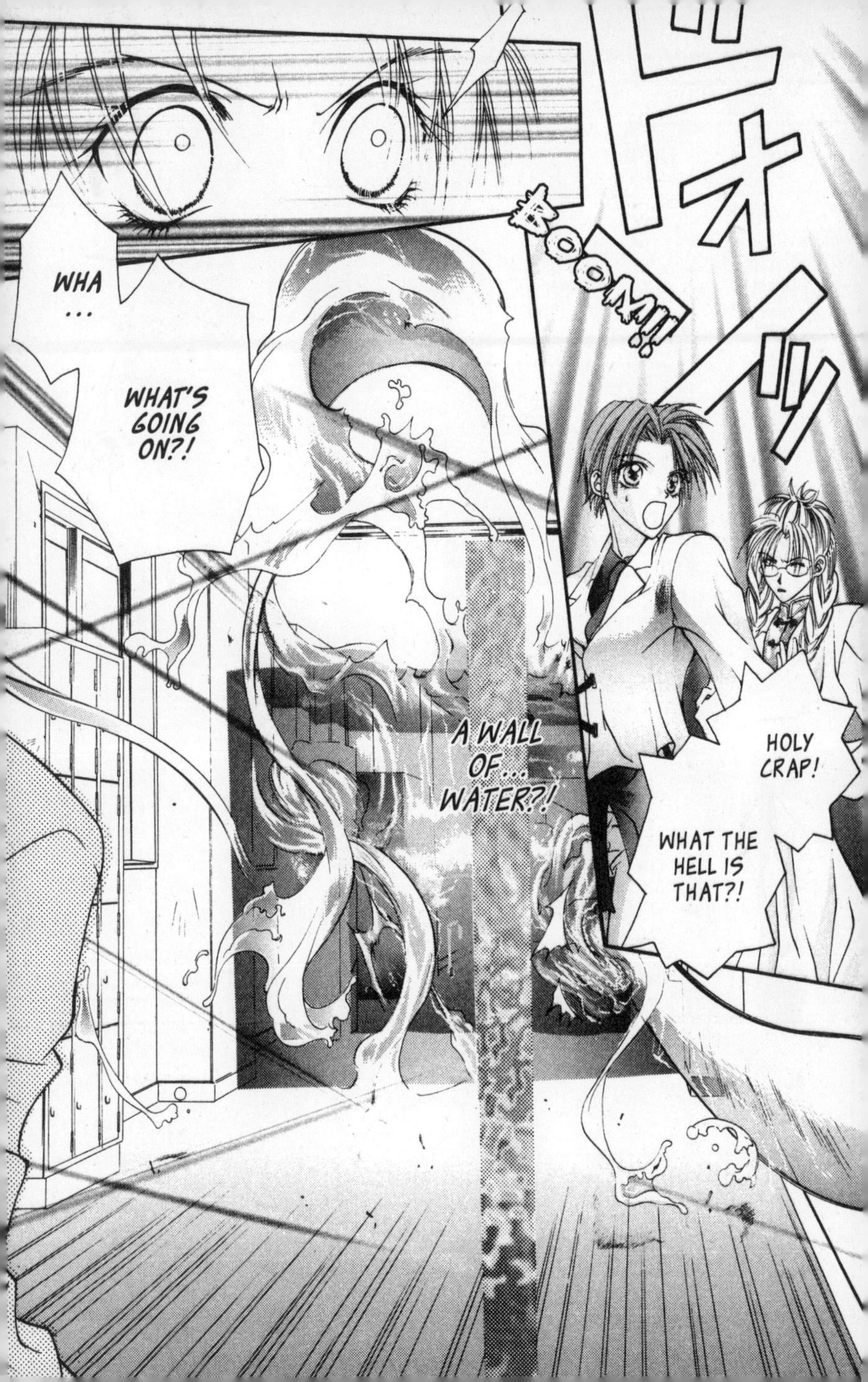
BOOM!!
HOLY CRAP!
WHAT THE HELL IS THAT?!
WHA ...
WHAT'S GOING ON?!
A WALL OF... WATER?!

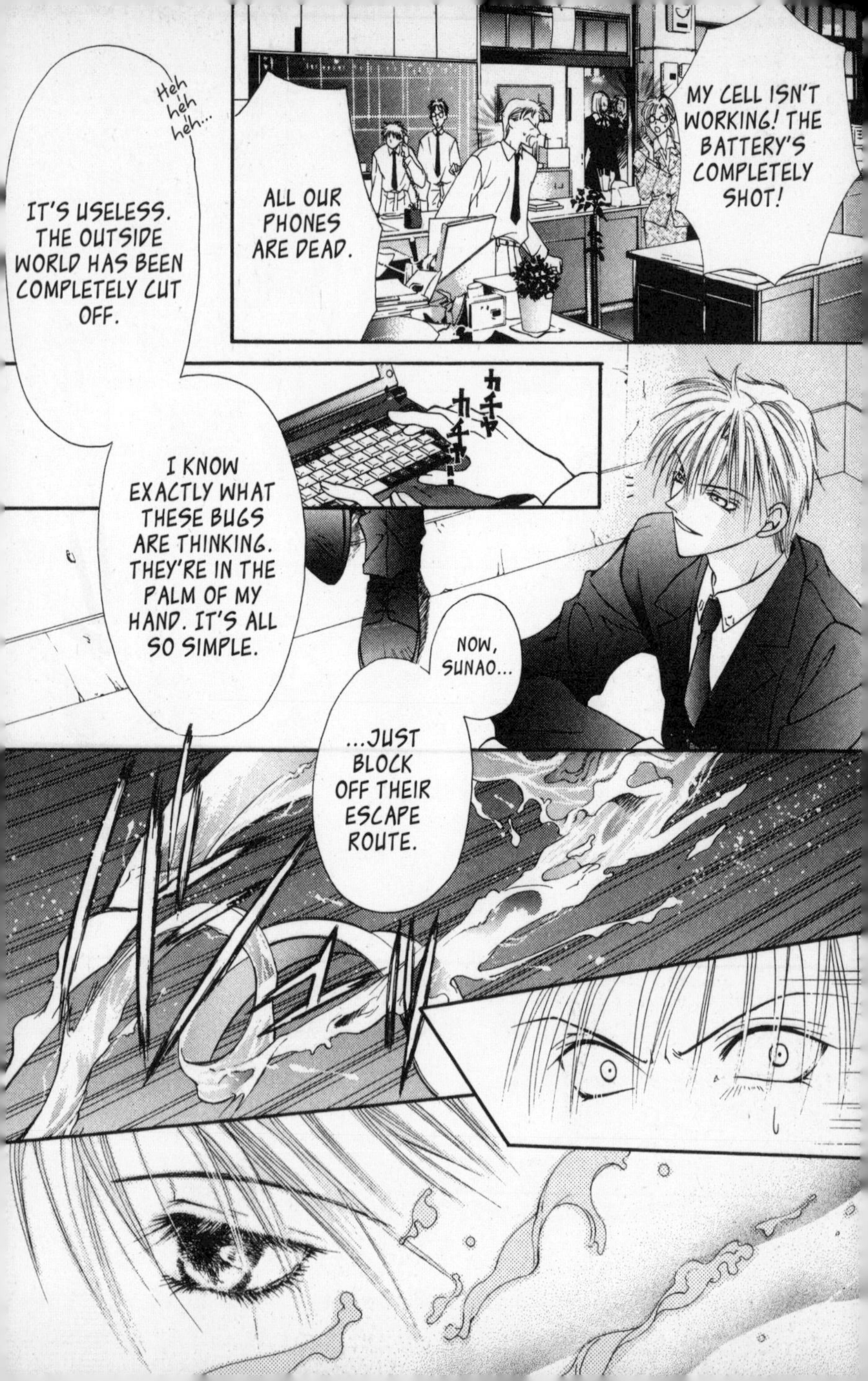
MY CELL ISN'T WORKING! THE BATTERY'S COMPLETELY SHOT!
ALL OUR PHONES ARE DEAD.
Heh heh heh...
IT'S USELESS. THE OUTSIDE WORLD HAS BEEN COMPLETELY CUT OFF.
カチャ
カチャ
I KNOW EXACTLY WHAT THESE BUGS ARE THINKING. THEY'RE IN THE PALM OF MY HAND. IT'S ALL SO SIMPLE.
NOW, SUNAO...
...JUST BLOCK OFF THEIR ESCAPE ROUTE.

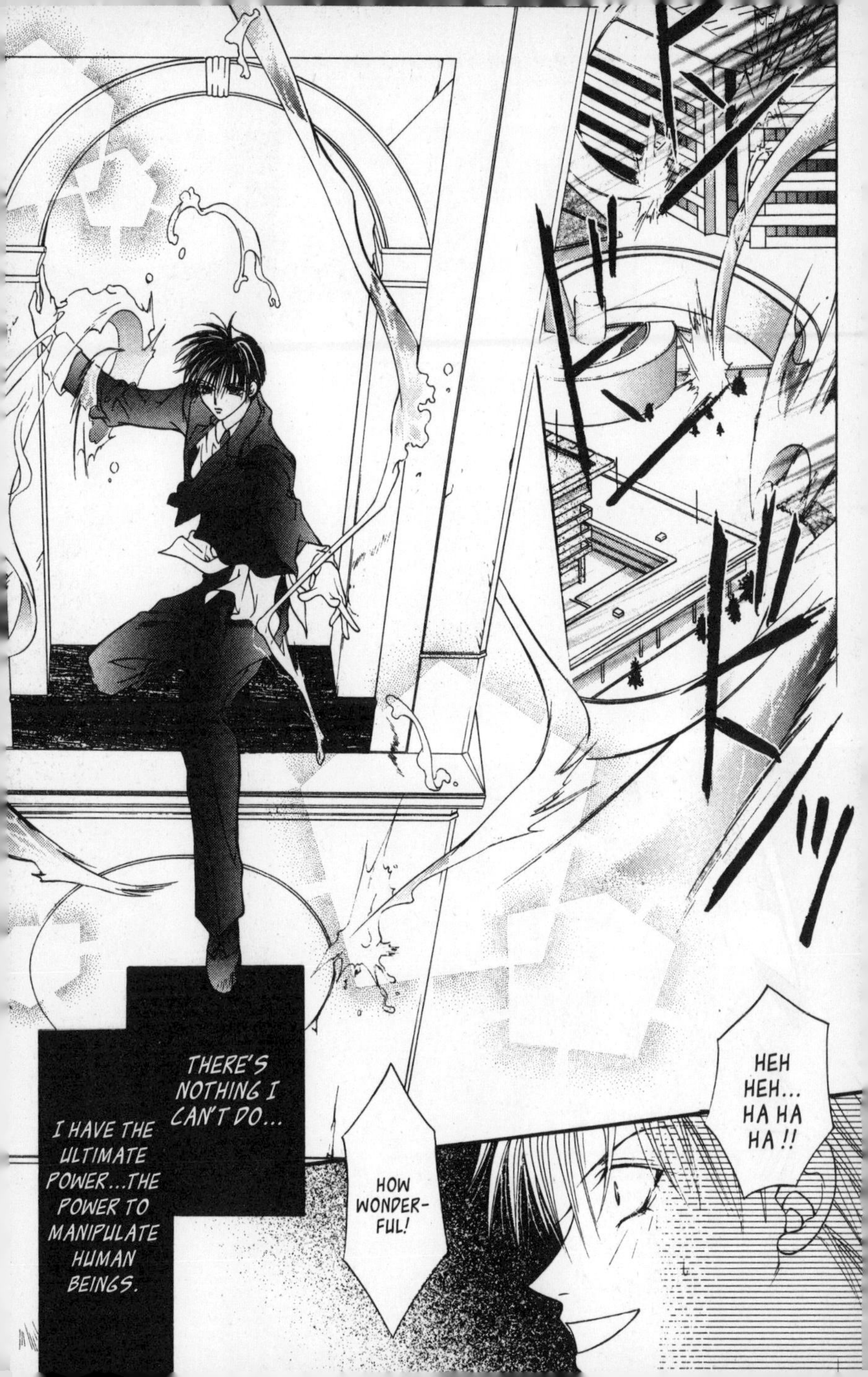
HEH HEH... HA HA HA!!
HOW WONDER-FUL!
THERE'S NOTHING I CAN'T DO...
I HAVE THE ULTIMATE POWER...THE POWER TO MANIPULATE HUMAN BEINGS.

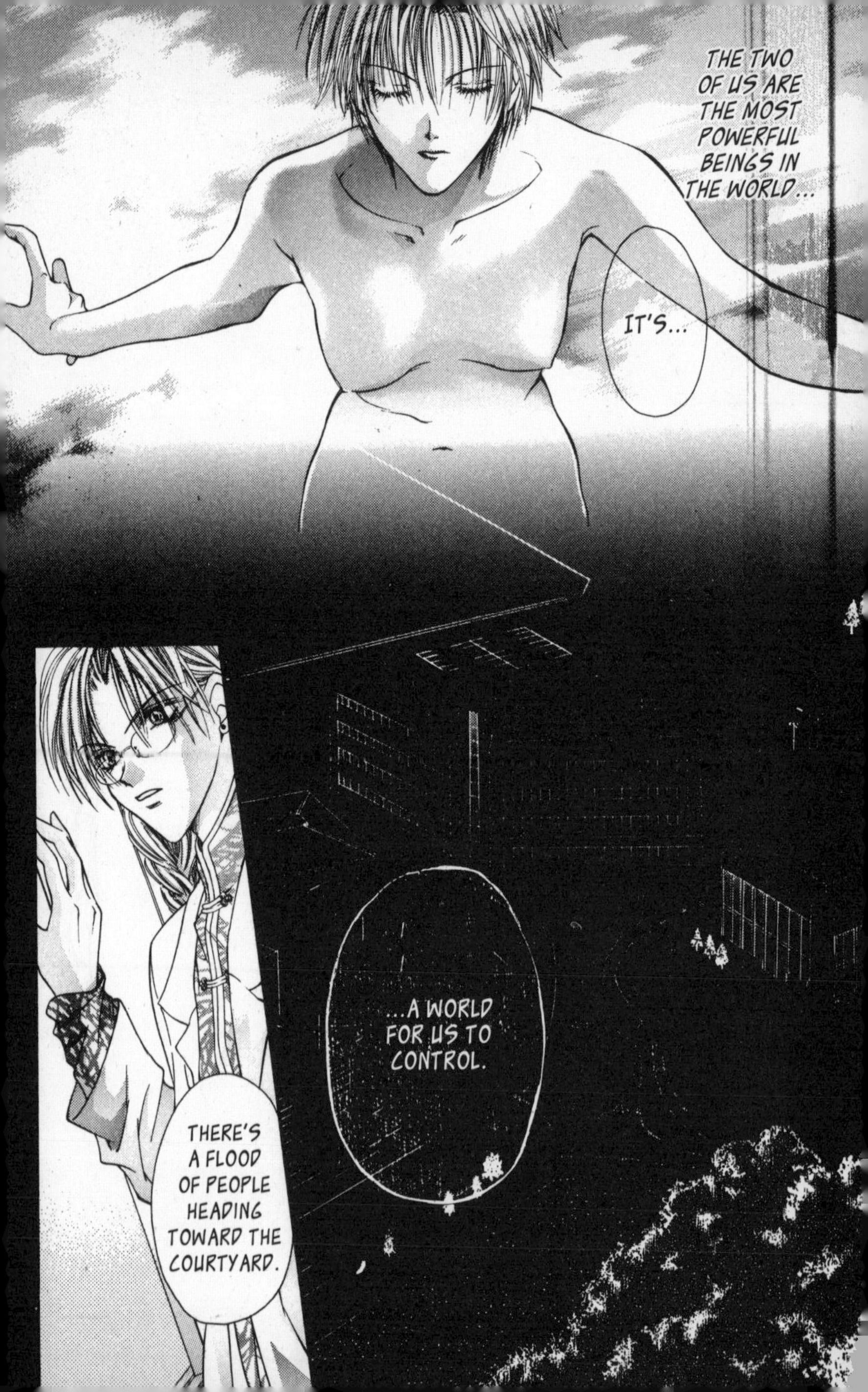
THE TWO OF US ARE THE MOST POWERFUL BEINGS IN THE WORLD...
IT'S...
...A WORLD FOR US TO CONTROL.
THERE'S A FLOOD OF PEOPLE HEADING TOWARD THE COURTYARD.

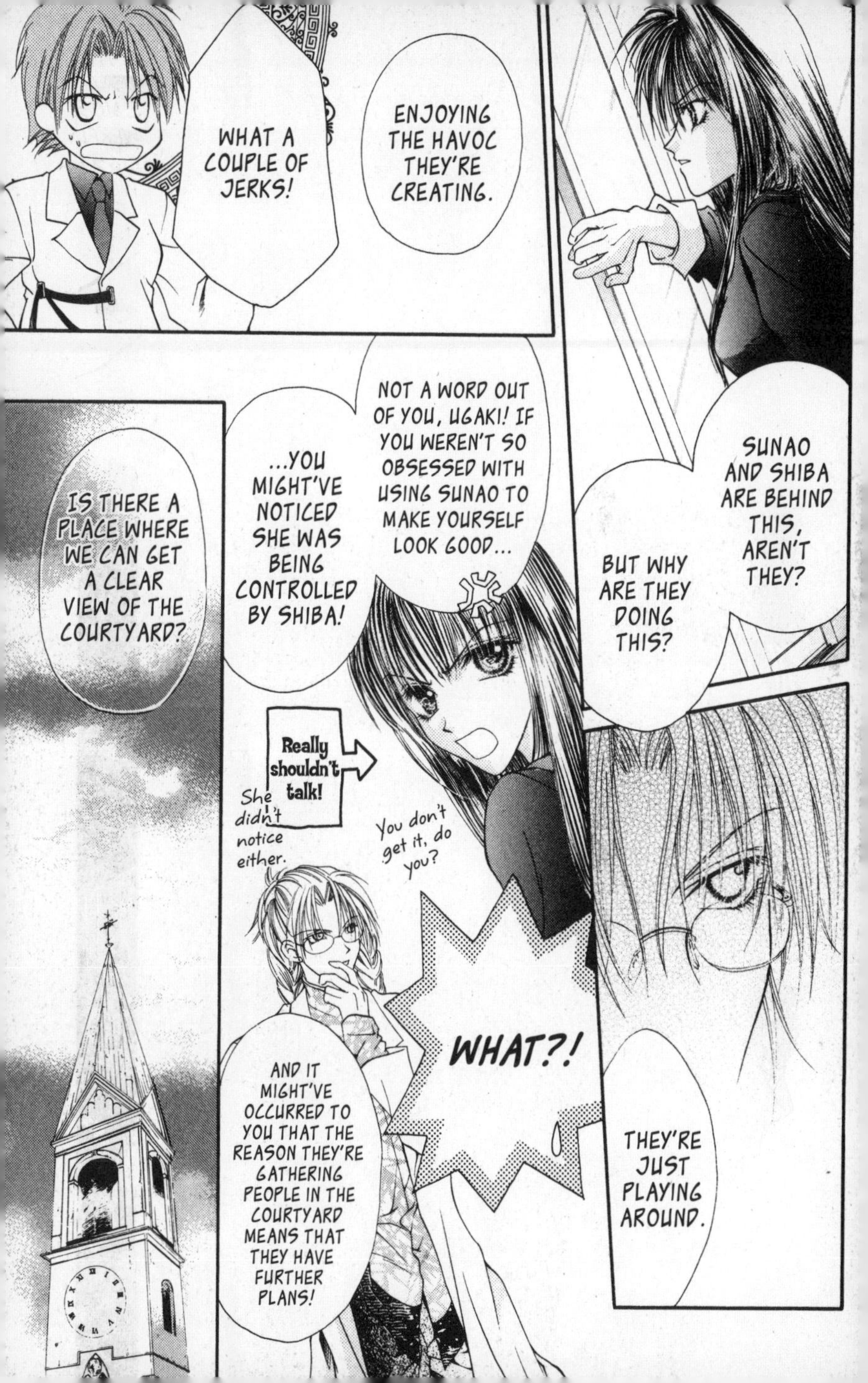
SUNAO AND SHIBA ARE BEHIND THIS, AREN'T THEY?
BUT WHY ARE THEY DOING THIS?
THEY'RE JUST PLAYING AROUND.
ENJOYING THE HAVOC THEY'RE CREATING.
WHAT A COUPLE OF JERKS!
NOT A WORD OUT OF YOU, UGAKI! IF YOU WEREN'T SO OBSESSED WITH USING SUNAO TO MAKE YOURSELF LOOK GOOD...
...YOU MIGHT'VE NOTICED SHE WAS BEING CONTROLLED BY SHIBA!
WHAT?!
AND IT MIGHT'VE OCCURRED TO YOU THAT THE REASON THEY'RE GATHERING PEOPLE IN THE COURTYARD MEANS THAT THEY HAVE FURTHER PLANS!
You don't get it, do you?
Really shouldn't talk!
She didn't notice either.
IS THERE A PLACE WHERE WE CAN GET A CLEAR VIEW OF THE COURTYARD?

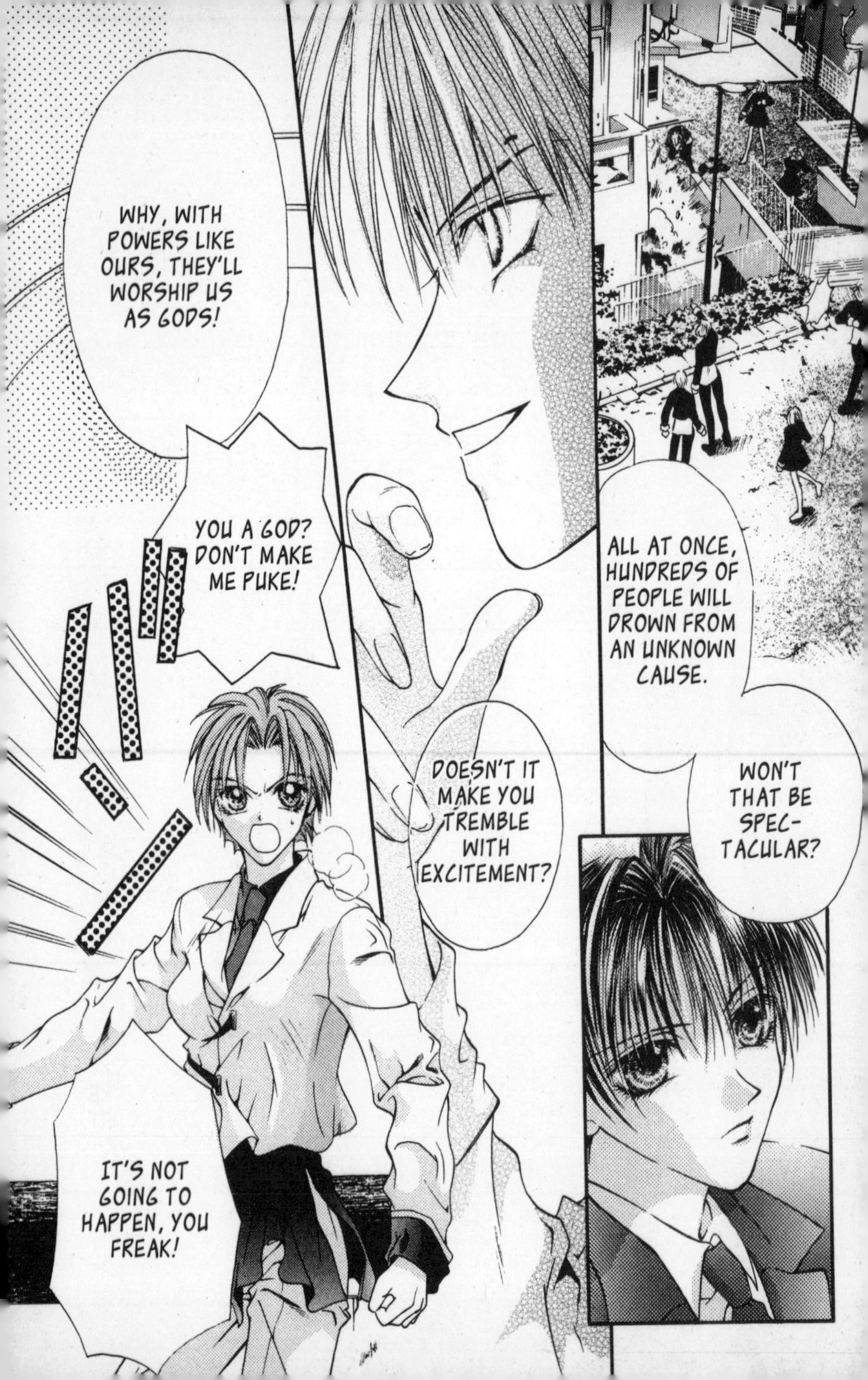
ALL AT ONCE, HUNDREDS OF PEOPLE WILL DROWN FROM AN UNKNOWN CAUSE.
WON'T THAT BE SPEC-TACULAR?
DOESN'T IT MAKE YOU TREMBLE WITH EXCITEMENT?
WHY, WITH POWERS LIKE OURS, THEY'LL WORSHIP US AS GODS!
YOU A GOD? DON'T MAKE ME PUKE!
IT'S NOT GOING TO HAPPEN, YOU FREAK!

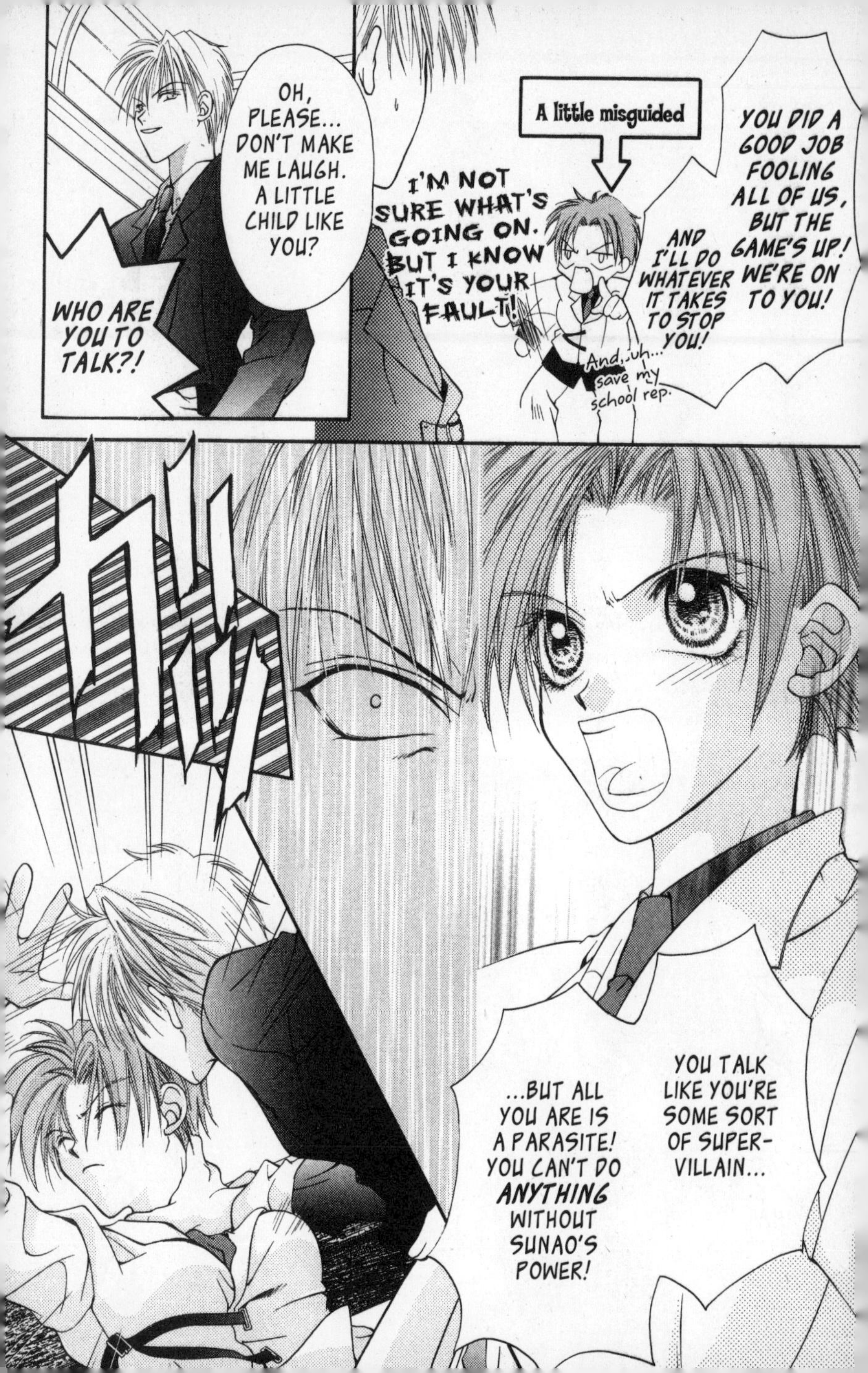
A little misguided
YOU DID A GOOD JOB FOOLING ALL OF US, BUT THE GAME'S UP! WE'RE ON TO YOU!
AND I'LL DO WHATEVER IT TAKES TO STOP YOU!
And, uh... save my school rep.
I'M NOT SURE WHAT'S GOING ON. BUT I KNOW IT'S YOUR FAULT!
OH, PLEASE... DON'T MAKE ME LAUGH. A LITTLE CHILD LIKE YOU?
WHO ARE YOU TO TALK?!
YOU TALK LIKE YOU'RE SOME SORT OF SUPER-VILLAIN...
...BUT ALL YOU ARE IS A PARASITE! YOU CAN'T DO ANYTHING WITHOUT SUNAO'S POWER!

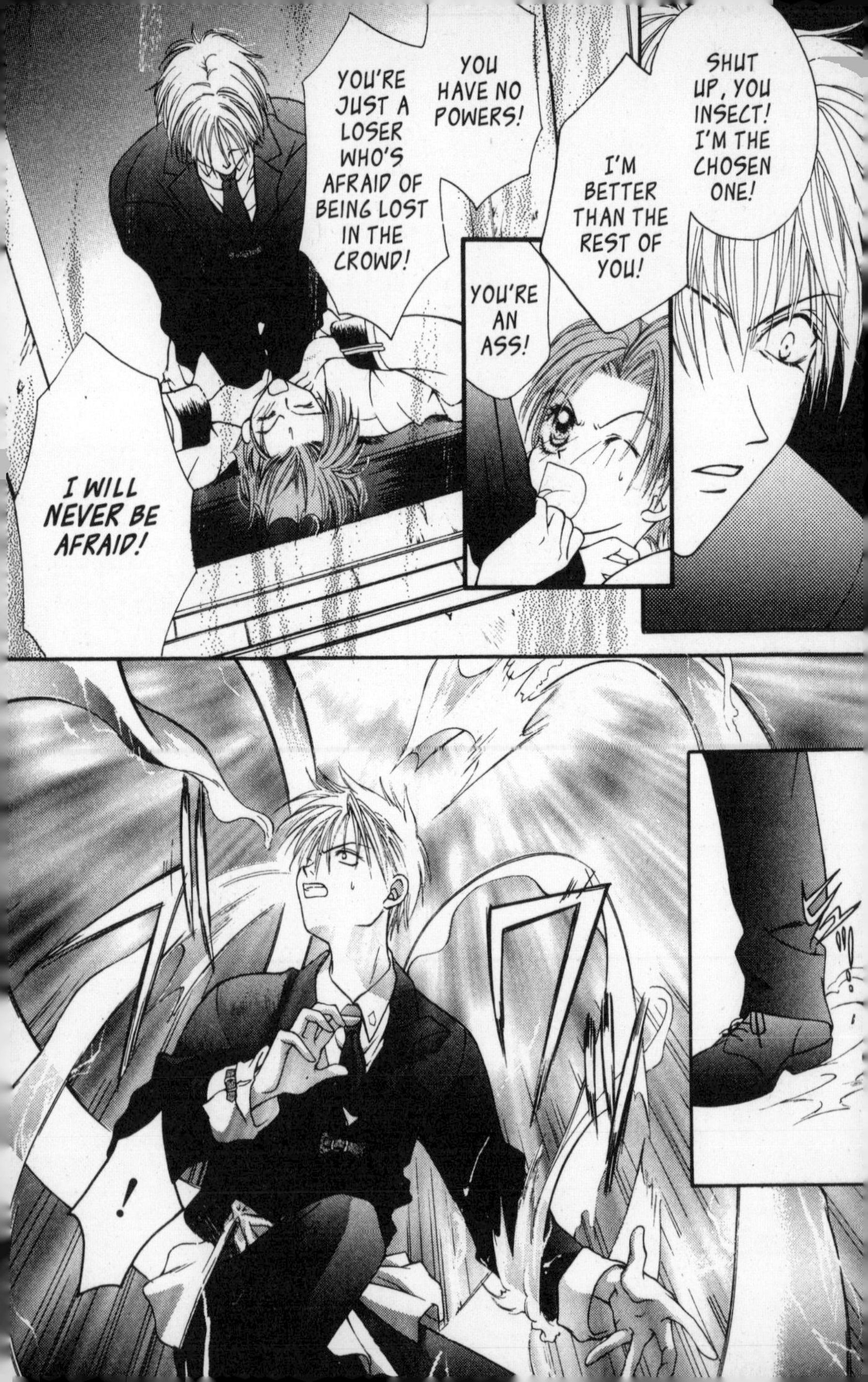

SHUT UP, YOU INSECT! I'M THE CHOSEN ONE!
I'M BETTER THAN THE REST OF YOU!
YOU'RE AN ASS!
YOU HAVE NO POWERS!
YOU'RE JUST A LOSER WHO'S AFRAID OF BEING LOST IN THE CROWD!
I WILL NEVER BE AFRAID!
!

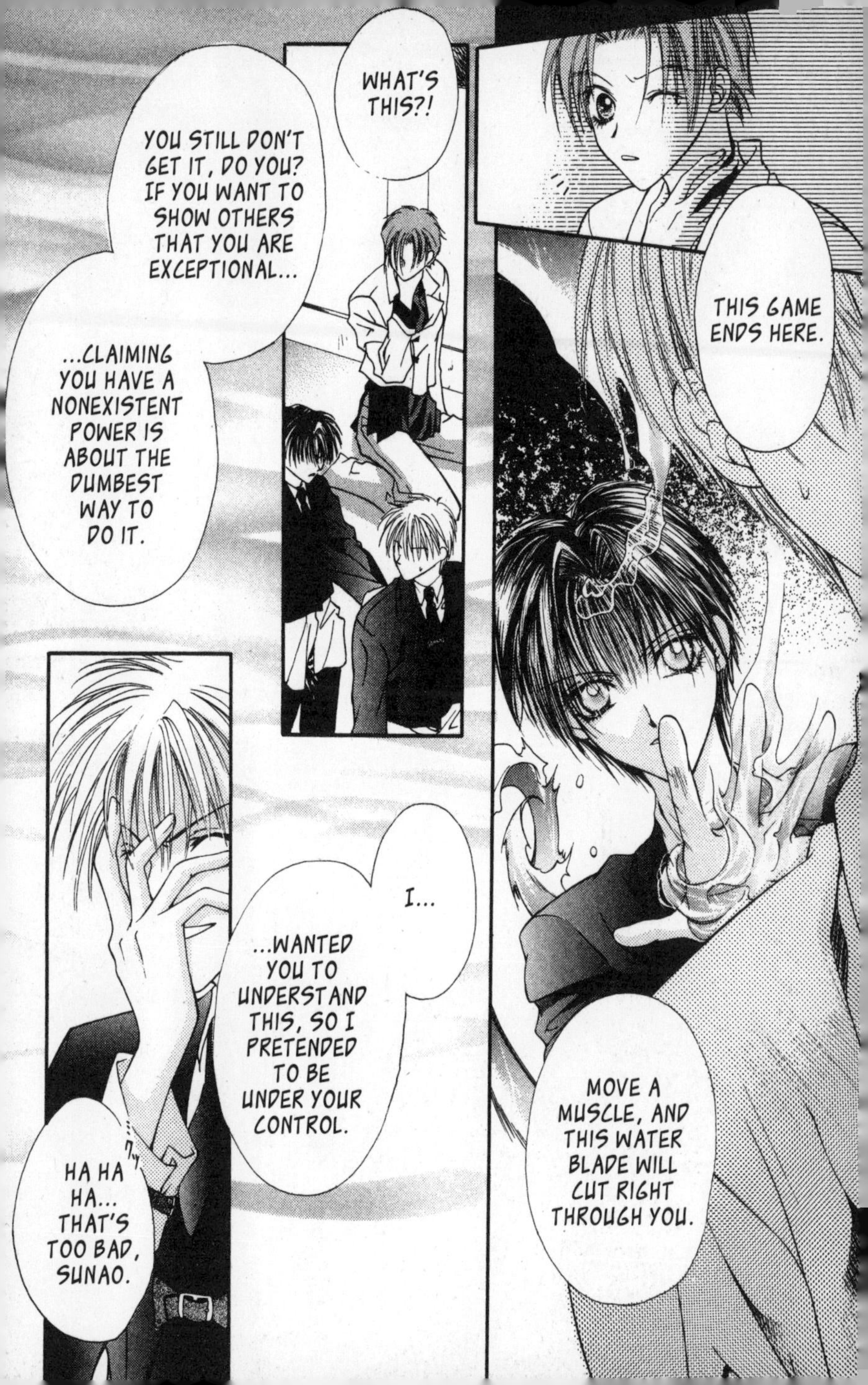
THIS GAME ENDS HERE.
MOVE A MUSCLE, AND THIS WATER BLADE WILL CUT RIGHT THROUGH YOU.
WHAT'S THIS?!
YOU STILL DON'T GET IT, DO YOU? IF YOU WANT TO SHOW OTHERS THAT YOU ARE EXCEPTIONAL...
...CLAIMING YOU HAVE A NONEXISTENT POWER IS ABOUT THE DUMBEST WAY TO DO IT.
I...
...WANTED YOU TO UNDERSTAND THIS, SO I PRETENDED TO BE UNDER YOUR CONTROL.
HA HA HA... THAT'S TOO BAD, SUNAO.

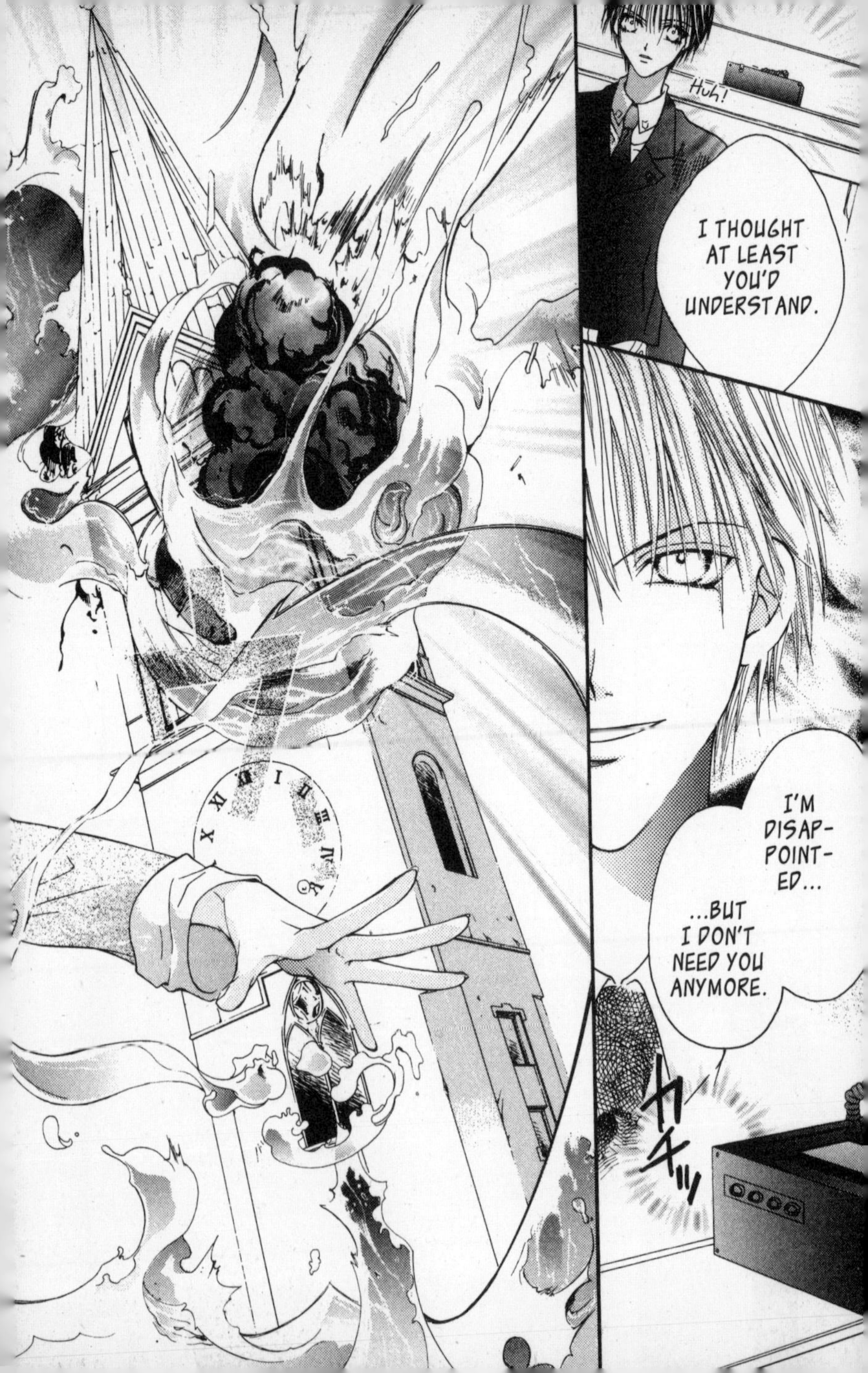
Huh!
I THOUGHT AT LEAST YOU'D UNDERSTAND.
I'M DISAPPOINTED...
...BUT I DON'T NEED YOU ANYMORE.
カチッ

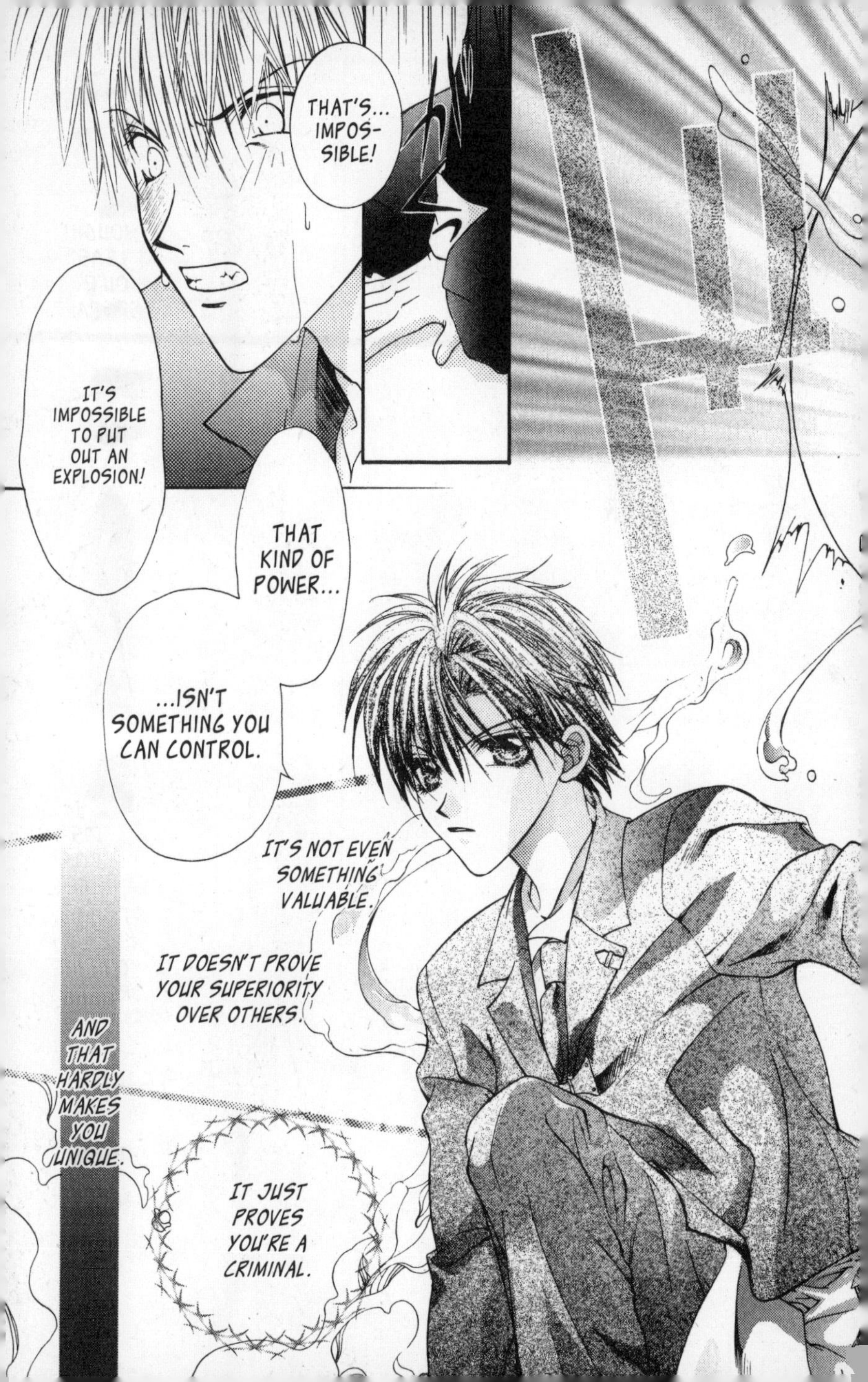
THAT'S... IMPOSSIBLE!
IT'S IMPOSSIBLE TO PUT OUT AN EXPLOSION!
THAT KIND OF POWER...
...ISN'T SOMETHING YOU CAN CONTROL.
IT'S NOT EVEN SOMETHING VALUABLE.
IT DOESN'T PROVE YOUR SUPERIORITY OVER OTHERS.
AND THAT HARDLY MAKES YOU UNIQUE.
IT JUST PROVES YOU'RE A CRIMINAL.

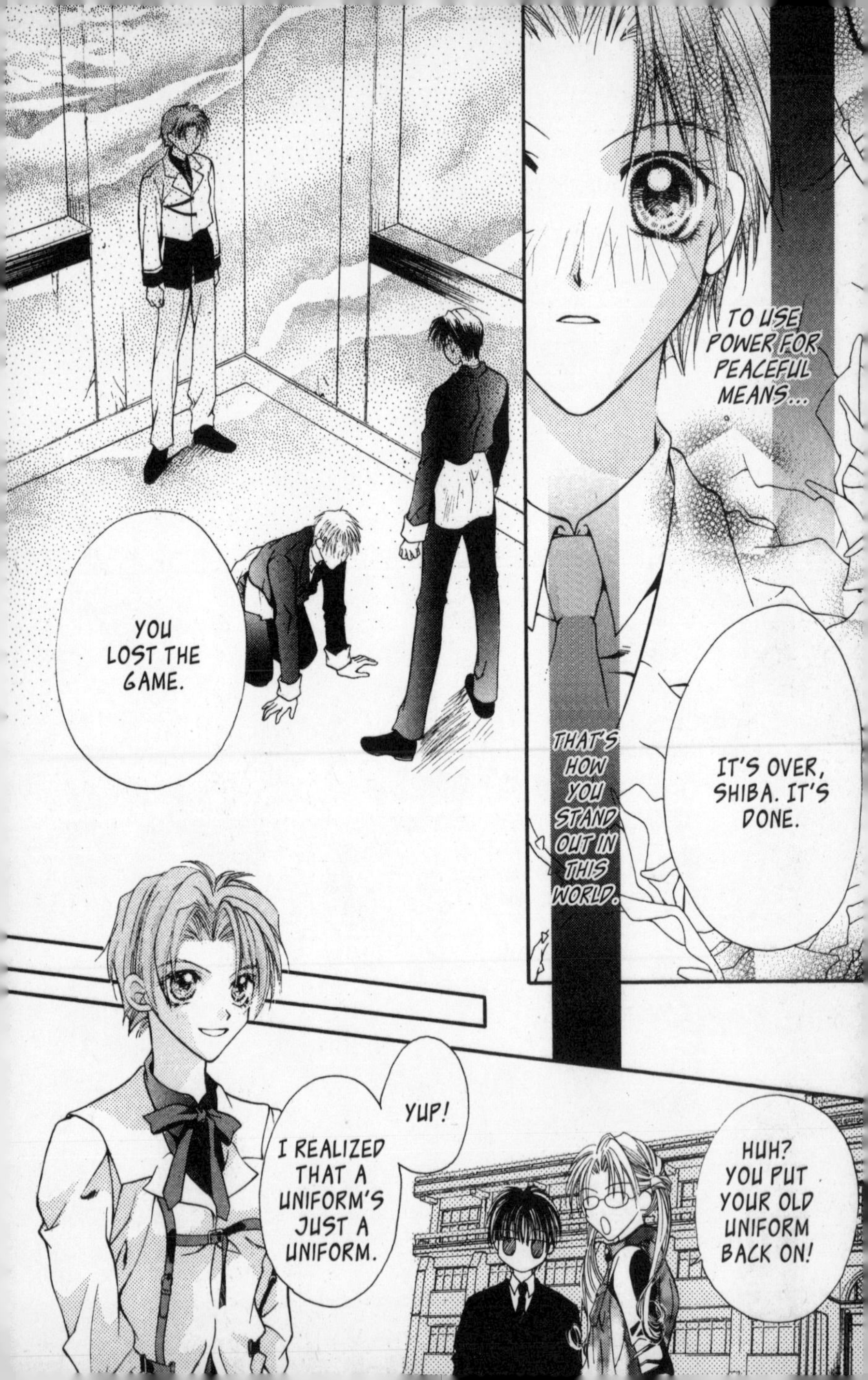

TO USE POWER FOR PEACEFUL MEANS...
THAT'S HOW YOU STAND OUT IN THIS WORLD.
IT'S OVER, SHIBA. IT'S DONE.
YOU LOST THE GAME.
HUH? YOU PUT YOUR OLD UNIFORM BACK ON!
YUP!
I REALIZED THAT A UNIFORM'S JUST A UNIFORM.

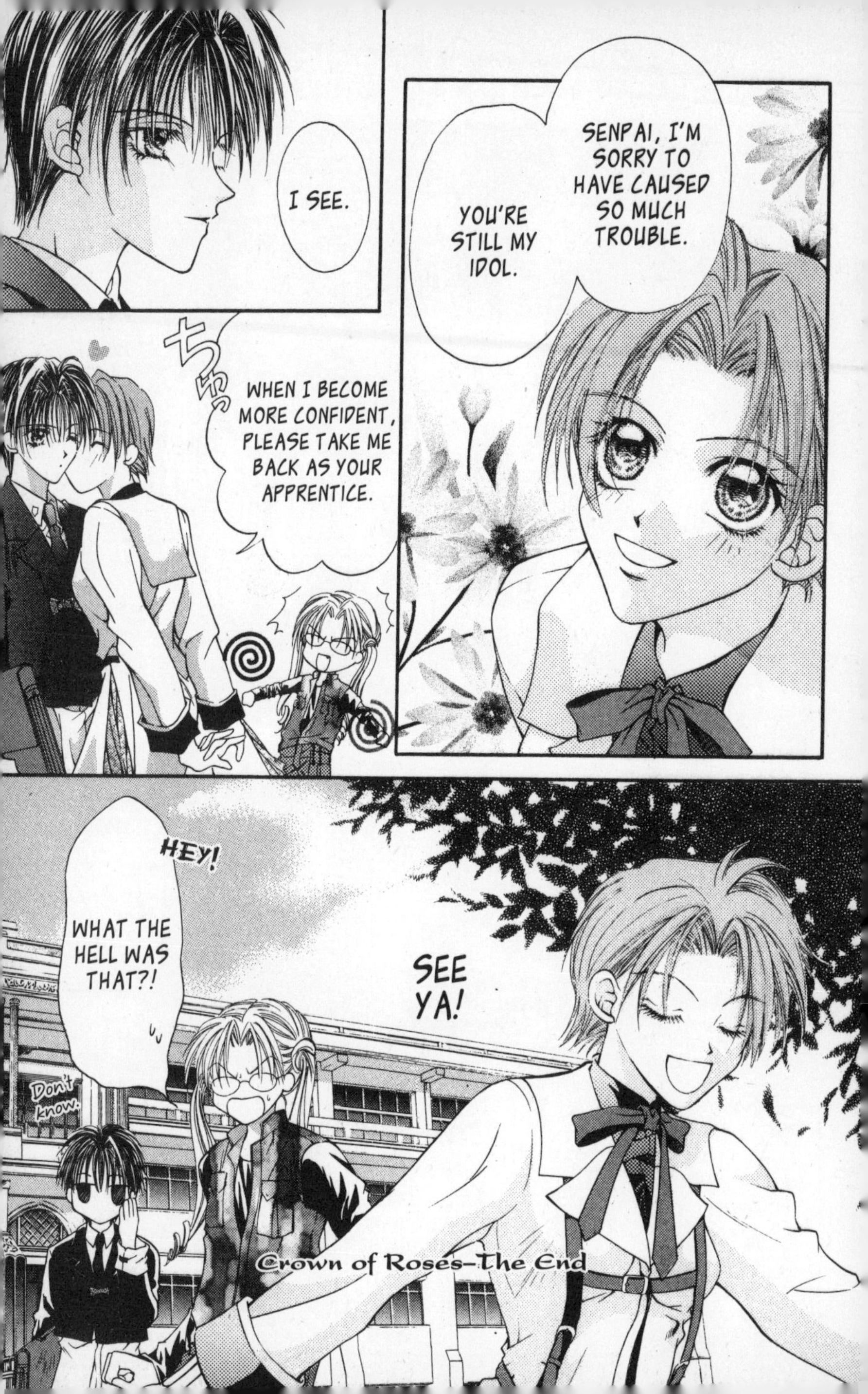
SENPAI, I'M SORRY TO HAVE CAUSED SO MUCH TROUBLE.
YOU'RE STILL MY IDOL.
I SEE.
ちゅっ
WHEN I BECOME MORE CONFIDENT, PLEASE TAKE ME BACK AS YOUR APPRENTICE.
SEE YA!
HEY!
WHAT THE HELL WAS THAT?!
Don't know.
Crown of Roses–The End

Love Machine

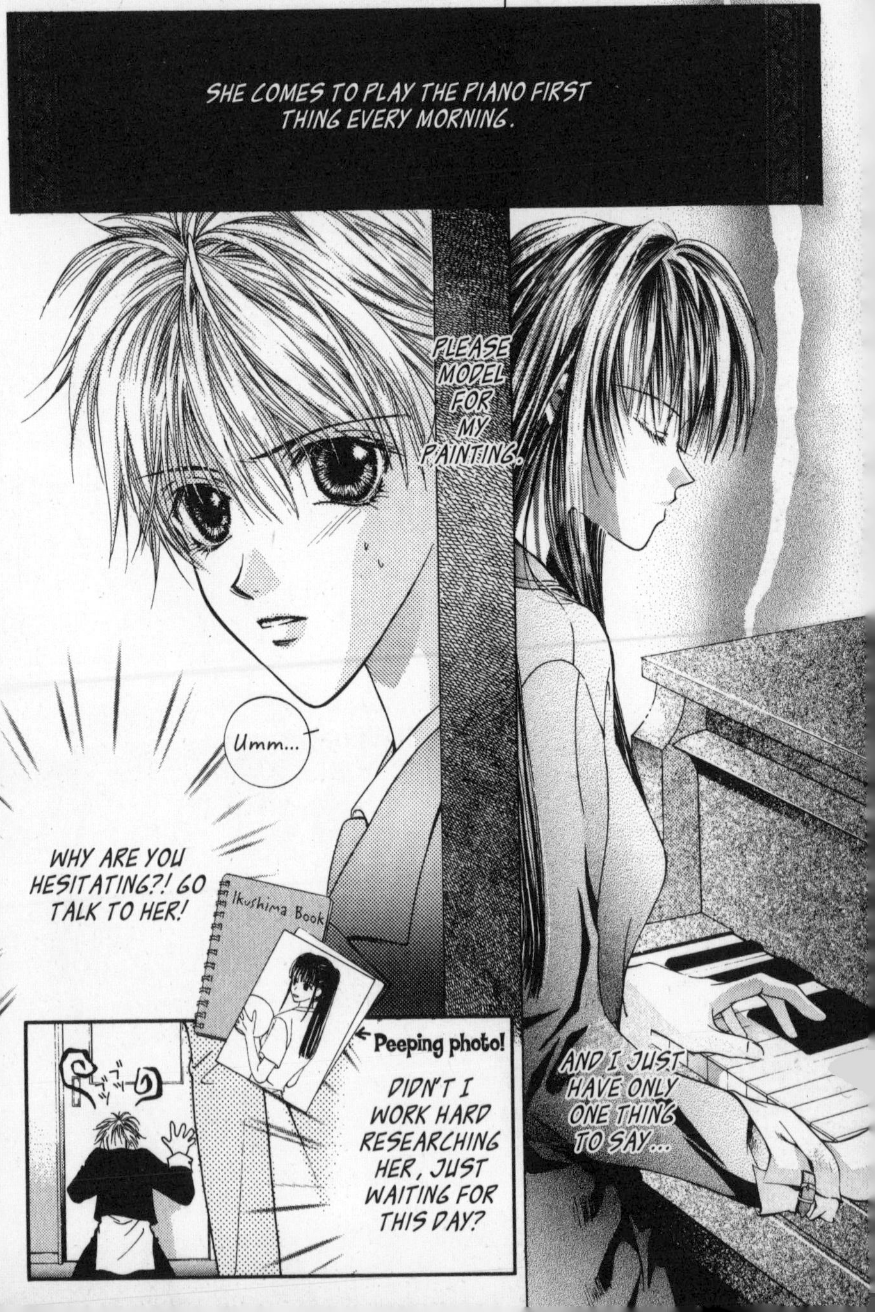
SHE COMES TO PLAY THE PIANO FIRST THING EVERY MORNING.
PLEASE MODEL FOR MY PAINTING.
Umm...
WHY ARE YOU HESITATING?! GO TALK TO HER!
Ikushima Book
Peeping photo!
AND I JUST HAVE ONLY ONE THING TO SAY...
DIDN'T I WORK HARD RESEARCHING HER, JUST WAITING FOR THIS DAY?

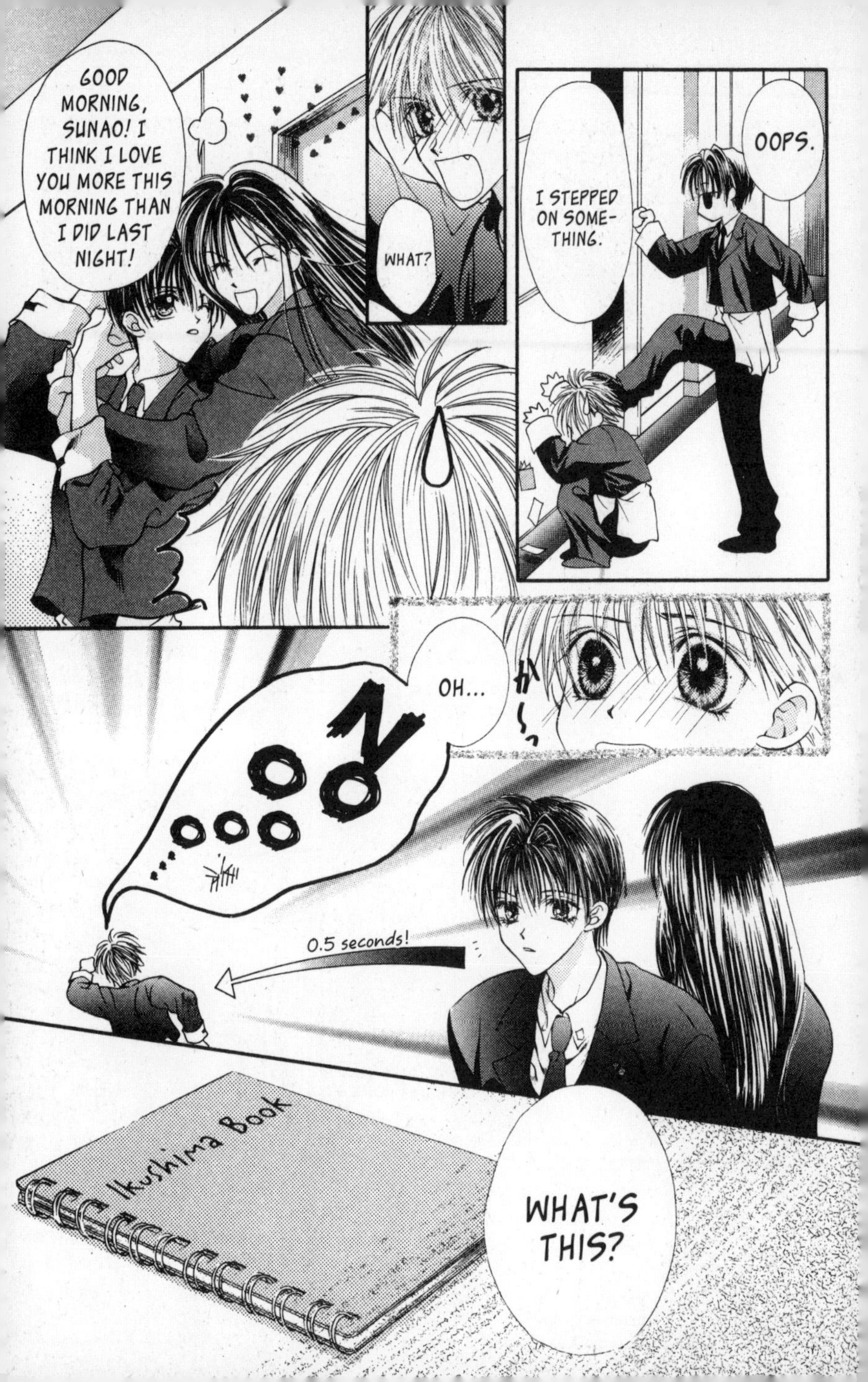
OOPS.
I STEPPED ON SOME-THING.
WHAT?
GOOD MORNING, SUNAO! I THINK I LOVE YOU MORE THIS MORNING THAN I DID LAST NIGHT!
OH...
NOOOOO...
0.5 seconds!
Ikushima Book
WHAT'S THIS?

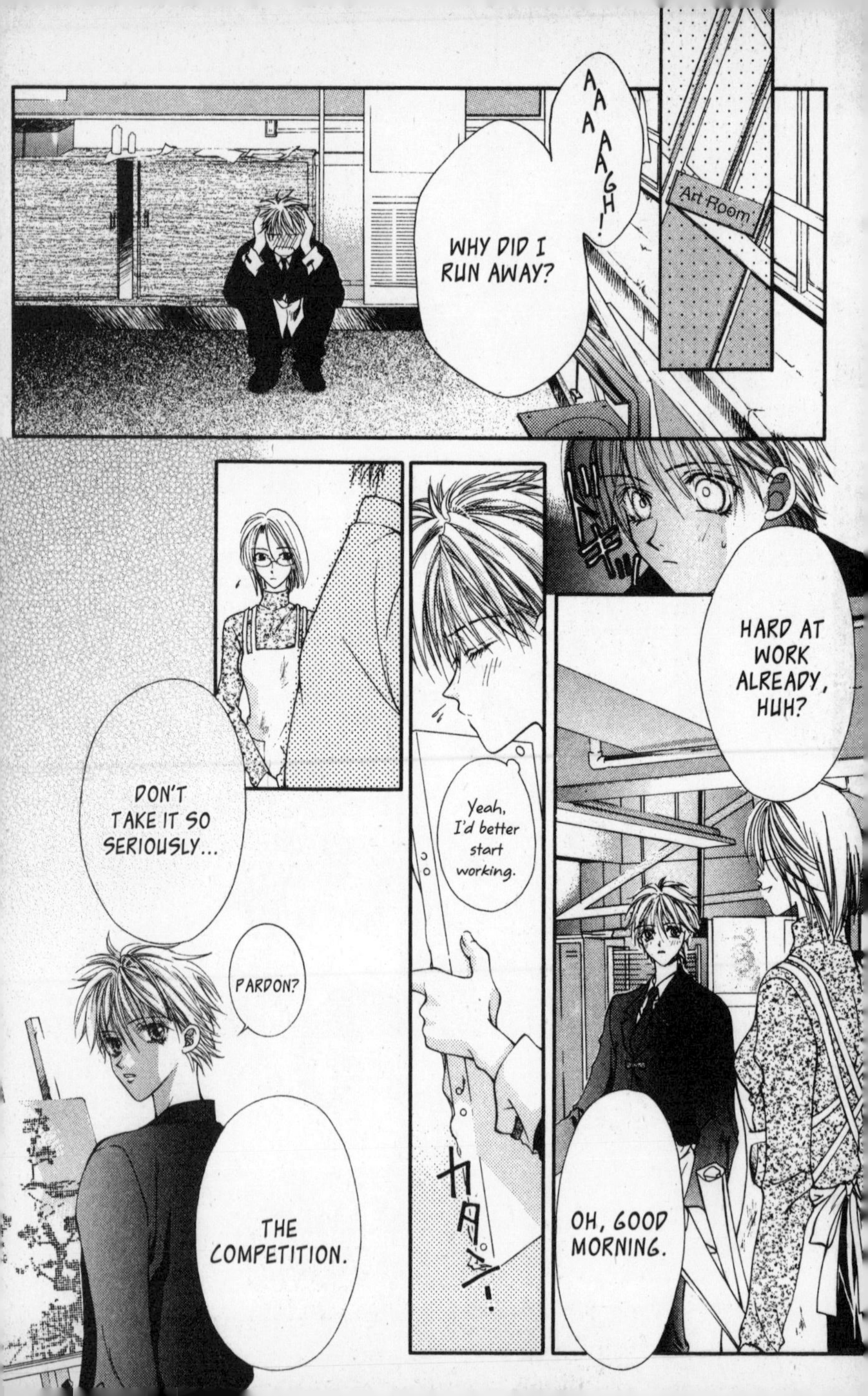
AAAAAGH!
'Art Room'
WHY DID I RUN AWAY?
HARD AT WORK ALREADY, HUH?
OH, GOOD MORNING.
Yeah, I'd better start working.
DON'T TAKE IT SO SERIOUSLY...
PARDON?
THE COMPETITION.

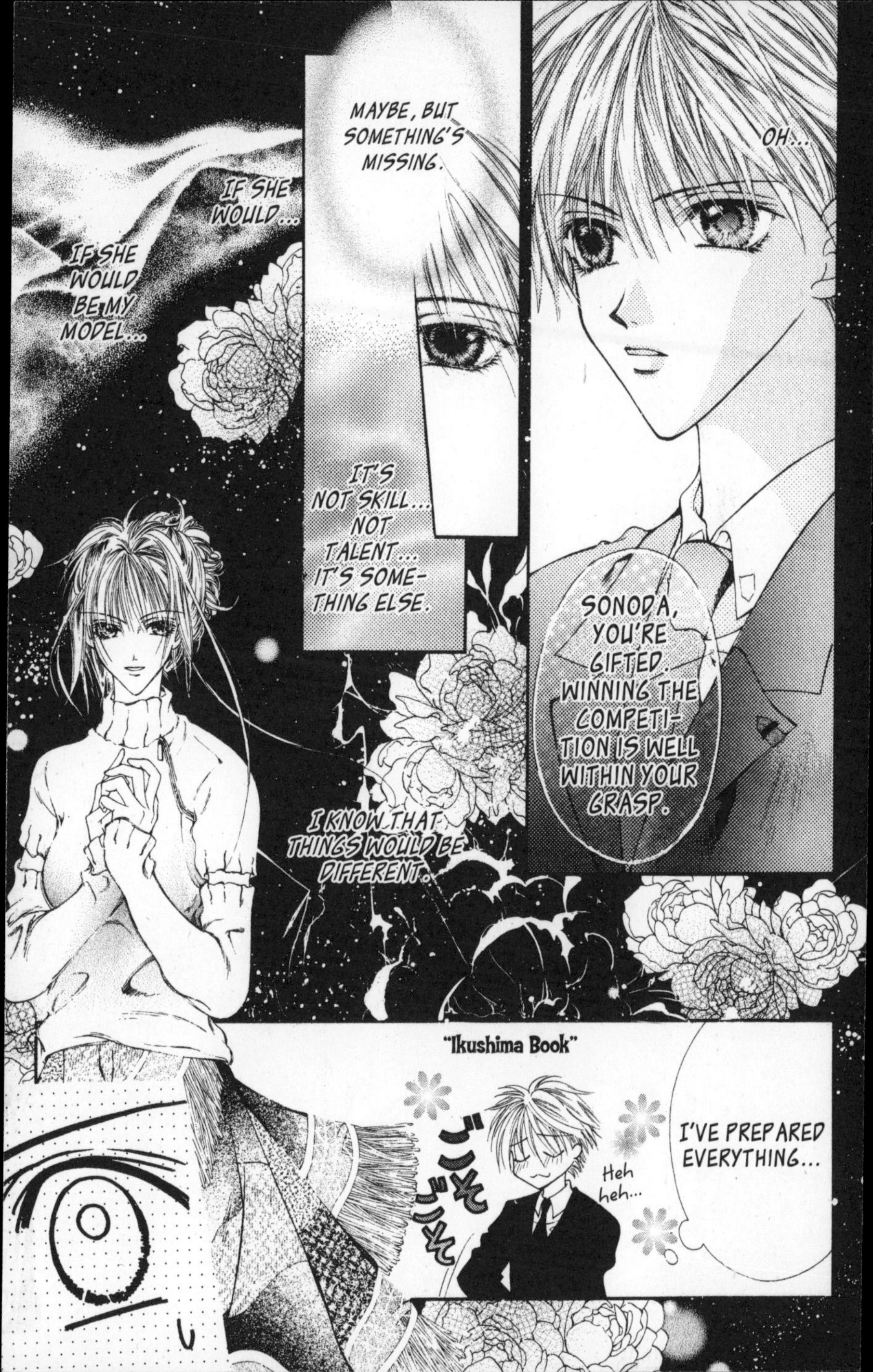
OH...
SONODA, YOU'RE GIFTED. WINNING THE COMPETITION IS WELL WITHIN YOUR GRASP.
MAYBE, BUT SOMETHING'S MISSING.
IT'S NOT SKILL... NOT TALENT... IT'S SOMETHING ELSE.
IF SHE WOULD...
IF SHE WOULD BE MY MODEL...
I KNOW THAT THINGS WOULD BE DIFFERENT.
"Ikushima Book"
I'VE PREPARED EVERYTHING...
Heh heh...

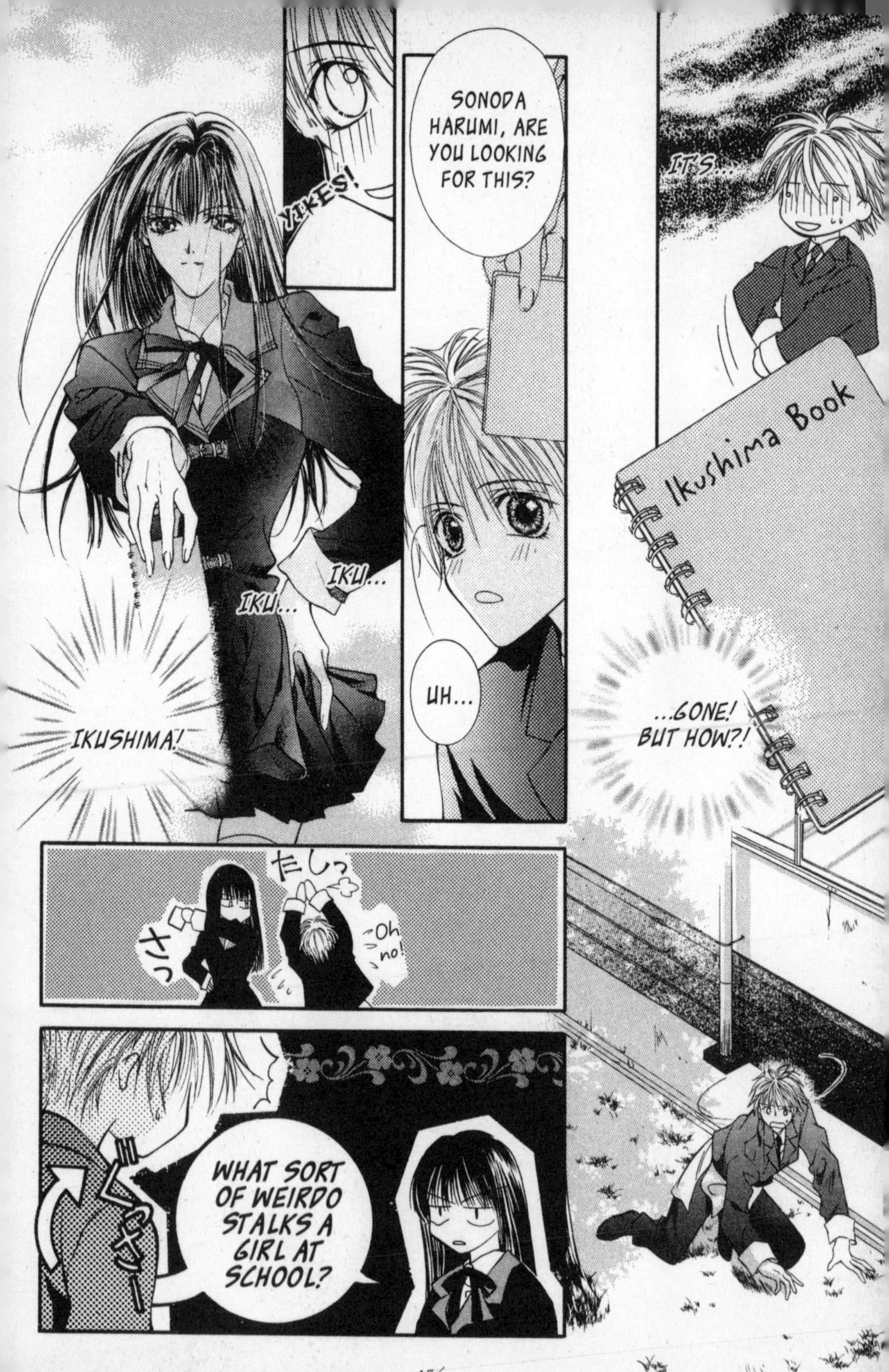
IT'S...
Ikushima Book
...GONE! BUT HOW?!
SONODA HARUMI, ARE YOU LOOKING FOR THIS?
UH...
YIKES!
IKU...
IKU...
IKUSHIMA!
たしっ
Oh no!
さっ
WHAT SORT OF WEIRDO STALKS A GIRL AT SCHOOL?

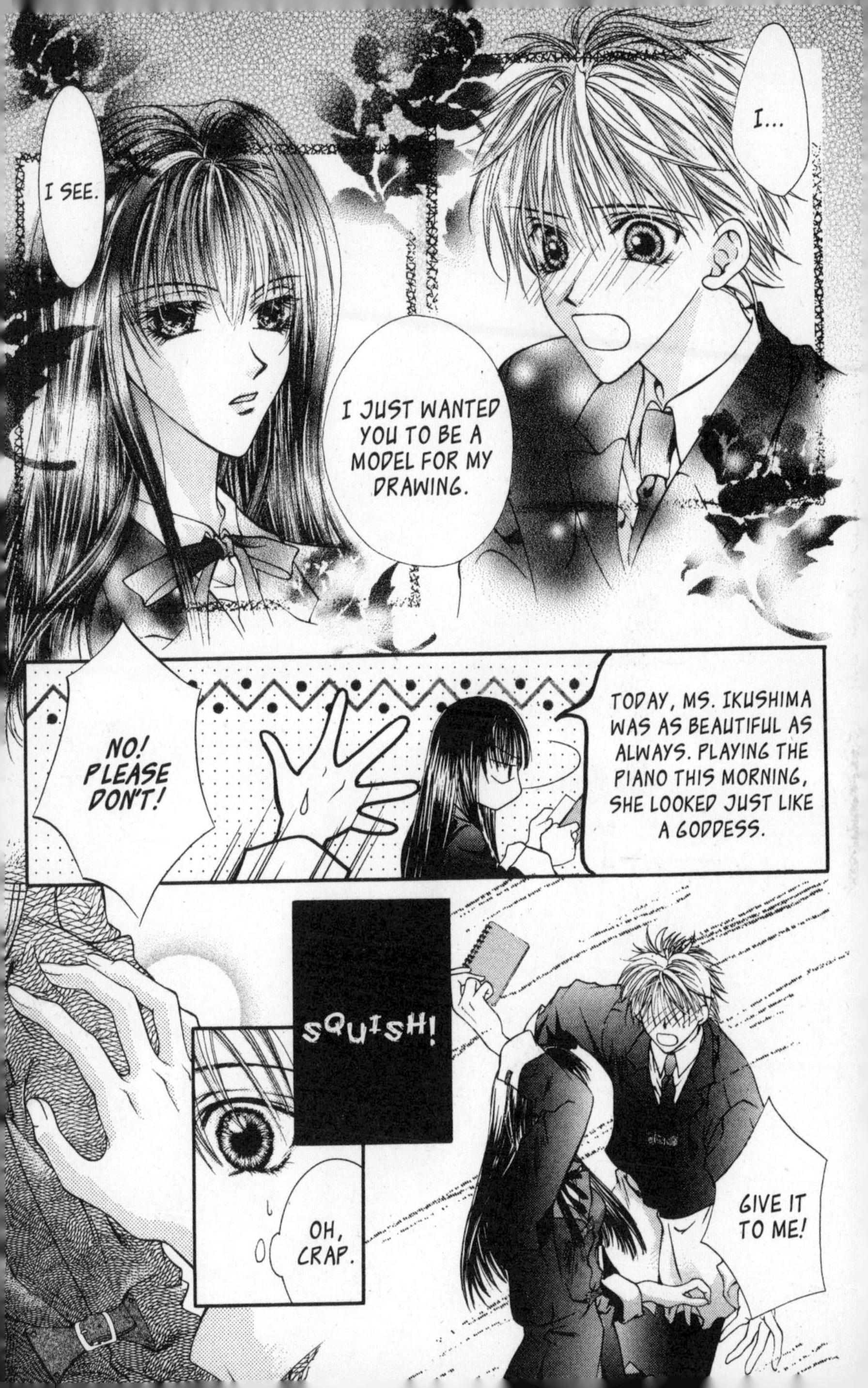
I...
I SEE.
I JUST WANTED YOU TO BE A MODEL FOR MY DRAWING.
TODAY, MS. IKUSHIMA WAS AS BEAUTIFUL AS ALWAYS. PLAYING THE PIANO THIS MORNING, SHE LOOKED JUST LIKE A GODDESS.
NO! PLEASE DON'T!
GIVE IT TO ME!
SQUISH!
OH, CRAP.

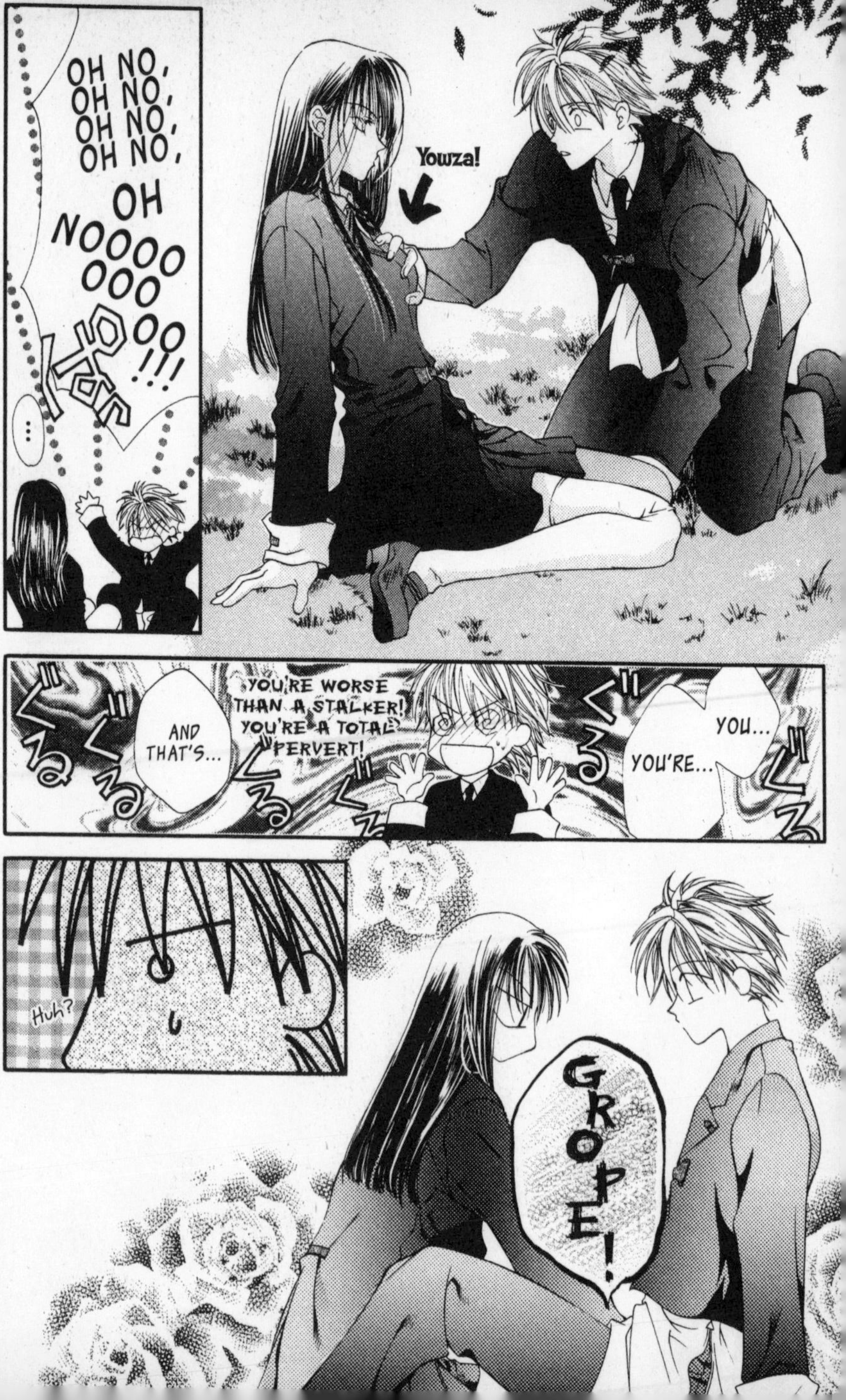

Yowza!
OH NO, OH NO, OH NO, OH NO, OH NOOOOOOOOOOO!!!
...
YOU... YOU'RE...
YOU'RE WORSE THAN A STALKER! YOU'RE A TOTAL PERVERT!
AND THAT'S...
GROPE!
Huh?

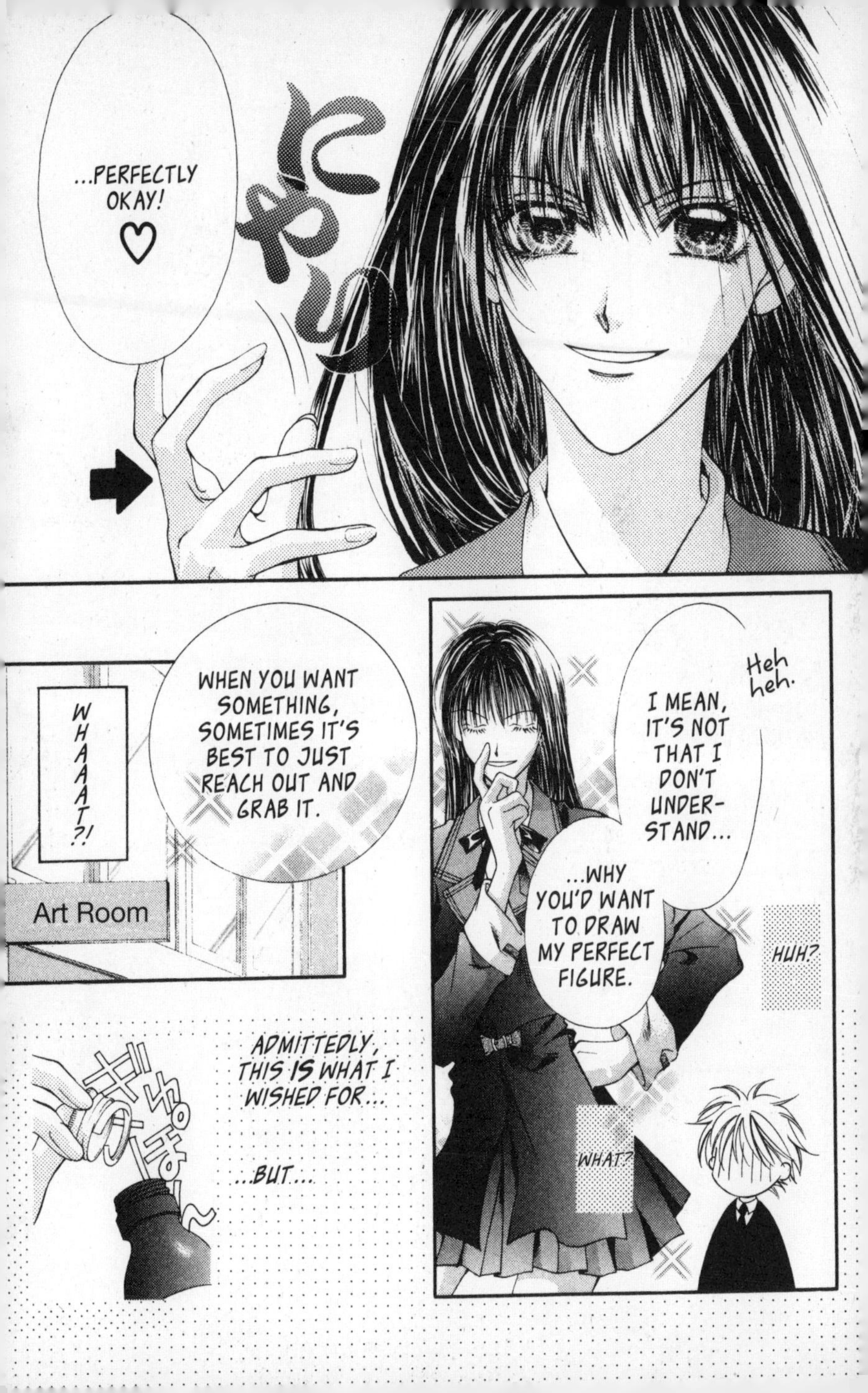
...PERFECTLY OKAY! ♡
Heh heh.
I MEAN, IT'S NOT THAT I DON'T UNDERSTAND...
...WHY YOU'D WANT TO DRAW MY PERFECT FIGURE.
HUH?
WHAT?
WHEN YOU WANT SOMETHING, SOMETIMES IT'S BEST TO JUST REACH OUT AND GRAB IT.
WHAAAAT?!
Art Room
ADMITTEDLY, THIS **IS** WHAT I WISHED FOR...
...BUT...

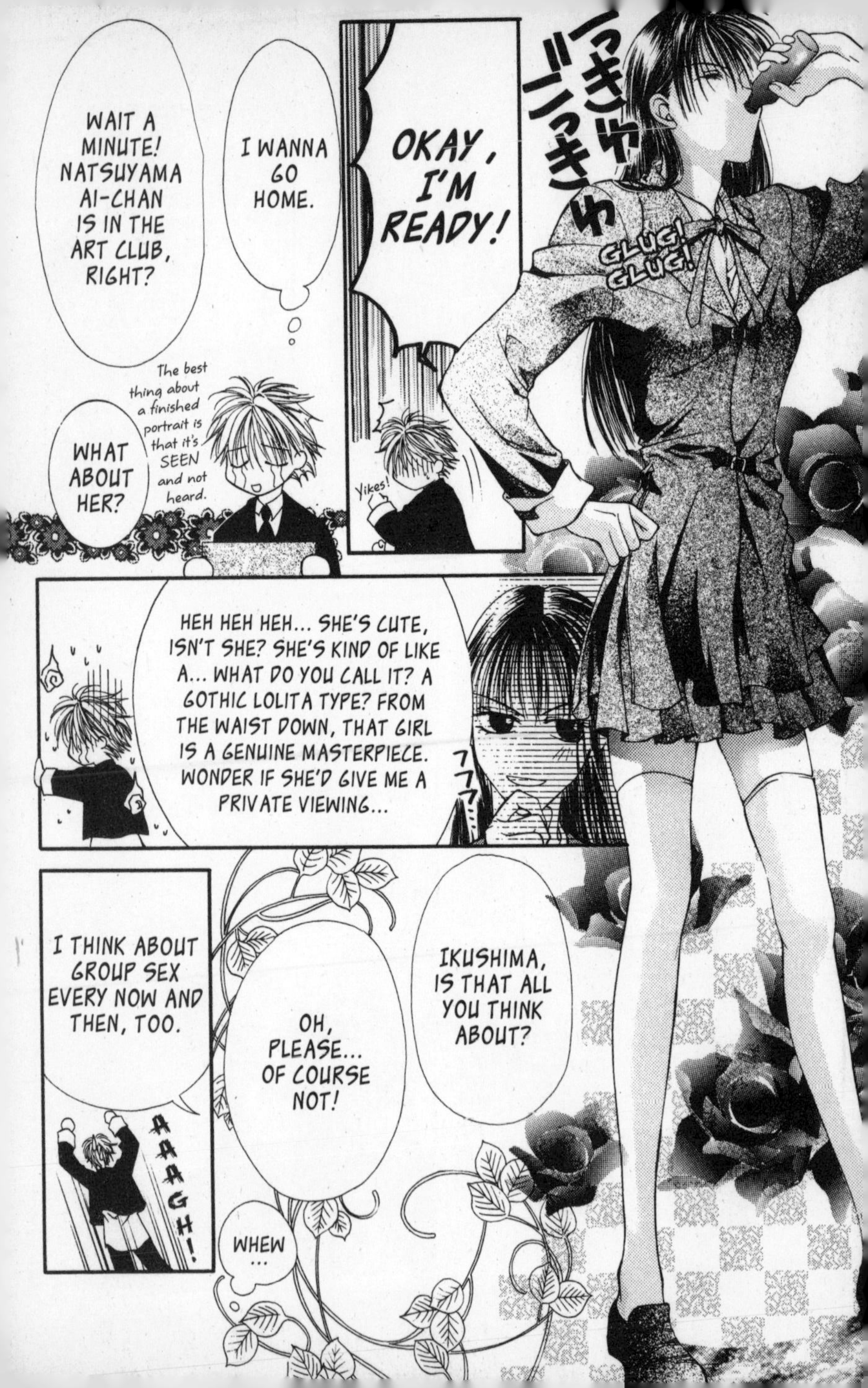
GLUG! GLUG!
OKAY, I'M READY!
Yikes!
I WANNA GO HOME.
WAIT A MINUTE! NATSUYAMA AI-CHAN IS IN THE ART CLUB, RIGHT?
The best thing about a finished portrait is that it's SEEN and not heard.
WHAT ABOUT HER?
HEH HEH HEH... SHE'S CUTE, ISN'T SHE? SHE'S KIND OF LIKE A... WHAT DO YOU CALL IT? A GOTHIC LOLITA TYPE? FROM THE WAIST DOWN, THAT GIRL IS A GENUINE MASTERPIECE. WONDER IF SHE'D GIVE ME A PRIVATE VIEWING...
IKUSHIMA, IS THAT ALL YOU THINK ABOUT?
OH, PLEASE... OF COURSE NOT!
WHEW...
I THINK ABOUT GROUP SEX EVERY NOW AND THEN, TOO.
AAAGH!

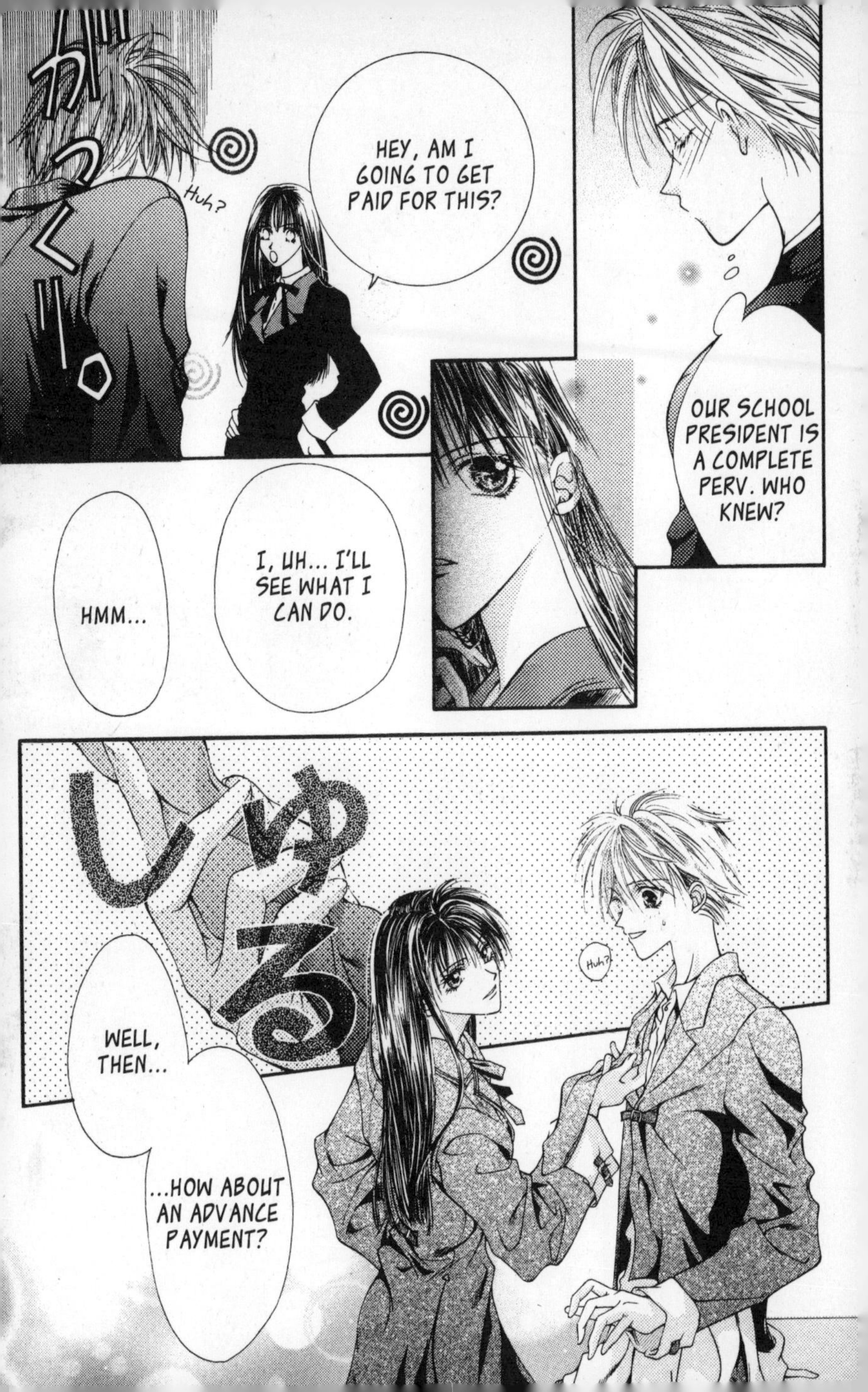
OUR SCHOOL PRESIDENT IS A COMPLETE PERV. WHO KNEW?
がっくし。
Huh?
HEY, AM I GOING TO GET PAID FOR THIS?
I, UH... I'LL SEE WHAT I CAN DO.
HMM...
しゅる
Huh?
WELL, THEN...
...HOW ABOUT AN ADVANCE PAYMENT?

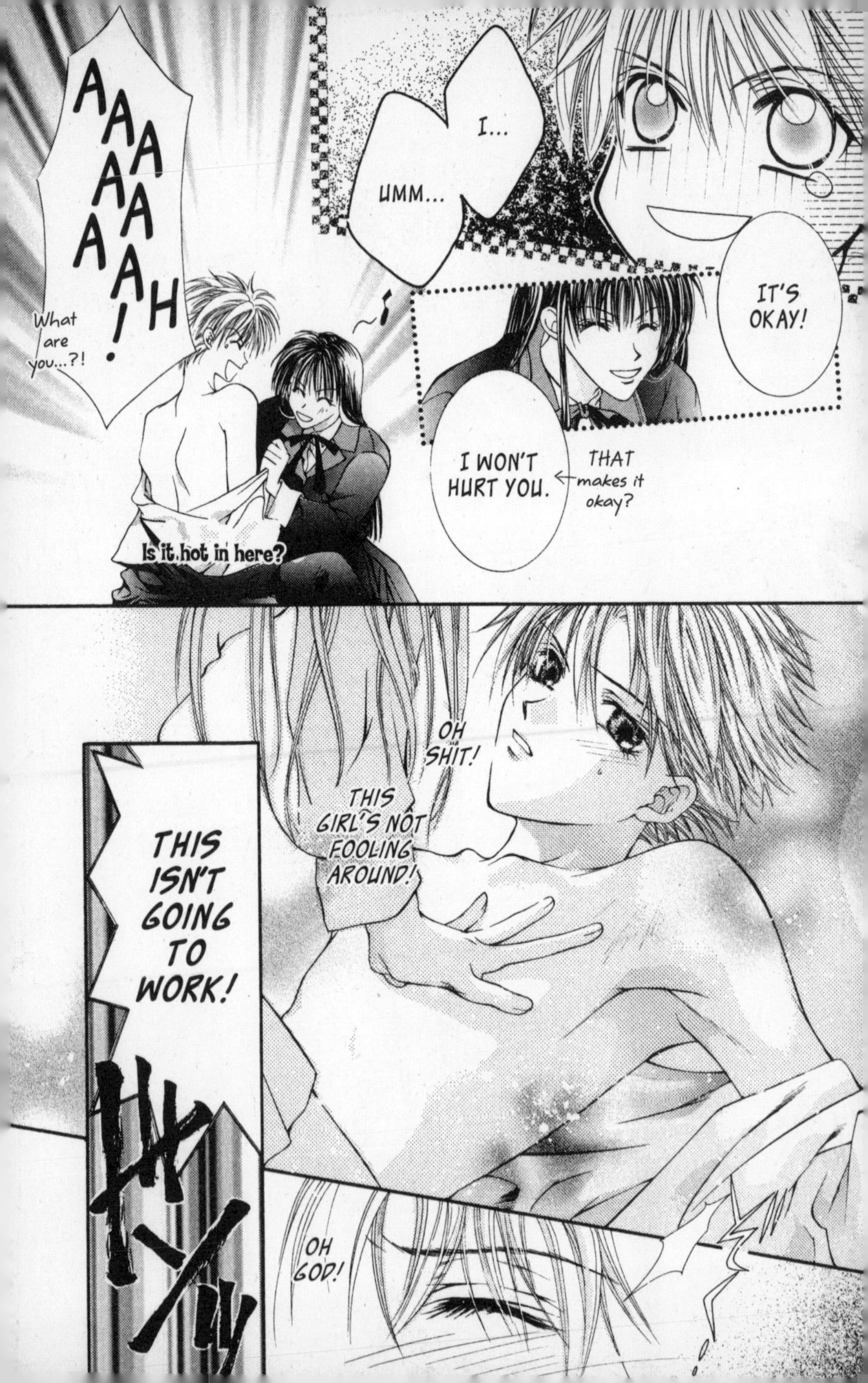

I...
UMM...
IT'S OKAY!
I WON'T HURT YOU.
THAT makes it okay?
AAAAAAAH!
What are you...?!
Is it hot in here?
OH SHIT!
THIS GIRL'S NOT FOOLING AROUND!
THIS ISN'T GOING TO WORK!
OH GOD!

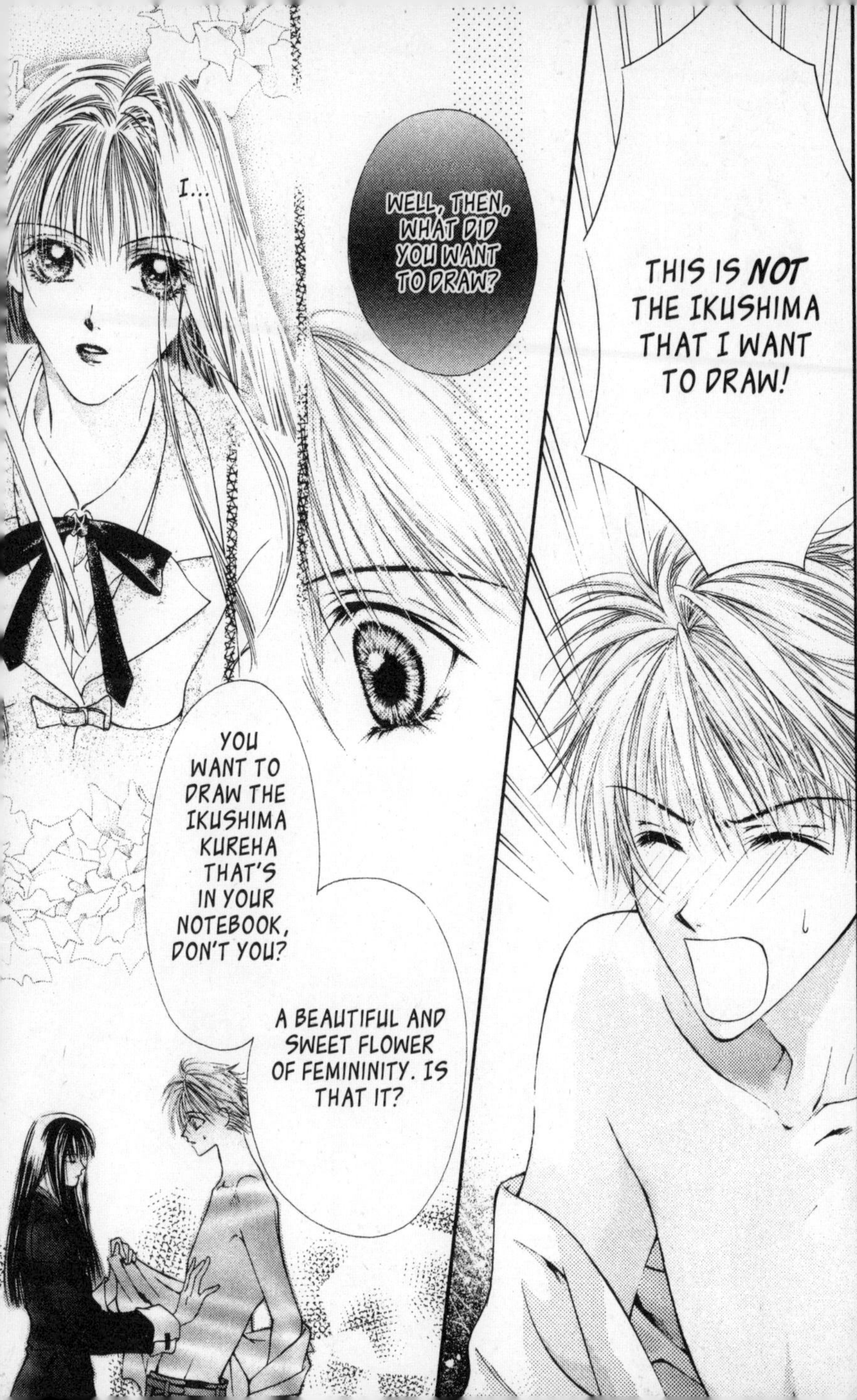
THIS IS *NOT* THE IKUSHIMA THAT I WANT TO DRAW!
WELL, THEN, WHAT DID YOU WANT TO DRAW?
I...
YOU WANT TO DRAW THE IKUSHIMA KUREHA THAT'S IN YOUR NOTEBOOK, DON'T YOU?
A BEAUTIFUL AND SWEET FLOWER OF FEMININITY. IS THAT IT?

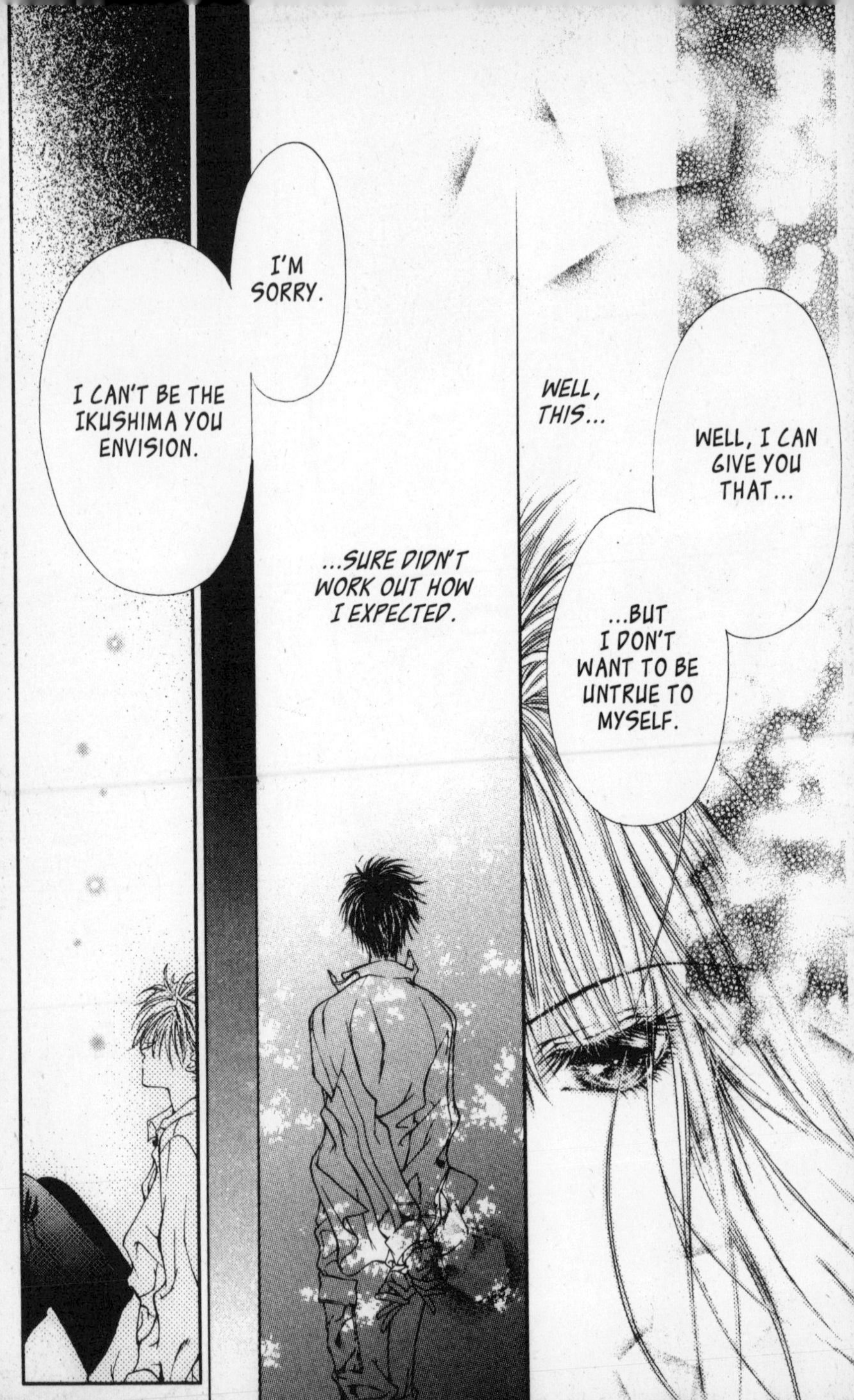
WELL, I CAN GIVE YOU THAT...
...BUT I DON'T WANT TO BE UNTRUE TO MYSELF.
WELL, THIS...
...SURE DIDN'T WORK OUT HOW I EXPECTED.
I'M SORRY.
I CAN'T BE THE IKUSHIMA YOU ENVISION.

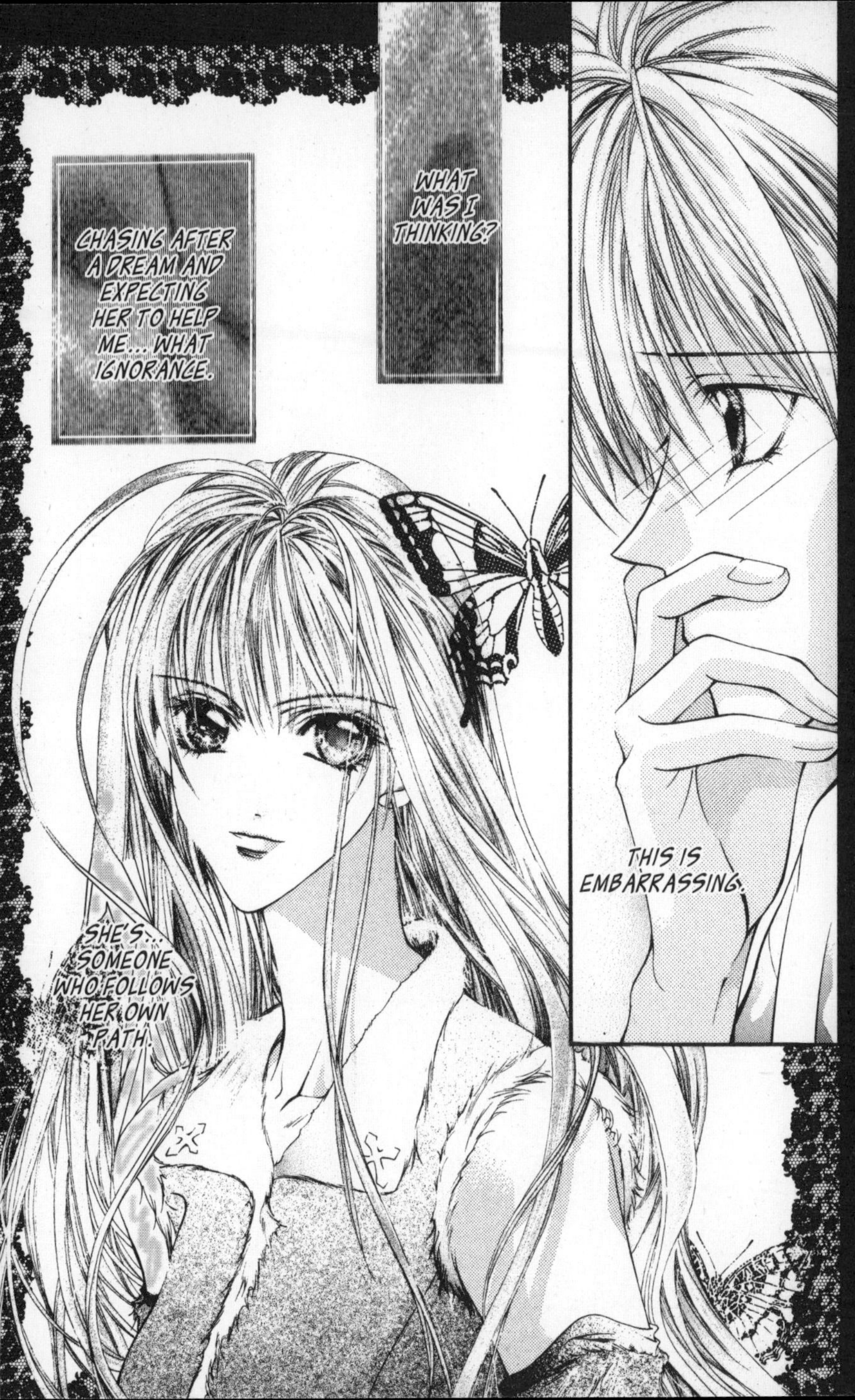
THIS IS EMBARRASSING.
WHAT WAS I THINKING?
CHASING AFTER A DREAM AND EXPECTING HER TO HELP ME... WHAT IGNORANCE.
SHE'S... SOMEONE WHO FOLLOWS HER OWN PATH.

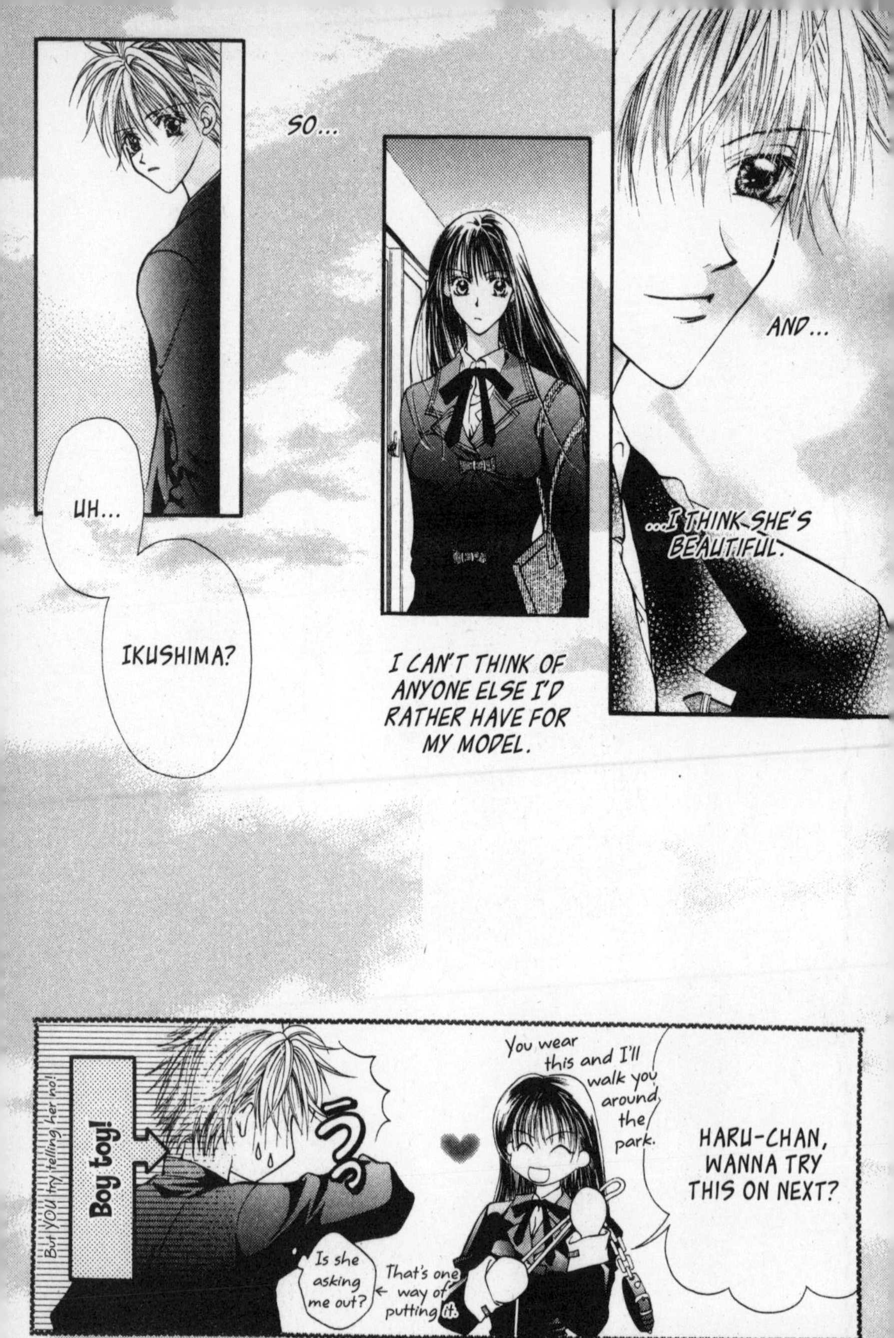
AND...
...I THINK SHE'S BEAUTIFUL.
SO...
I CAN'T THINK OF ANYONE ELSE I'D RATHER HAVE FOR MY MODEL.
UH...
IKUSHIMA?
HARU-CHAN, WANNA TRY THIS ON NEXT?
You wear this and I'll walk you around the park.
That's one way of putting it.
Is she asking me out?
Boy toy!
But YOU try telling her no!

Love Machine—The End

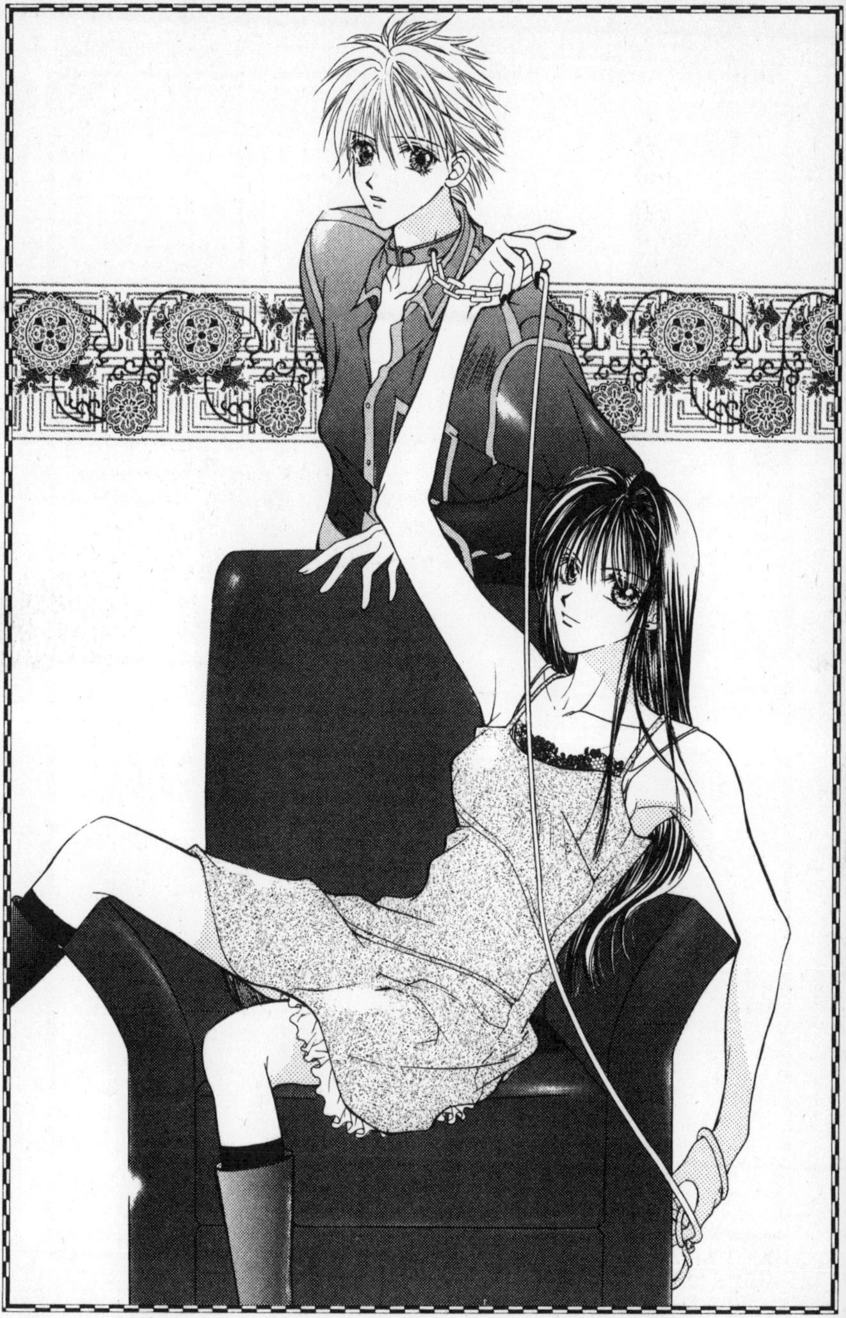

Lots of girls collect dolls, but Hinagi Ori is a doll designer that collects parts—human parts. Admired for his beautiful life-sized dolls, Ori has many fans, but there's a reason his dolls are so lifelike, and it's a horror that Sunao will come face-to-plastic face with when she's kidnapped by the doll-maker. However, to do this she'll have to confront something she's long since denied—her past.

Volume 2 also introduces us to Minamo, 15-year-old ghost hunter extraordinaire, and her partner Amane as they fight to rid their school of a frightening phantasm in the exciting side story, "The Good Times Never End."

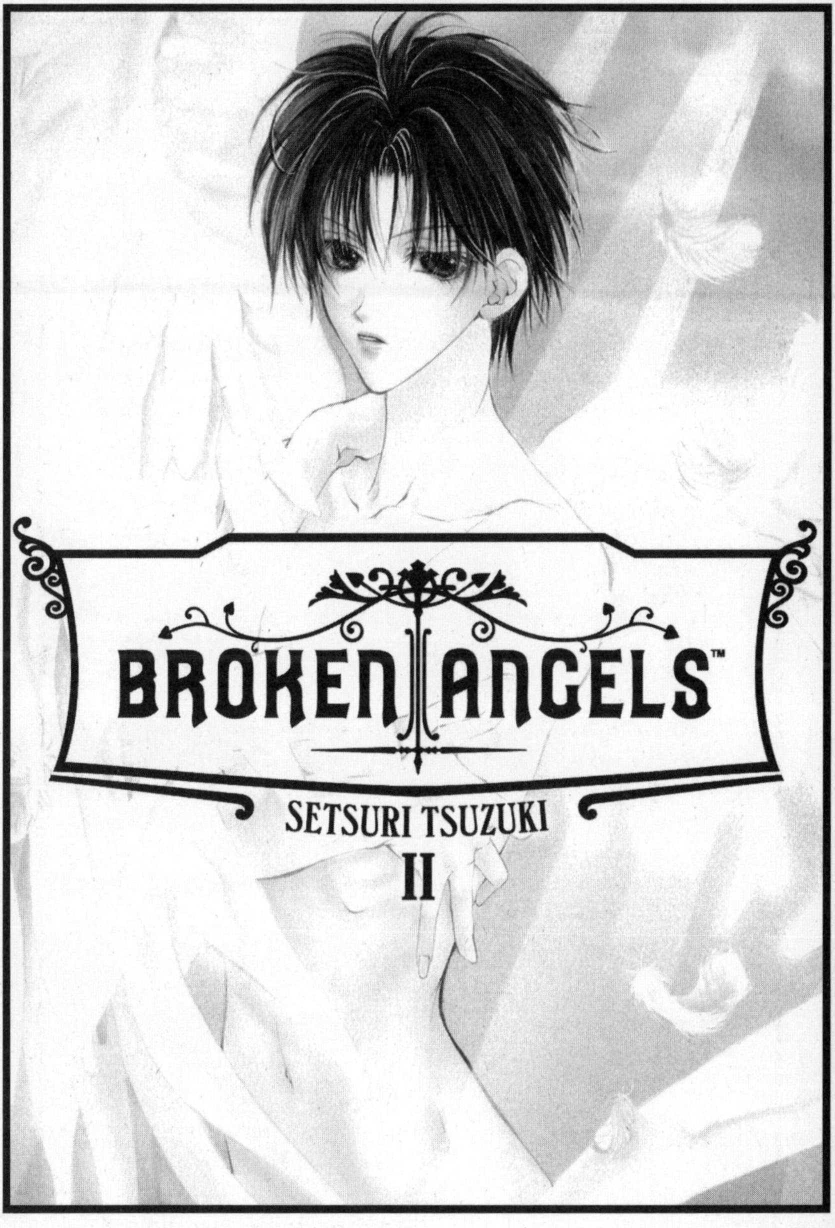
BROKEN ANGELS™
SETSURI TSUZUKI
II

TOKYOPOP SHOP

WWW.TOKYOPOP.COM/SHOP

HOT NEWS!

Check out the TOKYOPOP SHOP! The world's best collection of manga in English is now available online in one place!

BIZENGHAST POSTER

PRINCESS AI POSTCARDS

I Luv Halloween Glow-In-the-Dark STICKERS!

I LUV HALLOWEEN BUTTONS & STICKERS

• LOOK FOR SPECIAL OFFERS
• PRE-ORDER UPCOMING RELEASES
• COMPLETE YOUR COLLECTIONS

that I'm not like other people...

BIZENGHAST

*Dear Diary,
I'm starting to feel*

THIS FALL, TOKYOPOP CREATES A FRESH, NEW CHAPTER IN TEEN NOVELS...

For Adventurers...

Witches' Forest: The Adventures of Duan Surk

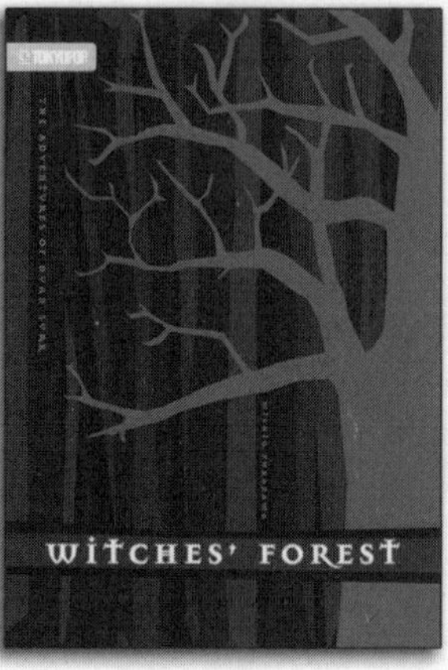
TOKYOPOP
WITCHES' FOREST

By Mishio Fukazawa

Duan Surk is a 16-year-old Level 2 fighter who embarks on the quest of a lifetime—battling mythical creatures and outwitting evil sorceresses, all in an impossible rescue mission in the spooky Witches' Forest!

BASED ON THE FAMOUS
FORTUNE QUEST WORLD

For Dreamers...

Magic Moon

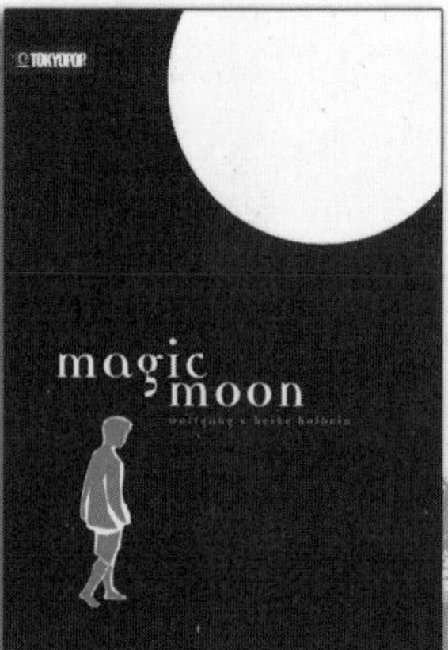
TOKYOPOP
magic moon

By Wolfgang and Heike Hohlbein

Kim enters the engimatic realm of Magic Moon, where he battles unthinkable monsters and fantastical creatures—in order to unravel the secret that keeps his sister locked in a coma.

THE WORLDWIDE BESTSELLING FANTASY
*THRILL*OGY ARRIVES IN THE U.S.!

STOP!

This is the back of the book.
You wouldn't want to spoil a great ending!

This book is printed "manga-style," in the authentic Japanese right-to-left format. Since none of the artwork has been flipped or altered, readers get to experience the story just as the creator intended. You've been asking for it, so TOKYOPOP® delivered: authentic, hot-off-the-press, and far more fun!

DIRECTIONS

If this is your first time reading manga-style, here's a quick guide to help you understand how it works.

It's easy... just start in the top right panel and follow the numbers. Have fun, and look for more 100% authentic manga from TOKYOPOP®!